contents
&

the contents o'th' story
Cymbeline II, 2, 27

To my mother, Julia Scheeder
L.S.

To my friend, R.N.W.
S.A.Y.

introduction

&

What's in a name?
Romeo and Juliet II, 2, 43

While *All the Words on Stage* is explicitly a pronunciation dictionary, there is another agenda behind the ostensibly prescriptive notion of the correct pronunciation of the Shakespearean vocabulary. In presenting our work, we hope that it will stir a greater interest on the part of actors and directors, as well as teachers and students, in Shakespeare's handling of language. We believe that a deeper understanding of Shakespeare's verse, specifically the rhythm and variants of the iambic pentameter line, can aid actors in their physical and psychological portrayals of his characters. The suggested pronunciations in this dictionary reflect the interweaving of word and rhythm produced by blank verse in its numerous variants.

In recent years, especially following a number of successful film adaptations, popular interest in Shakespeare has grown enormously. Despite this plethora of visual display, there still exists a major barrier to the plays for many students and actors. That barrier is language. At times, Shakespeare's language fosters intimidation and instills fear. The intent of this book is to assist in the dismantling of the barrier of language and to allow students, actors, and the general audience access not only to an articulation of individual words, but also to the world of these plays, which, after all, exists in and through words. We hope to guide the reader not only through the basic pronunciation of individual words, some of which are no longer in current use, but also through the complexities of how the words work in relation to each other.

In the past, editions of Shakespeare seem to have been created for the reader rather than the actor. However, some editions, like the Pelican, have included markings for stressed "ed" endings in the texts, and others have noted the syllabic divisions of a word in order to respect the rhythm of the verse. The third edition of the Arden series emphasizes the performance aspects of the plays in its introductory essays. Individual editors also suggest pronunciations by including instances of words that elongate (by the addition of a vowel) or shorten (by the deletion of a vowel). There seems to be a growing interest in and attention to the articulation of the plays and their relation to the verse form.

Previous reference works have partially provided what play editions omit. Theodora Irvine's *How to Pronounce the Names in Shakespeare* stems from a survey of leading English actors around 1900. The pronunciations reflect the upper class speech of the Edwardian era. Helge Kökeritz's *Shakespeare's Names: A Pronouncing Dictionary* was the standard work on the pronunciation of character names for many years. The pronunciations tend to be those of English speech with occasional American variants. The book also includes some indications of what Elizabethan pronunciations might have been like. Delbert Spain's *Shakespeare Sounded Soundly* contains much valuable information on the working of the verse. He includes an appendix of some 250 words, giving the stresses for polysyllabic words, though without phonetic transcription. Dale Coye's *Pronouncing Shakespeare's Words* is based primarily on a survey of professors in Britain, Canada, and the U.S. It embraces both names and words but does not include phonetics. Louis Colaianni's *Shakespeare's Names* is a pronunciation guide to the names in the plays, but does not include the rest of the Shakespearean vocabulary nor does it take into account the effects of the iambic pentameter line on pronunciation.

We began this project with a list of words that we had heard actors stumble over in the classroom or in rehearsal. We then added character names, as well as proper, geographic, and mythological names, and included words that seemed unfamiliar to a sampling of undergraduates, graduate students, and professional actors. The final step was the inclusion of words that are changed and altered by the play of the iambic pentameter line. Numerous dictionaries proved invaluable for the determination of the pronunciation of words in prose. The scansion of the verse line was the final arbiter for words in verse.

Invariably, at the beginning of one of our workshops or classes, a talented individual will stand in the performance space and either mangle the name of the character that is about to be portrayed or stumble over an unfamiliar word. Several years ago, one of those students turned and asked, "How come there isn't a book that tells you how to pronounce it?" Our work is an answer to that question.

Our suggested pronunciations are American. We believe that when American actors speak Shakespeare they should sound American. As recently as the 1960s, actors commonly affected English accents in their performances of Shakespeare. Others adopted an indeterminate mid-Atlantic sound. All too often however, such attempts resulted in a phony quality to their speech and, consequently, their acting became unbelievable. On the other hand, we have witnessed productions where the actors' desire to sound natural has led them to be unintelligible.

In order that the actor's voice serves the language, ideas, and world of the play, we believe in the close integration of voice and speech training. To this end, in our private studios and in our individual classes at New York University's Classical Studio and the Graduate Acting Department, we use the methods and techniques developed by Robert Neff Williams at Columbia University and The Juilliard School over the last thirty years. These techniques allow actors to develop voices that are flexible, varied, and expressive enough to convey the nuance, color, and subtle shading of the words that the character uses whether in an intellectual argument or an emotional outburst. We hope that our work on the pronunciation of the Shakespearean vocabulary contributes to this goal.

We have used the International Phonetic Alphabet (IPA) to transcribe the pronunciations in order to be as accurate and precise as possible. However, since many readers will not be familiar with the phonetic alphabet, we have also created a re-spelling system that we trust is clear, simple, and easy to use by both professional and layperson. This system is explained in the pages that follow, along with a brief section that reviews some basic principles of iambic pentameter. We have included sections devoted to Latin and accents, dialects, and foreign languages. We have also provided a section entitled "Afterthoughts," that considers each of Shakespeare's plays in turn. In this section, the reader will find examples of words whose pronunciation is altered by the meter, as well as information on difficult words and puns that are specific to each play. Shakespeare has always served as a measure of challenge and accomplishment for actors, students, and theater artists. We hope that this work will contribute to the growing interest in and increasing emphasis on the complexities of Shakespeare's language, especially his verse, and above all, on the articulation of these texts as performative speech.

acknowledgments
&

many thousand thanks
Henry VI Part Three III, 2, 56

We would like to thank our students in the Department of Drama and in the Graduate Acting Department at New York University, as well as the students in our private classes. We received invaluable encouragement and advice from colleagues at NYU including Deborah Hecht of Graduate Acting, who willingly shared her vast knowledge of Shakespeare and her point of view about speaking the texts, and Deloss Brown and Donna Germain of the Classical Studio, both of whom provided support, intelligence, and strong opinions. The Reference Librarians and staff at Bobst Library graciously assisted us with numerous tasks. Their help proved crucial.

Ned Jackson provided assistance on the pronunciation of Latin, as did Julie Crosby, who also shared her editorial acumen and grammatical wisdom. We would like to acknowledge Peter Meineck of the Aquila Theatre and Kelly Preston of NYU's Center for Ancient Studies for theoretical conversations and advice in this area.

Numerous friends encouraged and cheered along this lengthy project, including Nancy Kawalek, who was there with early support and thought-provoking questions, Lisa Reardon and Mick Weber, who lent their sharp eyes, keen ears and editorial skills, and J.R. Roessl and Peter Wise, who offered early and enthusiastic feed-back. Simon Opie produced timely assistance and shrewd suggestions, while Peter Webster was unrelenting in his enthusiasm and shared his insights freely. Kristin Stewart assisted in myriad ways. Richard Fitch not only proved to be a good friend throughout, but also a computer whiz with his prompt, efficient, and humorous technical support. Philip Gruber delivered critical eleventh hour aid with his Macintosh skills and creative wizardry. Our agents, Jack Tantleff and Charmaine Ferenczi, championed the book from the beginning and were a key factor in getting it into print.

Marisa Smith and Eric Kraus immediately saw the need for such a book and committed themselves wholeheartedly to the complexities of publishing a work that we trust is both scholarly and accessible. Julia Hill Gignoux was a joy to work with as she guided us through the intricacies of text design. They have our thanks.

For his generous spirit, for many years of friendly debates about speech, and for ongoing conversations about speaking the texts of Shakespeare, Shane Ann would like to thank Andrew Wade, Head of the Voice Department at the Royal Shakespeare Company. She would also like to acknowledge Zelda Fichandler, Chair of New York University's Graduate Acting Department, who has been a source of inspiration for her.

In a casual conversation, Marcia Siegel suggested to Louis that he write a book if he wanted to learn more about a subject. For this, and many other contributions to his intellectual growth, she has his thanks. He would also like to acknowledge the support and encouragement he received from Robert White-head and the late Roger Stevens in past endeavors.

Shane Ann wishes to thank Robert Neff Williams for intro-ducing her to Shakespeare and for sharing his love of the English language. Both of us are grateful and indebted to him for his extensive knowledge about voice, speech, and Shakespeare, and for his unflagging encouragement, extraordinary good taste, and sense of elegance. Finally, we must note that any mistakes and errors in this work are entirely our own.

play titles and abbreviations

Show me briefly

Much Ado About Nothing II, 2, 10

All's Well That Ends Well	AW
Antony and Cleopatra	A&C
As You Like It	AYL
The Comedy of Errors	CE
Coriolanus	COR
Cymbeline	CYM
Hamlet	HAM
Henry IV Part One	1HIV
Henry IV Part Two	2HIV
Henry V	HV
Henry VI Part One	1HVI
Henry VI Part Two	2HVI
Henry VI Part Three	3HVI
Henry VIII	HVIII
Julius Caesar	JC
King John	KJ
King Lear	LEAR
Love's Labor's Lost	LLL
Macbeth	MAC
Measure for Measure	MM
The Merchant of Venice	MVEN
The Merry Wives of Windsor	MW
A Midsummer Night's Dream	MID
Much Ado About Nothing	MADO
Othello	OTH
Pericles	PER
Richard II	RII
Richard III	RIII
Romeo and Juliet	R&J
The Taming of the Shrew	SHR
The Tempest	TEMP
Timon of Athens	TIMON
Titus Andronicus	TITUS
Troilus and Cressida	T&C
Twelfth Night	12th
Two Gentlemen of Verona	2GEN
The Two Noble Kinsmen	2NOB
The Winter's Tale	WT

key to pronunciations

Speak the speech, I pray you, as I pronounced it
Hamlet III, 2, 1

The following key gives the pronunciations in two ways—first in a respelled format for those who are not familiar with phonetics, and then phonetically using the IPA (International Phonetic Alphabet). The respelling system is our own invention. The first column contains the respelled sound, the second contains the phonetic symbol, and the third provides examples of the sound as used in a few common words.

RESPELLED	IPA SYMBOL	KEY WORDS
VOWELS		
EE	[i]	as in be, see, tea
I	[ɪ]	as in bit, hid, pin
EH	[ɛ]	as in bet, head, let
AA	[æ]	as in bat, fan, tackle
OO	[u]	as in boot, ooze, zoo
OO	[ʊ]	as in book, foot, put
AW	[ɔ]	as in bought, saw, dawn
AH	[ɑ]	as in father, calm, spa
ER	[ɝ]	as in bird, fur, learn
E(r)	[ɜ]	as in averring, whirring
UH	[ʌ]	as in cup, but, glove

Unstressed Vowels

er	[ɚ]	as in bett*er*, mod*er*n
uh	[ə]	as in foc*u*s, *a*go, fam*ou*s

Syllabics

(uh)	[‚]	as in mett*le*, rounde*l*, batte*n*

Diphthongs and Triphthongs

AY	[eɪ]	as in bay, take, say
EYE	[aɪ]	as in bite, high, time
OY	[ɔɪ]	as in boy, avoid, voice
OH	[oʊ]	as in boat, go, sew
OW	[aʊ]	as in how, town, out
YOO͞	[ɪu]	as in duke, new, tune
EAR	[ɪɚ]	as in beer, hear, fear
AIR	[ɛɚ]	as in bear, hair, fare
OO͞R	[ʊɚ]	as in tour, sure, poor
AWR	[ɔɚ]	as in bore, four, score
AHR	[ɑɚ]	as in bar, card, part
EYER	[aɪɚ]	as in sire, hire, fire
OWR	[aʊɚ]	as in hour, scour, sour

Consonants

P	[p]	as in pat, puppy, cap
B	[b]	as in bowl, rubbish, cab
T	[t]	as in top, better, cat
D	|d|	as in dip, moody, had
K	[k]	as in car, actor, pick
G	[g]	as in go, agree, hug
M	[m]	as in met, comma, aim
N	[n]	as in no, penny, chain
NG	[ŋ]	as in king, hang, banquet
L	[l]	as in low, salad, bell
R	[r]	as in red, ran, arrive
Y	[j]	as in yet, uniform, use
W	[w]	as in we, word, away
H	[h]	as in have, hid, help

HW	[hw]	as in what, where, wheat
S	[s]	as in soon, ask, toss
Z	[z]	as in zoo, busy, jazz
F	[f]	as in far, affirm, graph
V	[v]	as in vine, even, save
SH	[ʃ]	as in ship, nation, cash
ZH	[ʒ]	as in vision, casual, beige
TH	[θ]	as in thirty, nothing, path
<u>TH</u>	[ð]	as in then, other, breathe
CH	[tʃ]	as in child, future, watch
J	[dʒ]	as in just, fragile, ridge

NOTES ON SYLLABLES AND STRESS

Respellings
- A hyphen (-) separates the syllables.
- A syllable printed in **BOLD CAPITAL LETTERS** has the primary stress.
- A syllable printed in CAPITAL LETTERS has the secondary stress.
- All other syllables are in lower case letters.
- Unstressed vowels are always in lower case letters.
    Example: AY-dree-**AH**-nuh

Phonetics
- Phonetic symbols are surrounded by [brackets].
- Syllables are separated by a hyphen (-).
- ['] in front of a syllable indicates that the primary stress is on the following syllable.
    Example: [eɪ-dri-'ɑ-nə]

A detailed explanation of the respellings and phonetics is included in the next section, "How to Use the Dictionary."

how to use the dictionary
&

Well practiced wise directions
Henry IV Part Two V, 2, 121

"WORDS, WORDS, WORDS"
Hamlet II, 2, 191

All English words in this dictionary, including words absorbed into English from other languages, are listed alphabetically. Latin words and phrases are arranged alphabetically in their own section. We have chosen not to include malaprops or comic blunders. We believe that each actor should be free to develop a pronunciation for these words.

As much as possible, we have made the components of the respelling system reflect the sound that they represent. We have listed the respelled words first and then the phonetic symbols. (See "Key to Pronunciations" page 2.)

We follow the texts of the Pelican Shakespeare. For *The Two Noble Kinsmen* we employed the Arden edition. Occasionally we have used a spelling from another edition if it helps to clarify the pronunciation or if a majority of editions prefer a spelling that differs from the Pelican series:

popingay PAHP-in-gay ['pɑp-ɪn-geɪ] some editions "popin-jay" PAHP-in-jay ['pɑp-ɪn-ʤeɪ]

Sometimes a word that is spelled with a lower case letter is also a proper name. If the pronunciation is the same, these words are listed with the lower case first and the proper name second:

bedlam / Bedlam BEHD-luhm ['bɛd-ləm]

Nouns are listed in their singular form, and verbs are in the present tense, unless the word is used only one time in the plural or past tense form. For example *gallowglasses, gasted, sleeded,* and *smuched* are respelled with their *es* or *ed* endings because they appear only one time.

When an individual word has different spellings in the Pelican series, the variants are listed with a slash between them, followed by the respelling and phonetics:

lower / low'r / lour (to frown) LOWR [lɑʊɚ]

When a multi-syllabic word has more than one pronunciation, the syllables that are unchanged are indicated by a blank line:

scimitar SIM-i-ter ['sɪm-ɪ-tɚ] or ___-___-tahr [___-___-tɑɚ]

If alternate pronunciations are given, we leave the preference to the individual actor. Alternates are separated by the word *or:*

halberd HAAL-berd ['hæl-bɚd] or HAWL-___ ['hɔl-___]

The names of characters which appear in the Cast Lists are followed by the play's abbreviation, the respelling, and the phonetics. Pronunciations, altered by scansion, are given along with the act, scene and line reference. If the scanned version of the pronunciation is used more than one time *e.g.* (for example) precedes the line reference and the @ (at) symbol is placed in front of the act, scene and line:

Antiochus *(PER)* aan-TEYE-uh-kuhs [æn-'taɪ-ə-kəs]
scans to ___-TEYE-kuhs [__-'taɪ-kəs] e.g. @ I, 3, 19

Multiple entries, including family names, proper names of characters in the cast list and characters who are alluded to or mentioned in a play but are not in the cast list, are organized in the following manner: the first line of the main entry gives the basic pronunciation and any variant pronunciations due to scansion. Indented under the main entry, the characters in the cast are listed with their play abbreviation, the line references of variant pronunciations, and the respellings of any additional information. If no line reference is given, then the proper name does not alter in that play:

Katherine KAATH-uh-rin ['kæθ-ə-rɪn] scans to
KAATH-rin ['kæθ-rɪn]
Katherine *(HV)*
Katherine *(HVIII)*
Katherine *(SHR)* scans @ II, 1, 184, also called
"Katherina" KAATH-uh-REE-nuh [kæθ-ə-'ri-nə]
or KAAT-___-___-___ [kæt-___-___-___]
and "Kate" KAYT [keɪt]

Andronicus aan-DRAHN-i-kuhs [æn-'drɑn-ɪ-kəs]
Andronicus, Marcus *(TITUS)* MAHR-kuhs ['mɑɚ-kəs]
Andronicus, Titus *(TITUS)* TEYE-tuhs ['taɪ-təs]

"TAKE NOTE, TAKE NOTE"
Othello III, 3, 377

In order to assist the speaker, we give the syllable divisions and the levels of stress with as much detail as possible. Because most dictionaries are concerned with orthographic division in order to meet the needs of writers, proof readers, and typesetters, the syllable divisions for speakers are usually ignored and the indications of stress are often unclear. To clarify the spoken word, we place a hyphen between every syllable and include three levels of stress — primary, secondary, and unstressed.

The primary stress is the strongest level of emphasis, and it is indicated in the respelling system with **BOLD CAPITAL** letters and in the phonetics with an accent mark preceding the syllable with the primary stress:

lambkins LAAM-kinz [ˈlæm-kɪnz]

In certain multi-syllabic words, a secondary stress is indicated when it clarifies the pronunciation of the word. A secondary stress indicates the syllable that receives an intermediate level of stress and is written in the respelling system in CAPITAL letters without bold face type. For the secondary stress, speakers using the phonetic symbols will need to refer to the respelled version of the word:

palisadoes PAAL-i-SAY-dohz [pæl-ɪ-ˈseɪ-doʊz]

An unstressed syllable receives the lightest stress and is written in lower case letters:

supplyant suh-PLEYE-uhnt [sə-ˈplaɪ-ənt]

Often the verse demands a variant pronunciation. The variant follows the basic pronunciation. If the variant occurs more than once, the abbreviation *e.g.* precedes a citation:

lamentable luh-MEHN-tuh-b(uh)l [lə-ˈmɛn-tə-bl̩] scans to
 LAAM-uhn-__-__ [ˈlæm-ən-__-__] e.g. @ RII V, 1, 44
character (n) or (v) KAA-rik-ter [ˈkæ-rɪk-tɚ] scans to
 kuh-RAAK-___ [kə-ˈræk-__] e.g. @ RIII III, 1, 81

If the verse always demands a variant pronunciation, the phrase *always scans to* precedes the respelling and phonetics:

scorpion always scans to SKAWR-pyuhn [ˈskɔɚ-pjən]
Amazonian always scans to AAM-uh-ZOH-nyuhn
 [æm-ə-ˈzoʊ-njən]

If a word occurs only once in Shakespeare and needs to be elided to fulfill the demands of the meter, then just the elided pronunciation is given. Since the word appears only once, no reference is listed:

contumely scans to **KAHN**-ty$\overline{oo}$m-lee ['kɑn-tɪum-li]

The phrase *possibly scans to* precedes a word that might receive an alternate stress:

gallant GAAL-uhnt ['gæl-ənt] possibly scans to
   guh-**LAHNT** [gə-'lɑnt] @ RII V, 3, 15

If the scanned version of the word includes numerous changes, the entire word is respelled:

solemnized SAH-lehm-neyezd ['sɑ-lɛm-naɪzd] scans to
   suh-**LEHM**-neye-zid [sə-'lɛm-naɪ-zɪd] e.g. @ LLL II, 1, 42

When scansion of a verse line indicates that the primary stress of a two syllable word reverses, the word is respelled in its entirety:

complete kuhm-**PLEET** [kəm-'plit] scans to **KAHM**-pleet
   ['kɑm-plit] e.g. @ RIII IV, 4, 190

"The Dictionary" includes many, though not all, words that require an additional syllable to fulfill the demands of the meter. Other examples of these words are listed in "Afterthoughts." When an additional syllable is needed to elongate these words, the necessary metrical beat is indicated by the addition of an *ee* sound. This often combines with *sh*. The *shee* or *ee* syllable is never stressed and should be spoken as lightly as possible:

patrician puh-**TRI**-shuhn [pə-'trɪ-ʃən] scans to __-__-shee-uhn
   [__-__-ʃi-ən] @ COR V, 6, 82
marriage MAA-rij ['mæ-rɪʤ] scans to MAA-ree-ij ['mæ-ri-ɪʤ]
   e.g. @ R&J IV, 1, 11

9

One of the most common means of condensing a word to fulfill the demands of the meter is to remove an unstressed, internal vowel. No other sound is added to the remaining syllables:

stomacher STUHM-uh-ker ['stʌm-ə-kɚ] scans to STUHM-ker ['stʌm-kɚ] @ CYM III, 4, 84

The other common means of condensing a word is to remove the vowel in the penultimate syllable and replace it with *y* so that the two final syllables become one:

calumnious kuh-LUHM-nee-uhs [kə-'lʌm-ni-əs] scans to __-LUHM-nyuhs [__-'lʌm-njəs] e.g. @ HAM I, 3, 38
perfidious per-FID-ee-uhs [pɚ-'fɪd-i-əs] scans to ___-FID-yuhs [__-'fɪd-jəs] @ TEMP I, 2, 68

To clarify a pronunciation that changes depending on the word's usage, the abbreviations *(adj)* for adjective, *(adv)* for adverb, *(n)* for noun, *(v)* for verb, and *(part)* for participle are included when necessary:

consort (n) KAHN-sort ['kɑn-sɔɚt] scans to kuhn-SAWRT [kən-'sɔɚt] e.g. @ 2GEN IV, 1, 64
consort (v) kuhn-SAWRT [kən-'sɔɚt]

We offer definitions for apparent homonyms and other select instances:

bow (n) (weapon or collar of a yoke) BOH [boʊ] e.g. @ LLL IV, 1, 24 and AYL III, 3, 69
bow (v) (to bend into a curve or to play a stringed instrument with a bow) BOH [boʊ] @ PER IV, 2, 80
bow (v) (to incline the body) BOW [baʊ] e.g. @ RII I, 3, 47
covent (n) (a religious community) KUH-vehnt ['kʌ-vɛnt]

In this dictionary when the consonant *r* is between vowel sounds, it always indicates the beginning of a syllable. For example *orisons* is respelled **AW**-ri-zuhnz and not **AWR**-i-zuhnz, *Verona* is respelled vuh-**ROH**-nuh and not ver-**OH**-nuh, *environ* is respelled ehn-**VEYE**-ruhn and not ehn-**VEYER**-uhn. This placement of the consonant *r* at the beginning of a syllable gives a clean-cut definition to that syllable and adds clarity when speaking the text.

We have chosen to use the respelling Y$\overline{\text{OO}}$ to represent [ɪu]. Those who feel more comfortable using the simple vowel $\overline{\text{OO}}$ [u] should substitute it for words that have been respelled using Y$\overline{\text{OO}}$ [ɪu].

Syllabic consonants are those that form a syllable with a preceding consonant without the voicing of a vowel between the two. The syllabic is always an unstressed syllable and is indicated by placing the *uh* in parentheses (uh) in the respelled version. A small perpendicular mark is placed under the syllabic consonant in the phonetic version:

> **mettle** MEH-t(uh)l ['mɛ-tl̩]
> **batten** BAA-t(uh)n ['bæ-tn̩]

We give only one pronunciation for words in which the unstressed *i* [ɪ] and the *uh* [ə] are interchangeable, such as the first syllable in *bereft, denay,* and *requital.* Although the *uh* is more common in American speech, the unstressed *i* [ɪ] may be preferable because it has a clear, bright quality.

scanning the verse

Had in them more feet than the verses would bear
As You Like It III, 2, 159

Many of the suggested pronunciations in this dictionary are influenced by Shakespeare's use of iambic pentameter, which was the staple of English poetry from the time of Chaucer until the turn of the last century when free verse (that is, verse written outside of a metrical form) came into play. The verse form and the pronunciation of the Shakespearean vocabulary are intertwined. Shakespeare's verse often demands specific pronunciations, some of which are different than those used in colloquial speech. Pronunciations that respect the verse form can assist the actor not only with meaning and syntax but with acting intentions and emotional clarity.

Beginning students often ask how verse differs from prose. A short answer is that prose follows the rules of grammar, while verse obeys not only grammar but also additional principles, which serve to heighten our attention to the rhythm of the language. A line of iambic pentameter verse, indicated in print by its layout on the page, adheres to a set of metrical principles. An iamb is composed of two syllables, the first unstressed, the second stressed. This is called an iambic foot. A foot is merely a theoretical division of a verse line. Metrical refers to meter. Meter is the organization of the regularity of speech into a strict pattern that can be identified and counted. Pentameter means that there are five metrical units in each line of verse, since *penta* is the Greek word for five. Therefore, iambic pentameter is a line of five iambic feet, which contains ten syllables. For example:

> There is no virtue like necessity.
> *Richard II* I, 3, 278

Scansion is the orthographic or written attempt to represent the meter and stress of verse by noting the light and heavy stresses in the line. It seeks to capture the interplay of word and metrical stress. This interplay is often referred to as the rhythm of the language. Rhythm, however, can neither be seen, nor heard, nor read. Rhythm is something that is felt. It is a pulse, a beat, a sense of movement through time. Rhythm is innate, yet invisible. It is a pattern or series of beats that produce energy. Rhythm goes through time as movement goes through space. It is difficult, if not impossible, to portray rhythm on the page, though this is what scansion sets out to do. Capturing rhythm is like trying to capture breath. One can sense the act of breathing, but one does not see the air that is the component of the breath. In order for the audience to sense rhythm, the actor must establish it. And, once established, it must be maintained so that the variants, which heighten the expressiveness of the verse, can be *felt* as opposed to observed or heard. The variants need to be experienced as *variants*. The expressiveness and force of the language often stem from the variants to the iambic pentameter form employed by Shakespeare and his fellow dramatists. In the past, these variants were sometimes dismissed as an example of sloppy craftsmanship or ascribed to misguided typesetters. The actor should use and exploit variation and difference, not homogenize them. An individual line does not stand on its own but must be considered, eventually, both in relation to the other verse lines and to the prose surrounding it. As the variants are discovered and explored, the actor will find that they provide a map or sketch of the thought processes of the character, allowing the actor to create the verse line in the present moment.

It is important to note that Shakespeare and other writers of the period organized the arrangement of particular stresses — the beats and off-beats of the lines — not to fulfill arbitrary standards, but rather to reflect the emotional and psychological state of the character. Shakespeare wrote his plays over an approximately twenty-year period. He and his contemporaries sought to achieve a theatrical reality through the use of language. Consequently, they experimented with iambic pentameter, the English language, and the best theatrical forms for the expression of their ideas. One of his first plays *(Titus Andronicus)* was almost entirely in verse. Some early plays *(The Comedy of Errors, Two Gentlemen of Verona,* and *The Taming of the Shrew)* combine verse and prose. While a few *(Henry VI Part Two, Henry VI Part Three, Richard II,* and *King John)* are completely in verse, others *(Henry IV Part One, Henry IV Part Two, The Merry Wives of Windsor, Much Ado About Nothing,* and *As You Like It)* examine the potential of prose. In some early comedies *(A Midsummer Night's Dream* and *Love's Labor's Lost)* almost half of the play is in rhyming verse. However, a later tragedy *(Antony and Cleopatra)* contains 90 percent blank verse, i.e. verse that does not rhyme. Blank verse then becomes the predominate means of expression in the later tragedies and romances. In addition to these larger categories, Shakespeare investigates changes to the iambic pentameter line in individual plays. He experiments with long lines, epic caesuras, and short and shared lines, which are explained below. He was able to do this because iambic pentameter closely follows the rhythm of spoken English and, thus, has an extraordinary ability to accommodate a host of variations.

The most common variant to the ten syllable line is the longer line, specifically that which contains an eleventh or extra syllable, which is never stressed. (In the past, these line endings were referred to, in a form of literary misogyny, as "feminine" because of their "weak" or unstressed ending.) The most famous line in Shakespeare has an unstressed ending:

> To be or not to be, that is the question
> *Hamlet* III, 1, 55

The line is almost naturalistic in its simplicity, yet the iambic rhythm is present.

Some lines have twelve syllables. This type of line is referred to as either an alexandrine or a hexameter (six metric units to the line). An example is:

> Allow obedience, if you yourselves are old
> *King Lear* II, 4, 186

Whereas the iambic pentameter line of five units cannot divide itself in half, the hexameter line can. Two sections of three feet each give a sense of difference, perhaps a heightening of emotion or crisis in the character. When two characters share a twelve-syllable line, a sense of charged confrontation or heightened exchange exists between them. The twelve syllable line might also be reflective of a heightened emotional state in which the speaker is cramming twelve syllables into the time normally reserved for ten. The twelve-syllable line does something new, perhaps something disturbing, to the established iambic pentameter rhythm that has been set down for us. It is also possible for a hexameter line to have an additional unstressed syllable at the end, resulting in a line of thirteen beats. An example is:

> Yet are they passing cowardly. But, I beseech you
> *Coriolanus* I, 1, 198

Some lines when read appear to have more than ten syllables, but when spoken are actually regular iambic pentameter lines. A reverence for the printed text or a fixed belief in the efficacy of "proper" speech for Shakespearean production often leads actors to attempt to pronounce all the syllables that appear in a given line. Doing so creates havoc with the rhythm of the verse. However, contraction and elision will allow the rhythm to be maintained.

Contraction is the formation of a word by omitting or combining sounds of a longer phrase. Elision is the suppression of a weak, internal vowel or an unstressed syllable. We noted earlier that the verse line sometimes demands a pronunciation that is different than that used in contemporary speech. Conversely, the verse also demands contractions that are quite common in everyday life. The use of *I'm* for *I am* and *you'll* for *you will* often allows the actor to maintain the rhythm while ensuring that the ehm-**FAA**-sis does not fall on the wrong si-**LAA**-buhl. Elisions occur most often with the omission of the "uh" sound, known as the schwa. This is the unstressed sound found in words like *soda, forum,* and *bacon* and is the most common vowel sound in the English language. Given its prevalence in speech, one would expect listeners to be able to perceive the sound even if it is not actually spoken. Its elimination is most common in everyday speech in words like *natural* (**NAACH**–ruhl as opposed to **NAACH**–uh–ruhl) and *general* (**JEHN**–ruhl as opposed to **JEHN**-uh-ruhl). Some other words where this occurs are *liberal, factory, federal,* and *boundary.* This elimination occurs with increasing frequency through the later plays and might reach something of a peak in a line such as Hermione's

> The innocent milk in it most innocent mouth

Which, when the unstressed vowels are eliminated, becomes

> The inn'cent milk in it most inn'cent mouth
> *The Winter's Tale* III, 2, 99

This elision gives the line greater drive, provides for a stronger point of view, and with the closer antithetical alliteration of *n*'s and *m*'s allows the audience to hear a clearer version of her outrage and grief.

Another type of internal compression occurs when a word has contiguous vowels. Thus words like *glorious* scan to **GLAWR**-yuhs and *happier* scans to **HAAP**-yer. We have found that while actors sometimes find it strange to alter the printed text, once they achieve a certain specificity of action and level of emotional intensity, this elision becomes a part of their approach to the verse.

At times, it becomes necessary to expand a word in order to maintain the verse rhythm. The most common form of this, and one which is almost universally practiced, is pronouncing the *ed* endings to words as "id." This occurs in lines like Juliet's cry:

> Tybalt is dead and Romeo — banished
> That 'banished,' that one word 'banished.'
> *Romeo and Juliet* III, 2, 112–113

Some editions, such as the Pelican series, mark these stresses for the reader. Note also that Romeo with its contiguous vowels scans to two syllables, **ROHM**-yoh.

While contiguous vowels sometimes elide, they also can expand. This is most common with words ending in *ion*. It also occurs with words such as *patience, ocean,* and *marriage.* These syllabic expansions are an area of contention. Some feel that the full articulation of the *ion* ending (probably "ee-uhn" and rendered so in this dictionary) distances the audience from the play, short-circuits the emotional empathy between actor and audience, and thus should never be used. Others advocate the merest suggestion or hint of the extended sound, while still others prefer that the single syllabic sound be elongated to count for two beats. The pronunciation of these words remains anathema to some and controversial to others. We have begun to hear their occurrence in a number of professional productions. The third edition of the Arden series has taken to stating quite clearly that words like *invention* are "pronounced with four syllables" in the Prologue to *Henry V.* Within this Dictionary, we have offered expanded versions of some of these words and noted even more examples in "Afterthoughts" for those who wish to experiment with their usage. A far less controversial form of "stretching" occurs with the addition of a schwa between the existing syllables. With this addition, words like *business, entrance,* and *children,* expand to three syllables.

There are words in Shakespeare that can be pronounced with either one or two syllables. Some of the most common are *being, power, hour,* and *fire.* This syllabic variation will also allow the language to fulfill the demands of the meter. Odd as it may seem to those who still hold to an early 20th century elocutionary approach, the verse demands that certain words contract. This is especially true of words which possess a central *v, th,* or *r.* These interior consonants will disappear so that *ever* becomes *e'er* (as it is sometimes printed), *never* becomes *ne'er,* and *even* becomes *e'en. Either* and *whither* elide to monosyllabic *ei'er* and *wh'er.* Some would go so far as to elide *seven* to *se'n,* though this may challenge the comprehension of the audience. In this instance, the solution will be to speak the word quickly so as to give it one beat in the verse line, while still maintaining the *v* sound. Words with a central *r* that elide include *sirrah* and *warrant.*

In many cases, the text will provide instances of contractions, especially with prepositional phrases. Examples are:

> *o'th'* stands for "of the" pronounced as one syllable 'UH<u>TH</u>';
> *in't* stands for "in it" pronounced as one syllable 'INT';
> *to't* stands for "to it" pronounced as one syllable 'T$\overline{OO}$T';
> *i' th* stands for "in the" pronounced as one syllable '<u>I</u>T<u>H</u>';
> *th'other* stands for "the other" pronounced as two syllables
>   '<u>TH</u>UH<u>TH</u>-er'.

Elisions already printed in the text occur in words like *know'st, take't,* and *as't* and should be pronounced as one syllable "NOHST," "TAYKT," and "AAST."

Frequently, and especially in the later plays, there will be a line that seems to refuse to scan. Such a line often contains an epic caesura. The epic (or long) caesura is a form of the caesura, which is itself a break in the verse line. The caesura occurs after the fourth or sixth beat and often relates to the syntax of the sentence of which it is a part. While some refer to the caesura as a pause, it is perhaps more helpful to think of it either as a momentary spark of thought or as a shift of gears as the character embarks on a new thought or idea. Examples include:

> To sleep-perchance to dream: ay, there's the rub,
>> *Hamlet* III, 1, 65

in which the caesura appears after the sixth beat, and

> If you have tears, prepare to shed them now,
>> *Julius Caesar* III, 2, 169

and

> Be not afeard: The isle is full of noises,
>> *The Tempest* III, 2, 132

in both of which the caesura occurs after the fourth beat.

The epic (or long) caesura features a definite pause or full break in the line, which follows an extra weak or unstressed syllable in the foot before the break. After this full or deliberate pause, there seems to be a new beginning to the thought of the speaker. Quite often, there is a form of punctuation just before the epic caesura. The pause gives the line of eleven syllables the weight of twelve and allows the line to maintain an iambic rhythm without radically altering the pronunciation of everyday words. Examples are:

> And all the gods go with you. ( ) Upon your sword
>> *Antony and Cleopatra* I, 3, 99

> But for my sport and profit. ( ) I hate the Moor;
>> *Othello* I, 3, 380

Sometimes Shakespeare makes use of a short line which indicates a pause. The syllabic count falls short, but the iambic rhythm remains. The pause should be filled with some sort of non-verbal behavior, which can be either physical activity or silent psychological action, such as Horatio's anticipation of the Ghost's response to him in the first scene of *Hamlet*. On rare occasions, in plays filled with such articulate characters, the pause may reveal a character at a momentary loss for words. The duration of either the psychological action or the physical activity will, ideally, maintain the iambic rhythm of the verse.

At other times a line is shared. The full iambic line of five feet is split between two or more speakers. One character has two or three iambic feet, and another has the balance of the line. In the following, one line serves as an opportunity for two exchanges between the characters:

> LADY
>   I heard the owl scream and the crickets cry.
>   Did not you speak?
> MACBETH   When?
> LADY   Now.
> MACBETH   As I descended?
>   *Macbeth* II, 2, 15–16

Shakespeare occasionally uses both short, shared, and complete pentameter lines in combinations to stunning effect, as in the first scene of *Hamlet*.

Rarely, Shakespeare will employ a "headless" line. One example of this is Richard II casting his truncheon to the ground to stop the trial by combat of Bolingbroke and Mowbray, which prompts the Marshal to cry out:

> (—) Stay! the King hath thrown his warder down.
>   *Richard II* I, 3, 118

The beginning of the line is missing the unstressed syllable that normally precedes a stressed syllable in an iambic foot. The first word thus receives a heavy stress. The text calls for the briefest of pauses, which might allow an actor to register a sudden emotional shift or abrupt change in the scene.

Our attention to rhythm and Shakespeare's use of metrics in the compilation of this dictionary is intended to help the actor speak a living, breathing, supple language, rather than recite a printed text. As obvious as it seems, it might be good to note that the printed text is not the spoken word. The goal should be to experiment with the verse form in order to achieve a spoken language that is heightened yet realistic, thoughtful yet engaging. It is the unseen quality of the verse — its rhythm and the corresponding system of metrics — that gives the words their drive, power, and presence.

Readers who are interested in pursuing their study of Shakespeare's handling of metrics and the use of rhythm in poetic language are encouraged to consult *Shakespeare's Metrical Art* by George T. Wright and *Poetic Rhythm: An Introduction* by Derek Attridge, to whom we are indebted.

the dictionary

A fine volley of words
Two Gentlemen of Verona II, 4, 31

'a (corruption of the pronoun "he") uh [ə] an unstressed sound almost negligible to the ear; some productions substitute "he"

'a' (v) (to have) uh [ə]

a / 'a (prep) ("of" or "on") uh [ə]

Aaron *(TITUS)* **AA**-ruhn ['æ-rən] or **EH**-___ ['ɛ-___]

abate uh-**BAYT** [ə-'beɪt]

Abbess **AAB**-ehs ['æb-ɛs] or ___-is [___-ɪs]

Abel **AY**-buhl ['eɪ-bəl]

Aberga'ny see "Abergavenny"

Abergavenny, Lord *(HVIII)* **AAB**-er-**GEHN**-ee [æb-ə-'gɛn-i]

abhor aab-**HAWR** [æb-'hɔɚ] or uhb-___ [əb-___]

Abhorson *(MM)* aab-**HAWR**-suhn [æb-'hɔɚ-sən]

abject (adj) **AAB**-jehkt ['æb-ʤɛkt]

abjects (n) aab-**JEHKTS** [æb-'ʤɛkts]

abjure aab-**JOOR** [æb-'jʊɚ] or uhb-___ [əb-___]

abode uh-**BOHD** [ə-'boʊd]

abodements uh-**BOHD**-muhnts [ə-'boʊd-mənts]

abominably uh-**BAHM**-i-nuh-blee [ə-'bɑm-ɪ-nə-bli]

Abraham **AY**-bruh-haam ['eɪ-brə-hæm] scans to **AY**-bruhm ['eɪ-brəm] e.g. @ *RIII* IV, 3, 38

Abram **AY**-bruhm ['eɪ-brəm]
   Abram *(R&J)*

abram (light yellow color) **AY**-bruhm ['eɪ-brəm]

abroach uh-**BROHCH** [ə-'broʊʧ]

EE i be/ I ɪ bit/ EH ɛ bet/ AA æ bat/ O͞O u boot / O͞O ʊ book/ AW ɔ bought/ AH ɑ father/ ER ɝ bird/ UH ʌ cup/ AY eɪ bay/ EYE aɪ bite/ OY ɔɪ boy/ OH oʊ boat/ OW aʊ how/ YO͞O ɪu duke/ EAR ɪə beer/ AIR ɛə bear/ O͞OR ʊə tour/ AWR ɔə bore/ AHR ɑə bar/ NG ŋ king/ SH ʃ ship/ ZH ʒ vision/ TH θ thirty/ T͟H ð then/ CH ʧ child/ J ʤ just/ For complete list, see Key to Pronunciation p. 2.

abrogate AAB-ruh-gayt ['æb-rə-geɪt]

absent (v) aab-SEHNT [æb-'sɛnt]

Absey scans to AYB-see ['eɪb-si]

abstemious aab-STEE-mee-uhs [æb-'sti-mi-əs]

abstract (n) AAB-straakt ['æb-strækt]

Absyrtus uhb-SER-tuhs [əb-'sɝ-təs] or aab-___-___
   [æb-___-___]

aby uh-BEYE [ə-'baɪ]

abysm always scans to uh-BIZM [ə-'bɪzm]

academe AAK-uh-deem ['æk-ə-dim]

a-cap'ring uh-KAYP-ring [ə-'keɪp-rɪŋ]

access aak-SEHS [æk-'sɛs] scans to AAK-sehs ['æk-sɛs]
   @ *HAM* II, 1, 110

accessary (adj) AAK-sehs-uh-ree ['æk-sɛs-ə-ri] or possibly
   scans to AAK-sehs-ree ['æk-sɛs-ri] @ *RIII* I, 2, 191

accessary (n) aak-SEHS-uh-ree [æk-'sɛs-ə-ri] or AAK-sehs-ree
   ['æk-sɛs-ri]

accite aak-SEYET [æk-'saɪt]

accompt uh-KOWNT [ə-'kɑunt] (archaic form of
   "account" stems from Latin "computare" to count)
   Many productions use uh-KAHMPT [ə-'kɑmpt].

accordant uh-KAWR-d(uh)nt [ə-'kɔɚ-dn̩t]

accost uh-KAWST [ə-'kɔst]

accoustrements uh-KUHS-ter-muhnts [ə-'kʌs-tɚ-mənts]

accoutered / accoutred uh-KOO-terd [ə-'ku-tɚd]

accoutrement uh-KOO-truh-muhnt [ə-'ku-trə-mənt]

ache (the letter "H") AYCH [eɪtʃ]

ache (n) (a pain) (v) (to suffer pain) AYK [eɪk]

Acheron AAK-uh-rahn ['æk-ə-rɑn] scans to AAK-rahn ['æk-rɑn] @ *TITUS* IV, 3, 44

aches (pains) (pronounced like the letter "H" by the Elizabethans) AY-chiz ['eɪ-tʃɪz] e.g. @ *TEMP* I, 2, 370

Achilles uh-KIL-eez [ə-'kɪl-iz]
Achilles *(T&C)*

Achitophel uh-KIT-uh-fehl [ə-'kɪt-ə-fɛl]

acknown aak-NOHN [æk-'noʊn]

aconitum AA-kuh-NEYET-uhm [æ-kə-'naɪt-əm]

acquittance uh-KWIT-uhns [ə-'kwɪt-əns]

Actaeon aak-TEE-uhn [æk-'ti-ən]

Actium AAK-tee-uhm ['æk-ti-əm] or possibly scans to AAK-tyuhm ['æk-tjəm]

adage AAD-ij ['æd-ɪʤ]

Adallas uh-DAAL-uhs [ə-'dæl-əs]

Adam AAD-uhm ['æd-əm]
Adam *(AYL)*
Adam *(SHR)*

adamant AAD-uh-muhnt ['æd-ə-mənt] or ___-___-maant [___-___-mænt]

adder AAD-er ['æd-ɚ]

addle AA-d(uh)l ['æ-dl̩]

addrest uh-DREHST [ə-'drɛst]

adieu uh-DYOO [ə-'dɪu]

EE i be/ I ɪ bit/ EH ɛ bet/ AA æ bat/ OO u boot / OO ʊ book/ AW ɔ bought/ AH ɑ father/ ER ɝ bird/ UH ʌ cup/ AY eɪ bay/ EYE aɪ bite/ OY ɔɪ boy/ OH oʊ boat/ OW aʊ how/ YOO ɪu duke/ EAR ɪɚ beer/ AIR ɛɚ bear/ OOR ʊɚ tour/ AWR ɔɚ bore/ AHR ɑɚ bar/ NG ŋ king/ SH ʃ ship/ ZH ʒ vision/ TH θ thirty/ TH ð then/ CH tʃ child/ J ʤ just/ For complete list, see Key to Pronunciation p. 2.

27

Admiral AAD-muh-ruhl ['æd-mə-rəl]

Adonis uh-DAHN-is [ə-'dɑn-ɪs] or ___-DOHN-___
   [___-'doʊn-___]

adoptious uh-DAHP-shuhs [ə-'dɑp-ʃəs]

Adrian AY-dree-uhn ['eɪ-dri-ən]
   Adrian *(COR)*
   Adrian *(TEMP)*

Adriana *(CE)* AY-dree-AH-nuh [eɪ-dri-'ɑ-nə]

Adriatic AY-dree-AAT-ik [eɪ-dri-'æt-ɪk]

adverse aad-VERS [æd-'vɝs] scans to AAD-vers ['æd-vɚs]
   e.g. @ *12th* V, 1, 78

advertise always scans to aad-VER-teyez [æd-'vɝ-taɪz]

advertisement always scans to aad-VER-tiz-muhnt
   [æd-'vɝ-tɪz-mənt]

Aeacides ee-AAS-i-deez [i-'æs-ɪ-diz]

Aediles *(COR)* EE-deyelz ['i-daɪlz]

Aegles EE-gleez ['i-gliz]

Aemilius *(TITUS)* ee-MIL-ee-uhs [i-'mɪl-i-əs] scans to
   ___-MIL-yuhs [___-'mɪl-jəs] @ V, 1, 155

Aeneas i-NEE-uhs [ɪ-'ni-əs] or ee-__-__ [i-__-__]
   Aeneas *(T&C)*

Aeolus scans to EE-luhs ['i-ləs]

aery EH-ree ['ɛ-ri]

Aesculapius i-SKYOO͞-LAY-pee-uhs [ɪ-skju-'leɪ-pi-əs] or
   EH-__-__-__-__ [ɛ-__-__-__-__] scans to __-__-LAY-pyuhs
   [__-__-'leɪ-pjəs] @ *PER* III, 2, 111

Aeson EE-suhn ['i-sən]

Aesop EE-sahp ['i-sɑp]

Aetna EHT-nuh [ˈɛt-nə]

afeard uh-FEARD [ə-ˈfɪɚd]

affects (n) always scans to uh-FEHKTS [ə-ˈfɛkts]

affeered uh-FEARD [ə-ˈfɪɚd]

affiance (n) (confidence) uh-FEYE-uhns [ə-ˈfaɪ-əns]

affianced (pl) (betrothed) uh-FEYE-uhnst [ə-ˈfaɪ-ənst]

affined uh-FEYEND [əˈfaɪnd]

affray uh-FRAY [ə-ˈfreɪ]

affy uh-FEYE [ə-ˈfaɪ]

Afric AAF-rik [ˈæf-rɪk]

Agamemnon AAG-uh-MEHM-nahn [æg-ə-ˈmɛm-nɑn] or
___-___-___-nuhn [___-___-___-nən]
   Agamemnon *(T&C)*

agate AAG-it [ˈæg-ɪt]

Agenor uh-JEE-nawr [ə-ˈʤi-nɔɚ]

Agincourt AAJ-in-kawrt [ˈæʤ-ɪn-kɔɚt]

aglet AAG-lit [ˈæg-lɪt]

agnize aag-NEYEZ [æg-ˈnaɪz]

agone uh-GAWN [ə-ˈgɔn] or ___-GAHN [___-ˈgɑn]

Agrippa uh-GRIP-uh [ə-ˈgrɪp-ə]
   Agrippa *(A&C)*
   Agrippa *(COR)*

ague AY-gyo͞o [ˈeɪ-gju]

Aguecheek, Sir Andrew *(12th)* AY-gyo͞o-cheek [ˈeɪ-gju-ʧik]

EE i be/ I ɪ bit/ EH ɛ bet/ AA æ bat/ O͞O u boot / O͝O ʊ book/ AW ɔ bought/ AH ɑ father/ ER ɚ bird/
UH ʌ cup/ AY eɪ bay/ EYE aɪ bite/ OY ɔɪ boy/ OH oʊ boat/ OW aʊ how/ YO͞O ɪu duke/ EAR ɪɚ
beer/ AIR ɛɚ bear/ O͞OR ʊɚ tour/ AWR ɔɚ bore/ AHR ɑɚ bar/ NG ŋ king/ SH ʃ ship/ ZH ʒ vision/
TH θ thirty/ TH ð then/ CH ʧ child/ J ʤ just/ For complete list, see Key to Pronunciation p. 2.

aidance AY-d(uh)nts ['eɪ-dn̩ts]

aidant AY-d(uh)nt ['eɪ-dn̩t]

Ajax AY-jaaks ['eɪ-ʤæks]
　　Ajax *(T&C)*

alablaster AAL-uh-blaas-ter ['æl-ə-blæs-tɚ]

alack uh-LAAK [ə-'læk]

Alarbus *(TITUS)* uh-LAHR-buhs [ə-'lɑɚ-bəs]

alarum uh-LAH-ruhm [ə-'lɑ-rəm] or ___-LAA-___
　　[___-'læ-___]

alas uh-LAAS [ə-'læs]

Albans AWL-buhnz ['ɔl-bənz]

Albany, Duke of *(LEAR)* AWL-buh-nee ['ɔl-bə-ni] scans to
　　AWLB-nee ['ɔlb-ni] @ I, 1, 66

albeit always scans to awl-BEET [ɔl-'bit] except AWL-bee-it
　　['ɔl-bi-ɪt] @ *KJ* V, 2, 9

Albion AAL-bee-uhn ['æl-bi-ən] scans to AAL-byuhn
　　['æl-bjən] e.g. @ *2HVI* I, 3, 43

Al'ce AALS [æls]

alchemy AAL-kuh-mee ['æl-kə-mi]

Alcibiades *(TIMON)* AAL-si-BEYE-uh-deez [æl-sɪ-'baɪ-ə-diz]

Alcides aal-SEYE-deez [æl-'saɪ-diz]

alderliefest AWL-der-leef-ist ['ɔl-dɚ-lif-ɪst]

Alderman AWL-der-muhn ['ɔl-dɚ-mən]

Alecto uh-LEHK-toh [ə-'lɛk-toʊ]

Alencon uh-LEHN-suhn [ə-'lɛn-sən] scans to AAL-uhn-__
　　['æl-ən-__]
　　Alencon, Duke of *(1HVI)* scans @ I, 1, 95

Aleppo uh-LEHP-oh [ə-'lɛp-oʊ]

Alexander AAL-ig-ZAAN-der [æl-ɪg-'zæn-dɚ]
Alexander *(T&C)*

Alexandria AAL-ig-ZAAN-dree-uh [æl-ɪg-'zæn-dri-ə] scans
to __-__-ZAAN-druh [__-__-'zæn-drə] @ *A&C* IV, 8, 30

Alexandrian always scans to AAL-ig-ZAAN-druhn
[æl-ɪg-'zæn-drən]

Alexas *(A&C)* uh-LEHKS-uhs [ə-'lɛks-əs]

Alice AA-lis ['æ-lɪs]
Alice *(HV)* ah-LEES [ɑ-'lis] (since her name is only
spoken by Katherine, a native speaker of French)

Aliena AY-li-EE-nuh [eɪ-lɪ-'i-nə] possibly scans to
uh-LEE-uh-nuh [ə-'li-ə-nə] @ *AYL* I, 3, 124 if "Celia" is
SEE-lyuh ['si-ljə]

Alisander AAL-i-SAAN-der [æl-ɪ-'sæn-dɚ]

allay uh-LAY [ə-'leɪ]

allayment uh-LAY-muhnt [ə-'leɪ-mənt]

allegiant uh-LEE-juhnt [ə-'li-ʤənt]

Allhallond-Eve awl-HAAL-uhnd-eev [ɔl-'hæl-ənd-iv]

Allhallowmas awl-HAAL-oh-muhs [ɔl-'hæl-oʊ-məs]

Allhallown awl-HAAL-ohn [ɔ-'hæl-oʊn]

allicholy AAL-i-kahl-ee ['æl-ɪ-kɑl-i]

alligant AAL-uh-guhnt ['æl-ə-gənt]

allottery uh-LAHT-uh-ree [ə-'lɑt-ə-ri]

All-seer awl-SEE-er [ɔl-'si-ɚ]

EE i be/ I ɪ bit/ EH ɛ bet/ AA æ bat/ OO u boot / OO ʊ book/ AW ɔ bought/ AH ɑ father/ ER ɝ bird/
UH ʌ cup/ AY eɪ bay/ EYE aɪ bite/ OY ɔɪ boy/ OH oʊ boat/ OW aʊ how/ YOO ɪu duke/ EAR ɪɚ
beer/ AIR ɛɚ bear/ OOR ʊɚ tour/ AWR ɔɚ bore/ AHR ɑɚ bar/ NG ŋ king/ SH ʃ ship/ ZH ʒ vision/
TH θ thirty/ TH ð then/ CH ʧ child/ J ʤ just/ For complete list, see Key to Pronunciation p. 2.

ally (n) always scans to uh-**LEYE** [ə-'laɪ]

Almain **AHL**-mayn ['ɑl-meɪn]

almost **AWL**-mohst ['ɔl-moʊst] scans to awl-**MOHST** [ɔl-'moʊst] e.g. @ *MID* II, 2, 154

alms AHMZ [ɑmz]

Alonso *(TEMP)* uh-**LAHN**-zoh [ə-'lɑn-zoʊ]

Alow see "George Alow"

Althaea aal-**THEE**-uh [æl-'θi-ə]

Alton **AWL**-tuhn ['ɔl-tən]

Amaimon / Amamon uh-**MAY**-mahn [ə-'meɪ-mɑn]

amain uh-**MAYN** [ə-'meɪn]

Amazonian always scans to AAM-uh-**ZOH**-nyuhn [æm-ə-'zoʊ-njən]

ambuscadoes AAM-buh-**SKAY**-dohz [æm-bə-'skeɪ-doʊz]

amerce uh-**MERS** [ə-'mɝs]

ames-ace **AAMZ**-ays ['æmz-eɪs] or possibly aamz-**AYS** [æmz-'eɪs]

Amiens *(AYL)* scans to **AAM**-yuhnz ['æm-jənz]

amiss uh-**MIS** [ə-'mɪs]

amity **AAM**-i-tee ['æm-ɪ-ti]

amort uh-**MAWRT** [ə-'mɔɚt]

Amphimachus aam-**FIM**-uh-kuhs [æm-'fɪm-ə-kəs]

Ampthill **AAM**-t(uh)l ['æm-tl̩]

Amurath **AA**-muh-raat ['æ-mə-ræt] or __-__-raath [__-__-ræθ]

Amyntas uh-**MIN**-tuhs [ə-'mɪn-təs]

anathomize / anatomize uh-NAAT-uh-meyez [ə-'næt-ə-maɪz]
  possibly __-NOHT-__-__ [__-'nout-__-__] @ *LLL* IV, 1, 68

Anchises aan-KEYE-seez [æn-'kaɪ-siz]

ancientry AYN-shuhn-tree ['eɪn-ʃən-tri]

Ancus Marcius AANG-kuhs MAHR-shuhs ['æŋ-kəs]
  ['maɚ-ʃəs]

andirons AAND-eyernz ['ænd-aɪɚ-nz]

Andren AAN-druhn ['æn-drən]

Andromache *(T&C)* aan-DRAHM-uh-kee [æn-'drɑm-ə-ki]
  scans to __-DRAHM-kee [__-'drɑm-ki] @ V, 3, 84

Andronici aan-DRAHN-i-seye [æn-'drɑn-ɪ-saɪ]

Andronicus aan-DRAHN-i-kuhs [æn-'drɑn-ɪ-kəs]
  Andronicus, Marcus *(TITUS)* MAHR-kuhs ['maɚ-kəs]
  Andronicus, Titus *(TITUS)* TEYE-tuhs ['taɪ-təs]

Angelica aan-JEHL-i-kuh [æn-'dʒɛl-ɪ-kə]

Angelo AAN-ji-loh ['æn-dʒɪ-lou] scans to AANJ-loh
  ['ændʒ-lou]
  Angelo *(CE)*
  Angelo *(MM)* scans @ II, 1, 266

Angiers AAN-jearz ['æn-dʒɪɚ-z] scans to aan-JEARZ
  [æn-'dʒɪɚ-z] @ *KJ* II, 1, 1

Angus *(MAC)* AANG-guhs ['æŋ-gəs]

anhungry aan-HUHNG-gree [æn-'hʌŋ-gri]

Anjou aan-JOO [æn-'dʒu] scans to AAN-joo ['æn-dʒu]
  e.g. @ *1HVI* V, 3, 95

Anne, Lady *(RIII)* AAN [æn]

33

annexment uh-NEHKS-muhnt [ə-'nɛks-mənt]

anon uh-NAHN [ə-'nɑn]

Anselmo aan-SEHL-moh [æn-'sɛl-moʊ]

an't AANT [ænt]

Antenonidus AAN-ti-NOH-ni-duhs [æn-tɪ-'noʊ-nɪ-dəs]
some editions "Antenorides" AAN-ti-NAW-ri-deez
[æn-tɪ-'nɔ-rɪ-diz]

Antenor *(T&C)* aan-TEE-nawr [æn-'ti-nɔɚ]

anters AAN-terz ['æn-tɚz]

Anthropophagi AAN-thruh-PAHF-uh-jeye [æn-θrə-'pɑf-ə-ʤaɪ]

Anthropophaginian aan-thruh-PAHF-uh-JIN-ee-uhn
[æn-θrə-pɑf-ə-'ʤɪn-i-ən]

Antiates AAN-shee-ayts ['æn-ʃi-eɪts] possibly scans to
AAN-shyayts ['æn-ʃjeɪts] @ *COR* I, 6, 59

antic (n) or (v) or (adj) AAN-tik ['æn-tɪk]

Antigonus *(WT)* aan-TIG-uh-nuhs [æn-'tɪg-ə-nəs]

Antioch AAN-tee-ahk ['æn-ti-ɑk] scans to AAN-tyahk
['æn-tjɑk] e.g. @ *PER* I, Cho, 17

Antiochus *(PER)* aan-TEYE-uh-kuhs [æn-'taɪ-ə-kəs] scans
to ___-TEYE-kuhs [___-'taɪ-kəs] e.g. @ I, 3, 19

Antiopa aan-TEYE-uh-puh [æn-'taɪ-ə-pə]

Antipholus aan-TIF-uh-luhs [æn-'tɪf-ə-ləs]
Antipholus of Ephesus *(CE)* EHF-i-suhs ['ɛf-ɪ-səs]
Antipholus of Syracuse *(CE)* SI-ruh-kyo͞oz ['sɪ-rə-kjuz]

Antipodes aan-TIP-uh-deez [æn-'tɪp-ə-diz]

antiquary AAN-ti-kweh-ree ['æn-tɪ-kwɛ-ri]

antique (n) (a buffoon) AAN-tik ['æn-tɪk] (sometimes
spelled "antic")

antique (adj) (old or resembling antiquity) always scans to
AAN-teek ['æn-tik]

Antium AAN-tee-uhm ['æn-ti-əm] scans to AAN-tyuhm
['æn-tjəm] or AAN-shee-uhm ['æn-ʃi-əm] scans to
AAN-shyuhm ['æn-ʃjəm] e.g. @ *COR* III, 1, 11

Antoniad aan-TOH-nee-aad [æn-'toʊ-ni-æd]

Antonio aan-TOH-nee-oh [æn-'toʊ-ni-oʊ] scans to
___-TOH-nyoh [___-'toʊ-njoʊ]
Antonio *(MADO)*
Antonio *(MVEN)* scans e.g. @ II, 8, 10
Antonio *(TEMP)* scans e.g. @ I, 2, 129
Antonio *(12th)* scans e.g. @ IV, 3, 4
Antonio *(2GEN)* seems to scan @ II, 4, 51

Antonius, Marcus aan-TOH-nee-uhs [æn-'toʊ-ni-əs]
scans to ___-TOH-nyuhs [___-'toʊ-njəs] **MAHR**-kuhs
['mɑɚ-kəs]
Marcus Antonius *(JC)* also called "Mark Antony"
MAHRK **AAN**-tuh-nee [mɑɚk] ['æn-tə-ni] scans to
AANT-nee ['ænt-ni] e.g. @ II, 2, 52 (for the name in
A&C, see "Mark Antony")

Apemantus *(TIMON)* AAP-uh-**MAAN**-tuhs [æp-ə-'mæn-təs]

Apennines AAP-uh-neyenz ['æp-ə-naɪnz]

apish AY-pish ['eɪ-pɪʃ]

Apollo uh-**PAHL**-oh [ə-'pɑl-oʊ]

Apollodorus uh-**PAHL**-uh-**DAW**-ruhs [ə-pɑl-ə-'dɔ-rəs]

apoplexed AA-puh-plehkst ['æ-pə-plɛkst]

apoplexy AAP-uh-plehk-see ['æp-ə-plɛk-si] possibly scans to
AAP-plehk-___ ['æp-plɛk-___] @ *2HIV* IV, 4, 130

EE i be/ I ɪ bit/ EH ɛ bet/ AA æ bat/ O͞O u boot / O͝O ʊ book/ AW ɔ bought/ AH ɑ father/ ER ɝ bird/
UH ʌ cup/ AY eɪ bay/ EYE aɪ bite/ OY ɔɪ boy/ OH oʊ boat/ OW aʊ how/ Y O͞O ɪu duke/ EAR ɪɚ
beer/ AIR ɛɚ bear/ O͞OR ʊɚ tour/ AWR ɔɚ bore/ AHR ɑɚ bar/ NG ŋ king/ SH ʃ ship/ ZH ʒ vision/
TH θ thirty/ TH ð then/ CH tʃ child/ J dʒ just/ For complete list, see Key to Pronunciation p. 2.

35

apostrophus uh-PAHS-truh-fuhs [ə-'pɑs-trə-fəs]

apothecary uh-PAHTH-uh-KEH-ree [ə-'pɑθ-ə-kɛ-ri]
Apothecary *(R&J)*

appal uh-PAWL [ə-'pɔl]

appeach uh-PEECH [ə-'pitʃ]

appellant uh-PEHL-uhnt [ə-'pɛl-ənt] possibly scans to
AA-pehl-___ ['æ-pɛl-___] @ *RII* IV, 1, 104

apperil uh-PEH-ruhl [ə-'pɛ-rəl]

appertinent uh-PER-ti-nuhnt [ə-'pɝ-tɪ-nənt]

approbation AA-pruh-BAY-shuhn [æ-prə-'beɪ-ʃən] scans to
___-___-__-shee-uhn [___-__-__-ʃi-ən] e.g. @ *HV* I, 2, 19

approof uh-PROOF [ə-'pruf]

appurtenance uh-PER-t(uh)n-uhns [ə-'pɝ-tn̩-əns]

apricock AA-pri-kahk ['æ-prɪ-kɑk]

aptest AAPT-ist ['æpt-ɪst]

aqua vitae AH-kwuh VEE-teye or VEYE-tee ['ɑ-kwə]
['vi-taɪ] or ['vaɪ-ti]

Aquilon AAK-wi-lahn ['æk-wɪ-lɑn]

Aquitaine AAK-wi-tayn ['æk-wɪ-teɪn]

Arabia uh-RAY-bee-uh [ə-'reɪ-bi-ə] scans to ___-RAY-byuh
[___-'reɪ-bjə] e.g. @ *COR* IV, 2, 24

Arabian always scans to uh-RAY-byuhn [ə-'reɪ-bjən]

araise uh-RAYZ [ə-'reɪz]

arbitrament / arbitrement ahr-BI-truh-muhnt [ɑɚ-'bɪ-trə-mənt]

Arcas AHR-kuhs ['ɑɚ-kəs]

Archbishop ahrch-BISH-uhp [ɑɚtʃ-'bɪʃ-əp] scans to
AHRCH-bish-__ ['ɑɚtʃ-bɪʃ-__] e.g. @ *2HIV* I, 1, 189

archbishopric scans to **AHRCH**-bish-uhp-rik [ˈɑɚˈtʃ-bɪʃ-əp-rɪk]

Archelaus AHR-ki-**LAY**-uhs [ɑɚ-kɪ-ˈleɪ-əs]

Archibald, Earl of Douglas *(1HIV)* **AHR**-chi-bawld **DUHG**-luhs [ˈɑɚ-tʃɪ-bɔld] [ˈdʌg-ləs] scans to **DUHG**-uh-luhs [ˈdʌg-ə-ləs] @ V, 2, 32

Archidamus *(WT)* AHR-ki-**DAY**-muhs [ɑɚ-kɪ-ˈdeɪ-məs]

Arcite *(2NOB)* **AHR**-seyet [ˈɑɚ-saɪt]

Arde AHRD [ɑɚd]

Arden AHR-duhn [ˈɑɚ-dən]

argentine AHR-jin-teyen [ˈɑɚ-dʒɪn-taɪn]

Argier ahr-JEAR [ɑɚ-ˈdʒɪɚ]

argo AHR-goh [ˈɑɚ-goʊ]

argosy AHR-guh-see [ˈɑɚ-gə-si]

Argus AHR-guhs [ˈɑɚ-gəs]

Ariachne AA-ree-**AAK**-nee [æ-ri-ˈæk-ni]

Ariadne AA-ree-**AAD**-nee [æ-ri-ˈæd-ni] or EH-___-___-___ [ɛ-___-___-___]

Ariel *(TEMP)* **EH**-ree-uhl [ˈɛ-ri-əl] scans to **EH**-ryuhl [ˈɛ-rjəl] e.g. @ IV, 1, 57

Aries EH-reez [ˈɛ-riz]

Arion uh-REYE-uhn [ə-ˈraɪ-ən]

Aristotle AA-ri-**STAH**-t(uh)l [æ-rɪ-ˈstɑ-tl̩]

arithmetician uh-RITH-muh-TI-shuhn [ə-ˈrɪθ-mə-tɪ-ʃən] or scans to ___-___-___-___-shee-uhn [___-___-___-___-ʃi-ən]

EE i be/ I ɪ bit/ EH ɛ bet/ AA æ bat/ OO u boot / OO ʊ book/ AW ɔ bought/ AH ɑ father/ ER ɝ bird/ UH ʌ cup/ AY eɪ bay/ EYE aɪ bite/ OY ɔɪ boy/ OH oʊ boat/ OW aʊ how/ YOO ɪu duke/ EAR ɪɚ beer/ AIR ɛɚ bear/ OOR ʊɚ tour/ AWR ɔɚ bore/ AHR ɑɚ bar/ NG ŋ king/ SH ʃ ship/ ZH ʒ vision/ TH θ thirty/ TH ð then/ CH tʃ child/ J dʒ just/ For complete list, see Key to Pronunciation p. 2.

armado ahr-MAH-doh [ɑɚ-'mɑ-doʊ]

Armagnac AHRM-uhn-yaak ['ɑɚm-ən-jæk]

Armenia ahr-MEE-nee-uh [ɑɚ-'mi-ni-ə] possibly scans to
___-MEE-nyuh [___-'mi-njə] @ *A&C* III, 6, 35

Armigero ahr-MIJ-uh-roh [ɑɚ-'mɪʤ-ə-roʊ]

armipotent ahr-MI-puh-tuhnt [ɑɚ-'mɪ-pə-tənt]

aroint uh-ROYNT [ə-'rɔɪnt]

Arragon, Prince of *(MVEN)* AA-ruh-gahn ['æ-rə-gɑn]

arraign uh-RAYN [ə-'reɪn]

arrant AA-ruhnt ['æ-rənt]

arras AA-ruhs ['æ-rəs]

array uh-RAY [ə-'reɪ]

arrearages uh-RI-rij-iz [ə-'rɪ-rɪʤ-ɪz]

arrivance uh-REYE-vuhns [ə-'raɪ-vəns]

arrogancy AA-ruh-guhn-see ['æ-rə-gən-si]

Artemidorus *(JC)* AHR-tuh-mi-DAW-ruhs [ɑɚ-tə-mɪ-'dɔ-rəs]

artere scans to AHR-ter ['ɑɚ-tɚ]

Artesius *(2NOB)* ahr-TEE-zhuhs [ɑɚ-'ti-ʒəs] or ___-___-zyuhs
[___-___- zjəs]

Arthur, Duke of Britain *(KJ)* AHR-ther ['ɑɚ-θɚ]

artificer ahr-TIF-i-ser [ɑɚ-'tɪf-ɪ-sɚ]

Artois ahr-TOYZ [ɑɚ-'tɔɪz]

Arundel, Earl of AA-ruhn-d(uh)l ['æ-rən-dl̩]

Arviragus / Cadwal *(CYM)* AHR-vi-RAH-guhs [ɑɚ-vɪ-'rɑ-gəs]
or ___-___-RAY-___ [___-___-'reɪ-___] called KAAD-wawl
['kæd-wɔl]

Ascanius aas-**KAYN**-yuhs [æs-'keɪn-jəs]

ascribe uh-**SKREYEB** [ə-'skraɪb]

Asher AA-sher ['æ-ʃɚ]

Ashford AASH-ferd ['æʃ-fɚd]

Asia AY-zhuh ['eɪ-ʒə] scans to AY-zhee-uh ['eɪ-ʒi-ə]
    e.g. @ *CE* I, 1, 133

asinico AAS-i-**NEE**-koh [æs-ɪ-'ni-koʊ]

askant uh-**SKAANT** [ə-'skænt]

Asnath AAZ-nuhth ['æz-nəθ] some editions "Asmath"
    AAZ-muhth ['æz-məθ]

aspect always scans to aas-**PEHKT** [æs-'pɛkt]

aspic AAS-pik ['æs-pɪk]

asquint uh-**SKWINT** [ə-'skwɪnt]

assay (n) **AA**-say ['æ-seɪ] or aa-**SAY** [æ-'seɪ] in prose; always
    scans to aa-**SAY** [æ-'seɪ] in verse e.g. @ *MAC* IV, 3, 143

assay (v) **AA**-say ['æ-seɪ] scans to aa-**SAY** [æ-'seɪ]
    e.g. @ *AW* III, 7, 44

assembly uh-**SEHM**-blee [ə-'sɛm-bli] scans to __-__-buh-lee
    [__-__-bə-li] e.g. @ *MADO* V, 4, 34

assigns uh-**SEYENZ** [ə-'saɪnz]

assubjugate uh-**SUHB**-juh-gayt [ə-'sʌb-ʤə-geɪt]

Assyrian always scans to uh-**SI**-ryuhn [ə-'sɪ-rjən]

Astraea aas-**TREE**-uh [æs-'tri-ə]

asunder uh-**SUHN**-der [ə-'sʌn-dɚ]

EE i be/ I ɪ bit/ EH ɛ bet/ AA æ bat/ OO u boot / OO ʊ book/ AW ɔ bought/ AH ɑ father/ ER ɝ bird/
UH ʌ cup/ AY eɪ bay/ EYE aɪ bite/ OY ɔɪ boy/ OH oʊ boat/ OW aʊ how/ YOO ɪu duke/ EAR ɪə
beer/ AIR ɛə bear/ OOR ʊə tour/ AWR ɔə bore/ AHR ɑə bar/ NG ŋ king/ SH ʃ ship/ ZH ʒ vision/
TH θ thirty/ TH ð then/ CH ʧ child/ J ʤ just/ For complete list, see Key to Pronunciation p. 2.

39

Atalanta AA-tuh-LAAN-tuh [æ-tə-'læn-tə]

atasked uh-TAASKT [ə-'tæskt]

Ate AH-tay ['ɑ-teɪ] or **AY**-tee ['eɪ-ti]

Athenian (n) or (adj) uh-THEE-nee-uhn [ə-'θi-ni-ən] scans
    to __-THEE-nyuhn [__-'θi-njən] e.g. @ *MID* I, 1, 162

Athol AA-thuhl ['æ-θəl]

athwart uh-THWAWRT [ə-'θwɔɚt]

atomy AAT-uh-mee ['æt-ə-mi]

Atropos AA-truh-pahs ['æ-trə-pɑs] or ___-___-puhs
    [___-___-pəs]

attainder uh-TAYN-der [ə-'teɪn-dɚ]

attainture uh-TAYN-cher [ə-'teɪn-tʃɚ]

attendure uh-TEHN-der [ə-'tɛn-dɚ]

attent uh-TEHNT [ə-'tɛnt]

attributive uh-TRIB-yuh-tiv [ə-'trɪb-jə-tɪv]

atwain uh-TWAYN [ə-'tweɪn]

Aubrey Vere AW-bree VEAR ['ɔ-bri] [vɪɚ]

Audrey *(AYL)* AW-dree ['ɔ-dri]

Aufidius See "Tullus Aufidius"

auger AW-ger ['ɔ-gɚ]

aught AWT [ɔt]

augurer AW-guh-rer ['ɔ-gə-rɚ] or __-gyuh-__ [__-gjə-__]

augures AW-gerz ['ɔ-gɚz]

augury AW-gyuh-ree ['ɔ-gjə-ri]

Augustus aw-GUHS-tuhs [ɔ-'gʌs-təs]

auld AWLD [ɔld]

Aulis AW-lis ['ɔ-lɪs]

Aumerle, Duke of *(RII)* oh-MERL [oʊ-'mɝl]

auricular aw-RIK-yuh-ler [ɔ-'rɪk-jə-lɚ]

Aurora uh-RAW-ruh [ə-'rɔ-rə]

Autolycus *(WT)* aw-TAHL-uh-kuhs [ɔ-'tɑl-ə-kəs]

Auvergne, Countess of *(1HVI)* oh-VAIRN [oʊ-'vɛɚn] or __-VERN [__-'vɝn]

avaunt uh-VAWNT [ə-'vɔnt]

Ave Maries AH-vee or __-vay MEH-reez ['ɑ-vi] or [__-veɪ] ['mɛ-riz]

averring uh-VE(r)-ring [ə-'vɝ-rɪŋ]

aves AH-vayz ['ɑ-veɪz]

avised uh-VEYEZD [ə-'vaɪzd]

avoirdupois aav-er-duh-POYZ [æv-ɚ-də-'pɔɪz]

avouch uh-VOWCH [ə-'vaʊtʃ]

aweary uh-WI-ree [ə-'wɪ-ri]

awl AWL [ɔl]

awry uh-REYE [ə-'raɪ]

ay (yes) EYE [aɪ]

aye (ever) AY [eɪ]

azure AAZH-er ['æʒ-ɚ]

ba / baa BAA [bæ] or BAH [bɑ]

EE i be/ I ɪ bit/ EH ɛ bet/ AA æ bat/ OO u boot / OO ʊ book/ AW ɔ bought/ AH ɑ father/ ER ɝ bird/ UH ʌ cup/ AY eɪ bay/ EYE aɪ bite/ OY ɔɪ boy/ OH oʊ boat/ OW aʊ how/ YOO ɪu duke/ EAR ɪɚ beer/ AIR ɛɚ bear/ OOR ʊɚ tour/ AWR ɔɚ bore/ AHR ɑɚ bar/ NG ŋ king/ SH ʃ ship/ ZH ʒ vision/ TH θ thirty/ TH ð then/ CH tʃ child/ J ʤ just/ For complete list, see Key to Pronunciation p. 2.

41

baboon baa-BŌŌN [bæ-'bun] scans to **BAA**-bōōn ['bæ-bun] e.g. @ *MAC* IV, 1, 37

Babylon BAA-bi-lahn ['bæ-bɪ-lɑn] or __-__-luhn [__-__-lən]

Bacchanals BAAK-uh-naalz ['bæk-ə-nælz] or ___-___-nahlz [___-___-nɑlz]

Bacchus BAAK-uhs ['bæk-əs] or BAHK-___ ['bɑk-___]

backare (false Latin for "back-off") possibly BAAK-uh-ray ['bæk-ə-reɪ] or baak-AH-___ [bæk-'ɑ-___]

bad'st BAADST [bædst]

bade BAAD [bæd]

baes BAAZ [bæz] or BAHZ [bɑz]

Bagot *(RII)* BAAG-uht ['bæg-ət]

Bajazet baa-juh-ZEHT [bæ-ʤə-'zɛt]

baldrick BAWL-drik ['bɔl-drɪk]

bale BAYL [beɪl]

ballast BAAL-uhst ['bæl-əst]

ballet (a ballad) BAAL-it ['bæl-ɪt]

ballet-mongers BAAL-it-MUHNG-gerz ['bæl-ɪt-mʌŋ-gɚz] or ___-___-MAHNG-___ [___-___-mɑŋ-___]

balsamum BAWL-suh-muhm ['bɔl-sə-məm]

Balthasar / Balthazar BAAL-thuh-zahr ['bæl-θə-zɑɚ]
   Balthasar *(MVEN)*
   Balthasar *(MADO)*
   Balthasar *(R&J)*
   Balthazar *(CE)*

Banbury BAAN-buh-ree ['bæn-bə-ri]

banditto baan-DEE-toh [bæn-'di-toʊ]

bandogs BAAN-dawgz ['bæn-dɔgz]

bane BAYN [beɪn]

Banister BAAN-is-ter ['bæn-ɪs-tɚ]

bankrout BAANGK-rowt ['bæŋk-raʊt]

bannerets BAAN-uh-rehts ['bæn-ə-rɛts]

banning BAAN-ing ['bæn-ɪŋ]

banns BAANZ [bænz]

Banquo *(MAC)* BAANG-kwoh ['bæŋ-kwoʊ]

Baptista baap-TIS-tuh [bæp-'tɪs-tə] or __-TEES-__ [__-'tis-__]
Baptista Minola *(SHR)* MIN-uh-luh ['mɪn-ə-lə]

Bar BAHR [bɑɚ]

Barabbas scans to BAA-ruh-buhs ['bæ-rə-bəs]

Barbary BAHR-buh-ree ['bɑɚ-bə-ri] scans to BAHR-bree
['bɑɚ-bri] @ *RII* V, 5, 81

Barbason BAHR-buh-suhn ['bɑɚ-bə-sən]

barbermonger BAHR-ber-MUHNG-ger ['bɑɚ-bə-mʌŋ-gɚ]
or ___-___-MAHNG-___ [___-___-mɑŋ-___]

bard BAHRD [bɑɚd]

Bardolph BAHR-dahlf ['bɑɚ-dɑlf]
Bardolph *(1HIV, 2HIV, HV, MW)* possibly BAHR-d(uh)l
['bɑɚ-dl̩] based on spelling of "Bardol" in Quarto of 1HIV
Bardolph, Lord *(2HIV)*

Bargulus BAHR-guh-luhs ['bɑɚ-gə-ləs]

baring BEH-ring ['bɛ-rɪŋ]

EE i be/ I ɪ bit/ EH ɛ bet/ AA æ bat/ OO u boot / OO ʊ book/ AW ɔ bought/ AH ɑ father/ ER ɝ bird/
UH ʌ cup/ AY eɪ bay/ EYE aɪ bite/ OY ɔɪ boy/ OH oʊ boat/ OW aʊ how/ YOO ɪu duke/ EAR ɪɚ
beer/ AIR ɛɚ bear/ OOR ʊɚ tour/ AWR ɔɚ bore/ AHR ɑɚ bar/ NG ŋ king/ SH ʃ ship/ ZH ʒ vision/
TH θ thirty/ TH ð then/ CH tʃ child/ J dʒ just/ For complete list, see Key to Pronunciation p. 2.

43

Barkloughly bahrk-LOH-lee [bɑɚk-'loʊ-li] or possibly scans
  to **BAHRK**-loh-___ ['bɑɚk-loʊ-___] @ *RII* III, 2, 1

barm BAHRM [bɑɚm]

Barnardine *(MM)* **BAHR**-ner-deen ['bɑɚ-nɚ-din] possibly
  scans to ber-**NAHR**-___ [bɚ-'nɑɚ-___] @ IV, 2, 60

barne BAHRN [bɑɚn]

Barnet BAHR-nit ['bɑɚ-nɪt]

barony BAA-ruhn-ee ['bæ-rən-i]

barr'st BAHRST [bɑɚst]

barricado BAA-ri-KAY-doh [bæ-rɪ-'keɪ-doʊ] or ___-___-KAH-
  ___ [___-___-'kɑ-___]

Barson BAHR-s(uh)n ['bɑɚ-sn̩]

Barthol'mew *(SHR)* **BAHRTH**-uhl-myo͞o ['bɑɚθ-əl-mju] or
  BAHR-t(uh)l-___ ['bɑɚ-tl̩-___]

Bartholomew bahr-THAHL-uh-myo͞o [bɑɚ-'θɑl-ə-mju] or
  BAHR-t(uh)l-___ ['bɑɚ-tl̩-___] @ *HV* V, 2, 297

Basan BAY-suhn ['beɪ-sən]

Basilisco BAAS-i-LIS-koh [bæs-ɪ-'lɪs-koʊ] or BAAZ-___-___-___
  [bæz-___-___-___]

basilisk BAAS-i-lisk ['bæs-ɪ-lɪsk] or BAAZ-___-___ ['bæz-___-___]

Basingstoke BAY-zing-stohk ['beɪ-zɪŋ-stoʊk]

Bassanio *(MVEN)* always scans to buh-SAH-nyoh
  [bə-'sɑ-njoʊ] possibly buh-SAH-nee-oh [bə-'sɑ-ni-oʊ] in
  prose

Basset *(1HVI)* BAAS-it ['bæs-ɪt]

Bassianus *(TITUS)* BAA-see-AY-nuhs [bæ-si-'eɪ-nəs]

basta BAHS-tuh ['bɑs-tə]

Bastard of Orleans *(1HVI)* AWR-lee-uhnz [ˈɔɚ-li-ənz] scans to awr-LEENZ [ɔɚ-ˈlinz] e.g. @ I, 1, 93

bastinado BAAS-tuh-NAY-doh [bæs-tə-ˈneɪ-doʊ] or __-__-NAH-__ [__-__-ˈnɑ-__]

bate BAYT [beɪt]

Bates, John *(HV)* BAYTS [beɪts]

batler BAAT-ler [ˈbæt-lɚ]

battalia buh-TAYL-yuh [bə-ˈteɪl-jə] or __-TAHL-__ [__-ˈtɑl-__]

batten BAA-t(uh)n [ˈbæ-tn̩]

bauble BAW-b(uh)l [ˈbɔ-bl̩]

Bavian BAY-vee-uhn [ˈbeɪ-vi-ən]

bavin BAAV-in [ˈbæv-ɪn]

bawcock BAW-kahk [ˈbɔ-kɑk]

bawd / Bawd *(PER)* BAWD [bɔd]

bawdry BAW-dree [ˈbɔ-dri]

Baynard BAY-nerd [ˈbeɪ-nɚd]

Bayonne bay-OHN [beɪ-ˈoʊn]

be'st see "beest (v)"

beadle / Beadle BEE-d(uh)l [ˈbi-dl̩]

bearherd BE(r)-rerd [ˈbɜ-rɚd]

Beatrice *(MADO)* BEE-uh-tris [ˈbi-ə-trɪs] scans to BEE-tris [ˈbi-trɪs] e.g. @ III, 1, 21

EE i be/ I ɪ bit/ EH ɛ bet/ AA æ bat/ OŌ u boot / OŌ ʊ book/ AW ɔ bought/ AH ɑ father/ ER ɝ bird/ UH ʌ cup/ AY eɪ bay/ EYE aɪ bite/ OY ɔɪ boy/ OH oʊ boat/ OW ɑʊ how/ YOŌ ɪu duke/ EAR ɪɚ beer/ AIR ɛɚ bear/ OŌR ʊɚ tour/ AWR ɔɚ bore/ AHR ɑɚ bar/ NG ŋ king/ SH ʃ ship/ ZH ʒ vision/ TH θ thirty/ TH ð then/ CH ʧ child/ J ʤ just/ For complete list, see Key to Pronunciation p. 2.

45

Beauchamp, Richard, Earl of Warwick *(1HVI)* BOH-chaamp ['boʊ-ʧæmp] WAW-rik ['wɔ-rɪk] or WAH-__ ['wɑ-__]

Beaufort BOH-fert ['boʊ-fət]
    Beaufort, Cardinal Henry, Bishop of Winchester *(1HVI, 2HVI)* WIN-chehs-ter ['wɪn-ʧɛs-tɚ]
    Beaufort, Edmund, Duke of Somerset *(1HVI, 2HVI)* SUHM-er-seht ['sʌm-ɚ-sɛt] scans to SUHM-seht ['sʌm-sɛt]
    Beaufort, Henry, Duke of Somerset *(1HVI)*
    Beaufort, John, Duke of Somerset *(1HVI)*
    Beaufort, Thomas, Duke of Exeter *(1HVI)* EHK-si-ter ['ɛk-sɪ-tɚ]
    Beaufort, Thomas, Duke of Exeter *(3HVI)*

Beaumond BOH-muhnd ['boʊ-mənd]

Beaumont BOH-mahnt ['boʊ-mɑnt] possibly scans to boh-MAHNT [boʊ-'mɑnt] e.g. @ *HV* III, 5, 44

Bedford BEHD-ferd ['bɛd-fɚd]
    Bedford, Duke of, John *(HV, 1HVI)*

bedlam / Bedlam BEHD-luhm ['bɛd-ləm]

bedrid BEHD-rid ['bɛd-rɪd]

bedtime always scans to behd-TEYEM [bɛd-'taɪm]

bedward BEHD-werd ['bɛd-wɚd]

beest / be'st (v) BEEST [bist]

beest (n) BEEST [bist]

beget bi-GEHT [bɪ-'gɛt]

begot bi-GAHT [bɪ-'gɑt]

beguile bi-GEYEL [bɪ-'gaɪl]

behoof bi-HOOF [bɪ-'huf]

behoove bi-HOOV [bɪ-'huv]

behove bi-HOHV [bɪ-ˈhoʊv]

Bel BAYL [beɪl] or BEHL [bɛl]

Belarius / Morgan *(CYM)* bi-LEH-ree-uhs [bɪ-ˈlɛ-ri-əs] called MAWR-guhn [ˈmɔɚ-gən]

Belch, Sir Toby *(12th)* BEHLCH TOH-bee [bɛltʃ] [ˈtoʊ-bi]

beldam / beldame BEHL-daam [ˈbɛl-dæm] or ___- duhm [___- dəm]

belee'd bi-LEED [bɪ-ˈlid]

Belgia BEHL-juh [ˈbɛl-dʒə] scans to BEHL-jee-uh [ˈbɛl-dʒi-ə] @ *3HVI* IV, 3, 1

belie bi-LEYE [bɪ-ˈlaɪ]

belike bi-LEYEK [bɪ-ˈlaɪk]

Bellario buh-LAH-ree-oh [bə-ˈlɑ-ri-oʊ] scans to __-LAH-ryoh [__-ˈlɑ-rjoʊ] e.g. @ *MVEN* IV, 1, 164

Bellona beh-LOH-nuh [bɛ-ˈloʊ-nə]

bell-wether BEHL-wehth-er [ˈbɛl-wɛð-ɚ]

Belzebub BEHL-zuh-buhb [ˈbɛl-zə-bəb]

bemadding bi-MAAD-ing [bɪ-ˈmæd-ɪŋ]

bemete bi-MEET [bɪ-ˈmit]

bemock bi-MAHK [bɪ-ˈmɑk]

bemoiled bi-MOYLD [bɪ-ˈmɔɪld]

bemonster bi-MAHNS-ter [bɪ-ˈmɑns-tɚ]

Benedick *(MADO)* BEHN-uh-dik [ˈbɛn-ə-dɪk] or ___-i-___ [___-ɪ-___]

EE i be/ I ɪ bit/ EH ɛ bet/ AA æ bat/ OŌ u boot / OO ʊ book/ AW ɔ bought/ AH ɑ father/ ER ɝ bird/ UH ʌ cup/ AY eɪ bay/ EYE aɪ bite/ OY ɔɪ boy/ OH oʊ boat/ OW aʊ how/ YOŌ ɪu duke/ EAR ɪɚ beer/ AIR ɛɚ bear/ OŌR ʊɚ tour/ AWR ɔɚ bore/ AHR ɑɚ bar/ NG ŋ king/ SH ʃ ship/ ZH ʒ vision/ TH θ thirty/ TH ð then/ CH tʃ child/ J dʒ just/ For complete list, see Key to Pronunciation p. 2.

benefice BEHN-i-fis [ˈbɛn-ɪ-fɪs]

benetted bi-NEHT-id [bɪ-ˈnɛt-ɪd]

benign scans to BEE-neyen [ˈbi-naɪn]

benison BEHN-i-suhn [ˈbɛn-ɪ-sən] or ___-___-zuhn [___-___- zən]

Bentii BEHN-shee-eye [ˈbɛn-ʃi-aɪ]

Bentivolii BEHN-ti-VOH-lee-eye [bɛn-tɪ-ˈvoʊ-li-aɪ]

Benvolio *(R&J)* behn-VOH-lee-oh [bɛn-ˈvoʊ-li-oʊ] scans to ___-VOH-lyoh [___-ˈvoʊ-ljoʊ]

bequeath bi-KWEE<u>TH</u> [bɪ-ˈkwið] or __-KWEETH [__-ˈkwiθ]

berard BEH-rerd [ˈbɛ-rɚd]

bereft bi-REHFT [bɪ-ˈrɛft]

Bergamo BER-guh-moh [ˈbɝ-gə-moʊ]

Bergomask BER-guh-maask [ˈbɝ-gə-mæsk]

Berkeley (the name of a place in *1HIV* and RII) BAHRK-lee [ˈbɑɚk-li] scans to BAHRK-uh-lee [ˈbɑɚk-ə-li] or BERK-lee [ˈbɝk-li] scans to BERK-uh-lee [ˈbɝk-ə-li] @ *RII* II, 2, 119

Berkeley *(RIII)* BAHRK-lee [ˈbɑɚk-li] or BERK-lee [ˈbɝk-li]

Berkeley, Lord *(RII)* BAHRK-lee [ˈbɑɚk-li] or BERK-lee [ˈbɝk-li]

Bermoothes ber-MOOTH-iz [bɚ-ˈmuð-ɪz]

Bernardo *(HAM)* ber-NAHR-doh [bɚ-ˈnɑɚ-doʊ]

Berowne *(LLL)* bi-ROON [bɪ-ˈrun] possibly scans to BROON [brun] @ II, 1, 213

Berri BEH-ree [ˈbɛ-ri]

berrord BEH-rerd [ˈbɛ-rɚd]

Bertram see "Rossillion"

Berwick BEH-rik [ˈbɛ-rɪk]

beseech bi-SEECH [bɪ-ˈsitʃ]

beshrew bi-SHR$\overline{OO}$ [bɪ-ˈʃru]

beshrow bi-SHROH [bɪ-ˈʃroʊ]

besom BEE-zuhm [ˈbi-zəm]

Besonian scans to bi-ZOH-nyuhn [bɪ-ˈzoʊ-njən]

bestead bi-STEHD [bɪ-ˈstɛd]

bestial BEHS-chuhl [ˈbɛs-tʃəl]

bestraught bi-STRAWT [bɪ-ˈstrɔt]

bestrid bi-STRID [bɪ-ˈstrɪd]

betid bi-TID [bɪ-ˈtɪd]

betide bi-TEYED [bɪ-ˈtaɪd]

betroth bi-TROH<u>TH</u> [bɪ-ˈtroʊð] or __-TROHTH
  [__-ˈtroʊθ]

Bevis BEHV-is [ˈbɛv-ɪs] or BEEV-___ [ˈbiv-___]

bevy BEHV-ee [ˈbɛv-i]

bewet bi-WEHT [bɪ-ˈwɛt]

bewray bi-RAY [bɪ-ˈreɪ]

bezonians bi-ZOH-nee-uhnz [bɪ-ˈzoʊ-ni-ənz]

Bianca bee-AHNG-kuh [bi-ˈɑŋ-kə] or __-AANG-__
  [__-ˈæŋ-__]
  Bianca *(OTH)*
  Bianca *(SHR)*

bier BEAR [bɪɚ]

EE i be/ I ɪ bit/ EH ɛ bet/ AA æ bat/ $\overline{OO}$ u boot / $\overline{OO}$ ʊ book/ AW ɔ bought/ AH ɑ father/ ER ɝ bird/ UH ʌ cup/ AY eɪ bay/ EYE aɪ bite/ OY ɔɪ boy/ OH oʊ boat/ OW ɑʊ how/ Y$\overline{OO}$ ɪu duke/ EAR ɪɚ beer/ AIR ɛɚ bear/ $\overline{OO}$R ʊɚ tour/ AWR ɔɚ bore/ AHR ɑɚ bar/ NG ŋ king/ SH ʃ ship/ ZH ʒ vision/ TH θ thirty/ <u>TH</u> ð then/ CH tʃ child/ J dʒ just/ For complete list, see Key to Pronunciation p. 2.

biggen BIG-in ['bɪg-ɪn]

Bigot, Lord *(KJ)* BIG-uht ['bɪg-ət]

bilberry BIL-buh-ree ['bɪl-bə-ri]

bilbo BIL-boh ['bɪl-boʊ]

billeted BIL-i-tid ['bɪl-ɪ-tɪd]

billets BIL-its ['bɪl-ɪts]

Biondello *(SHR)* bee-uhn-**DEHL**-oh [bi-ən-'dɛl-oʊ] possibly scans to byuhn-**DEHL**-__ [bjən-'dɛl-__] @ I, 2, 223

Birnam Wood BER-nuhm WO͞OD ['bɝ-nəm] [wʊd]

bisson BIS-uhn ['bɪs-ən]

bitumed BI-tyo͞omd ['bɪ-tɪumd]

blackamoor BLAAK-uh-mo͞or ['blæk-ə-mʊɚ]

Blackfriars scans to blaak-**FREYERZ** [blæk-'fraɪɚz]

Blackheath scans to blaak-**HEETH** [blæk-'hiθ]

Blackmere BLAAK-mear ['blæk-mɪɚ]

blains BLAYNZ [bleɪnz]

Blanch BLAANCH [blænʧ]
Blanch *(KJ)*

blaspheme blaas-**FEEM** [blæs-'fim]

blastments BLAAST-muhnts ['blæst-mənts]

blazon BLAY-z(uh)n ['bleɪ-zn̩]

blench BLEHNCH [blɛnʧ]

blent BLEHNT [blɛnt]

blithe BLEYETH [blaɪð] or BLEYETH [blaɪθ]

blither (happier) **BLEYETH**-er ['blaɪð-ɚ]

Blithild BLITH-ild ['blɪθ-ɪld] or BLITH-___ ['blɪð-___]

Blois BLOYZ [blɔɪz]

blowse BLOWZ [blaʊz]

Blunt BLUHNT [blʌnt]
Blunt, Sir James *(RIII)*
Blunt, Sir John *(2HIV)*
Blunt, Sir Walter *(1HIV)*

boatswain / Boatswain *(TEMP)* BOH-s(uh)n ['boʊ-sn̩]

Bocchus BAHK-uhs ['bɑk-əs]

bode BOHD [boʊd]

bodements BOHD-muhnts ['boʊd-mənts]

bodged BAHJD [bɑʤd]

bodkin BAHD-kin ['bɑd-kɪn]

bodykins BAH-dee-kinz ['bɑ-di-kɪnz]

boggle BAHG-uhl ['bɑg-əl]

boggler BAH-guh-ler ['bɑ-gə-lɚ]

Bohemia boh-HEE-mee-uh [boʊ-'hi-mi-ə] scans to
___-HEE-myuh [___-'hi-mjə] e.g. @ *WT* I, 2, 333

Bohun BO͞ON [bun]

Bolingbroke BAH-ling-bro͝ok ['bɑ-lɪŋ-brʊk] or BOH-___-___
['boʊ-___-___] or BO͞O-___-___ ['bu-___-___]
Bolingbroke, Henry, Duke of Hereford, afterward Henry IV
(RII) HER-ferd ['hɝ-fɚd]
Bolingbroke, Roger

bolins BOH-linz ['boʊ-lɪnz]

EE i be/ I ɪ bit/ EH ɛ bet/ AA æ bat/ O͞O u boot / O͝O ʊ book/ AW ɔ bought/ AH ɑ father/ ER ɝ bird/
UH ʌ cup/ AY eɪ bay/ EYE aɪ bite/ OY ɔɪ boy/ OH oʊ boat/ OW aʊ how/ YO͞O ɪu duke/ EAR ɪə
beer/ AIR ɛə bear/ O͞OR ʊə tour/ AWR ɔə bore/ AHR ɑə bar/ NG ŋ king/ SH ʃ ship/ ZH ʒ vision/
TH θ thirty/ TH ð then/ CH ʧ child/ J ʤ just/ For complete list, see Key to Pronunciation p. 2.

51

bombard BAHM-berd ['bɑm-bɚd]

bombast BAHM-baast ['bɑm-bæst]

Bona *(3HVI)* BOH-nuh ['boʊ-nə]

bona-robas BOH-nuh-roh-buhz ['boʊ-nə-roʊ-bəz]

bonny BAHN-ee ['bɑn-i]

Bonville BAHN-vil ['bɑn-vɪl]

boon BŌON [bun]

boor BŌOR [bʊɚ]

booteless BŌOT-uh-luhs ['but-ə-ləs]   scans to bōo-TUH-luhs [bu-'tʌ-ləs] @ *1HIV* III, 1, 67

Borachio *(MADO)* boh-RAH-chee-oh [boʊ-'rɑ-ʧi-oʊ]

Bordeaux scans to BAWR-doh ['bɔɚ-doʊ]

Boreas scans to BAWR-yuhs ['bɔɚ-jəs]

boresprit BAWR-sprit ['bɔɚ-sprɪt]

borne BAWRN [bɔɚn]

borough BUH-roh ['bʌ-roʊ]

bosky BAHS-kee ['bɑs-ki]

Bosworth BAHZ-werth ['bɑz-wɚθ]

botcher BAHCH-er ['bɑʧ-ɚ]

botchy BAHCH-ee ['bɑʧ-i]

bots BAHTS [bɑts]

Bottom, Nick / Pyramus *(MID)* BAH-tuhm ['bɑ-təm] PI-ruh-muhs ['pɪ-rə-məs]

Bouciqualt BŌO-si-kawlt ['bu-sɪ-kɔlt]

bough BOW [baʊ]

Boult *(PER)* BOHLT [boʊlt]

bounden BOWN-duhn [ˈbaʊn-dən]

Bourbon BŌOR-buhn [ˈbʊɚ-bən] or BER-___ [ˈbɝ-___]
Bourbon, Duke of *(HV)*

Bourchier, Cardinal, Archbishop of Canterbury *(RIII)*
BOW-cher [ˈbaʊ-tʃɚ]

bourn BAWRN [bɔɚn] or BŌORN [bʊɚn]

bow (n) (weapon or collar of a yoke) BOH [boʊ] e.g. @
LLL IV, 1, 24 and *AYL* III, 3, 69

bow (v) (to bend into a curve or to play a stringed instrument
with a bow) BOH [boʊ] @ *PER* IV, 2, 80

bow (v) (to incline the body) BOW [baʊ] e.g. @ *RII* I, 3, 47

Boyet *(LLL)* boy-EHT [bɔɪ-ˈɛt]

Brabant BRAA-buhnt [ˈbræ-bənt]

Brabantio *(OTH)* bruh-BAHN-shyoh [brə-ˈbɑn-ʃjoʊ] or
__-BAAN-__ [__-ˈbæn-__] possibly scans to __-__-shee-oh
[__-__-ʃi-oʊ] @ I, 2, 78

brabbler / Brabbler BRAAB-ler [ˈbræb-lɚ]

brach BRAACH [brætʃ]

braggardism scans to BRAAG-er-dizm [ˈbræg-ɚ-dɪzm]

braggart BRAAG-ert [ˈbræg-ɚt]

Brainford BRAYN-ferd [ˈbreɪn-fɚd]

Brakenbury, Sir Robert *(RIII)* BRAAK-uhn-buh-ree
[ˈbræk-ən-bə-ri] or ___-___-beh-___ [___-___-bɛ-___]

brandish BRAAN-dish [ˈbræn-dɪʃ]

Brandon BRAAN-duhn ['bræn-dən]
Brandon *(HVIII)*
Brandon, Sir William *(RIII)*

bray BRAY [breɪ]

brazed BRAYZD [breɪzd]

brazier BRAY-zher ['breɪ-ʒɚ]

breach BREECH [britʃ]

Brecknock BREHK-nuhk ['brɛk-nək]

breech (n) (leg covering) BRICH [brɪtʃ] or BREECH [britʃ] usually in the plural BRICH-iz ['brɪtʃ-ɪz] or BREECH-___ ['britʃ-___]

breech (v) (to sheathe or to flog) BREECH [britʃ]

breedbate BREED-bayt ['brid-beɪt]

breese BREEZ [briz]

Bretagne BREHT-uhn ['brɛt-ən] possibly scans to breh-**TAHN** [brɛ-'tɑn]

brethren BREH<u>TH</u>-rehn ['brɛð-rɛn] scans to BREH-<u>th</u>uh-rehn ['brɛ-ðə-rɛn] e.g. @ *TITUS* I, 1, 92

Briareus breye-AH-ree-uhs [braɪ-'ɑ-ri-əs] or ___-EH-___-___ [___-'ɛ-___-___]

Bridget BRIJ-it ['brɪdʒ-ɪt]

brinded BRIND-id ['brɪnd-ɪd]

brinish BREYEN-ish ['braɪn-ɪʃ]

Bristol BRIS-t(uh)l ['brɪs-tl̩]

Bristow BRIS-toh ['brɪs-toʊ]

Britaine bri-TAYN [brɪ-'teɪn]

Britaine, Duke of *(KJ)* BRI-t(uh)n ['brɪ-tn̩]

Briton BRI-t(uh)n [ˈbrɪ-tn̩]

Brittaine BRI-t(uh)n-ee [ˈbrɪ-tn̩-i]

Brittany BRI-t(uh)n-ee [ˈbrɪ-tn̩-i]

broach BROHCH [broʊtʃ]

Brocas BRAHK-uhs [ˈbrɑk-əs] or BROHK-__ [ˈbroʊk-__]

brogues BROHGZ [broʊgz]

brooch BROHCH [broʊtʃ]

brothel BRAHTH-uhl [ˈbrɑθ-əl]

Brownist BROWN-ist [ˈbrɑʊn-ɪst]

bruit BROOT [brut]

Brundusium bruhn-DYOO-zee-uhm [brən-ˈdɪu-zi-əm]

Brutus BROO-tuhs [ˈbru-təs]
    Brutus, Decius *(JC)* DEE-shee-uhs [ˈdi-ʃi-əs] scans to
    DEE-shuhs [ˈdi-ʃəs] e.g. @ I, 3, 148
    Brutus, Marcus *(JC)* MAHR-kuhs [ˈmɑɚ-kəs]

bubukles BYOO-buh-kuhlz [ˈbju-bə-kəlz]

Buckingham BUHK-ing-uhm [ˈbʌk-ɪŋ-əɪn]
    Buckingham, Duke of *(2HVI)*
    Buckingham, Duke of *(HVIII)*
    Buckingham, Duke of *(RIII)*

Bucklersbury BUHK-lerz-buh-ree [ˈbʌk-lɚz-bə-ri]

buckram BUHK-ruhm [ˈbʌk-rəm]

buffet (n) (a blow) BUHF-it [ˈbʌf-ɪt]

buffet (v) (to hit) BUHF-it [ˈbʌf-ɪt]

bull-beeves bool-BEEVZ [bʊl-ˈbivz]

EE i be/ I ɪ bit/ EH ɛ bet/ AA æ bat/ OO u boot / OO ʊ book/ AW ɔ bought/ AH ɑ father/ ER ɝ bird/
UH ʌ cup/ AY eɪ bay/ EYE aɪ bite/ OY ɔɪ boy/ OH oʊ boat/ OW ɑʊ how/ YOO ɪu duke/ EAR ɪɚ
beer/ AIR ɛɚ bear/ OOR ʊɚ tour/ AWR ɔɚ bore/ AHR ɑɚ bar/ NG ŋ king/ SH ʃ ship/ ZH ʒ vision/
TH θ thirty/ TH ð then/ CH tʃ child/ J dʒ just/ For complete list, see Key to Pronunciation p. 2.

55

Bullcalf, Peter *(2HIV)* BOOL-kaaf ['bʊl-kæf]

Bullen, Anne *(HVIII)* BOOL-in ['bʊl-ɪn]

bullock BOOL-uhk ['bʊl-ək]

Bulmer BOOL-mer ['bʊl-mɚ]

bulwark BOOL-werk ['bʊl-wɚk]

bunghole BUHNG-hohl ['bʌŋ-hoʊl]

burbolt BER-bohlt ['bɝ-boʊlt]

burgher BER-ger ['bɝ-gɚ]

burgomasters BER-guh-maas-terz ['bɝ-gə-mæs-tɚz]

burgonet BER-guh-neht ['bɝ-gə-nɛt]

Burgundy, Duke of BER-guhn-dee ['bɝ-gən-di]
    Burgundy, Duke of *(HV, 1HVI)*
    Burgundy, Duke of *(LEAR)*

burnet BER-neht ['bɝ-nɛt] or ___-nuht [___-nət]

burthen BER-thuhn ['bɝ-ðən]

Burton-heath BER-t(uh)n-heeth ['bɝ-tn̩-hiθ]

Bury BEH-ree ['bɛ-ri]

Bushy *(RII)* BOOSH-ee ['bʊʃ-i]

business BIZ-niz ['bɪz-nɪs] scans to BIZ-uh-nis ['bɪz-ə-nɪs]
    e.g. @ *WT* IV, 4, 403

buskined BUHS-kind ['bʌs-kɪnd]

buss BUHS [bʌs]

Butts, Doctor *(HVIII)* BUHTS [bʌts]

by'r BEYER [baɪɚ]

Byzantium bi-ZAAN-tee-uhm [bɪ-'zæn-ti-əm] or __-__-shee-__
    [__-__-ʃi-__]

cabileros KAA-bi-LEH-rohz [kæ-bɪ-'lɛ-roʊz]

cacodemon KAA-kuh-dee-muhn ['kæ-kə-di-mən]

caddis KAAD-is ['kæd-ɪs]

Cade, Jack *(2HVI)* KAYD [keɪd]

cadent KAY-d(uh)nt ['keɪ-dn̩t]

Cadmus KAAD-muhs ['kæd-məs]

caduceus kuh-DYOO-see-uhs [kə-'dɪu-si-əs] or __-__-shee-__
     [__-__-ʃi-__]

Cadwallader kaad-WAWL-uh-der [kæd-'wɔl-ə-dɚ]

Caelius scans to SEEL-yuhs ['sil-jəs]

Caesar SEE-zer ['si-zɚ]

Caesarion always scans to si-ZEH-ryuhn [sɪ-'zɛ-rjən] or see-
     ___-___ [si-___-___]

Cain KAYN [keɪn]

Caithness *(MAC)* KAYTH-nehs ['keɪθ-nɛs]

caitiff KAY-tif ['keɪ-tɪf]

Caius KEYE-uhs ['kaɪ-əs] or possibly KAY-___ ['keɪ-___]
     Caius *(TITUS)*
     Caius Lucius *(CYM)* LOO-shuhs ['lu-ʃəs] scans to
         LOO-see-uhs ['lu-si-əs] @ II, 3, 55
     Caius Marcius Coriolanus *(COR)* MAHR-shuhs ['mɑɚ-ʃəs]
         scans to MAHR-shee-uhs ['mɑɚ-ʃi-əs] e.g. @ III, 1, 195
         KAW-ree-oh-LAY-nuhs [kɔ-ri-oʊ-'leɪ-nəs] scans to
         KAWR-yoh-LAY-nuhs [kɔɚ-joʊ-'leɪ-nəs] e.g. @ II, 2, 65

Caius, Doctor *(MW)* KEEZ [kiz] possibly scans to KAY-uhs
     ['keɪ-əs] or KEE-__ ['ki-__] @ IV, 6, 27

EE i be/ I ɪ bit/ EH ɛ bet/ AA æ bat/ OO u boot / OO ʊ book/ AW ɔ bought/ AH ɑ father/ ER ɝ bird/
UH ʌ cup/ AY eɪ bay/ EYE aɪ bite/ OY ɔɪ boy/ OH oʊ boat/ OW aʊ how/ YOO ɪu duke/ EAR ɪɚ
beer/ AIR ɛɚ bear/ OOR ʊɚ tour/ AWR ɔɚ bore/ AHR ɑɚ bar/ NG ŋ king/ SH ʃ ship/ ZH ʒ vision/
TH θ thirty/ TH ð then/ CH tʃ child/ J dʒ just/ For complete list, see Key to Pronunciation p. 2.

Calaber KAAL-uh-ber ['kæl-ə-bɚ] or scans to KAAL-ber ['kæl-bɚ]

Calais KAA-lis ['kæ-lɪs] (if French pronunciation is preferred in prose kaa-**LAY** [kæ-'leɪ])

Calchas *(T&C)* KAAL-kuhs ['kæl-kəs]

Caliban *(TEMP)* KAAL-i-baan ['kæl-ɪ-bæn]

Calipolis kuh-**LIP**-uh-lis [kə-'lɪp-ə-lɪs]

caliver KAAL-i-ver ['kæl-ɪ-vɚ]

calkin KAW-kin ['kɔ-kɪn]

callet KAAL-it ['kæl-ɪt]

Calphurnia *(JC)* kaal-**PER**-nee-uh [kæl-'pɚ-ni-ə] scans to ___-**PER**-nyuh [___-'pɚ-njə] e.g. @ I, 2, 7

calumniate kuh-**LUHM**-nee-ayt [kə-'lʌm-ni-eɪt]

calumniating kuh-**LUHM**-nee-**AYT**-ing [kə-'lʌm-ni-eɪt-ɪŋ]

calumnious kuh-**LUHM**-nee-uhs [kə-'lʌm-ni-əs] scans to ___-**LUHM**-nyuhs [___-'lʌm-njəs] e.g. @ *HAM* I, 3, 38

calumny KAAL-uhm-nee ['kæl-əm-ni]

Calydon KAAL-i-duhn ['kæl-ɪ-dən] or __-__-dahn [__-__-dɑn]

Cambio see "Lucentio"

Cambria KAAM-bree-uh ['kæm-bri-ə] scans to KAAM-bryuh ['kæm-brjə] @ *CYM* V, 5, 17

cambric KAAM-brik ['kæm-brɪk] or KAYM-___ ['keɪm-___]

Cambridge KAYM-brij ['keɪm-brɪʤ]
   Cambridge, Earl of *(HV)*

Cambyses kaam-**BEYE**-seez [kæm-'baɪ-siz]

Camelot KAAM-uh-laht ['kæm-ə-lɑt]

Camillo *(WT)* kuh-**MIL**-oh [kə-'mɪl-oʊ]

camomile KAAM-uh-meyel ['kæm-ə-maɪl] or ___-___-meel [___-___-mil]

Campeius, Cardinal *(HVIII)* kaam-PEE-uhs [kæm-'pi-əs]

canakin KAA-nuh-kin ['kæ-nə-kɪn]

canary (a sweet wine or a dance) kuh-NEH-ree [kə-'nɛ-ri]

Canidius *(A&C)* kuh-NID-ee-uhs [kə-'nɪd-i-əs] scans to ___-NI-dyuhs [___-'nɪ-djəs] @ IV, 6, 16 if Epic Caesura

canker KAANG-ker ['kæŋ-kɚ]

cannibally KAAN-i-buh-lee ['kæn-ɪ-bə-li]

cannoneer kaa-nuh-NEAR [kæ-nə-'nɪɚ]

canonized KAA-nuhn-eyezd ['kæ-nən-aɪzd] scans to kuh-NUHN-___ [kə-'nʌn-___] e.g. @ *HAM* I, 4, 47

canstick KAAN-stik ['kæn-stɪk]

Canterbury KAAN-tuh-buh-ree ['kæn-tə-bə-ri] scans to ___-tuh-bree [___-tə-bri]
Canterbury, Archbishop of *(HV)*

cantle KAAN-t(uh)l ['kæn-tl̩]

canton KAAN-tuhn ['kæn-tən]

canvass (v) KAAN-vuhs ['kæn-vəs]

canzonet kaan-zuh-NEHT [kæn-zə-'nɛt]

Capaneus KAAP-uh-NEE-uhs [kæp-ə-'ni-əs]

cap-a-pe kaap-uh-PEE [kæp-ə-'pi] or KAAP-uh-pee ['kæp-ə-pi]

caparison kuh-PAA-ri-suhn [kə-'pæ-rɪ-sən]

Capel KAA-p(uh)l ['kæ-pl̩]

EE i be/ I ɪ bit/ EH ɛ bet/ AA æ bat/ OO u boot / OO ʊ book/ AW ɔ bought/ AH ɑ father/ ER ɝ bird/ UH ʌ cup/ AY eɪ bay/ EYE aɪ bite/ OY ɔɪ boy/ OH oʊ boat/ OW aʊ how/ YOO ɪu duke/ EAR ɪɚ beer/ AIR ɛɚ bear/ OOR ʊɚ tour/ AWR ɔɚ bore/ AHR ɑɚ bar/ NG ŋ king/ SH ʃ ship/ ZH ʒ vision/ TH θ thirty/ TH ð then/ CH ʧ child/ J ʤ just/ For complete list, see Key to Pronunciation p. 2.

59

Capet KAY-pit ['keɪ-pɪt] or **KAA-___** ['kæ-___]

Caphis *(TIMON)* KAY-fis ['keɪ-fɪs]

Capilet KAAP-uh-lit ['kæp-ə-lɪt]
   Capilet, Widow of Florence *(AW)* FLAW-rehns ['flɔ-rɛns]
   or FLAH-___ ['flɑ-___]

capitulate kuh-PICH-uh-layt [kə-'pɪtʃ-ə-leɪt]

capocchia kuh-POH-kee-uh [kə-'poʊ-ki-ə]

capon KAY-pahn ['keɪ-pɑn] or ___-puhn [___-pən]

Cappadocia KAAP-uh-DOH-shuh [kæp-ə-'doʊ-ʃə]

capriccio scans to kuh-PREE-chyoh [kə-'pri-tʃjoʊ]

capricious kuh-PRISH-uhs [kə-'prɪʃ-əs]

Captain *(Various)*
   The Captains Dumain *(AW)* dyōō-MAYN [dɪu-'meɪn]

captious KAAP-shuhs ['kæp-ʃəs]

captivate KAAP-ti-vayt ['kæp-tɪ-veɪt]

Capuchius *(HVIII)* kuh-PYŌŌ-shuhs [kə-'pju-ʃəs]

Capulet KAAP-yōō-lit ['kæp-ju-lɪt]
   Capulet *(R&J)*
   Capulet, Lady *(R&J)*

carack / carrack KAA-rik ['kæ-rɪk]

caracts KAA-rikts ['kæ-rɪkts]

caraways KAA-ruh-wayz ['kæ-rə-weɪz]

carbonado KAHR-buh-NAH-doh [kɑɚ-bə-'nɑ-doʊ] or
   ___-___-NAY-___ [___-___-'neɪ-___]

carbuncle KAHR-buhng-kuhl ['kɑɚ-bəŋ-kəl]

carcanet KAHR-kuh-neht ['kɑɚ-kə-nɛt]

carcase / carcass KAHR-kuhs ['kɑɚ-kəs]

cardecue KAHR-duh-kyōō ['kɑɚ-də-kju]

cardinal / Cardinal KAHR-di-nuhl ['kɑɚ-dɪ-nəl] scans to KAHRD-nuhl ['kɑɚd-nəl] e.g. @ *1HVI* I, 3, 36

carduus benedictus KAHR-jōō-uhs BEHN-i-DIK-tuhs ['kɑɚ-ʤu-əs] [bɛn-ɪ-'dɪk-təs]

Carlisle, Bishop of *(RII)* kahr-LEYEL [kɑɚ-'laɪl]

carlot KAHR-luht ['kɑɚ-lət]

carman KAHR-maan ['kɑɚ-mæn]

Carnarvonshire kahr-NAHR-vuhn-sher [kɑɚ-'nɑɚ-vən-ʃɚ] or ___-___-___-shear [___-___-___ʃɪɚ]

carouse (n) (a hearty drink) kuh-ROWZ [kə-'rɑʊz]

carpet-monger KAHR-pit-MUHNG-ger ['kɑɚ-pɪt-mʌŋ-gɚ] or ___-___-MAHNG-___ [___-___-mɑŋ-___]

carriage KAA-rij ['kæ-rɪʤ] scans to KAA-ree-ij ['kæ-ri-ɪʤ] e.g. @ *R&J* I, 4, 94

carrion KAA-ree-uhn ['kæ-ri-ən] scans to KAA-ryuhn ['kæ-rjən] e.g. @ *2HVI* V, 2, 11

carters KAHR-terz ['kɑɚ-tɚz]

Carthage KAHR-thij ['kɑɚ-θɪʤ]

Casca *(JC)* KAAS-kuh ['kæs-kə]

casement KAYS-muhnt ['keɪs-mənt]

casketed KAAS-ki-tid ['kæs-kɪ-tɪd]

casque KAASK [kæsk]

Cassandra *(T&C)* kuh-SAAN-druh [kə-'sæn-drə]

Cassibelan kaa-SIB-uh-luhn [kæ-'sɪb-ə-lən]

EE i be/ I ɪ bit/ EH ɛ bet/ AA æ bat/ ŌŌ u boot / ŌO ʊ book/ AW ɔ bought/ AH ɑ father/ ER ɝ bird/ UH ʌ cup/ AY eɪ bay/ EYE aɪ bite/ OY ɔɪ boy/ OH oʊ boat/ OW aʊ how/ YŌŌ ɪu duke/ EAR ɪɚ beer/ AIR ɛɚ bear/ ŌOR ʊɚ tour/ AWR ɔɚ bore/ AHR ɑɚ bar/ NG ŋ king/ SH ʃ ship/ ZH ʒ vision/ TH θ thirty/ TH ð then/ CH ʧ child/ J ʤ just/ For complete list, see Key to Pronunciation p. 2.

Cassio *(OTH)* KAAS-ee-oh ['kæs-i-oʊ] scans to KAASH-yoh ['kæʃ-joʊ] e.g. @ V, 2, 319

Cassius KAASH-uhs ['kæʃ-əs] scans to KAASH-ee-uhs ['kæʃ-i-əs] or KAAS-yuhs ['kæs-jəs] scans to KAAS-ee-uhs ['kæs-i-əs]
Cassius *(JC)* scans e.g. @ I, 2, 182

cassocks KAAS-uhks ['kæs-əks]

Castilian King-Urinal kaa-STIL-yuhn king-YŎŎ-ri-nuhl [kæ-'stɪl-jən] [kɪŋ-'jʊ-rɪ-nəl]

Castor KAAS-ter ['kæs-tɚ]

Cataian kuh-TAY-uhn [kə-'teɪ-ən]

cataplasm scans to KAAT-uh-plaazm ['kæt-ə-plæzm]

catarrhs kuh-TAHRZ [kə-'tɑɚz]

catechise / catechize KAAT-i-keyez ['kæt-ɪ-kaɪz]

catechism KAAT-uh-kiz-uhm ['kæt-ə-kɪz-əm]

cate-log KAYT-lahg ['keɪt-lɑg]

cater-cousins KAY-ter-KUHZ-inz ['keɪ-tɚ-kʌz-ɪnz]

caterwauling KAAT-er-wawl-ing ['kæt-ɚ-wɔl-ɪŋ]

cates KAYTS [keɪts]

Catesby, Sir William *(RIII)* KAYTS-bee ['keɪts-bi] scans to KAY-tis-bee ['keɪ-tɪs-bi] or KAATS-bee ['kæts-bi] scans to KAA-tis-bee ['kæ-tɪs-bi] e.g. @ III, 7, 83

catlings KAAT-lingz ['kæt-lɪŋz]

Cato KAY-toh ['keɪ-toʊ]

Caucasus KAW-kuh-suhs ['kɔ-kə-səs]

caudle KAW-d(uh)l ['kɔ-dl̩]

cautel KAW-t(uh)l ['kɔ-tl̩]

cautelous KAW-tuh-luhs ['kɔ-tə-ləs] scans to **KAWT**-luhs ['kɔt-ləs] @ *COR* IV, 1, 33

Cavalery KAA-vuh-LI-ree [kæ-və-'lɪ-ri]

Cavaliero KAA-vuh-LEE-roh [kæ-və-'li-roʊ]

cavalleria KAA-vuh-LEH-ree-uh [kæ-və-'lɛ-ri-ə]

caviary KAAV-ee-eh-ree ['kæv-i-ɛ-ri]

cavil KAA-vuhl ['kæ-vəl]

Cawdor KAW-dawr ['kɔ-dɔ˞] or ___-der [___-də˞]

Cedius SEE-dee-uhs ['si-di-əs] or scans to SEE-dyuhs ['si-djəs]

ceinture SEHN-cher ['sɛn-tʃə˞]

celerity si-LEH-ri-tee [sɪ-'lɛ-rɪ-ti]

Celia *(AYL)* SEE-lee-uh ['si-li-ə] possibly scans to SEE-lyuh ['si-ljə] @ I, 3, 124 if "Aliena" scans to uh-LEE-uh-nuh [ə-'li-ə-nə]

cellarage SEH-luh-rij ['sɛ-lə-rɪdʒ]

cement (n) or (v) always scans to SEE-mehnt ['si-mɛnt]

censer SEHN-ser ['sɛn-sə˞]

Censorinus SEHN-suh-REYE-nuhs [sɛn-sə-'raɪ-nəs]

censure SEHN-sher ['sɛn-ʃə˞]

Centaur SEHN-tawr ['sɛn-tɔ˞]

centry SEHN-tree ['sɛn-tri]

centurions sehn-TYOO-ree-uhnz [sɛn-'tjʊ-ri-ənz]

Cerberus SER-buh-ruhs ['sɝ-bə-rəs] scans to SER-bruhs ['sɝ-brəs] e.g. @ *TITUS* II, 4, 51

EE i be/ I ɪ bit/ EH ɛ bet/ AA æ bat/ OO u boot / OO ʊ book/ AW ɔ bought/ AH ɑ father/ ER ɝ bird/ UH ʌ cup/ AY eɪ bay/ EYE aɪ bite/ OY ɔɪ boy/ OH oʊ boat/ OW aʊ how/ YOO ɪu duke/ EAR ɪə˞ beer/ AIR ɛə˞ bear/ OOR ʊə˞ tour/ AWR ɔə˞ bore/ AHR ɑə˞ bar/ NG ŋ king/ SH ʃ ship/ ZH ʒ vision/ TH θ thirty/ TH ð then/ CH tʃ child/ J dʒ just/ For complete list, see Key to Pronunciation p. 2.

cere SEAR [sɪɚ]

cerecloth SEAR-klawth ['sɪɚ-klɔθ]

cerements SEAR-muhnts ['sɪɚ-mənts]

Ceres SI-reez ['sɪ-riz]
Ceres *(TEMP)*

Cerimon SEH-ri-mahn ['sɛ-rɪ-mɑn]

certes SER-teez ['sɝ-tiz] scans to SERTS [sɝts] e.g. @ *HVIII*
I, 1, 48

Cesario suh-ZAH-ree-oh [sə-'zɑ-ri-ou] scans to __-ZAH-
ryoh [__-'zɑ-rjou] e.g. @ *12th* II, 4, 2

cess / cesse SEHS [sɛs]

chafe CHAYF [ʧeɪf]

chaff CHAAF [ʧæf]

chaffy CHAAF-ee ['ʧæf-i]

chalice (n) CHAA-lis ['ʧæ-lɪs]

Cham KAAM [kæm]

Chamberlain CHAYM-ber-lin ['ʧeɪm-bɚ-lɪn]
Chamberlain *(1HIV)*
Chamberlain, Lord *(HVIII)*

chamblet KAAM-blit ['kæm-blɪt] some editions "camlet"
KAAM-lit ['kæm-lɪt]

chameleon kuh-MEEL-yuhn [kə-'mil-jən] scans to KAA-
mee-leye-uhn ['kæ-mi-laɪ-ən] @ *3HVI* 3, 2, 191

Champagne shaam-PAYN [ʃæm-'peɪn]

champain CHAAM-payn ['ʧæm-peɪn]

champian CHAAM-pee-uhn ['ʧæm-pi-ən] or CHAAM-
payn ['ʧæm-peɪn]

Chancellor CHAAN-suh-ler ['ʧæn-sə-lɚ]
Chancellor, Lord *(HVIII)*

changeling CHAYNJ-ling ['ʧeɪnʤ-lɪŋ] scans to CHAYNJ-uh-ling ['ʧeɪnʤ-ə-lɪŋ] @ *MID* II, 1, 23

chanson shahn-SOHN [ʃan-'soʊn] or CHAAN-suhn ['ʧæn-sən]

chanticleer CHAAN-tuh-klear ['ʧæn-tə-klɪɚ] or SHAAN-___-___ ['ʃæn-___-___]

chantry CHAAN-tree ['ʧæn-tri]

chape CHAYP [ʧeɪp]

chapeless CHAYP-lis ['ʧeɪp-lɪs]

chapfall'n CHAAP-fawln ['ʧæp-fɔln]

chaplet CHAAP-lit ['ʧæp-lɪt]

chapmen CHAAP-mehn ['ʧæp-mɛn]

character (n) or (v) KAA-rik-ter ['kæ-rɪk-tɚ] scans to kuh-RAAK-___ [kə-'ræk-___] e.g. @ *RIII* III, 1, 81

characterless scans to kuh-RAAK-ter-lis [kə-'ræk-tɚ-lɪs]

charactery always scans to kuh-RAAK-tuh-ree [kə-'ræk-tə-ri]

Charbon SHAHR-bahn ['ʃaɚ-bɑn]

chare CHAIR [ʧɛɚ]

chariest scans to CHEH-ryuhst ['ʧɛ-rjəst]

chariness CHEH-ree-nuhs ['ʧɛ-ri-nəs]

Charing Cross CHEH-ring KRAWS ['ʧɛ-rɪŋ] [krɔs]

Charlemain SHAHR-luh-mayn ['ʃaɚ-lə-meɪn]

EE i be/ I ɪ bit/ EH ɛ bet/ AA æ bat/ OO u boot / OO ʊ book/ AW ɔ bought/ AH ɑ father/ ER ɝ bird/ UH ʌ cup/ AY eɪ bay/ EYE aɪ bite/ OY ɔɪ boy/ OH oʊ boat/ OW aʊ how/ YOO ɪu duke/ EAR ɪɚ beer/ AIR ɛɚ bear/ OOR ʊɚ tour/ AWR ɔɚ bore/ AHR ɑɚ bar/ NG ŋ king/ SH ʃ ship/ ZH ʒ vision/ TH θ thirty/ TH ð then/ CH ʧ child/ J ʤ just/ For complete list, see Key to Pronunciation p. 2.

Charles CHAHRLZ [ʧɑɚlz] scans to **CHAH**-ruhlz [ˈʧɑ-rəlz]
Charles *(AYL)*
Charles VI *(HV)*
Charles, Dauphin *(1HVI)* scans @ IV, 4, 26

Charmian *(A&C)* **CHAHR**-mee-uhn [ˈʧɑɚ-mi-ən] scans to
CHAHR-myuhn [ˈʧɑɚ-mjən] or **SHAHR**-__-__
[ˈʃɑɚ-__-__] scans to **SHAHR**-__ [ˈʃɑɚ-__] or **KAHR**-__-__
[ˈkɑɚ-__-__] scans to **KAHR**-__ [ˈkɑɚ-__] e.g. @ I, 3, 15

charneco shahr-**NAY**-koh [ʃɑɚ-ˈneɪ-koʊ] or **CHAHR**-ni-___
[ˈʧɑɚ-nɪ-___]

charnel CHAHR-nuhl [ˈʧɑɚ-nəl]

Charolois SHAA-ruh-loyz [ˈʃæ-rə-lɔɪz]

Charon KEH-ruhn [ˈkɛ-rən] or **KAA**-___ [ˈkæ-___]

Chartreux SHAHR-trōō [ˈʃɑɚ-tru]

Charybdis kuh-**RIB**-dis [kə-ˈrɪb-dɪs]

chastise always scans to **CHAAS**-teyez [ˈʧæs-taɪz] except
possibly chaas-**TEYEZ** [ʧæs-ˈtaɪz] @ *T&C* V, 5, 4

chastisement CHAAS-tiz-muhnt [ˈʧæs-tɪz-mənt]

Chatillion *(KJ)* shaa-**TIL**-yuhn [ʃæ-ˈtɪl-jən] scans to __-__-ee-uhn
[__-__-i-ən] @ I, 1, 30

Chatillon SHAA-til-yuhn [ˈʃæ-tɪl-jən] if "Jacques" is JAYKS
[ʤeɪks] or JAAKS [ʤæks] or shaa-**TIL**-yuhn [ʃæ-ˈtɪl-jən]
if "Jacques" is JAY-kweez [ˈʤeɪ-kwiz] @ *HV* III, 5, 43

chattels CHAA-t(uh)lz [ˈʧæ-tl̩z]

Chaucer CHAW-ser [ˈʧɔ-sɚ]

chaudron CHAW-druhn [ˈʧɔ-drən]

chaunt CHAANT [ʧænt]

chawed CHAWD [ʧɔd]

checkins CHEH-kinz ['ʧɛ-kɪnz]

cheerly CHEAR-lee ['ʧɪɚ-li]

Chertsey CHERT-see ['ʧɝt-si]

cherubin CHEH-ruh-bin ['ʧɛ-rə-bɪn]

Chetas KEE-tuhs ['ki-təs]

chev'ril SHEHV-ruhl ['ʃɛv-rəl]

chevalier sheh-vuh-LEAR [ʃɛ-və-'lɪɚ]

cheveril SHEHV-uh-ruhl ['ʃɛv-ə-rəl] scans to SHEHV-ruhl ['ʃɛv-rəl] @ *HVIII* II, 3, 32

chewet CHŌŌ-it ['ʧu-ɪt]

chid CHID [ʧɪd]

chidden CHI-d(uh)n ['ʧɪ-dn̩]

chide CHEYED [ʧaɪd]

chiders CHEYED-erz ['ʧaɪd-ɚz]

Chief Justice, Lord *(2HIV)* CHEEF JUHS-tis [ʧif] ['ʤʌs-tɪs]

Childeric CHIL-duh-rik ['ʧɪl-də-rɪk]

children CHIL-drehn ['ʧɪl-drɛn] or __-druhn [__-drən] scans to CHIL-duh-rehn ['ʧɪl-də-rɛn] or CHIL-duh-ruhn ['ʧɪl-də-rən] e.g. @ *CE* V, 1, 361

chine CHEYEN [ʧaɪn]

chink CHINGK [ʧɪŋk]

Chiron *(TITUS)* KEYE-ruhn ['kaɪ-rən] or __-rahn [__-rɑn]

chirurgeonly keye-RER-juhn-lee [kaɪ-'rɝ-ʤən-li]

Chitopher CHIT-uh-fer ['ʧɪt-ə-fɚ] or KIT-__-__ ['kɪt-__-__]

EE i be/ I ɪ bit/ EH ɛ bet/ AA æ bat/ ŌŌ u boot / ŌŌ ʊ book/ AW ɔ bought/ AH ɑ father/ ER ɝ bird/
UH ʌ cup/ AY eɪ bay/ EYE aɪ bite/ OY ɔɪ boy/ OH oʊ boat/ OW aʊ how/ YŌŌ ɪu duke/ EAR ɪɚ
beer/ AIR ɛɚ bear/ ŌŌR ʊɚ tour/ AWR ɔɚ bore/ AHR ɑɚ bar/ NG ŋ king/ SH ʃ ship/ ZH ʒ vision/
TH θ thirty/ TH ð then/ CH ʧ child/ J ʤ just/ For complete list, see Key to Pronunciation p. 2.

choler KAHL-er ['kɑl-ɚ]

choleric KAH-luh-rik ['kɑ-lə-rɪk] scans to KAHL-rik ['kɑl-rɪk] e.g. @ *MM* II, 2, 130

chopine choh-PEEN [tʃou-'pin]

chopt CHAHPT [tʃɑpt]

Chorus KAW-ruhs ['kɔ-rəs]
    Chorus *(HV)*
    Chorus *(R&J)*
    Chorus *(WT)*

chough CHUHF [tʃʌf]

christen KRIS-uhn ['krɪs-ən]

christendom / Christendom KRIS-uhn-duhm ['krɪs-ən-dəm] scans to KRIS-duhm ['krɪs-dəm] @ *HVIII* III, 2, 67

christom KRIZ-uhm ['krɪz-əm]

Christophero kris-TAHF-uh-roh [krɪs-'tɑf-ə-rou] scans to __-TAHF-roh [__-'tɑf-rou] @ *SHR* Ind, 2, 71

chrysolite KRIS-uh-leyet ['krɪs-ə-laɪt]

chuffs CHUHFS [tʃʌfs]

churl CHERL [tʃɝl]

Chus KUHS [kʌs] or KUHSH [kʌʃ]

cicatrice SI-kuh-tris ['sɪ-kə-trɪs]

Cicely always scans to SIS-lee ['sɪs-li]

Cicero *(JC)* SIS-uh-roh ['sɪs-ə-rou] scans to SIS-roh ['sɪs-rou] @ IV, 3, 178

Ciceter SIS-i-ter ['sɪs-ɪ-tɚ]

Cilicia scans to si-LI-shuh [sɪ-'lɪ-ʃə]

Cimber, Metellus *(JC)* See "Metellus Cimber"

Cimmerian si-MI-ree-uhn [sɪ-'mɪ-ri-ən]

Cinna SIN-uh ['sɪn-ə]
Cinna *(JC)*
Cinna, a Poet *(JC)*

cinque-pace SINGK-uh-pays ['sɪŋk-ə-peɪs] or SINGK-pays ['sɪŋk-peɪs]

Cinque-Ports singk-PAWRTS [sɪŋk-'pɔɚts]

cinque-spotted singk-SPAHT-id [sɪŋk-'spɑt-ɪd]

cipher SEYE-fer ['saɪ-fɚ]

Circe SER-see ['sɝ-si]

circummured SER-kuhm-myoōrd ['sɝ-kəm-mjʊɚd]

cistern SIS-tern ['sɪs-tɚn]

cital SEYE-t(uh)l ['saɪ-tl̩]

cittern-head SIT-ern-hehd ['sɪt-ɚn-hɛd]

civet SIV-it ['sɪv-ɪt]

clamber KLAAM-ber ['klæm-bɚ]

clangor KLAANG-er ['klæŋ-ɚ] or ___-ger [___-gɚ]

Clare KLAIR [klɛɚ]

Clarence KLAA-ruhns ['klæ-rəns]

claret KLAA-rit ['klæ-rɪt]

Claribel KLAA-ri-behl ['klæ-rɪ-bɛl]

Claudio KLAW-dee-oh ['klɔ-di-oʊ] scans to KLAW-dyoh ['klɔ-djoʊ]
Claudio *(MM)* scans @ III, 1, 74
Claudio *(MADO)* scans @ I, 1, 264

EE i be/ I ɪ bit/ EH ɛ bet/ AA æ bat/ OŌ u boot/ OŌ ʊ book/ AW ɔ bought/ AH ɑ father/ ER ɝ bird/ UH ʌ cup/ AY eɪ bay/ EYE aɪ bite/ OY ɔɪ boy/ OH oʊ boat/ OW aʊ how/ YOŌ ɪu duke/ EAR ɪɚ beer/ AIR ɛɚ bear/ OŌR ʊɚ tour/ AWR ɔɚ bore/ AHR ɑɚ bar/ NG ŋ king/ SH ʃ ship/ ZH ʒ vision/ TH θ thirty/ TH ð then/ CH ʧ child/ J ʤ just/ For complete list, see Key to Pronunciation p. 2.

Claudius KLAW-dee-uhs [ˈklɔ-di-əs] scans to **KLAW**-dyuhs
[ˈklɔ-djəs]
Claudius *(HAM)*
Claudius *(JC)* scans @ IV, 3, 242

cleft KLEHFT [klɛft]

Cleitus KLEYE-tuhs [ˈklaɪ-təs]

clement KLEHM-uhnt [ˈklɛm-ənt]

Cleomenes *(WT)* klee-**AHM**-i-neez [kli-ˈɑm-ɪ-niz]

Cleon *(PER)* KLEE-ahn [ˈkli-ɑn]

Cleopatra KLEE-uh-**PAA**-truh [kli-ə-ˈpæ-trə]
Cleopatra *(A&C)* possibly scans to klee-**PAA**-___
[kli-ˈpæ-___] e.g. @ V, 2, 124

clepe KLEEP [klip]

clepeth KLEEP-ith [ˈklip-ɪθ]

clept KLEHPT [klɛpt]

clerestories KLEAR-staw-reez [ˈklɪɚ-stɔ-riz]

clerk KLERK [klɝk] possibly KLAHRK [klɑɚk] in *MVEN*
to follow rhyme scheme in final speech

Clerk of Chartham *(2HVI)* CHAA-tuhm [ˈtʃæ-təm] or
CHAHR-tuhm [ˈtʃɑɚ-təm]

clew KLŌŌ [klu]

Clifford KLIF-erd [ˈklɪf-ɚd]
Clifford, Lord John *(3HVI)*
Clifford, Lord Thomas *(2HVI)*

climatures KLEYE-muh-cherz [ˈklaɪ-mə-tʃɚz]

clime KLEYEM [klaɪm]

clinquant KLING-kuhnt [ˈklɪŋ-kənt]

Clitus *(JC)* KLEYE-tuhs [ˈklaɪ-təs]

clo'es KLOHZ [kloʊz]

clodpoll KLAHD-pohl [ˈklɑd-poʊl]

cloistress KLOY-stris [ˈklɔɪ-strɪs]

close (adj) or (adv) KLOHS [kloʊs]

close (n) or (v) KLOHZ [kloʊz]

close-stool KLOHS-stool [ˈkloʊs-stul]

Cloten *(CYM)* KLAH-t(uh)n [ˈklɑ-tn̩] or KLOH-___
    [ˈkloʊ-___]

Clothair KLOH-thair [ˈkloʊ-θɛɚ] or ___-tair [___-tɛɚ]

Clotharius kloh-<u>TH</u>EH-ree-uhs [kloʊ-ˈðɛ-ri-əs] or
    __-TEH-__-__ [__-ˈtɛ-__-__]

clothier KLOH-<u>th</u>ee-er [ˈkloʊ-ði-ɚ] scans to KLOH<u>TH</u>-yer
    [ˈkloʊð-jɚ] @ *HVIII* I, 2, 31

clotpoll KLAHT-pohl [ˈklɑt-poʊl]

clout KLOWT [klaʊt]

cloven KLOH-vuhn [ˈkloʊ-vən]

Clowder KLOW-der [ˈklaʊ-dɚ]

cloyment KLOY-muhnt [ˈklɔɪ-mənt]

clyster KLIS-ter [ˈklɪs-tɚ]

Cobham KAH-buhm [ˈkɑ-bəm]
    Cobham, Eleanor, Duchess of Gloucester *(2HVI)* EHL-i-
        nawr [ˈɛl-ɪ-nɔɚ] or __-__-ner [__-__-nɚ] scans to
        EHL-nawr [ˈɛl-nɔɚ] or __-ner [__-nɚ] e.g. @ II, 3, 1

cobloaf KAHB-lohf [ˈkɑb-loʊf]

Cobweb *(MID)* KAHB-wehb [ˈkɑb-wɛb]

EE i be/ I ɪ bit/ EH ɛ bet/ AA æ bat/ O͞O u boot / O͞O ʊ book/ AW ɔ bought/ AH ɑ father/ ER ɝ bird/
UH ʌ cup/ AY eɪ bay/ EYE aɪ bite/ OY ɔɪ boy/ OH oʊ boat/ OW aʊ how/ YO͞O ɪu duke/ EAR ɪɚ
beer/ AIR ɛɚ bear/ O͞OR ʊɚ tour/ AWR ɔɚ bore/ AHR ɑɚ bar/ NG ŋ king/ SH ʃ ship/ ZH ʒ vision/
TH θ thirty/ <u>TH</u> ð then/ CH ʧ child/ J ʤ just/ For complete list, see Key to Pronunciation p. 2.

cock'rel KAHK-ruhl ['kɑk-rəl]

cockatrice KAHK-uh-tris ['kɑk-ə-trɪs]

cockle KAHK-uhl ['kɑk-əl]

Cocytus koh-SEYE-tuhs [koʊ-'saɪ-təs]

codding KAHD-ing ['kɑd-ɪŋ]

Coeur-de-Lion KAWR-duh-leye-uhn ['kɔɚ-də-laɪ-ən] or
    KER-__-lee-__ ['kɝ-__-li-__]

coffer KAW-fer ['kɔ-fɚ] or KAH-___ ['kɑ-___]

cognizance KAHG-ni-zuhns ['kɑg-nɪ-zəns]

cohere koh-HEAR [koʊ-'hɪɚ]

cohorts KOH-hawrts ['koʊ-hɔɚts]

coign KOYN [kɔɪn]

Coint, Francis KOYNT [kɔɪnt] some editions "Quoint"
    KWOYNT [kwɔɪnt]

coistrel KOYS-truhl ['kɔɪs-trəl]

Colbrand / Colebrand KOHL-braand ['koʊl-brænd]

Colchos KAHL-kis ['kɑl-kɪs]

Colebrook KOHL-brook ['koʊl-brʊk]

Coleville, Sir John *(2HIV)* KOHL-vil ['koʊl-vɪl] scans to
    KOHL-uh-vil ['koʊl-ə-vɪl] e.g. @ IV, 3, 70

colic KAHL-ik ['kɑl-ɪk]

colleagued kuh-LEE-gid [kə-'li-gɪd]

collied KAH-leed ['kɑ-lid]

collier KAHL-yer ['kɑl-jɚ]

collop KAHL-uhp ['kɑl-əp]

Colmekill KOHM-kil ['koʊm-kɪl]

Colme's Inch KAHL-meez INCH ['kɑl-miz] [ɪntʃ]

coloquintida KAH-luh-KWIN-ti-duh [kɑ-lə-'kwɪn-tɪ-də]

colossus / Colossus kuh-LAH-suhs [kə-'lɑ-səs]

columbine KAHL-uhm-beyen ['kɑl-əm-baɪn]

Comagene KAHM-uh-jeen ['kɑm-ə-dʒin]

comart koh-MAHRT [koʊ-'mɑɚt]

combat (n) KAHM-baat ['kɑm-bæt]

combat (v) KAHM-baat ['kɑm-bæt] possibly scans to
  kuhm-BAAT [kəm-'bæt] @ *1HVI* I, 1, 54

combatants always scans to KAHM-buh-tuhnts
  ['kɑm-bə-tənts]

combated (pl) KAHM-buh-tid ['kɑm-bə-tɪd] or __-baa-__
  [__-bæ-__]

combating KAHM-baat-ing ['kɑm-bæt-ɪŋ]

combinate KAHM-bi-nit ['kɑm-bɪ-nɪt]

Comfect KAHM-fehkt ['kɑm-fɛkt]

comfit-maker KUHM-fit-may-ker ['kʌm-fɪt-meɪ-kɚ]

comfortable KUHMF-ter-b(uh)l ['kʌmf-tɚ-bl̩] scans to
  KUHM-fer-tuh-b(uh)l ['kʌm-fɚ-tə-bl̩] e.g. @ *RIII* IV, 4, 174

Cominius *(COR)* kuh-MIN-ee-uhs [kə-'mɪn-i-əs] scans to
  __-MIN-yuhs [__-'mɪn-jəs] e.g. @ I, 1, 232

commandement kuh-MAAN-duh-munt [kə-'mæn-də-mənt]

commeddled koh-MEH-d(uh)ld [koʊ-'mɛ-dl̩d]

commend (n) kuh-MEHND [kə-'mɛnd]

EE i be/ I ɪ bit/ EH ɛ bet/ AA æ bat/ O͞O u boot / O͞O ʊ book/ AW ɔ bought/ AH ɑ father/ ER ɝ bird/
UH ʌ cup/ AY eɪ bay/ EYE aɪ bite/ OY ɔɪ boy/ OH oʊ boat/ OW aʊ how/ YO͞O ɪu duke/ EAR ɪə
beer/ AIR ɛə bear/ O͞OR ʊə tour/ AWR ɔɚ bore/ AHR ɑɚ bar/ NG ŋ king/ SH ʃ ship/ ZH ʒ vision/
TH θ thirty/ TH ð then/ CH tʃ child/ J dʒ just/ For complete list, see Key to Pronunciation p. 2.

commendable always scans to **KAH**-mehn-duh-b(uh)l
['kɑ-mɛn-də-bl̩] except possibly kuh-**MEHN**-__-__
[kə-'mɛn-__-__] @ *MVEN* I, 1, 111

commerce **KAH**-mers ['kɑ-mɚs] scans to kah-**MERS**
[kɑ-'mɝs] e.g. @ *T&C* III, 3, 205

commit kuh-**MIT** [kə-'mɪt] scans to **KOH**-mit ['koʊ-mɪt]
@ *TIMON* III, 5, 72

commix kuh-**MIKS** [kə-'mɪks]

commixtion kuh-**MIKS**-chuhn [kə-'mɪks-tʃən]

commixture koh-**MIKS**-cher [koʊ-'mɪks-tʃɚ]

commonalty **KAHM**-uh-nuhl-tee ['kɑm-ə-nəl-ti] scans to
KAHM-nuhl-___ ['kɑm-nəl-___] @ *HVIII* I, 2, 170

commonweal **KAHM**-uhn-weel ['kɑm-ən-wil]

commune (v) **KAH**-myo͞on ['kɑ-mjun] possibly scans to
kuh-**MYO͞ON** [kə-'mjun] @ *WT* II, 1, 162

commutual scans to kuh-**MYO͞O**-chuhl [kə-'mju-tʃəl]

compact (n) or (adj) kuhm-**PAAKT** [kəm-'pækt] scans to
KAHM-paakt ['kɑm-pækt] @ *1HVI* V, 4, 163

compact (v) **KAHM**-paakt ['kɑm-pækt]

compeers kuhm-**PEARZ** [kəm-'pɪɚz]

compel kuhm-**PEHL** [kəm-'pɛl] scans to **KAHM**-pehl
['kɑm-pɛl] e.g. @ *2NOB* III, 1, 68

complete kuhm-**PLEET** [kəm-'plit] scans to **KAHM**-pleet
['kɑm-plit] e.g. @ *RIII* IV, 4, 190

complices **KAHM**-plis-iz ['kɑm-plɪs-ɪz]

complot (n) **KAHM**-plaht ['kɑm-plɑt] scans to kuhm-
PLAHT [kəm-'plɑt] e.g. @ *RIII* III, 1, 192

complot (v) kuhm-**PLAHT** [kəm-'plɑt] scans to **KAHM**-plaht ['kɑm-plɑt] @ *RII* I, 3, 189

composture kuhm-**PAHS**-tyer [kəm-'pɑs-tjɚ] or __-__-cher [__-__-tʃɚ]

compremise **KAHM**-pruh-meyez ['kɑm-prə-maɪz]

compt KOWNT [kɑʊnt] (archaic form of "count" stems from Latin "computare" to count) Many productions use KAHMPT [kɑmpt].

comptible KOWNT-uh-b(uh)l ['kɑʊnt-ə-bl̩] (archaic form of "count" stems from Latin "computare" to count) Many productions use **KAHMP**-tuh-b(uh)l ['kɑmp-tə-bl̩].

comptroller kuhn-**TROH**-ler [kən-'troʊ-lɚ] or kuhmp-__-__ [kəmp-__-__]

compunctious kuhm-**PUHNGK**-shuhs [kəm-'pʌŋk-ʃəs]

comrade **KAHM**-raad ['kɑm-ræd] scans to kahm-**RAAD** [kɑm-'ræd] @ *1HIV* IV, 1, 96

concavities kahn-**KAAV**-i-teez [kɑn-'kæv-ɪ-tiz]

conceal kuhn-**SEEL** [kən-'sil] scans to **KAHN**-seel ['kɑn-sil] e.g. @ *R&J* III, 3, 98

concernancy **KAHN**-ser-nuhn-see ['kɑn-sɚ-nən-si]

concubine **KAHNG**-kyoo-beyen ['kɑŋ-kju-baɪn]

Concolinel (unexplained lyric or title) possibly kahn-**KAH**-li-nehl [kɑn-'kɑ-lɪ-nɛl]

concupiscible scans to kuhn-**KYOOP**-si-b(uh)l [kən-'kjup-sɪ-bl̩] with "intemperate" as three syllables @ *MM* V, 1, 98

concupy **KAHN**-kyoo-peye ['kɑn-kju-paɪ]

EE i be/ I ɪ bit/ EH ɛ bet/ AA æ bat/ OO u boot / OO ʊ book/ AW ɔ bought/ AH ɑ father/ ER ɝ bird/ UH ʌ cup/ AY eɪ bay/ EYE aɪ bite/ OY ɔɪ boy/ OH oʊ boat/ OW ɑʊ how/ YOO ɪu duke/ EAR ɪɚ beer/ AIR ɛɚ bear/ OOR ʊɚ tour/ AWR ɔɚ bore/ AHR ɑɚ bar/ NG ŋ king/ SH ʃ ship/ ZH ʒ vision/ TH θ thirty/ TH ð then/ CH tʃ child/ J dʒ just/ For complete list, see Key to Pronunciation p. 2.

condemn kuhn-DEHM [kən-'dɛm] scans to **KAHN**-dehm ['kɑn-dɛm] e.g. @ *A&C* I, 3, 49

condign kuhn-DEYEN [kən-'daɪn] scans to **KAHN**-deyen ['kɑn-daɪn] @ *2HVI* III, 1, 130

condole kuhn-DOHL [kən-'doʊl]

condolements kuhn-DOHL-muhnts [kən-'doʊl-mənts]

conduce kuhn-DYO͞OS [kən-'dɪus]

conduct (n) **KAHN**-duhkt ['kɑn-dəkt] scans to kuhn-DUHKT [kən-'dʌkt] @ *TITUS* IV, 4, 64

conduit **KAHN**-dyo͞o-it ['kɑn-dɪu-ɪt] scans to **KAHN**-dit ['kɑn-dɪt] or **KAHN**-dwit ['kɑn-dwɪt] e.g. @ *COR* II, 3, 237

confessor kuhn-FEHS-er [kən-'fɛs-ɚ] scans to **KAHN**-fehs-er ['kɑn-fɛs-ɚ] e.g. @ *HVIII* I, 1, 218

confine (n) **KAHN**-feyen ['kɑn-faɪn] scans to kuhn-FEYEN [kən-'faɪn] e.g. @ *HAM* I, 1, 155

confiners **KAHN**-feyen-erz ['kɑn-faɪn-ɚz]

confirm kuhn-FERM [kən-'fɝm] scans to **KAHN**-ferm ['kɑn-fɚm] e.g. @ *MADO* V, 4, 17

confiscate **KAHN**-fi-skayt ['kɑn-fɪ-skeɪt] scans to kuhn-FI-___ [kən-'fɪ-___] e.g. @ *CE* I, 1, 20

conflux scans to kahn-FLUHKS [kɑn-'flʌks]

conformable kuhn-FAWR-muh-b(uh)l [kən-'fɔɚ-mə-bl̩]

conger (an eel) **KAHNG**-ger ['kɑŋ-gɚ]

congied **KAHN**-jeed ['kɑn-ʤid]

congreeing kuhn-GREE-ing [kən-'gri-ɪŋ]

congreeted kuhn-GREET-id [kən-'grit-ɪd]

congruing **KAHN**-gro͞o-ing ['kɑn-gru-ɪŋ]

conjoin kuhn-JOYN [kən-'ʤɔɪn]

conjointly kuhn-JOYNT-lee [kən-'ʤɔɪnt-li]

conjunct kuhn-JUHNGKT [kən-'ʤʌŋkt]

conjunctive kuhn-JUHNGK-tiv [kən-'ʤʌŋk-tɪv]

conjuration KAHN-juh-RAY-shuhn [kɑn-ʤə-'reɪ-ʃən]

conjure KAHN-jer ['kɑn-ʤɚ] scans to kuhn-JOOR [kən-'ʤʊɚ] e.g. @ *R&J* II, 1, 26

Conrade *(MADO)* KAHN-raad ['kɑn-ræd]

consanguineous KAHN-saang-GWIN-ee-uhs [kɑn-sæŋ-'gwɪn-i-əs]

consanguinity KAHN-saang-GWIN-i-tee [kɑn-sæŋ-'gwɪn-ɪ-ti]

consecrate KAHN-si-krayt ['kɑn-sɪ-kreɪt]

conserves (n) KAHN-servz ['kɑn-sɚvz] scans to kuhn-SERVZ [kən-'sɝvz] @ *SHR* Ind, 2, 3

consign kuhn-SEYEN [kən-'saɪn] scans to KAHN-seyen ['kɑn-saɪn] @ *T&C* IV, 4, 44

consistory KAHN-sis-taw-ree ['kɑn-sɪs-tɔ-ri] possibly scans to ___-sis-tree [___-sɪs-tri] e.g. @ *HVIII* II, 4, 91

consolate KAHN-suh-layt ['kɑn-sə-leɪt]

consonancy KAHN-suh-nuhn-see ['kɑn-sə-nən-si]

consort (n) KAHN-sawrt ['kɑn-sɔɚt] scans to kuhn-SAWRT [kən-'sɔɚt] e.g. @ *2GEN* IV, 1, 64

consort (v) kuhn-SAWRT [kən-'sɔɚt]

conspectuities kuhn-SPEHK-TYOO-i-teez [kən-spɛk-'tɪu-ɪ-tiz] or kahn-__-__-__-__ [kɑn-__-__-__-__]

EE i be/ I ɪ bit/ EH ɛ bet/ AA æ bat/ OO u boot / OO ʊ book/ AW ɔ bought/ AH ɑ father/ ER ɝ bird/ UH ʌ cup/ AY eɪ bay/ EYE aɪ bite/ OY ɔɪ boy/ OH oʊ boat/ OW aʊ how/ YOO ɪu duke/ EAR ɪɚ beer/ AIR ɛɚ bear/ OOR ʊɚ tour/ AWR ɔɚ bore/ AHR ɑɚ bar/ NG ŋ king/ SH ʃ ship/ ZH ʒ vision/ TH θ thirty/ TH ð then/ CH tʃ child/ J ʤ just/ For complete list, see Key to Pronunciation p. 2.

conspirant kuhn-SPEYE-ruhnt [kən-'spaɪ-rənt]

Constable of France *(HV)* KAHN-stuh-b(uh)l ['kɑn-stə-bl̩]

Constance *(KJ)* KAHN-stuhns ['kɑn-stəns]

Constantine KAHN-stuhn-teen ['kɑn-stən-tin]

Constantinople KAHN-staan-ti-NOH-p(uh)l
   [kɑn-stæn-tɪ-'noʊ-pl̩]

conster KAHN-ster ['kɑn-stɚ]

constringed kuhn-STRINJD [kən-'strɪndʒd]

consul KAHN-suhl ['kɑn-səl]

contagion kuhn-TAY-juhn [kən-'teɪ-dʒən] scans to __-__-jee-uhn
   [__-__-dʒi-ən] @ *CE* II, 2, 143 if "being" is one syllable

contemn kuhn-TEHM [kən-'tɛm]

contemplative kuhn-TEHM-pluh-tiv [kən-'tɛm-plə-tɪv]

contents (n) KAHN-tehnts ['kɑn-tɛnts] scans to kuhn-
   TEHNTS [kən-'tɛnts] e.g. @ *AYL* IV, 3, 9

contestation KAHN-teh-STAY-shuhn [kɑn-tɛ-'steɪ-ʃən]

continency KAHN-tuh-nuhn-see ['kɑn-tə-nən-si]

continuance kuhn-TIN-yoo-uhns [kən-'tɪn-ju-əns] scans to
   __-TIN-yuhns [__-'tɪn-jəns] e.g. @ *R&J* Pro, 10

continuantly kuhn-TIN-YOO-uhnt-lee [kən-'tɪn-ju-ənt-li]

continuate always scans to kuhn-TIN-wit [kən-'tɪn-wɪt]

contract (n) KAHN-traakt ['kɑn-trækt] scans to kuhn-
   TRAAKT [kən-'trækt] e.g. @ *1HVI* III, 1, 143

contrariety KAHN-truh-REYE-i-tee [kɑn-trə-'raɪ-ɪ-ti]

contrarious always scans to kuhn-TRAIR-yuhs [kən-'trɛɚ-jəs]

contrary (adj) KAHN-treh-ree ['kɑn-trɛ-ri] scans to kuhn-
   TREH-__ [kən-'trɛ-__] e.g. @ *KJ* IV, 2, 198

contrary (n) **KAHN**-treh-ree [ˈkɑn-trɛ-ri]

contrary (v) kuhn-**TREH**-ree [kən-ˈtrɛ-ri]

contumelious KAHN-tyo͞o-**MEE**-li-uhs [kɑn-tɪu-ˈmi-lɪ-əs]
scans to ___-___-**MEEL**-yuhs [___-___-ˈmil-jəs]
e.g. @ *1HVI* I, 4, 39

contumeliously scans to KAHN-tyo͞o-**MEEL**-yuhs-lee
[kɑn-tɪu-ˈmil-jəs-li]

contumely scans to **KAHN**-tyo͞om-lee [ˈkɑn-tɪum-li]

convent (v) (to summon) kuhn-**VEHNT** [kən-ˈvɛnt]

conventicles scans to **KAHN**-vehn-ti-k(uh)lz [ˈkɑn-vɛn-tɪ-kl̩z]

conversant **KAHN**-ver-suhnt [ˈkɑn-və˞-sənt]

converse (n) kuhn-**VERS** [kən-ˈvɝs]

convertite **KAHN**-ver-teyet [ˈkɑn-və˞-taɪt]

convive kuhn-**VEYEV** [kən-ˈvaɪv]

cony **KOH**-nee [ˈkou-ni]

copatain **KAHP**-uh-tayn [ˈkɑp-ə-teɪn]

coped KOHPT [koupt]

Cophetua koh-**FEH**-tyo͞o-uh [kou-ˈfɛ-tɪu-ə] scans to __-**FEH**-
tyuh [__-ˈfɛ-tjə] e.g. @ *R&J* II, 1, 14

copped KAHPT [kɑpt]

coppice **KAHP**-is [ˈkɑp-ɪs]

cop'st KOHPST [koupst]

copulatives **KAH**-pyo͞o-lay-tivz [ˈkɑ-pju-leɪ-tɪvz]

coragio kuh-**RAH**-zhoh [kə-ˈrɑ-ʒou]

EE i be/ I ɪ bit/ EH ɛ bet/ AA æ bat/ O͞O u boot / O͞O ʊ book/ AW ɔ bought/ AH ɑ father/ ER ɝ bird/
UH ʌ cup/ AY eɪ bay/ EYE aɪ bite/ OY ɔɪ boy/ OH ou boat/ OW aʊ how/ YO͞O ɪu duke/ EAR ɪə
beer/ AIR ɛə bear/ O͞OR ʊə tour/ AWR ɔə bore/ AHR ɑə bar/ NG ŋ king/ SH ʃ ship/ ZH ʒ vision/
TH θ thirty/ TH ð then/ CH ʧ child/ J ʤ just/ For complete list, see Key to Pronunciation p. 2.

79

Coram KOH-ruhm ['koʊ-rəm]

Corambus koh-RAAM-buhs [koʊ-'ræm-bəs]

coranto kuh-RAHN-toh [kə-'rɑn-toʊ]

Cordelia *(LEAR)* kawr-DEE-lyuh [kɔɚ-'di-ljə] scans to ___-
__-lee-uh [__-__-li-ə] @ V, 3, 272 first citation

Cordelion KAWR-duh-leye-uhn ['kɔɚ-də-laɪ-ən] some editions use French spelling "Coeur de Lion" KAWR-duh-
leye-uhn ['kɔɚ-də-laɪ-ən] or KER-__-lee-__ ['kɝ-__-li-__]

cordial (adj) KAWR-juhl ['kɔɚ-ʤəl] scans to KAWR-jee-uhl
['kɔɚ-ʤi-əl] @ CYM IV, 2, 327

cordial (n) KAWR-juhl ['kɔɚ-ʤəl]

Corin KAW-rin ['kɔ-rɪn]
    Corin *(AYL)*

Corinth KAW-rinth ['kɔ-rɪnθ]

Corinthian kuh-RIN-thee-uhn [kə-'rɪn-θi-ən]

Coriolanus KAW-ree-oh-LAY-nuhs [kɔ-ri-oʊ-'leɪ-nəs]   scans
    to KAW-ryoh-LAY-__ [kɔ-rjoʊ-'leɪ-__]
    Coriolanus *(COR)* see "Caius Marcius Coriolanus"
    Coriolanus scans @ TITUS IV, 4, 67

Corioles kuh-REYE-uh-luhs [kə-'raɪ-ə-ləs] scans to
    ___-REYE-luhs [___-'raɪ-ləs] e.g. @ COR V, 3, 179

cormorant KAWR-muh-raant ['kɔɚ-mə-rænt] scans to
    KAWRM-raant ['kɔɚm-rænt] or __-__- ruhnt [__-__-rənt]
    scans to __-ruhnt [__-rənt] e.g. @ T&C II, 2, 6

Cornelia kawr-NEE-lyuh [kɔɚ-'ni-ljə] scans to __-__-lee-uh
    [__-__-li-ə] @ TITUS IV, 2, 141

Cornelius kawr-NEE-lyuhs [kɔɚ-'ni-ljəs]
    Cornelius *(CYM)*
    Cornelius *(HAM)*

cornets KAWR-nets ['kɔɚ-nɛts] or ____-nits [___-nɪts]

cornuto kawr-NOO-toh [kɔɚ-'nu-toh] or __-NYOO-__ [__-'nɪu-__]

Cornwall, Duke of *(LEAR)* KAWRN-wawl ['kɔɚn-wɔl]

corollary KAW-ruh-leh-ree ['kɔ-rə-lɛ-ri]

coronet KAW-ruh-neht ['kɔ-rə-nɛt] scans to KAWR-neht ['kɔɚ-nɛt] e.g. @ *LEAR* I, 1, 139

corrival kuh-REYE-vuhl [kə-'raɪ-vəl] or koh-___-___ [koʊ-___-___]

corroborate kuh-RAHB-uh-rit [kə-'rɑb-ə-rɪt]

corrosive (n) or (adj) always scans to KAW-ruh-siv ['kɔ-rə-sɪv]

corslet KAWRS-lit ['kɔɚs-lɪt]

Cosmo KAHZ-moh ['kaz-moʊ]

costard / Costard *(LLL)* KAHS-terd ['kas-tɚd]

costermonger KAHS-ter-MUHNG-ger ['kas-tɚ-mʌŋ-gɚ] or ___-___-MAHNG-___ [___-___-maŋ-___]

cote (n) KOHT [koʊt]

coted KOHT-id ['koʊt-ɪd]

Cotsall KAHT-s(uh)l ['kat-sl̩]

Cotswold KAHTS-wohld ['kats-woʊld]

Cotus KOH-tuhs ['koʊ-təs]

coulter KOHL-ter ['koʊl-tɚ]

counterpoise KOWN-ter-poyz ['kaʊn-tɚ-pɔɪz]

countervail KOWN-ter-vayl ['kaʊn-tɚ-veɪl]

EE i be/ I ɪ bit/ EH ɛ bet/ AA æ bat/ OO u boot / OO ʊ book/ AW ɔ bought/ AH ɑ father/ ER ɝ bird/ UH ʌ cup/ AY eɪ bay/ EYE aɪ bite/ OY ɔɪ boy/ OH oʊ boat/ OW aʊ how/ YOO ɪu duke/ EAR ɪɚ beer/ AIR ɛɚ bear/ OOR ʊɚ tour/ AWR ɔɚ bore/ AHR ɑɚ bar/ NG ŋ king/ SH ʃ ship/ ZH ʒ vision/ TH θ thirty/ TH ð then/ CH ʧ child/ J ʤ just/ For complete list, see Key to Pronunciation p. 2.

81

County KOWN-tee [ˈkɑʊn-ti]

courage (n) (bravery) KE(r)-rij [ˈkɜ-rɪdʒ] or KUH-__ [ˈkʌ-__]

courage (n) (a fiery young person) kuh-RAHJ [kə-ˈrɑdʒ]

courier KOO-ree-er [ˈkʊ-ri-ɚ] scans to KOOR-yer [ˈkʊɚ-jɚ] @ *MAC* I, 7, 23

courser KAWR-ser [ˈkɔɚ-sɚ]

coursing KAWR-sing [ˈkɔɚ-sɪŋ]

Court, Alexander KAWRT AAL-ig-ZAAN-der [kɔɚt] [æl-ɪg-ˈzæn-dɚ]

court'sy (contraction of "courtesy") KERT-see [ˈkɝt-si]

courtesan KAWR-tuh-zuhn [ˈkɔɚ-tə-zən] Courtesan *(CE)*

courtier KAWR-tee-er [ˈkɔɚ-ti-ɚ] scans to KAWR-tyer [ˈkɔɚ-tjɚ] e.g. @ *2HVI* IV, 4, 36

covent (n) (a religious community) KUH-vehnt [ˈkʌ-vɛnt]

Coventry KUHV-uhn-tree [ˈkʌv-ən-tri]

covert (adj) KOH-vert [ˈkoʊ-vɚt] or KUHV-ert [ˈkʌv-ɚt]

covert (n) KUHV-ert [ˈkʌv-ɚt] or KOH-vert [ˈkoʊ-vɚt]

covertly (adv) koh-VERT-lee [koʊ-ˈvɝt-li] or KUHV-ert-lee [ˈkʌv-ɚt-li]

coverture KUHV-er-cher [ˈkʌv-ɚ-tʃɚ]

covetousness KUHV-i-tuhs-nuhs [ˈkʌv-ɪ-təs-nəs]

cowish KOW-ish [ˈkɑʊ-ɪʃ]

cowl-staff KOWL-staaf [ˈkɑʊl-stæf]

cowslip KOW-slip [ˈkɑʊ-slɪp]

coxcomb KAHKS-kohm [ˈkɑks-koʊm]

coz KUHZ [kʌz]

coz'nage KUHZ-nij [ˈkʌz-nɪʤ]

cozenage KUHZ-uh-nij [ˈkʌz-ə-nɪʤ]

cozener KUHZ-uhn-er [ˈkʌz-ən-ɚ]

coziers KOH-zherz [ˈkou-ʒɚz]

Crab KRAAB [kræb]

Cranmer, Archbishop of Canterbury *(HVIII)* KRAAN-mer [ˈkræn-mɚ]

crants KRAANTS [krænts]

crare KRAIR [krɛɚ]

crasing KRAYZ-ing [ˈkreɪz-ɪŋ] some editions "crazing" KRAYZ-ing [ˈkreɪz-ɪŋ] or "grazing" GRAYZ-ing [ˈgreɪz-ɪŋ]

Crassus KRAAS-uhs [ˈkræs-əs]

craven KRAY-vuhn [ˈkreɪ-vən]

Crécy KREHS-ee [ˈkrɛs-i]

credence KREE-d(uh)nts [ˈkri-dn̩ts]

credent KREE-d(uh)nt [ˈkri-dn̩t]

credulity kruh-DYOO-li-tee [krə-ˈdɪu-lɪ-ti]

Creon KREE-ahn [ˈkri-ɑn]

crept KREHPT [krɛpt]

crescent KREHS-uhnt [ˈkrɛs-ənt] (KREHS-kint [ˈkrɛs-kɪnt] is sometimes heard)

crescive KREH-siv [ˈkrɛ-sɪv]

cressets KREH-sits [ˈkrɛ-sɪts]

EE i be/ I ɪ bit/ EH ɛ bet/ AA æ bat/ OO u boot / OO ʊ book/ AW ɔ bought/ AH ɑ father/ ER ɝ bird/
UH ʌ cup/ AY eɪ bay/ EYE aɪ bite/ OY ɔɪ boy/ OH ou boat/ OW aʊ how/ YOO ɪu duke/ EAR ɪɚ
beer/ AIR ɛɚ bear/ OOR ʊɚ tour/ AWR ɔɚ bore/ AHR ɑɚ bar/ NG ŋ king/ SH ʃ ship/ ZH ʒ vision/
TH θ thirty/ TH ð then/ CH tʃ child/ J ʤ just/ For complete list, see Key to Pronunciation p. 2.

83

Cressid KREHS-id ['krɛs-ɪd]

Cressida KREHS-i-duh ['krɛs-ɪ-də]
Cressida *(T&C)* also called "Cressid" KREHS-id ['krɛs-ɪd]

Cretan KREE-t(uh)n ['kri-tn̩]

Crete KREET [krit]

Crispian KRIS-pee-uhn ['krɪs-pi-ən]

Crispianus KRIS-pee-AY-nuhs [krɪs-pi-'eɪ-nəs]

Crispin KRIS-pin ['krɪs-pɪn]

Cromer KROH-mer ['kroʊ-mɚ]

Cromwell *(HVIII)* KRAHM-wehl ['krɑm-wɛl] or
____-wuhl [___-wəl]

crotchets KRAH-chits ['krɑ-tʃɪts]

crownet KROW-nit ['kraʊ-nɪt]

crudy KROO-dee ['kru-di]

crupper KRUHP-er ['krʌp-ɚ]

crusadoes kroo-SAH-dohz [kru-'sɑ-doʊz]

cubiculo kyoo-BIK-yuh-loh [kju-'bɪk-jə-loʊ]

cuckold KUHK-uhld ['kʌk-əld]

cudgel KUHJ-uhl ['kʌdʒ-əl]

cull KUHL [kʌl]

cullion KUHL-yuhn ['kʌl-jən] scans to KUHL-ee-uhn
['kʌl-i-ən] @ *SHR* IV, 2, 20

culverin KUHL-vuh-rin ['kʌl-və-rɪn]

cumber KUHM-ber ['kʌm-bɚ]

Cumberland KUHM-ber-luhnd ['kʌm-bɚ-lənd]

Curan *(LEAR)* KUH-ruhn ['kʌ-rən] or KE(r)-__ ['kɜ-__]

curate KYOO-rit [ˈkjʊ-rɪt]

Curio *(12th)* KYOO-ree-oh [ˈkjʊ-ri-oʊ]]

currance KUH-ruhns [ˈkʌ-rəns]

currish KUH-rish [ˈkʌ-rɪʃ]

cursitory KER-si-taw-ree [ˈkɝ-sɪ-tɔ-ri]

curst KERST [kɝst]

cursy KER-see [ˈkɝ-si]

curtail (v) ker-TAYL [kɚ-ˈteɪl] scans to KER-tayl [ˈkɝ-teɪl]
@ *RIII* I, 1, 18

curtal / Curtal KER-t(uh)l [ˈkɝ-tl̩]

Curtis *(SHR)* KER-tis [ˈkɝ-tɪs]

curtle-axe KER-t(uh)l-aaks [ˈkɝ-tl̩-æks]

curvet ker-VEHT [kɚ-ˈvɛt]

cushes KOOSH-iz [ˈkʊʃ-ɪz]

Cyclops SEYE-klahps [ˈsaɪ-klɑps]

Cydnus SID-nuhs [ˈsɪd-nəs]

cygnet SIG-nit [ˈsɪg-nɪt]

Cymbeline *(CYM)* SIM-buh-leen [ˈsɪm-bə-lin]

Cynthia always scans to SIN-thyuh [ˈsɪn-θjə]

Cyprus SEYE-pruhs [ˈsaɪ-prəs]

Cyrus SEYE-ruhs [ˈsaɪ-rəs]

Cytherea SITH-uh-REE-uh [sɪθ-ə-ˈri-ə]

d. (abbreviation for "pence") PEHNS [pɛns]

EE i be/ I ɪ bit/ EH ɛ bet/ AA æ bat/ OO u boot / OO ʊ book/ AW ɔ bought/ AH ɑ father/ ER ɝ bird/
UH ʌ cup/ AY eɪ bay/ EYE aɪ bite/ OY ɔɪ boy/ OH oʊ boat/ OW aʊ how/ YOO ɪu duke/ EAR ɪɚ
beer/ AIR ɛɚ bear/ OOR ʊɚ tour/ AWR ɔɚ bore/ AHR ɑɚ bar/ NG ŋ king/ SH ʃ ship/ ZH ʒ vision/
TH θ thirty/ TH ð then/ CH tʃ child/ J dʒ just/ For complete list, see Key to Pronunciation p. 2.

Daedalus DEHD-uh-luhs ['dɛd-ə-ləs]

daff DAAF [dæf]

daffadilly DAAF-uh-dil-ee ['dæf-ə-dɪl-i]

Dagonet DAA-goh-neht ['dæ-goʊ-nɛt] or ___-guh-nit [___-gə-nɪt]

Daintry DAYN-tree ['deɪn-tri]

dalliance DAAL-ee-uhns ['dæl-i-əns] scans to DAAL-yuhns ['dæl-jəns] e.g. @ *HAM* I, 3, 50

Dalmatians daal-MAY-shunz [dæl-'meɪ-ʃənz] scans to ___-___-shee-uhnz [___-___-ʃi-ənz] @ *CYM* III, 7, 3

dam DAAM [dæm]

Damascus duh-MAAS-kuhs [də-'mæs-kəs]

damask DAAM-uhsk ['dæm-əsk]

damned DAAMD [dæmd] scans to DAAM-nid ['dæm-nɪd] e.g. @ *RIII* II, 4, 64

Damon DAY-muhn ['deɪ-mən]

damosella daam-oh-ZEHL-uh [dæm-oʊ-'zɛl-ə]

damsons DAAM-zuhnz ['dæm-zənz] or ___-suhnz [___-sənz]

dandle DAAN-d(uh)l ['dæn-dl̩]

Daniel DAAN-yuhl ['dæn-jəl] scans to DAAN-ee-uhl ['dæn-i-əl] @ *MVEN* IV, 1, 331 first citation

Danskers DAANSK-erz ['dænsk-ɚz]

Daphne DAAF-nee ['dæf-ni]

dar'st DAIRST [dɛɚst]

Dardan DAHR-d(uh)n ['dɑɚ-dn̩]

Dardanian scans to dahr-DAY-nyuhn [dɑɚ-'deɪ-njən]

Dardanius *(JC)* dahr-DAY-nee-uhs [dɑɚ-'deɪ-ni-əs]

Darius duh-REYE-uhs [də-'raɪ-əs]

darnel DAHR-nuhl ['dɑɚ-nəl]

darraign di-RAYN [dɪ-'reɪn]

dastard DAAS-terd ['dæs-tɚd]

Datchet Mead DAACH-it MEED ['dætʃ-ɪt] [mid]

daub DAWB [dɔb]

daubery DAWB-uh-ree ['dɔb-ə-ri]

Daughter of Antiochus *(PER)* aan-TEYE-uh-kuhs [æn-'taɪ-ə-kəs]

daunt DAWNT [dɔnt]

Dauphin DAW-fin ['dɔ-fɪn]

Daventry DAAV-uhn-tree ['dæv-ən-tri]

Davy DAY-vee ['deɪ-vi]
Davy *(2HIV)*

daw DAW [dɔ]

de Armado, Don Adriano *(LLL)* duh-ahr-MAH-doh DAHN AY-dree-AH-noh [də-ɑɚ-'ma-doʊ] [dɑn] [eɪ-dri-'a-noʊ]

de Burgh, Hubert *(KJ)* duh-BERG HYOO-bert [də-'bɝg] ['hju-bɚt]

de Champ dyoo-CHAAMP [dɪu-'tʃæmp]

de la Car deh-luh-KAHR [dɛ-lə-'kɑɚ]

de la Pole, William, Earl afterward Duke of Suffolk *(1HVI, 2HVI)* deh-luh-POHL [dɛ-lə-'poʊl] or __-__-POOL [__-__-'pul] SUHF-uhk ['sʌf-ək]

EE i be/ I ɪ bit/ EH ɛ bet/ AA æ bat/ OO u boot / OO ʊ book/ AW ɔ bought/ AH ɑ father/ ER ɝ bird/ UH ʌ cup/ AY eɪ bay/ EYE aɪ bite/ OY ɔɪ boy/ OH oʊ boat/ OW aʊ how/ YOO ɪu duke/ EAR ɪɚ beer/ AIR ɛɚ bear/ OOR ʊɚ tour/ AWR ɔɚ bore/ AHR ɑɚ bar/ NG ŋ king/ SH ʃ ship/ ZH ʒ vision/ TH θ thirty/ TH ð then/ CH tʃ child/ J dʒ just/ For complete list, see Key to Pronunciation p. 2.

de Pucelle, Joan *(1HVI)* duh-pōō-SEHL [də-pu-'sɛl] scans to
__-PUH-suhl [__-'pʌ-səl] or __-PUH-zuhl [__-'pʌ-zəl]
e.g. @ I, 6, 3

de Vere, John, Earl of Oxford duh-VEAR [də-'vɪɚ]
de Vere, John, Earl of Oxford *(3HVI, RIII)*

dearth DERTH [dɝθ]

debile DEH-buhl ['dɛ-bəl] or DEE-beyel ['di-baɪl]

Deborah DEHB-uh-ruh ['dɛb-ə-rə]

deboshed di-BAHSHT [dɪ-'baʃt]

decimation DEH-si-MAY-shuhn [dɛ-sɪ-'meɪ-ʃən]

decoct dee-KAHKT [di-'kɑkt]

Decretas *(A&C)* duh-KREE-tuhs [də-'kri-təs] scans to
DEHK-ruh-__ ['dɛk-rə-__] @ V, 1, 5 if "I am" elides; some
editions "Dercetas" der-SEE-tuhs [dɚ-'si-təs]

defunction di-FUHNGK-shuhn [dɪ-'fʌŋk-ʃən]

deign DAYN [deɪn]

deifying DEE-uh-feye-ing ['di-ə-faɪ-ɪŋ]

Deiphobus *(T&C)* dee-IF-uh-buhs [di-'ɪf-ə-bəs]

deity DEE-i-tee ['di-ɪ-ti] scans to DEE-tee ['di-ti]
e.g. @ *12th* V, 1, 219

Delabreth DEH-luh-brehth ['dɛ-lə-brɛθ]

delated di-LAY-tid [dɪ-'leɪ-tɪd]

delectable scans to DEE-lehk-tuh-b(uh)l ['di-lɛk-tə-bl̩] possibly the same in prose

Delphos DEHL-fahs ['dɛl-fɑs] or __-fuhs [__-fəs]

deluge DEHL-yōōj ['dɛl-juʤ]

Delver DEHL-ver ['dɛl-vɚ]

demesnes di-MAYNZ [dɪ-'meɪnz]

Demetrius di-MEE-tree-uhs [dɪ-'mi-tri-əs] scans to
    __-MEE-truhs [__-'mi-trəs]
  Demetrius *(A&C)*
  Demetrius *(MID)* scans e.g. @ I, 1, 52
  Demetrius *(TITUS)*

demise di-MEYEZ [dɪ-'maɪz]

demonstrable scans to DEHM-uhn-struh-b(uh)l
    ['dɛm-ən-strə-bl̩]

demonstrate DEH-muhn-strayt ['dɛ-mən-streɪt] scans to
    duh-MAHN-___ [də-'mɑn-___] e.g. @ *TIMON* I, 1, 91

denay di-NAY [dɪ-'neɪ]

denier di-NEAR [dɪ-'nɪɚ]

Dennis DEHN-is ['dɛn-ɪs]

Denny, Sir Anthony *(HVIII)* DEHN-ee ['dɛn-i]

depart (n) di-PAHRT [dɪ-'paɚt]

depositaries di-PAHZ-i-TEH-reez [dɪ-'pɑz-ɪ-tɛ-riz]

deputation DEHP-yuh-TAY-shuhn [dɛp-jə-'teɪ-ʃən]

depute di-PYOOT [dɪ-'pjut]

deracinate di-RAAS-in-ayt [dɪ-'ræs-ɪn-eɪt]

Derby DAHR-bee ['daɚ-bi] or DER-___ ['dɝ-___]

dern DERN [dɝn]

derogate (v) DEH-ruh-gayt ['dɛ-rə-geɪt]

derogate (adj) scans to DAIR-guht ['dɛɚ-gət]

derogately DEH-roh-gayt-lee ['dɛ-rou-geɪt-li]

EE i be/ I ɪ bit/ EH ɛ bet/ AA æ bat/ OO u boot / OO ʊ book/ AW ɔ bought/ AH ɑ father/ ER ɝ bird/
UH ʌ cup/ AY eɪ bay/ EYE aɪ bite/ OY ɔɪ boy/ OH ou boat/ OW aʊ how/ YOO ɪu duke/ EAR ɪɚ
beer/ AIR ɛɚ bear/ OOR ʊɚ tour/ AWR ɔɚ bore/ AHR ɑɚ bar/ NG ŋ king/ SH ʃ ship/ ZH ʒ vision/
TH θ thirty/ <u>TH</u> ð then/ CH tʃ child/ J dʒ just/ For complete list, see Key to Pronunciation p. 2.

derogation DEH-roh-GAY-shuhn [dɛ-roʊ-'geɪ-ʃən]

descant DEHS-kaant ['dɛs-kænt]

descension di-SEHN-shuhn [dɪ-'sɛn-ʃən]

descry (n) or (v) di-SKREYE [dɪ-'skraɪ]

Desdemona *(OTH)* DEHZ-di-MOH-nuh [dɛz-dɪ-'moʊ-nə] also called "Desdemon" DEHZ-di-mohn ['dɛz-dɪ-moʊn]

desert (an uninhabited land) DEH-zert ['dɛ-zɚt] e.g. @ *WT* III, 3, 2

desert (that which is due to a person) di-ZERT [dɪ-'zɝt] e.g. @ *3HVI* III, 3, 192

designment di-ZEYEN-muhnt [dɪ-'zaɪn-mənt]

desist di-SIST [dɪ-'sɪst] or ___-ZIST [___-'zɪst]

despised di-SPEYEZD [dɪ-'spaɪzd] scans to DIS-peyezd ['dɪs-paɪzd] @ *HAM* III, 1, 72

despite di-SPEYET [dɪ-'spaɪt]

detestable always scans to DEE-tehs-tuh-b(uh)l ['di-tɛs-tə-bl̩]

Deucalion dyōō-KAY-lee-uhn [dɪu-'keɪ-li-ən] scans to __-KAY-lyuhn [__-'keɪ-ljən] @ *WT* IV, 4, 424

devesting di-VEHST-ing [dɪ-'vɛst-ɪŋ]

Devonshire DEHV-uhn-sher ['dɛv-ən-ʃɚ] or ___-___-shear [___-___-ʃɪɚ]

dewlap DYŌŌ-laap ['dɪu-læp]

dexter DEHK-ster ['dɛk-stɚ]

dexteriously dehk-STEH-ree-uhs-lee [dɛk-'stɛ-ri-əs-li]

diadem DEYE-uh-dehm ['daɪ-ə-dɛm] scans to DEYE-dehm ['daɪ-dɛm] e.g. @ *HAM* III, 4, 101

dial DEYEL [daɪl] scans to DEYE-uhl ['daɪ-əl] e.g. @ *3HVI* II, 5, 24

diamond DEYE-muhnd ['daɪ-mənd] scans to DEYE-uh-muhnd ['daɪ-ə-mənd] e.g. @ *CE* IV, 3, 64

Dian DEYE-uhn ['daɪ-ən]

Diana deye-AAN-uh [daɪ-'æn-ə]
Diana *(AW)*
Diana *(PER)*

dibble DIB-uhl ['dɪb-əl]

dich DICH [dɪtʃ]

Dickon DIK-uhn ['dɪk-ən]

Dictynna dik-TIN-uh [dɪk-'tɪn-ə]

diddest DID-dist ['dɪd-dɪst]

Dido DEYE-doh ['daɪ-dou]

different DIF-uh-ruhnt ['dɪf-ə-rənt] possibly scans to di-FE(r)-ruhnt [dɪ-'fɝ-rənt] @ *CE* V, 1, 46

Dighton DEYE-t(uh)n ['daɪ-tn̩]

dilatory DIL-uh-taw-ree ['dɪl-ə-tɔ-ri]

dild DEELD [dild]

diminitives di-MIN-i-tivz [dɪ-'mɪn-ɪ-tɪvz]

diminution DIM-i-NYOO-shuhn [dɪm-ɪ-'nɪu-ʃən]

din DIN [dɪn]

dint DINT [dɪnt]

Diomede DEYE-uh-meed ['daɪ-ə-mid]

EE i be/ I ɪ bit/ EH ɛ bet/ AA æ bat/ O̅O̅ u boot / O̅O̅ ʊ book/ AW ɔ bought/ AH ɑ father/ ER ɝ bird/ UH ʌ cup/ AY eɪ bay/ EYE aɪ bite/ OY ɔɪ boy/ OH ou boat/ OW aʊ how/ YO̅O̅ ɪu duke/ EAR ɪə beer/ AIR ɛə bear/ O̅OR ʊə tour/ AWR ɔə bore/ AHR ɑə bar/ NG ŋ king/ SH ʃ ship/ ZH ʒ vision/ TH θ thirty/ TH ð then/ CH tʃ child/ J ʤ just/ For complete list, see Key to Pronunciation p. 2.

91

Diomedes DEYE-uh-MEE-deez [daɪ-ə-ˈmi-diz] also called
    "Diomed" **DEYE**-uh-mehd [ˈdaɪ-ə-mɛd] scans to
    DEYE-mehd [ˈdaɪ-mɛd]
  Diomedes *(A&C)* scans @ IV, 14, 116
  Diomedes *(T&C)* scans @ V, 2, 133

Dion *(WT)* DEYE-ahn [ˈdaɪ-ɑn] or ___-uhn [___-ən]

Dionyza *(PER)* DEYE-uh-NEYE-zuh [daɪ-ə-ˈnaɪ-zə]

dire DEYER [daɪɚ]

direct (adj) di-REHKT [dɪ-ˈrɛkt] scans to DEYE-rehkt
    [ˈdaɪ-rɛkt] e.g. @ *OTH* I, 2, 86

directitude di-REHK-ti-tyōōd [dɪ-ˈrɛk-tɪ-tɪud]

dirge DERJ [dɝʤ]

Dis DIS [dɪs]

disannul dis-uh-NUHL [dɪs-ə-ˈnʌl]

discandying scans to dis-KAAN-dying [dɪs-ˈkæn-djɪŋ]

discomfit dis-KUHM-fit [dɪs-ˈkʌm-fɪt]

discomfiture dis-KUHM-fi-chōōr [dɪs-ˈkʌm-fɪ-ʧʊɚ] or
    ___-___-___-cher [___-___-___-ʧɚ]

discourse (n) DIS-kawrs [ˈdɪs-kɔɚs] scans to dis-KAWRS
    [dɪs-ˈkɔɚs] e.g. @ *R&J* III, 5, 53

disedged dis-EHJD [dɪs-ˈɛʤd]

disgest dis-JEHST [dɪs-ˈʤɛst]

dishclout DISH-klowt [ˈdɪʃ-klɑʊt]

disinsanity DIS-in-SAAN-i-tee [dɪs-ɪn-ˈsæn-ɪ-ti]

dislimns dis-LIMZ [dɪs-ˈlɪmz]

dismes DEYEMZ [daɪmz]

dismission dis-MISH-uhn [dɪs-ˈmɪʃ-ən]

dispatch (n) dis-PAACH [dɪs-'pætʃ]

displant dis-PLAANT [dɪs-'plænt]

disponge di-SPUHNJ [dɪ-'spʌnʤ]

disport di-SPAWRT [dɪ-'spɔɚ-t]

dispose di-SPOHZ [dɪ-'spoʊz]

disputation dis-pyōō-TAY-shuhn [dɪs-pju-'teɪ-ʃən] scans to
___-__-__-shee-uhn [__-__-__-ʃi-ən] @ *1HIV* II, 1, 203

disseat dis-SEET [dɪs-'sit]

dissemble di-SEHM-b(uh)l [dɪ-'sɛm-bļ]

dissentious di-SEHN-shuhs [dɪ-'sɛn-ʃəs]

dissever dis-SEHV-er [dɪs-'sɛv-ɚ]

distaff DIS-taaf ['dɪs-tæf]

distain di-STAYN [dɪ-'steɪn]

distemperature dis-TEHM-pruh-chŏŏr [dɪs-'tɛm-prə-tʃʊɚ]
or ___-___-___-cher [__-___-___-tʃɚ]

distinct dis-TINGKT [dɪs-'tɪŋkt] scans to DIS-tingkt
['dɪs-tɪŋkt] e.g. @ *T&C* IV, 4, 44

distrain dis-TRAYN [dɪs-'treɪn]

distressed dis-TREHST [dɪs-'trɛst] scans to DIS-trehst
['dɪs-trɛst] @ *1HVI* IV, 3, 30

diurnal deye-ER-nuhl [daɪ-'ɝ-nəl]

divers DEYE-verz ['daɪ-vɚz]

Dives DEYE-veez ['daɪ-viz]

dividable scans to DI-vi-duh-b(uh)l ['dɪ-vɪ-də-bļ]

EE i be/ I ɪ bit/ EH ɛ bet/ AA æ bat/ O̅O̅ u boot / O̅O̅ ʊ book/ AW ɔ bought/ AH ɑ father/ ER ɝ bird/
UH ʌ cup/ AY eɪ bay/ EYE aɪ bite/ OY ɔɪ boy/ OH oʊ boat/ OW aʊ how/ YO̅O̅ ɪu duke/ EAR ɪɚ
beer/ AIR ɛɚ bear/ O̅O̅R ʊɚ tour/ AWR ɔɚ bore/ AHR ɑɚ bar/ NG ŋ king/ SH ʃ ship/ ZH ʒ vision/
TH θ thirty/ TH ð then/ CH tʃ child/ J ʤ just/ For complete list, see Key to Pronunciation p. 2.

dividant di-VEYE-duhnt [dɪ-ˈvaɪ-dənt]

dividual di-VIJ-ōō-uhl [dɪ-ˈvɪʤ-u-əl]

divination DIV-uh-NAY-shuhn [dɪv-ə-ˈneɪ-ʃən]

Dobbin DAHB-in [ˈdɑb-ɪn]

do'ee DŌŌ-ee [ˈdu-i]

doers DŌŌ-erz [ˈdu-ɚz]

doff DAWF [dɔf] or DAHF [daf]

Dogberry *(MADO)* DAWG-beh-ree [ˈdɔg-bɛ-ri]

doit / Doit DOYT [dɔɪt]

Dolabella *(A&C)* DAH-luh-BEH-luh [dɑ-lə-ˈbɛ-lə]

dolor / dolour DOH-ler [ˈdoʊ-lɚ]

dolorous DOH-luh-ruhs [ˈdoʊ-lə-rəs]

dolphin / Dolphin DAHL-fin [ˈdɑl-fɪn]

dolt DOHLT [doʊlt]

Dombledon DUHM-uhl-duhn [ˈdʌm-əl-dən]

Domine DAH-min-ee [ˈdɑ-mɪn-i]

dominical duh-MIN-i-k(uh)l [də-ˈmɪn-ɪ-kl̩]

dominie DAH-min-ee [ˈdɑ-mɪn-i]

Domitius Enobarbus *(A&C)* always scans to doh-MI-shuhs
[doʊ-ˈmɪ-ʃəs] or duh-__-__ [də-__-__] EE-nuh-BAHR-buhs
[i-nə-ˈbaɚ-bəs] scans to een-BAHR-buhs [in-ˈbaɚ-bəs]
e.g. @ III, 13, 1; also called "Enobarb" EE-nuh-barb
[ˈi-nə-baɚb] @ II, 7, 121

Don Alphonso DAHN aal-FAHN-zoh [dɑn] [æl-ˈfɑn-zoʊ]

Donalbain *(MAC)* DAHN-uhl-bayn [ˈdɑn-əl-beɪn]

Doncaster DAHNG-kuhs-ter [ˈdɑŋ-kəs-tɚ]

donned DAHND [dɑnd]

Dorcas *(WT)* DAWR-kuhs ['dɔɚ-kəs]

Doreus scans to DAWR-yuhs ['dɔɚ-jəs]

Doricles DAW-ri-kleez ['dɔ-rɪ-kliz]

Dorset, Marquess of *(RIII)* DAWR-sit ['dɔɚ-sɪt]

Dorsetshire DAWR-sit-sher ['dɔɚ-sɪt-ʃɚ] or ___-___-shear [___-___-ʃɪɚ]

dost DUHST [dʌst]

dotage DOH-tij ['doʊ-tɪdʒ]

dotant DOH-tuhnt ['doʊ-tənt]

dotard DOH-terd ['doʊ-tɚd]

dote DOHT [doʊt]

doth DUHTH [dʌθ]

doublet DUHB-lit ['dʌb-lɪt]

doubly DUHB-lee ['dʌb-li]

doughty-handed DOW-tee-HAAND-id ['dɑu-ti-hænd-ɪd]

dout DOWT [dɑut]

dovecote DUHV-koht ['dʌv-koʊt]

Dover DOH-ver ['doʊ-vɚ]

dowager DOW-uh-jer ['dɑu-ə-dʒɚ]

dower DOW-er ['dɑu-ɚ] scans to DOWR [dɑuɚ] e.g. @ *LEAR* I, 1, 128

dowlas DOW-luhs ['dɑu-ləs]

EE i be/ I ɪ bit/ EH ɛ bet/ AA æ bat/ OO u boot / OO ʊ book/ AW ɔ bought/ AH ɑ father/ ER ɝ bird/ UH ʌ cup/ AY eɪ bay/ EYE aɪ bite/ OY ɔɪ boy/ OH oʊ boat/ OW ɑu how/ YOO ɪu duke/ EAR ɪɚ beer/ AIR ɛɚ bear/ OOR ʊɚ tour/ AWR ɔɚ bore/ AHR ɑɚ bar/ NG ŋ king/ SH ʃ ship/ ZH ʒ vision/ TH θ thirty/ TH ð then/ CH tʃ child/ J dʒ just/ For complete list, see Key to Pronunciation p. 2.

dowle DOWL [daʊl]

Dowsabel DOW-suh-behl ['daʊ-sə-bɛl] or ___-zuh-___
[___-zə-___]

dowset DOW-sit ['daʊ-sɪt]

doxy DAHK-see ['dɑk-si]

dozy DOH-zee ['doʊ-zi]

drab DRAAB [dræb]

drachma DRAAK-muh ['dræk-mə]

draff DRAAF [dræf]

dram DRAAM [dræm]

draught DRAAFT [dræft]

drave DRAYV [dreɪv]

drawer (waiter / tapster) DRAW-er ['drɔ-ɚ]

drayman DRAY-muhn ['dreɪ-mən]

Dromio DROH-mee-oh ['droʊ-mi-oʊ] scans to DROH-myoh
['droʊ-mjoʊ]
  Dromio of Ephesus *(CE)* scans e.g. @ I, 2, 68 EHF-i-suhs
  ['ɛf-ɪ-səs]
  Dromio of Syracuse *(CE)* scans e.g. @ I, 2, 10 SI-ruh-kyōōz
  ['sɪ-rə-kjuz]

dross DRAWS [drɔs] or DRAHS [drɑs]

drossy DRAWS-ee ['drɔs-i] or DRAHS-__ ['drɑs-__]

drouth DROWTH [draʊθ]

drovier DROHV-er ['droʊv-ɚ]

drudge DRUHJ [drʌʤ]

drumble DRUHM-b(uh)l ['drʌm-bl̩]

ducat DUHK-it ['dʌk-ɪt]

ducdame (a nonsense word) possibly duhk-**DAH**-may
  [dək-'dɑ-meɪ]

duchy DUHCH-ee ['dʌtʃ-i]

dudgeon DUHJ-uhn ['dʌdʒ-ən]

duello dyo͞o-EHL-oh [dɪu-'ɛl-oʊ]

duer DYO͞O-er ['dɪu-ɚ]

Duff DUHF [dʌf]

Duke DYO͞OK [dɪuk]
  Duke Frederick *(AYL)* FREH-duh-rik ['frɛ-də-rɪk] scans
    to FREH-drik ['frɛ-drɪk] @ V, 4, 148
  Duke Senior *(AYL)* SEEN-yer ['sin-jɚ]

dukedom DYO͞OK-duhm ['dɪuk-dəm]

dulcet DUHL-sit ['dʌl-sɪt]

Dull *(LLL)* DUHL [dʌl]

Dumaine *(LLL)* dyo͞o-MAYN [dɪu-'meɪn]

Dumbe DUHM [dʌm]

dun DUHN [dʌn]

Dun Adramadio DUHN AH-drah-MAH-dee-oh [dʌn]
  [ɑ-drɑ-'mɑ-di-oʊ]

Duncan *(MAC)* DUHNG-kuhn ['dʌŋ-kən]

dungy DUHNG-ee ['dʌŋ-i]

Dunsinane Hill DUHN-si-nayn ['dʌn-sɪ-neɪn] scans to
  duhn-SI-nayn [dən-'sɪ-neɪn] @ *MAC* IV, 1, 93

Dunsmore DUHNZ-mawr ['dʌnz-mɔɚ]

Dunstable DUHN-stuh-b(uh)l ['dʌn-stə-bl̩]

EE i be/ I ɪ bit/ EH ɛ bet/ AA æ bat/ O͞O u boot / O͞O ʊ book/ AW ɔ bought/ AH ɑ father/ ER ɚ bird/
UH ʌ cup/ AY eɪ bay/ EYE aɪ bite/ OY ɔɪ boy/ OH oʊ boat/ OW aʊ how/ YO͞O ɪu duke/ EAR ɪɚ
beer/ AIR ɛɚ bear/ O͞OR ʊɚ tour/ AWR ɔɚ bore/ AHR ɑɚ bar/ NG ŋ king/ SH ʃ ship/ ZH ʒ vision/
TH θ thirty/ TH ð then/ CH tʃ child/ J dʒ just/ For complete list, see Key to Pronunciation p. 2.

dupped DUHPT [dʌpt]

durance DYŌO-ruhns ['djʊ-rəns]

dure DYŌOR [djʊɚ]

durst DERST [dɜ˞st]

duteous DYŌO-tee-uhs ['dɪu-ti-əs]

e'en EEN [in]

e'er AIR [ɛɚ]

ean EEN [in]

eanling EEN-ling ['in-lɪŋ]

earing (cultivating or plowing) I-ring ['ɪ-rɪŋ]

Eastcheap EEST-cheep ['ist-tʃip]

eat EHT [ɛt] (archaic form of "eaten")

ebon EHB-uhn ['ɛb-ən]

eche EECH [itʃ]

Edgar *(LEAR)* EHD-ger ['ɛd-gɚ]

edict EE-dikt ['i-dɪkt] scans to ee-**DIKT** [i-'dɪkt]
e.g. @ *MID* I, 1, 151

Edmund EHD-muhnd ['ɛd-mənd]
Edmund *(LEAR)*
Edmund of Langley, Duke of York *(RII)* LAANG-lee
['læŋ-li]
Edmund, Earl of Rutland *(3HVI)* RUHT-luhnd ['rʌt-lənd]

Edmundsbury EHD-muhndz-buh-ree ['ɛd-məndz-bə-ri]

Edward EHD-werd ['ɛd-wɚd]
Edward IV *(3HVI, RIII)*
Edward, Earl of March *(1HIV)* MAHRCH [mɑɚtʃ]
Edward, Prince of Wales *(3HVI)*
Edward, Prince of Wales, afterward Edward V *(RIII)*

effigies scans to i-FI-jeez [ɪ-'fɪ-ʤiz]

effuse i-FYOOZ [ɪ-'fjuz] or __-FYOOS [__-'fjus]

eftsoons ehft-SOONZ [ɛft-'sunz] scans to EHFT-soonz ['ɛft-sunz] @ 2NOB III, 1, 12

egal EE-guhl ['i-gəl]

egally EE-guh-lee ['i-gə-li]

Egeon *(CE)* ee-JEE-uhn [i-'ʤi-ən] or i-__-__ [ɪ-__-__]

Egeus *(MID)* ee-JEE-uhs [i-'ʤi-əs] or i-__-__ [ɪ-__-__]

Eglamour *(2GEN)* EHG-luh-mawr ['ɛg-lə-mɔɚ] or __-__- moor [__-__-mʊɚ]

eglantine EHG-luhn-teyen ['ɛg-lən-taɪn]

egregious i-GREE-juhs [ɪ-'gri-ʤəs]

eke EEK [ik]

Elbe EHLB [ɛlb]

Elbow *(MM)* EHL-boh ['ɛl-boʊ]

eld EHLD [ɛld]

elflocks EHLF-lahks ['ɛlf-lɑks]

eliads EHL-yuhdz ['ɛl-jədz]

Elinor, Queen *(KJ)* EHL-i-nawr ['ɛl-ɪ-nɔɚ] or __-__-ner [__-__-nɚ]

ell EHL [ɛl]

Elsinore EHL-si-nawr ['ɛl-sɪ-nɔɚ]

Eltham EHL-tuhm ['ɛl-təm] or __-thuhm [__-θəm]

elvish-marked EHL-vish-mahrkt ['ɛl-vɪʃ-mɑɚkt]

EE i be/ I ɪ bit/ EH ɛ bet/ AA æ bat/ OO u boot/ OO ʊ book/ AW ɔ bought/ AH ɑ father/ ER ɝ bird/ UH ʌ cup/ AY eɪ bay/ EYE aɪ bite/ OY ɔɪ boy/ OH oʊ boat/ OW aʊ how/ YOO ɪu duke/ EAR ɪɚ beer/ AIR ɛɚ bear/ OOR ʊɚ tour/ AWR ɔɚ bore/ AHR ɑɚ bar/ NG ŋ king/ SH ʃ ship/ ZH ʒ vision/ TH θ thirty/ TH ð then/ CH ʧ child/ J ʤ just/ For complete list, see Key to Pronunciation p. 2.

Ely EE-lee ['i-li]
   Ely, Bishop of *(HV)*

Elysium i-LIZ-ee-uhm [ɪ-'lɪz-i-əm] scans to ___-LIZ-yuhm
   [___-'lɪz-jəm] or ___-LIZH-___-___ [___-'lɪʒ-___-___] scans
   to ___-LIZH-yuhm [___-'lɪʒ-jəm] e.g. @ *HV* IV, 1, 260

embargements ehm-BAHRJ-muhnts [ɛm-'bɑɚʤ-mənts]

embassade EHM-buh-sahd ['ɛm-bə-sɑd]

embassage EHM-buh-sij ['ɛm-bə-sɪʤ]

embattailed scans to ehm-BAA-t(uh)l-id [ɛm-'bæ-tl̩-ɪd]

embayed ehm-BAYD [ɛm-'beɪd]

embolden ehm-BOHL-d(uh)n [ɛm-'boʊl-dn̩]

embowel ehm-BOWL [ɛm-'baʊl]

embrasures ehm-BRAY-zherz [ɛm-'breɪ-ʒɚz]

Emilia i-MEEL-ee-uh [ɪ-'mil-i-ə] scans to __-MEEL-yuh
   [__-'mil-jə] or __-MIL-__-__ [__-'mɪl-__-__] scans to
   __-MIL-yuh [__-'mɪl-jə]
   Emilia *(CE)*
   Emilia *(OTH)* scans e.g. @ V, 3, 92
   Emilia *(2NOB)* scans e.g. @ II, 5, 49
   Emilia *(WT)* scans e.g. @ II, 2, 15

Emmanuel i-MAAN-yo͞o-ehl [ɪ-'mæn-ju-ɛl]

emperor EHM-puh-rer ['ɛm-pə-rɚ] scans to EHM-prer
   ['ɛm-prɚ] e.g. @ *A&C* IV, 14, 90

empery EHM-puh-ree ['ɛm-pə-ri]

empirics scans to EHM-pi-riks ['ɛm-pɪ-rɪks]

empiricutic ehm-PI-ri-KYO͞O-tik [ɛm-pɪ-rɪ-'kju-tɪk]

empoison ehm-POY-zuhn [ɛm-'pɔɪ-zən]

emulous EHM-yuh-luhs ['ɛm-jə-ləs] scans to EHM-luhs
   ['ɛm-ləs] e.g. @ *T&C* II, 3, 224

enactures ehn-AAK-cherz [ɛn-'æk-ʧɚz]

Enceladus ehn-SEHL-uh-duhs [ɛn-'sɛl-ə-dəs]

enchafed in-CHAYFT [ɪn-'ʧeɪft]

endart ehn-DAHRT [ɛn-'dɑɚt]

endite ehn-DEYET [ɛn-'daɪt]

Endymion ehn-DIM-ee-uhn [ɛn-'dɪm-i-ən]

enew i-NYŌŌ [ɪ-'nɪu]

enfeoffed ehn-FEEFT [ɛn-'fift]

enfranched ehn-FRAANCH-id [ɛn-'frænʧ-ɪd] or in-___-___ [ɪn-___-___]

enfranchise ehn-FRAAN-cheyez [ɛn-'fræn-ʧaɪz] or in-__-__ [ɪn-__-__]

enfranchisement ehn-FRAAN-chuhz-muhnt [ɛn-'fræn-ʧəz-mənt] or ___-FRAAN-cheyez-___ [___-'fræn-ʧaɪz-___]

enfreed ehn-FREED [ɛn-'frid]

engild ehn-GILD [ɛn-'gɪld]

enginer EHN-ji-ner ['ɛn-ʤɪ-nɚ]

engirt ehn-GERT [ɛn-'gɝt]

englut ehn-GLUHT [ɛn-'glʌt]

enjailed ehn-JAYLD [ɛn-'ʤeɪld] or in-___ [ɪn-___]

enjoin ehn-JOYN [ɛn-'ʤɔɪn] scans to EHN-joyn ['ɛn-ʤɔɪn] @ *AW* III, 5, 90

enlard ehn-LAHRD [ɛn-'lɑɚd]

Enobarbus see "Domitius Enobarbus"

---

enow i-NOW [ɪ-'nɑʊ]

ensconce ehn-SKAHNS [ɛn-'skɑns]

ensear ehn-SEAR [ɛn-'sɪɚ]

ensign EHN-sin ['ɛn-sɪn]

enskied in-SKEYED [ɪn-'skaɪd] or ehn-____ [ɛn-___]

ensure ehn-SHŌOR [ɛn-'ʃʊɚ]

entrails EHN-traylz ['ɛn-treɪlz]

envenom ehn-VEHN-uhm [ɛn-'vɛn-əm]

environ ehn-VEYE-ruhn [ɛn-'vaɪ-rən]

Ephesian i-FEE-zhuhn [ɪ-'fi-ʒən]

Ephesus EHF-i-suhs ['ɛf-ɪ-səs]

epicure EHP-i-kyŌor ['ɛp-ɪ-kʊɚ]

Epicurean EHP-i KYŌO-ree-uhn [ɛp-ɪ-'kjʊ-ri-ən] scans to
    __-__-KYŌO-ryuhn [__-__-'kʊ-rjən] @ *A&C* II, 1, 24

epicurism scans to eh-PI-kyŌo-rizm [ɛ-'pɪ-kjʊ-rɪzm]

Epicurus EH-pi-KYŌO-ruhs [ɛ-pɪ-'kjʊ-rəs]

Epidamnum EHP-i-DAAM-nuhm [ɛp-ɪ-'dæm-nəm]

Epidaurus EHP-i-DAW-ruhs [ɛp-ɪ-'dɔ-rəs]

epistle i-PIS-uhl [ɪ-'pɪs-əl]

Epistrophus i-PIS-truh-fuhs [ɪ-'pɪs-trə-fəs]

epitaph EHP-i-taaf ['ɛp-ɪ-tæf]

epithet EHP-i-theht ['ɛp-ɪ-θɛt]

epitheton i-PITH-uh-tahn [ɪ-'pɪθ-ə-tɑn]

equinoctial EH-kwuh-NAHK-shuhl [ɛ-kwə-'nɑk-ʃəl]

equipage EHK-wuh-pij ['ɛk-wə-pɪʤ]

equivocal i-KWIV-uh-k(uh)l [ɪ-'kwɪv-ə-kl̩]

equivocation i-KWIV-uh-KAY-shuhn [ɪ-kwɪv-ə-'keɪ-ʃən]

equivocator i-KWIV-uh-KAY-ter [ɪ-'kwɪv-ə-keɪ-tɚ]

ere AIR [ɛɚ] scans @ *1HVI* I, 3, 88, perhaps EH-er ['ɛ-ɚ]

Erebus EH-ruh-buhs ['ɛ-rə-bəs]

ergo ER-goh ['ɝ-goʊ] or AIR-___ ['ɛɚ-___]

Ermengard ER-muhn-gahrd ['ɝ-mən-gɑɚd]

erned ERND [ɝnd]

Eros *(A&C)* EH-rahs ['ɛ-rɑs] or __-rohs [__-roʊs]

Erpingham ER-ping-uhm ['ɝ-pɪŋ-əm] or ___-___-haam
   [___-___-hæm]
   Erpingham, Sir Thomas *(HV)*

err ER [ɝ]

errant EH-ruhnt ['ɛ-rənt]

erst ERST [ɝst]

erudition scans to AIR-yuh-DI-shee-uhn [ɛɚ-jə-'dɪ-ʃi-ən]

eryngoes i-RING-gohz [ɪ-'rɪŋ-goʊz]

Escalus EHS-kuh-luhs ['ɛs-kə-ləs]
   Escalus *(MM)*
   Escalus, Prince of Verona *(R&J)* vuh-ROH-nuh [və-'roʊ-nə]

Escanes *(PER)* EHS-kuh-neez ['ɛs-kə-niz]

escapend i-SKAY-puhnd [ɪ-'skeɪ-pənd]

eschewed ehs-CHOOD [ɛs-'tʃud]

escoted eh-SKAHT-id [ɛ-'skɑt-ɪd]

EE i be/ I ɪ bit/ EH ɛ bet/ AA æ bat/ OO u boot / OO ʊ book/ AW ɔ bought/ AH ɑ father/ ER ɝ bird/
UH ʌ cup/ AY eɪ bay/ EYE aɪ bite/ OY ɔɪ boy/ OH oʊ boat/ OW ɑʊ how/ YOO ɪu duke/ EAR ɪɚ
beer/ AIR ɛɚ bear/ OOR ʊɚ tour/ AWR ɔɚ bore/ AHR ɑɚ bar/ NG ŋ king/ SH ʃ ship/ ZH ʒ vision/
TH θ thirty/ TH ð then/ CH tʃ child/ J dʒ just/ For complete list, see Key to Pronunciation p. 2.

esill AY-suhl ['eɪ-səl] or EE-__ ['i-__]

especial i-SPEHSH-uhl [ɪ-'spɛʃ-əl] scans to __-__-ee-uhl [__-__-i-əl] @ *HAM* IV, 7, 97

esperance EHS-puh-ruhns ['ɛs-pə-rəns] scans to ___-___-ruhns-ay [___-___-rəns-eɪ] @ *1HIV* V, 2, 96

espial i-SPEYE-uhl [ɪ-'spaɪ-əl] scans to I-speyel ['ɪ-spaɪl] @ *1HVI* I, 4, 8

espouse i-SPOWZ [ɪ-'spɑʊz]

espy i-SPEYE [ɪ-'spaɪ]

esquire EHS-kweyer ['ɛs-kwaɪɚ] scans to ehs-KWEYER [ɛs-'kwaɪɚ] e.g. @ *HV* I, 1, 14

Essex, Earl of *(KJ)* EHS-iks ['ɛs-ɪks]

estridge EHS-trij ['ɛs-trɪʤ]

eterne i-TERN [ɪ-'tɝn]

eternized i-TER-neyezd [ɪ-'tɝ-naɪzd]

Ethiop / Ethiope EE-thee-ohp ['i-θi-oʊp] scans to EE-thyohp ['i-θjoʊp] e.g. @ *PER* II, 2, 20

Ethiopian always scans to EE-thee-OH-pyuhn [i-θi-'oʊ-pjən]

Etna EHT-nuh ['ɛt-nə]

Eton EE-t(uh)n ['i-tn̩]

eunuch YŌO-nuhk ['ju-nək]

Euphrates scans to YŌO-fray-teez ['ju-freɪ-tiz]

Euriphile yōo-RI-fi-lee [jʊ-'rɪ-fɪ-li]

Europa yōo-ROH-puh [jʊ-'roʊ-pə]

Evans, Sir Hugh *(MW)* EH-vuhnz HYŌO ['ɛ-vənz] [hju]

evitate EH-vi-tayt ['ɛ-vɪ-teɪt]

104

ewe $Y\overline{OO}$ [ju]

ewer $Y\overline{OO}$-er ['ju-ɚ] scans to $Y\overline{OO}R$ ['juɚ] e.g. @ *SHR* II, 1, 350

exact (adj) ig-**ZAAKT** [ɪg-'zækt] scans to **EHG**-zaakt ['ɛg-zækt] e.g. @ *1HIV* IV, 1, 46

excess always scans to ik-**SEHS** [ɪk-'sɛs]

exchequer ehks-**CHEHK**-er [ɛks-'tʃɛk-ɚ]

exclaim (n) always scans to iks-**KLAYM** [ɪks-'kleɪm]

execrable **EHKS**-i-kruh-b(uh)l ['ɛks-ɪ-krə-bl̩]

execrations **EHK**-si-**KRAY**-shuhnz [ɛk-sɪ-'kreɪ-ʃənz]

executor ig-**ZEHK**-yuh-ter [ɪg-'zɛk-jə-tɚ] scans to **EHK**-si-kyōō-ter ['ɛk-sɪ-kju-tɚ] @ *HV* I, 2, 203

exequies **EHKS**-uh-kweez ['ɛks-ə-kwiz]

Exeter **EHK**-si-ter ['ɛk-sɪ-tɚ] scans to **EHK**-ster ['ɛk-stɚ] Exeter, Duke of *(HV)* scans @ IV, 8, 52

exhale ehks-**HAYL** [ɛks-'heɪl]

exhort ig-**ZAWRT** [ɪg-'zɔɚt]

exigent **EHK**-suh-juhnt ['ɛk-sə-ʤənt]

exile **EHK**-seyel ['ɛk-saɪl] scans to ehg-**ZEYEL** [ɛg-'zaɪl] e.g. @ *2GEN* III, 2, 3

exorciser **EHK**-sawr-seyez-er ['ɛk-sɔɚ-saɪz-ɚ]

expiate **EHKS**-pee-ayt ['ɛks-pi-eɪt]

exploit (n) always scans to ehks-**PLOYT** [ɛks-'plɔɪt]

expositor ehks-**PAHZ**-i-tawr [ɛks-'pɑz-ɪ-tɔɚ]

EE i be/ I ɪ bit/ EH ɛ bet/ AA æ bat/ $\overline{OO}$ u boot / $\overline{OO}$ ʊ book/ AW ɔ bought/ AH ɑ father/ ER ɝ bird/ UH ʌ cup/ AY eɪ bay/ EYE aɪ bite/ OY ɔɪ boy/ OH oʊ boat/ OW aʊ how/ $Y\overline{OO}$ ɪu duke/ EAR ɪɚ beer/ AIR ɛɚ bear/ $\overline{OO}R$ ʊɚ tour/ AWR ɔɚ bore/ AHR ɑɚ bar/ NG ŋ king/ SH ʃ ship/ ZH ʒ vision/ TH θ thirty/ TH ð then/ CH tʃ child/ J ʤ just/ For complete list, see Key to Pronunciation p. 2.

expostulate ik-SPAHS-chuh-layt [ɪk-'spɑs-tʃə-leɪt]

expostulation ik-SPAHS-chuh-LAY-shuhn [ɪk-spɑs-tʃə-'leɪ-ʃən]

exposture ik-SPAHS-cher [ɪk-'spɑs-tʃɚ] or __-SPOHS-__ [__-'spoʊs-__]

expressure ehks-PREH-shŏŏr [ɛks-'prɛ-ʃʊɚ]

expulsed ehks-PUHLST [ɛks-'pʌlst]

exquisite ik-SKWIZ-it [ɪk-'skwɪz-ɪt] scans to EHK-skwi-zit ['ɛk-skwɪ-zɪt] e.g. @ *R&J* I, 1, 227

exsufflicate ik-SUHF-li-kit [ɪk-'sʌf-lɪ-kɪt]

extant EHK-stuhnt ['ɛk-stənt] or possibly ehk-STAANT [ɛk-'stænt] in prose

extemporal ik-STEHM-puh-ruhl [ɪk-'stɛm-pə-rəl] scans to ___-STEHM-pruhl [___-'stɛm-prəl] e.g. @ *1HVI* III, 1, 6

extempore ik-STEHM-puh-ree [ɪk-'stɛm-pə-ri] scans to ___-STEHM-pree [___-'stɛm-pri] @ *SHR* II, 1, 265

exteriorly ehks-TEAR-yer-lee [ɛks-'tɪɚ-jɚ-li]

extermined ehks-TER-mind [ɛks-'tɝ-mɪnd]

extern scans to ik-STERN [ɪk-'stɝn]

extirp ehk-STERP [ɛk-'stɝp]

extirpate scans to iks-TER-payt [ɪks-'tɝ-peɪt]

Exton, Sir Pierce of *(RII)* EHKS-t(uh)n PEARS ['ɛks-tṇ] [pɪɚs]

extraordinary always scans to EHK-struh-**AWR**-din-eh-ree [ɛk-strə-'ɔɚ-dɪn-ɛ-ri] possibly the same in prose

extraught ehks-TRAWT [ɛks-'trɔt]

extreme ik-STREEM [ɪk-'strim] scans to EHK-streem ['ɛk-strim] e.g. @ *COR* IV, 5, 70

eyases EYE-uhs-iz ['aɪ-əs-ɪz]

eyas-musket EYE-uhs-MUHS-kit ['aɪ-əs-mʌs-kɪt]

eyed EYED [aɪd]

eyne EYEN [aɪn]

eyrie EH-ree ['ɛ-ri] or I-ree ['ɪ-ri]

Fabian *(12th)* FAY-bee-uhn ['feɪ-bi-ən] scans to FAY-byuhn ['feɪ-bjən] @ V, 1, 305

facinerious FAAS-i-NI-ree-uhs [fæs-ɪ-'nɪ-ri-əs]

factionary FAAK-shuhn-eh-ree ['fæk-ʃən-ɛ-ri]

factious FAAK-shuhs ['fæk-ʃəs]

fadge FAAJ [fædʒ]

fagot / faggot FAAG-uht ['fæg-ət]

fain FAYN [feɪn]

falc'ner FAWLK-ner ['fɔlk-nɚ] or FAALK-__ ['fælk-__]

falchion FAWL-chuhn ['fɔl-tʃən]

Falconbridge FAW-kuhn-brij ['fɔ-kən-brɪdʒ] or FAWL-__-__ ['fɔl-__-__] or FAAL-__-__ ['fæl-__-__] or FAHL-__-__ ['fɑl-__-__]
Falconbridge, Jacques JAY-kweez ['dʒeɪ-kwiz]

falconer FAWL-kuhn-er ['fɔl-kən-ɚ] or FAAL-__-__ ['fæl-__-__]

fallow FAAL-oh ['fæl-oʊ]

Falstaff FAWL-staaf ['fɔl-stæf]
Falstaff, Sir John *(1HIV, 2HIV, MW)*
Falstaff, Sir John *(1HVI)*
Falstaff's Page *(2HIV)*

---

familiar fuh-MIL-yer [fə-'mɪl-jɚ] scans to __-__-ee-er [__-__-i-ɚ] e.g. @ *R&J* III, 3, 6

fancy-monger FAAN-see-MUHNG-ger ['fæn-si-mʌŋ-gɚ] or __-__-MAHNG-__ [__-__-mɑŋ-__]

fanes FAYNZ [feɪnz]

Fang *(2HIV)* FAANG [fæŋ]

fantasticoes faan-TAAS-ti-kohz [fæn-'tæs-tɪ-koʊz]

fap FAAP [fæp]

farborough FAHR-buh-roh ['fɑɚ-bə-roʊ]

fardel FAHR-d(uh)l ['fɑɚ-dl̩]

farewell fair-WEHL [fɛɚ-'wɛl] scans to FAIR-wehl ['fɛɚ-wɛl] e.g. @ *RII* II, 2, 8

farre FAHR [fɑɚ]

farthingale FAHR-<u>th</u>ing-gayl ['fɑɚ-ðɪŋ-geɪl] or __-<u>th</u>in-__ [__-ðɪn-__]

farthings FAHR-<u>th</u>ingz ['fɑɚ-ðɪŋz]

fashion-monger FAA-shuhn-MUHNG-ger ['fæ-ʃən-mʌŋ-gɚ] or __-__-MAHNG-__ [__-__-mɑŋ-__]

fashion-monging FAA-shuhn-MUHNG-ging ['fæ-ʃən-'mʌŋ-gɪŋ] or __-__-MAHNG-__ [__-__-mɑŋ-__]

fathom FAA-<u>th</u>uhm ['fæ-ðəm]

fatigate FAA-ti-gayt ['fæ-tɪ-geɪt]

Faulconbridge FAWL-kuhn-brij ['fɔl-kən-brɪʤ] or FAW-__-__ ['fɔ-__-__]
    Faulconbridge, Lady *(KJ)*
    Faulconbridge, Robert *(KJ)*

Faustuses FOWS-tuhs-iz ['faʊs-təs-ɪz]

fay FAY [feɪ]

fealty FEE-uhl-tee ['fi-əl-ti] scans to FEEL-tee ['fil-ti]
    e.g. @ *RII* V, 2, 45

feat FEET [fit]

featly FEET-lee ['fit-li]

fecks FEHKS [fɛks]

fedary FEHD-uh-ree ['fɛd-ə-ri] scans to FEHD-ree ['fɛd-ri]
    @ *CYM* III, 2, 21

federary scans to FEHD-ruh-ree ['fɛd-rə-ri] or FEHD-uh-ree
    ['fɛd-ə-ri]

Feeble, Francis *(2HIV)* FEE-b(uh)l FRAAN-sis ['fi-bḷ]
    ['fræn-sɪs]

feeze FEEZ [fiz]

feign FAYN [feɪn]

felicitate fi-LIS-i-tayt [fɪ-'lɪs-ɪ-teɪt]

felicity fi-LIS-i-tee [fɪ-'lɪs-ɪ-ti]

fellies FEH-leez ['fɛ-liz]

fen FEHN [fɛn]

fennel FEHN-uhl ['fɛn-əl]

fenny FEHN-ee ['fɛn-i]

Fenton *(MW)* FEHN-tuhn ['fɛn-tən]

Fer see "le Fer"

Ferdinand FER-di-naand ['fɝ-dɪ-nænd]
    Ferdinand *(TEMP)*
    Ferdinand, King of Navarre *(LLL)* nuh-VAHR [nə-'vɑɚ]

fere FEAR [fɪɚ]

EE i be/ I ɪ bit/ EH ɛ bet/ AA æ bat/ O͞O u boot / O͞O ʊ book/ AW ɔ bought/ AH ɑ father/ ER ɝ bird/
UH ʌ cup/ AY eɪ bay/ EYE aɪ bite/ OY ɔɪ boy/ OH oʊ boat/ OW aʊ how/ YO͞O ɪu duke/ EAR ɪɚ
beer/ AIR ɛɚ bear/ O͞OR ʊɚ tour/ AWR ɔɚ bore/ AHR ɑɚ bar/ NG ŋ king/ SH ʃ ship/ ZH ʒ vision/
TH θ thirty/ TH ð then/ CH tʃ child/ J dʒ just/ For complete list, see Key to Pronunciation p. 2.

Ferrara fuh-RAH-ruh [fə-'rɑ-rə]

Ferrers scans to feh-RERZ [fɛ-'rɝz]

ferret FEH-rit ['fɛ-rɪt]

ferula FAIR-yōō-luh ['fɛɚ-ju-lə]

fervency FER-vuhn-see ['fɝ-vən-si]

fescue FEHS-kyōō ['fɛs-kju]

Feste *(12th)* FEHS-tee ['fɛs-ti]

festinate FEHS-ti-nit ['fɛs-tɪ-nɪt]

festinately FEHS-ti-nit-lee ['fɛs-tɪ-nɪt-li]

fet FEHT [fɛt]

fetlocks FEHT-lahks ['fɛt-lɑks]

fetter FEHT-er ['fɛt-ɚ]

feverous always scans to FEEV-ruhs ['fiv-rəs]

fia FEE-uh ['fi-ə]

Fidele fi-DAY-lee [fɪ-'deɪ-li] or ___-DEE-___ [___-'di-___]

fidiused FID-ee-uhst ['fɪd-i-əst]

fie FEYE [faɪ]

Fiennes, James, Lord Say *(2HVI)* FEYENZ [faɪnz]

fife / Fife FEYEF [faɪf]

figo FI-goh ['fɪ-goʊ] or FEE-___ ['fi-___]

filberts FIL-berts ['fɪl-bɚts]

filch FILCH [fɪltʃ]

filed FEYELD [faɪld]

filial always scans to FIL-yuhl ['fɪl-jəl]

fillet FIL-it ['fɪl-ɪt]

fillip FIL-ip ['fɪl-ɪp]

finical FIN-i-k(uh)l ['fɪn-ɪ-kl̩]

finny FIN-ee ['fɪn-i]

Finsbury possibly scans to **FINZ**-bree ['fɪnz-bri] or finz-**BREE** [fɪnz-'bri]

firago fuh-**RAH**-goh [fə-'rɑ-goʊ]

fire FEYER [faɪɚ] scans to **FEYE**-er ['faɪ-ɚ] e.g. @ *JC* III, 1, 171 first citation

firk FERK [fɝk]

fishmonger FISH-muhng-ger ['fɪʃ-məŋ-gɚ] or ___-mahng-___ [___-mɑŋ-___]

fisnomy FIZ-nuh-mee ['fɪz-nə-mi]

fistula FIS-chuh-luh ['fɪs-tʃə-lə]

fitchew FITCH-ōō ['fɪtʃ-u]

Fitzwater, Lord *(RII)* always scans to fits-**WAWT**-er [fɪts-'wɔt-ɚ]

fixure FIK-sher ['fɪk-ʃɚ]

flagon FLAAG-uhn ['flæg-ən]

flamen FLAY-muhn ['fleɪ-mən]

Flaminius *(TIMON)* fluh-**MIN**-ee-uhs [flə-'mɪn-i-əs]

Flanders FLAAN-derz ['flæn-dɚz]

Flavina fluh-**VEE**-nuh [flə-'vi-nə]

Flavius FLAY-vee-uhs ['fleɪ-vi-əs] scans to **FLAY**-vyuhs ['fleɪ-vjəs]

EE i be/ I ɪ bit/ EH ɛ bet/ AA æ bat/ ŌŌ u boot / ŌŌ ʊ book/ AW ɔ bought/ AH ɑ father/ ER ɝ bird/ UH ʌ cup/ AY eɪ bay/ EYE aɪ bite/ OY ɔɪ boy/ OH oʊ boat/ OW aʊ how/ YŌŌ ɪu duke/ EAR ɪɚ beer/ AIR ɛɚ bear/ ŌŌR ʊɚ tour/ AWR ɔɚ bore/ AHR ɑɚ bar/ NG ŋ king/ SH ʃ ship/ ZH ʒ vision/ TH θ thirty/ TH ð then/ CH tʃ child/ J ʤ just/ For complete list, see Key to Pronunciation p. 2.

Flavius *(JC)* scans @ V, 3, 108
Flavius *(TIMON)*

Fleance *(MAC)* FLEE-uhns ['fli-əns] possibly scans to FLEENS [flins] @ III, 1, 35

fledge FLEHJ [flɛʤ]

fleer FLEAR [fliɚ]

fleshment FLEHSH-muhnt ['flɛʃ-mənt]

fleshmonger FLEHSH-muhng-ger ['flɛʃ-məŋ-gɚ] or ___-mahng-___ [___-mɑŋ-___]

fleur-de-luce FLER-duh-lōōs ['flɝ-də-lus] or FLŌŌR-__-__ ['flʊɚ-__-__]

flewed FLŌŌD [flud]

flexure FLEHK-sher ['flɛk-ʃɚ]

Flibbertigibbet FLI-ber-tee-JI-bit ['flɪ-bɚ-ti-ʤɪ-bɪt]

Flint FLINT [flɪnt]

flirt-gills FLERT-jilz ['flɝt-ʤɪlz]

Florence FLAW-rehns ['flɔ-rɛns] or FLAH-___ ['flɑ-___] Florence, Duke of *(AW)*

Florentine FLAW-ruhn-teen ['flɔ-rən-tin] or __-__-teyen [__-__-taɪn]

Florentius flaw-REHN-shuhs [flɔ-'rɛn-ʃəs]

Florizel *(WT)* FLAW-ri-zehl ['flɔ-rɪ-zɛl] or FLAH-__-__ ['flɑ-__-__]

flote FLOHT [floʊt]

flouriets scans to FLOW-rits ['flɑʊ-rɪts] @ *MID* IV, 1, 54

flourish FLUH-rish ['flʌ-rɪʃ] or FLŌŌ-___ ['flu-___]

flout FLOWT [flɑʊt]

flower-de-luce scans to FLOWR-duh-loos ['flauɚ-də-lus]
e.g. @ *1HVI* I, 1, 80

Fluellen *(HV)* floo-EHL-in [flu-'ɛl-ɪn]

flurted FLERT-id ['flɝt-ɪd]

Flute, Francis / Thisbe *(MID)* FLOOT [flut] THIZ-bee
['θɪz-bi]

fob FAHB [fɑb]

foh FOH [fou]

foin FOYN [fɔɪn]

foison FOY-zuhn ['fɔɪ-zən]

Foix FOYZ [fɔɪz]

font FAHNT [fɑnt]

Fontybell FAHN-ti-behl ['fɑn-tɪ-bɛl]

Fool FOOL [ful]
Fool *(LEAR)*
Fool *(TIMON)*

fopp'ry FAHP-ree ['fɑp-ri]

fopped FAHPT [fɑpt]

foppery FAHP-uh-ree ['fɑp-ə-ri]

for't FAWRT [fɔrt]

forbade fer-BAAD [fɚ-'bæd] or fawr-___ [fɔɚ-___]

Ford FAWRD [fɔɚd]
Ford *(MW)*
Ford, Mistress *(MW)*

fordo fawr-DOO [fɔɚ-'du]

EE i be/ I ɪ bit/ EH ɛ bet/ AA æ bat/ OO u boot / OO ʊ book/ AW ɔ bought/ AH ɑ father/ ER ɝ bird/
UH ʌ cup/ AY eɪ bay/ EYE aɪ bite/ OY ɔɪ boy/ OH ou boat/ OW aʊ how/ YOO ɪu duke/ EAR ɪɚ
beer/ AIR ɛɚ bear/ OOR ʊɚ tour/ AWR ɔɚ bore/ AHR ɑɚ bar/ NG ŋ king/ SH ʃ ship/ ZH ʒ vision/
TH θ thirty/ TH ð then/ CH tʃ child/ J dʒ just/ For complete list, see Key to Pronunciation p. 2.

113

forepast FAWR-paast ['fɔɚ-pæst]

fore-spurrer fawr-SPE(r)-rer [fɔɚ-'spɝ-rɚ]

Forester *(LLL)* FAW-ri-ster ['fɔ-rɪ-stɚ] or FAH-__-__ ['fɑ-__-__]

forfeit FAWR-fit ['fɔɚ-fɪt]

forfeiture FAWR-fi-cher ['fɔɚ-fɪ-tʃɚ]

forgetive FAWR-ji-tiv ['fɔɚ-dʒɪ-tɪv]

forlorn fer-LAWRN [fɚ-'lɔɚn] scans to FAWR-lawrn ['fɔɚ-lɔɚn] e.g. @ *1HVI* I, 2, 19

fornicatress FAWR-ni-KAY-tris [fɔɚ-nɪ-'keɪ-trɪs]

Forres FAW-ris ['fɔ-rɪs] or FAH-___ ['fɑ-___]

Forrest FAW-rist ['fɔ-rist] or FAH-___ ['fɑ-___]

forset-seller FAWR-sit-sehl-er ['fɔɚ-sɪt-sɛl-ɚ] some editions "faucet" FAW-sit ['fɔ-sɪt]

forsooth fawr-SOOTH [fɔɚ-'suθ]

forswear fawr-SWAIR [fɔɚ-'swɛɚ]

forsworn fawr-SWAWRN [fɔɚ-'swɔɚn]

Fortinbras *(HAM)* FAWR-tin-brahs ['fɔɚ-tɪn-brɑs] or ___-___-braas [___-___-bræs]

fortnight FAWRT-neyet ['fɔɚt-naɪt]

fortune / Fortune FAWR-chuhn ['fɔɚ-tʃən]

forwhy fawr-HWEYE [fɔɚ-'hwaɪ]

foughten FAW-t(uh)n ['fɔ-tn̩]

foutra FOO-truh ['fu-trə]

fracted FRAAK-tid ['fræk-tɪd]

frampold FRAAM-pohld ['fræm-poʊld]

frampul FRAAM-puhl ['fræm-pəl]

France FRAANS [fræns]
France, King of *(AW)*
France, King of *(LEAR)*
France, Princess of *(LLL)*

Frances / Francis FRAAN-sis ['fræn-sɪs]
Francis *(1HIV)*
Francis, Friar *(MADO)* FREYER [fraɪɚ] scans to
FREYE-er ['fraɪ-ɚ] e.g. @ V, 4, 18

Francisca *(MM)* fraan-SIS-kuh [fræn-'sɪs-kə]

Francisco fraan-SIS-koh [fræn-'sɪs-koʊ]
Francisco *(HAM)*
Francisco *(TEMP)*

Frankford FRAANGK-ferd ['fræŋk-fɚd]

Frateretto FRAA-tuh-REH-toh [fræ-tə-'rɛ-toʊ]

fraught FRAWT [frɔt]

fraughtage FRAW-tij ['frɔ-tɪʤ]

fray FRAY [freɪ]

freelier FREE-lee-er ['fri-li-ɚ]

frequent (v) always scans to free-KWEHNT [fri-'kwɛnt]

fret FREHT [frɛt]

Friar FREYER [fraɪɚ] scans to FREYE-er ['fraɪ-ɚ]
e.g. @ *R&J* V, 2, 1

Friar Penker scans to FREYE-er PEHNG-ker ['fraɪ-ɚ]
['pɛŋ-kɚ]

frieze FREEZ [friz]

EE i be/ I ɪ bit/ EH ɛ bet/ AA æ bat/ OO u boot / OO ʊ book/ AW ɔ bought/ AH ɑ father/ ER ɝ bird/
UH ʌ cup/ AY eɪ bay/ EYE aɪ bite/ OY ɔɪ boy/ OH oʊ boat/ OW aʊ how/ YOO ɪu duke/ EAR ɪə
beer/ AIR ɛə bear/ OOR ʊə tour/ AWR ɔə bore/ AHR ɑə bar/ NG ŋ king/ SH ʃ ship/ ZH ʒ vision/
TH θ thirty/ TH ð then/ CH ʧ child/ J ʤ just/ For complete list, see Key to Pronunciation p. 2.

115

frippery FRIP-uh-ree ['frɪp-ə-ri]

friskins FRIS-kinz ['frɪs-kɪnz]

Frogmore FRAHG-mawr ['frɑg-mɔɚ]

Froissart FROY-sahrt ['frɔɪ-sɑɚ-t]

frontier always scans to FRUHN-tear ['frʌn-tɪɚ]

frontlet FRUHNT-lit ['frʌnt-lɪt]

Froth *(MM)* FRAWTH [frɔθ] or FRAHTH [frɑθ]

froward FROH-werd ['froʊ-wɚd]

fructful FRŌŌKT-fool ['frukt-fʊl] or FRUHKT-___
['frʌkt-___]

fructify FRUHK-tuh-feye ['frʌk-tə-faɪ] or FRŌŌK-__-__
['frʊk-__-__]

frush FRUHSH [frʌʃ]

frustrate (adj) (ineffectual) FRUHS-trayt ['frʌs-treɪt]

fubbed FUHBD [fʌbd]

fullam FŌŌL-uhm ['fʊl-əm]

fulsome FŌŌL-suhm ['fʊl-səm]

Fulvia FŌŌL-vee-uh ['fʊl-vi-ə] scans to FŌŌL-vyuh
['fʊl-vjə] e.g. @ *A&C* I, 2, 103

fumiter FYŌŌ-mi-ter ['fju-mɪ-tɚ]

fumitory FYŌŌ-mi-taw-ree ['fju-mɪ-tɔ-ri]

funeral FYŌŌN-ruhl ['fjun-rəl] scans to FYŌŌ-nuh-ruhl
['fju-nə-rəl] e.g. @ *JC* III, 1, 233

furbish FER-bish ['fɝ-bɪʃ]

furlong FER-lawng ['fɝ-lɔŋ]

Furnival FER-ni-vuhl ['fɝ-nɪ-vəl]

furze FERZ [fɜz]

fust FUHST [fʌst]

fustian FUHS-chuhn [ˈfʌs-tʃən] or ___-tee-uhn [___-ti-ən]

fustilarian FUHS-ti-LAA-ree-uhn [fʌs-tɪ-ˈlæ-ri-ən]

fusty FUHS-tee [ˈfʌs-ti]

fut FUHT [fʌt] or FŌOT [fʊt]

gabble GAAB-uhl [ˈgæb-əl]

gaberdine GAAB-er-deen [ˈgæb-ɚ-din]

gad GAAD [gæd]

Gadshill *(1HIV)* GAADZ-hil [ˈgædz-hɪl]

gage GAYJ [geɪʤ]

gainsaid gayn-SAYD [geɪn-ˈseɪd] or ___-SEHD [___-ˈsɛd]

gainsay gayn-SAY [geɪn-ˈseɪ]

Galathe GAAL-uh-thee [ˈgæl-ə-θi]

Galen GAY-lin [ˈgeɪ-lɪn]

gall GAWL [gɔl]

gallant GAAL-uhnt [ˈgæl-ənt] possibly scans to guh-LAHNT [gə-ˈlɑnt] @ *RII* V, 3, 15

Gallia GAAL-ee-uh [ˈgæl-i-ə] scans to GAAL-yuh [ˈgæl-jə] e.g. @ *HV* I, 2, 217

Gallian always scans to GAAL-yuhn [ˈgæl-jən]

galliard GAAL-yerd [ˈgæl-jɚd]

galliasses GAAL-ee-aas-iz [ˈgæl-i-æs-ɪz] possibly scans to GAAL-yuhs-iz [ˈgæl-jəs-ɪz] @ *SHR* II, 1, 380

EE i be/ I ɪ bit/ EH ɛ bet/ AA æ bat/ ŌO u boot / ŌO ʊ book/ AW ɔ bought/ AH ɑ father/ ER ɝ bird/ UH ʌ cup/ AY eɪ bay/ EYE aɪ bite/ OY ɔɪ boy/ OH oʊ boat/ OW aʊ how/ YŌO ɪu duke/ EAR ɪɚ beer/ AIR ɛɚ bear/ ŌOR ʊɚ tour/ AWR ɔɚ bore/ AHR ɑɚ bar/ NG ŋ king/ SH ʃ ship/ ZH ʒ vision/ TH θ thirty/ TH ð then/ CH tʃ child/ J ʤ just/ For complete list, see Key to Pronunciation p. 2.

gallimaufry GAAL-i-MAW-free [gæl-ɪ-'mɔ-fri] or __-__-
 MAH-__ [__-__-'mɑ-__]

Galloway GAAL-uh-way ['gæl-ə-weɪ]

gallowglasses GAAL-oh-glaas-iz ['gæl-ou-glæs-ɪz]

gallowses GAAL-ohz-iz ['gæl-ouz-ɪz]

Gallus *(A&C)* GAAL-uhs ['gæl-əs]

Gam GAAM [gæm]

gambol GAAM-b(uh)l ['gæm-bl̩]

gamester GAYM-ster ['geɪm-stɚ]

gammon GAAM-uhn ['gæm-ən]

gamut GAAM-uht ['gæm-ət]

gangrened GAANG-greend ['gæŋ-grind]

Ganymede GAAN-i-meed ['gæn-ɪ-mid]

gaol JAYL [ʤeɪl]

gaoler / Gaoler JAYL-er ['ʤeɪl-ɚ]
 Gaoler *(2NOB)*
 Gaoler *(WT)*
 Gaoler's Daughter *(2NOB)*

gaping GAY-ping ['geɪ-pɪŋ]

garboils GAHR-boylz ['gɑɚ-bɔɪlz]

Gardiner, afterward Bishop of Winchester *(HVIII)*
 GAHRD-ner ['gɑɚd-nɚ]

Gargantua gahr-GAAN-choo-uh [gɑɚ-'gæn-tʃu-ə]

Gargrave, Sir Thomas *(1HVI)* GAHR-grayv ['gɑɚ-greɪv]

gaskins GAAS-kinz ['gæs-kɪnz]

gasted GAAST-id ['gæst-ɪd]

gastness GAAST-nis ['gæst-nɪs]

gat GAAT [gæt]

gaud see "gawd"

Gaul GAWL [gɔl]

Gaultier GAW-ter ['gɔ-tɚ]

Gaultree GAWL-tree ['gɔl-tri]

gaunt / Gaunt GAWNT [gɔnt]

gauntlet GAWNT-lit ['gɔnt-lɪt]

gawd GAWD [gɔd]

Gawsey GAW-zee ['gɔ-zi] or ___-see [__-si]

geck GEHK [gɛk]

gelt GEHLT [gɛlt]

geminy JEHM-i-neye ['ʤɛm-ɪ-naɪ]

gennets JEHN-its ['ʤɛn-ɪts]

Genoa JEHN-oh-uh ['ʤɛn-oʊ-ə]

Geoffrey JEHF-ree ['ʤɛf-ri]

George Alow uh-LOH [ə-'loʊ]

George, Duke of Clarence *(RIII)* JAWRJ KLAA-ruhns [ʤɔɚ-ʤ] ['klæ-rəns]

Gerard de Narbon juh-RAHRD duh-NAHR-buhn [ʤə-'rɑɚ-d] [də-'nɑɚ-bən]

germain JER-muhn ['ʤɝ-mən]

germane jer-MAYN [ʤɚ-'meɪn]

119

germans JER-muhnz ['ʤɝ-mənz]

Gertrude *(HAM)* GER-trōōd ['gɝ-trud]

gests JEHSTS [ʤɛsts]

Ghost of Hamlet's Father *(HAM)* GOHST [goʊst]

gi'in GIN [gɪn]

gib GIB [gɪb]

gibber JIB-er ['ʤɪb-ɚ]

gibbet JIB-it ['ʤɪb-ɪt]

gib-cat GIB-kaat ['gɪb-kæt]

gibe JEYEB [ʤaɪb]

giber JEYEB-er ['ʤaɪb-ɚ]

gibing JEYEB-ing ['ʤaɪb-ɪŋ]

gig GIG [gɪg]

giglet / giglot GIG-lit ['gɪg-lɪt]

gild GILD [gɪld]

Gilliams GIL-yuhmz ['gɪl-jəmz]

Gillian scans to JIL-yuhn ['ʤɪl-jən]

gillyvors JIL-ee-vawrz ['ʤɪl-i-vɔɚz]

gimmaled GIM-uhld ['gɪm-əld] or JIM-___ ['ʤɪm-___]

gimmors JIM-erz ['ʤɪm-ɚz]

gin (n) (a snare or trap) JIN [ʤɪn]

gin (v) (to begin) GIN [gɪn]

ging GING [gɪŋ]

Ginn JIN [ʤɪn]

Giraldo juh-RAHL-doh [ʤə-'rɑl-dou] or __-RAAL-__
[__-'ræl-__]

girt GERT [gɝt]

Gis JIS [ʤɪs]

Glamis GLAHM-is ['glɑm-ɪs] possibly scans to GLAHMZ
[glɑmz] e.g. @ *MAC* I, 5, 20

glanders GLAAN-derz ['glæn-dɚz]

Glansdale, Sir William *(1HVI)* GLAANZ-d(uh)l ['glænz-dl̩]

gleek GLEEK [glik]

Glendower GLEHN-dow-er ['glɛn-dɑu-ɚ] scans to GLEHN-
dowr ['glɛn-dɑuɚ] or glehn-DOWR [glɛn-'dɑuɚ]
Glendower, Owen *(1HIV)* scans to first syllable stress
e.g. @ V, 5, 40; scans to second syllable stress e.g.
@ I, 3, 101

glikes GLEYEKS [glaɪks]

glister GLIS-ter ['glɪs-tɚ]

globy GLOH-bee ['glou-bi]

glose GLOHZ [glouz]

Gloucester GLAHS-ter ['glɑs-tɚ] scans to GLAHS-i-ter
['glɑs-ɪ-tɚ] or GLAH-sis-ter ['glɑ-sɪs-tɚ]
Gloucester, Duchess of *(RII)*
Gloucester, Duke of *(RIII)* scans e.g. @ III, 4, 46
Gloucester, Duke of, Humphrey *(1HVI)* scans e.g. @ I, 3, 6
Gloucester, Earl of *(LEAR)*

Gloucestershire GLAHS-ter-sher ['glɑs-tɚ-ʃɚ] or ___-___-
shear [___-___-ʃɪɚ]

gloze GLOHZ [glouz]

EE i be/ I ɪ bit/ EH ɛ bet/ AA æ bat/ OO u boot / OO ʊ book/ AW ɔ bought/ AH ɑ father/ ER ɝ bird/
UH ʌ cup/ AY eɪ bay/ EYE aɪ bite/ OY ɔɪ boy/ OH ou boat/ OW ɑu how/ YOO ɪu duke/ EAR ɪɚ
beer/ AIR ɛɚ bear/ OOR ʊɚ tour/ AWR ɔɚ bore/ AHR ɑɚ bar/ NG ŋ king/ SH ʃ ship/ ZH ʒ vision/
TH θ thirty/ TH ð then/ CH ʧ child/ J ʤ just/ For complete list, see Key to Pronunciation p. 2.

gnaw NAW [nɔ]

Gneius NEE-uhs ['ni-əs]

gobbets GAH-bits ['gɑ-bɪts]

Gobbo GAH-boh ['gɑ-boʊ]
  Gobbo, Launcelot *(MVEN)* LAHNS-uh-laht ['lɑns-ə-lɑt]
    scans to LAHNS-laht ['lɑns-lɑt] or LAANS-___-___
    ['læns-___-___] scans to LAANS-___ ['læns-___] or
    LAWNS-___-___ ['lɔns-___-___] scans to LAWNS-___
    ['lɔns-___]
  Gobbo, Old *(MVEN)*

God 'ield gahd-EELD [gɑd-'ild]

God be w' you GAHD BEYE YOO [gɑd] [baɪ] [ju] or
  GAHD BWEE YOO [gɑd] [bwi] [ju]

God bye you GAHD BEYE YOO [gɑd] [baɪ] [ju] alternate
  spellings include "God b'uy you"

god-den / God-den gōod-EHN [gʊd-'ɛn]

Goffe, Matthew *(2HVI)* GAHF [gɑf]

gogs-wouns gahgz-WOONZ [gɑgz-'wunz]

Golgotha GAHL-guh-thuh ['gɑl-gə-θə]

Goliases goh-LEYE-uh-siz [goʊ-'laɪ-ə-sɪz]

Goliath guh-LEYE-uhth [gə-'laɪ-əθ]

gondola GAHN-duh-luh ['gɑn-də-lə]

gondolier gahn-duh-LEAR [gɑn-də-'lɪɚ]

Goneril *(LEAR)* GAHN-uh-ruhl ['gɑn-ə-rəl] scans to
  GAHN-ruhl ['gɑn-rəl] @ I, 1, 82

Gonzago guhn-ZAH-goh [gən-'za-goʊ]

Gonzalo *(TEMP)* guhn-ZAH-loh [gən-'za-loʊ] possibly
  GAHN-zuh-loh ['gɑn-zə-loʊ] @ V, 1, 68

good-den / good den gōod-DEHN [gʊd-'dɛn]

Goodrig GŌOD-rig ['gʊd-rɪg]

Goodwin GŌOD-win ['gʊd-wɪn]

Goodwin Sands GŌOD-win SAANDZ ['gʊd-wɪn] [sændz]

gorbellied GAWR-behl-eed ['gɔɚ-bɛl-id]

Gorboduc GAWR-buh-duhk ['gɔɚ-bə-dək]

Gordian always scans to GAWR-dyuhn ['gɔɚ-djən]

gorget GAWR-jit ['gɔɚ-ʤɪt]

Gorgon GAWR-guhn ['gɔɚ-gən]

gormandize GAWR-muhn-deyez ['gɔɚ-mən-daɪz]

gosling GAHZ-ling ['gɑz-lɪŋ]

goss GAWS [gɔs] or GAHS [gɑs]

Goths GAHTHS [gɑθs] except GOHTS [goʊts]
  @ *AYL* III, 3, 7 to make the pun with "goats"

gourd GAWRD [gɔɚd]

gouts GOWTS [gaʊts]

Governor of Harfleur *(HV)* HAHR-fler ['hɑɚ-flɚ] or
  ___-flōo [___-flu]

Gower GOW-er ['gaʊ-ɚ]
  Gower *(2HIV, HV)*
  Gower *(PER)*

graff GRAAF [græf]

gramercy gruh-MER-see [grə-'mɝ-si]

grandam / Grandam GRAAN-daam ['græn-dæm]

EE i be/ I ɪ bit/ EH ɛ bet/ AA æ bat/ ŌO u boot / ŌO ʊ book/ AW ɔ bought/ AH ɑ father/ ER ɝ bird/
UH ʌ cup/ AY eɪ bay/ EYE aɪ bite/ OY ɔɪ boy/ OH oʊ boat/ OW aʊ how/ YŌO ɪu duke/ EAR ɪɚ
beer/ AIR ɛɚ bear/ ŌOR ʊɚ tour/ AWR ɔɚ bore/ AHR ɑɚ bar/ NG ŋ king/ SH ʃ ship/ ZH ʒ vision/
TH θ thirty/ TH ð then/ CH ʧ child/ J ʤ just/ For complete list, see Key to Pronunciation p. 2.

Grandpré graand-PRAY [grænd-'preɪ]
　Grandpré *(HV)*

grandsire GRAAND-seyer ['grænd-saɪɚ]

Gratiano GRAH-shee-AH-noh [grɑ-ʃi-'ɑ-noʊ] scans to
　___-SHYAH-noh [__-'ʃjɑ-noʊ]
　Gratiano *(MVEN)* scans @ I, 1, 58
　Gratiano *(OTH)* scans @ V, 2, 365

Gratii GRAY-shee-eye ['greɪ-ʃi-aɪ]

gratillity gruh-TIL-i-tee [grə-'tɪl-ɪ-ti]

gratis GRAA-tis ['græ-tɪs] or GRAH-___ ['grɑ-___]

gratulate GRAA-chuh-layt ['græ-tʃə-leɪt]

Graymalkin gray-MAWL-kin [greɪ-'mɔl-kɪn]

Grecian GREE-shuhn ['gri-ʃən]

Green *(RII)* GREEN [grin]

greensward GREENZ-werd ['grinz-wɚd]

Greenwich GREHN-ich ['grɛn-ɪtʃ] or GRIN-ij ['grɪn-ɪdʒ]

Gregory GREHG-uh-ree ['grɛg-ə-ri] scans to GREHG-ree
　['grɛg-ri]
　Gregory *(R&J)*
　Gregory de Cassado scans @ *HVIII* III, 2, 321 duh-kuh-
　SAH-doh [də-kə-'sɑ-doʊ]

Gremio *(SHR)* GREHM-ee-oh ['grɛm-i-oʊ] scans to
　GREHM-yoh ['grɛm-joʊ] e.g. @ I, 1, 96

Grey GRAY [greɪ]
　Grey, Lady, afterward Queen Elizabeth *(3HVI)*
　Grey, Lord *(RIII)*
　Grey, Sir Thomas *(HV)*

griffin GRIF-in ['grɪf-ɪn]

Griffith *(HVIII)* GRIF-ith ['grɪf-ɪθ]

griffon GRIF-uhn ['grɪf-ən]

Grindstone GREYEND-stohn ['graɪnd-stoʊn]

gripe GREYEP [graɪp] or GRIP [grɪp]

grise GREYES [graɪs] or GREYEZ [graɪz]

grisly GRIZ-lee ['grɪz-li]

Grissel GRI-s(uh)l ['grɪ-sl̩]

grize GREYEZ [graɪz]

groat GROHT [groʊt]

grovel GRAHV-uhl ['grɑv-əl] or GRUHV-__ ['grʌv-__]

Grumio *(SHR)* GROOM-ee-oh ['grum-i-oʊ] scans to
    GROOM-yoh ['grum-joʊ] e.g. @ I, 2, 27

guardage GAHR-dij ['gɑɚ-dɪdʒ]

guardant GAHR-d(uh)nt ['gɑɚ-dn̩t]

gudgeon GUHJ-uhn ['gʌdʒ-ən]

guerdon GER-d(uh)n ['gɝ-dn̩]

Guiana gee-AAN-uh [gi-'æn-ə] or __-AHN-__ [__-'ɑn-__]

Guichard GICH-erd ['gɪtʃ-ɚd]

Guiderius / Polydore *(CYM)* scans to gwi-DI-ryuhs
    [gwɪ-'dɪ-rjəs] called PAH-li-dawr ['pɑ-lɪ-dɔɚ]

Guildenstern *(HAM)* GIL-d(uh)n-stern ['gɪl-dn̩-stɚn]

guilders GIL-derz ['gɪl-dɚz]

Guildhall GILD-hawl ['gɪld-hɔl] @ *RIII* III, 5, 73 with
    "Mayor" as one syllable; scans to gild-HAWL [gɪld-'hɔl]
    @ *RIII* III, 5, 102

EE i be/ I ɪ bit/ EH ɛ bet/ AA æ bat/ OO̅ u boot / OO̅ ʊ book/ AW ɔ bought/ AH ɑ father/ ER ɝ bird/
UH ʌ cup/ AY eɪ bay/ EYE aɪ bite/ OY ɔɪ boy/ OH oʊ boat/ OW aʊ how/ YOO̅ ɪu duke/ EAR ɪɚ
beer/ AIR ɛɚ bear/ OO̅R ʊɚ tour/ AWR ɔɚ bore/ AHR ɑɚ bar/ NG ŋ king/ SH ʃ ship/ ZH ʒ vision/
TH θ thirty/ TH ð then/ CH tʃ child/ J dʒ just/ For complete list, see Key to Pronunciation p. 2.

125

guile GEYEL [gaɪl]

Guilford GIL-ferd [ˈgɪl-fɚd]
  Guilford, Sir Henry *(HVIII)*

Guiltian GIL-tee-uhn [ˈgɪl-ti-ən] or ___-shee-___ [___-ʃi-___]

guinea GIN-ee [ˈgɪn-i]

Guinever GWIN-uh-ver [ˈgwɪn-ə-vɚ] some editions
  "Guinevere" GWIN-uh-vear [ˈgwɪn-ə-vɪɚ]

guise GEYEZ [gaɪz]

gules GYOOLZ [gjulz]

gundello GUHN-duh-loh [ˈgʌn-də-loʊ]

gurnet GER-nit [ˈgɝ-nɪt]

Gurney, James *(KJ)* GER-nee [ˈgɝ-ni]

Guyenne gee-EHN [gi-ˈɛn] or geye-___ [gaɪ-___]

Guynes GEEN [gin]

Guysors jee-ZAWRZ [ʤi-ˈzɔɚz]

gyve JEYEV [ʤaɪv]

H (the letter) AYCH [eɪʧ]

Haberdasher *(SHR)* HAAB-er-dash-er [ˈhæb-ɚ-dæʃ-ɚ]

habiliment huh-BIL-uh-muhnt [hə-ˈbɪl-ə-mənt]

hackney HAAK-nee [ˈhæk-ni]

Hagar's HAY-gahrz [ˈheɪ-gɑɚ-z]

haggard HAAG-erd [ˈhæg-ɚd]

haggish HAAG-ish [ˈhæg-ɪʃ]

halberd HAAL-berd [ˈhæl-bɚd] or HAWL-___ [ˈhɔl-___]

halcyon always scans to HAAL-syuhn [ˈhæl-sjən]

hale HAYL [heɪl]

halfpence HAY-puhnts [ˈheɪ-pənts]

halfpenny HAY-puh-nee [ˈheɪ-pə-ni]

halidom / holidam / holidame HAAL-i-duhm [ˈhæl-ɪ-dəm]
scans to HAAL-duhm [ˈhæl-dəm] @ *SHR* V, 2, 104

hallo huh-LOH [hə-ˈloʊ] or hah-___ [hɑ-___] possibly scans
to HAH-loh [ˈhɑ-loʊ] @ *12th* I, 5, 258

halloed / hallooed huh-LOHD [hə-ˈloʊd] or hah-___
[hɑ-___]

halloing huh-LOO-ing [hə-ˈlu-ɪŋ] or ___-LOH-___
[___-ˈloʊ-___] scans to HAAL-wing [ˈhæl-wɪŋ] or
HAHL-___ [ˈhɑl-___] @ *2GEN* V, 4, 13

Hallowmas HAAL-oh-muhs [ˈhæl-oʊ-məs] or __-__-maas
[__-__-mæs]

Hames HAAMZ [hæmz] or HAYMZ [heɪmz]

Hamlet *(HAM)* HAAM-lit [ˈhæm-lɪt]

handkercher HAANG-ker-cher [ˈhæŋ-kɚ-tʃɚ]

handkerchief HAANG-ker-chif [ˈhæŋ-kɚ-tʃɪf]

Hannibal HAAN-uh-b(uh)l [ˈhæn-ə-bl̩]

hap HAAP [hæp]

haply HAAP-lee [ˈhæp-li]

harbinger HAHR-bin-jer [ˈhɑɚ-bɪn-dʒɚ]

Harcourt *(2HIV)* HAHR-kawrt [ˈhɑɚ-kɔɚt] or ___-kert
[___-kɚt]

hardiment HAHR-di-muhnt [ˈhɑɚ-dɪ-mənt]

EE i be/ I ɪ bit/ EH ɛ bet/ AA æ bat/ OO u boot / OO ʊ book/ AW ɔ bought/ AH ɑ father/ ER ɝ bird/
UH ʌ cup/ AY eɪ bay/ EYE aɪ bite/ OY ɔɪ boy/ OH oʊ boat/ OW aʊ how/ YOO ɪu duke/ EAR ɪɚ
beer/ AIR ɛɚ bear/ OOR ʊɚ tour/ AWR ɔɚ bore/ AHR ɑɚ bar/ NG ŋ king/ SH ʃ ship/ ZH ʒ vision/
TH θ thirty/ TH ð then/ CH tʃ child/ J dʒ just/ For complete list, see Key to Pronunciation p. 2.

hardocks HAHR-dahks ['hɑɚ-dɑks]

harebell HAIR-behl ['hɛɚ-bɛl]

Harfleur HAHR-fler ['hɑɚ-flɚ] or ___-floo [___-flu]

Ha'rford-West HAHR-ferd-wehst ['hɑɚ-fɚd-wɛst]

harlot HAHR-luht ['hɑɚ-lət]

harlotry HAHR-luh-tree ['hɑɚ-lə-tri]

Harpier HAHR-pear ['hɑɚ-pɪɚ] or ___-per [___-pɚ]

harrow HAA-roh ['hæ-roʊ]

Hastings HAYS-tingz ['heɪs-tɪŋz]
　　Hastings, Lord *(2HIV)*
　　Hastings, Lord William *(3HVI, RIII)*

haught HAWT [hɔt]

hautboy HOH-boy ['hoʊ-bɔɪ] or OH-___ ['oʊ-___]

haver (a possessor) HAAV-er ['hæv-ɚ]

havior HAYV-yer ['heɪv-jɚ]

havoc HAAV-uhk ['hæv-ək]

hawthorn HAW-thawrn ['hɔ-θɔɚn]

he'ld HEELD [hild]

hebona huh-BOH-nuh [hə-'boʊ-nə] or __-BUH-__ [__-'bʌ-__]
　　or __-BAH-__ [__-'bɑ-__] possibly scans to HEHB-nuh
　　['hɛb-nə] @ *HAM* I, 5, 62 if "cursed" two syllables

Hecate HEHK-it ['hɛk-ɪt] scans to HEHK-i-tee ['hɛk-ɪ-ti]
　　Hecate *(MAC)*
　　Hecate scans @ *1HVI* III, 2, 64

Hector HEHK-ter ['hɛk-tɚ] or possibly ___-tawr [___-tɔɚ]
　　Hector *(T&C)*

Hecuba HEHK-yuh-buh ['hɛk-jə-bə] or __-yoo-__ [__-ju-__]
　　scans to HEHK-buh ['hɛk-bə] @ *CYM* IV, 2, 313

128

heigh HAY [heɪ]

heigh-ho HAY-hoh ['heɪ-hoʊ] or hay-HOH [heɪ-'hoʊ]

heighth HEYETTH [haɪtθ] or HEYETH [haɪθ]

heinous HAY-nuhs ['heɪ-nəs]

heir AIR [ɛɚ]

Helen HEHL-in ['hɛl-ɪn]
   Helen *(CYM)*
   Helen *(T&C)*

Helena HEHL-i-nuh ['hɛl-ɪ-nə]
   Helena *(AW)*
   Helena *(MID)*

Helenus *(T&C)* HEHL-i-nuhs ['hɛl-ɪ-nəs]

Helias scans to HEEL-yuhs ['hil-jəs] @ *T&C* Pro, 16

Helicanus *(PER)* HEH-li-KAY-nuhs [hɛ-lɪ-'keɪ-nuhs] also
   called "Helicane" HEH-li-kayn ['hɛ-lɪ-keɪn] e.g. @ II, Cho, 17

Helicons HEH-li-kuhnz ['hɛ-lɪ-kənz]

Hellespont HEHL-i-spahnt ['hɛl-ɪ-spɑnt]

hempen HEHM-puhn ['hɛm-pən]

henceforth HEHNS-fawrth ['hɛns-fɔɚ-θ] scans to hehns-
   FAWRTH [hɛns-'fɔɚ-θ] e.g. @ *2HVI* V, 1, 80

Henry HEHN-ree ['hɛn-ri] scans to HEHN-uh-ree ['hɛn-ə-ri]
   Henry, Earl of Richmond, afterward Henry VII *(3HVI, RIII)*
     scans e.g. @ *3HVI* I, 1, 107
   Henry, King IV *(RII, 1HIV, 2HIV)* scans e.g. @ *RII* IV, 1, 112
   Henry, King V *(2HIV, HV)*
   Henry, King VI *(1HVI, 2HVI, 3HVI)* scans e.g. @ *1HVI*
     II, 5, 82

EE i be/ I ɪ bit/ EH ɛ bet/ AA æ bat/ OO u boot / OO ʊ book/ AW ɔ bought/ AH ɑ father/ ER ɝ bird/
UH ʌ cup/ AY eɪ bay/ EYE aɪ bite/ OY ɔɪ boy/ OH oʊ boat/ OW aʊ how/ YOO ɪu duke/ EAR ɪɚ
beer/ AIR ɛɚ bear/ OOR ʊɚ tour/ AWR ɔɚ bore/ AHR ɑɚ bar/ NG ŋ king/ SH ʃ ship/ ZH ʒ vision/
TH θ thirty/ TH ð then/ CH ʧ child/ J ʤ just/ For complete list, see Key to Pronunciation p. 2.

Henry, King VIII *(HVIII)*
Henry, Prince of Wales, also called "Hal" *(1HIV, 2HIV)*
Henry, Prince *(KJ)*

hent HEHNT [hɛnt]

Henton see "Nicholas Henton"

Herbert HER-bert ['hɝ-bɚt]
Herbert, Sir Walter *(RIII)*
Herbert, William, Earl of Pembroke *(3HVI)* PEHM-bro͞ok
['pɛm-brʊk] or PEHM-brohk ['pɛm-broʊk]

Herculean scans to her-KYO͞OL-yuhn [hɝ-'kjul-jən]

Hercules HER-kyo͞o-leez ['hɝ-kju-liz] scans to HER-kleez
['hɝ-kliz] or her-KLEEZ [hɚ-'kliz] @ *2NOB* I, 1, 66

Hereford / Herford HER-ferd ['hɝ-fɚd]

Herefordshire HER-ferd-sher ['hɝ-fɚd-ʃɚ] or __-__-shear
[__-__-ʃɪɚ]

heresy HEH-ri-see ['hɛ-rɪ-si]

heretic HEH-ri-tik ['hɛ-rɪ-tɪk]

Hermes HER-meez ['hɝ-miz]

Hermia *(MID)* HER-mee-uh ['hɝ-mi-ə] scans to HER-
myuh ['hɝ-mjə] e.g. @ I, 1, 46

Hermione *(WT)* her-MEYE-i-nee [hɚ-'maɪ-ɪ-ni] scans to
__-MEYE-nee [__-'maɪ-ni] e.g. @ V, 3, 28

Herne HERN [hɝn]

Hero HI-roh ['hɪ-roʊ]
Hero *(MADO)*

Herod HEH-ruhd ['hɛ-rəd]

Hesperides heh-SPEH-ri-deez [hɛ-'spɛ-rɪ-diz]

Hesperus HEHS-puh-ruhs ['hɛs-pə-rəs]

hest HEHST [hɛst]

hie HEYE [haɪ]

Hiems HEYE-uhmz [ˈhaɪ-əmz]

hight HEYET [haɪt]

highway / high way HEYE-way [ˈhaɪ-weɪ] scans to heye-WAY [haɪ-ˈweɪ] e.g. @ *MVEN* V, 1, 263

hilding HILD-ing [ˈhɪld-ɪŋ]

hilloa hi-LOH [hɪ-ˈloʊ]

hilt HILT [hɪlt]

Hinckley HINGK-lee [ˈhɪŋk-li]

hind HEYEND [haɪnd]

Hipparchus hi-PAHR-kuhs [hɪ-ˈpɑɚ-kəs]

Hippolyta hi-PAH-li-tuh [hɪ-ˈpɑ-lɪ-tə]
   Hippolyta *(MID)*
   Hippolyta *(2NOB)*

Hiren HEYE-ruhn [ˈhaɪ-rən]

Hirtius HER-shuhs [ˈhɝ-ʃəs]

Hisperia his-PI-ree-uh [hɪs-ˈpɪ-ri-ə]

hither HITH-er [ˈhɪð-ɚ]

hitherward HITH-er-werd [ˈhɪð-ɚ-wɚd]

hoar HAWR [hɔɚ]

Hob HAHB [hɑb]

Hobbididence HAH-bi-DI-d(uh)ns [hɑ-bɪ-ˈdɪ-dn̩s]

Hobgoblin HAHB-gahb-lin [ˈhɑb-gɑb-lɪn]

EE i be/ I ɪ bit/ EH ɛ bet/ AA æ bat/ OO u boot / OO ʊ book/ AW ɔ bought/ AH ɑ father/ ER ɝ bird/ UH ʌ cup/ AY eɪ bay/ EYE aɪ bite/ OY ɔɪ boy/ OH oʊ boat/ OW aʊ how/ YOO ɪu duke/ EAR ɪɚ beer/ AIR ɛɚ bear/ OOR ʊɚ tour/ AWR ɔɚ bore/ AHR ɑɚ bar/ NG ŋ king/ SH ʃ ship/ ZH ʒ vision/ TH θ thirty/ TH ð then/ CH tʃ child/ J ʤ just/ For complete list, see Key to Pronunciation p. 2.

131

hoise HOYZ [hɔɪz]

Holborn HOHL-bern ['hoʊl-bɚn] or HOH-___ ['hoʊ-___]

holidam / holidame HAAL-i-duhm ['hæl-ɪ-dəm]

holily HOH-li-lee ['hoʊ-lɪ-li]

holla (an interjection) hoh-LAH [hoʊ-'la] or huh-___ [hə-___]

Hollander HAHL-uhn-der ['hɑl-ən-dɚ]

hollo HAH-loh ['hɑ-loʊ] possibly scans to huh-LOH
    [hə-'loʊ] e.g. @ *COR* I, 8, 7

holloed HAHL-ohd ['hɑl-oʊd]

Holmedon HOHM-duhn ['hoʊm-dən]

Holofernes *(LLL)* HAHL-oh-FER-neez [hɑl-oʊ-'fɝ-niz] or
    ___-uh-___-___ [__-ə-___-___]

holp HOHLP [hoʊlp]

Holy-rood scans to HOHL-rōōd ['hoʊl-rud]

homage HAH-mij ['hɑ-mɪʤ] or AH-___ ['ɑ-___]

homager HAHM-ij-er ['hɑm-ɪʤ-ɚ] or AHM-___-___
    ['ɑm-___-___]

Hoppedance HAHP-daans ['hɑp-dæns]

Horace HAW-ruhs ['hɔ-rəs]

Horatio *(HAM)* huh-RAY-shyoh [hə-'reɪ-ʃjoʊ] scans to
    ___-___-shee-oh [__-__-ʃi-oʊ] e.g. @ I, 2, 180

Horner, Thomas *(2HVI)* HAWR-ner ['hɔɚ-nɚ]

horologe HAW-ruh-lohj ['hɔ-rə-loʊʤ]

horrider HAW-ri-der ['hɔ-rɪ-dɚ] or HAH-__-__ ['hɑ-__-__]

Hortensio *(SHR)* hawr-TEHN-shee-oh [hɔɚ-'tɛn-ʃi-oʊ]
    scans to ___-TEHN-shyoh [__-'tɛn-ʃjoʊ] e.g. @ I, 2, 63 later

posing as "Litio" **LI**-shee-oh [ˈlɪ-ʃi-ou] scans to **LI**-shyoh [ˈlɪ-ʃjou] e.g. @ II, 1, 60

Hortensius *(TIMON)* hawr-**TEHN**-see-uhs [hɔɚ-ˈtɛn-si-əs] or possibly scans to ___-**TEHN**-shyuhs [___-ˈtɛn-ʃjəs]

Hostilius hahs-**TIL**-ee-uhs [hɑs-ˈtɪl-i-əs] scans to ____-**TIL**-yuhs [___-ˈtɪl-jəs] @ *COR* II, 3, 235, possibly scans to **HAHS**-til-___ [ˈhɑs-tɪl-___] @ *TIMON* III, 2, 62

hour OWR [ɑʊɚ] scans to OW-er [ˈɑʊ-ɚ] e.g. @ *CE* III, 1, 122

house (v) HOWZ [hɑʊz]

housewifery hows-**WEYE**-fuh-ree [hɑʊs-ˈwaɪ-fə-ri] or scans to **HOWS**-wif-ree [hɑʊs-ˈwɪf-ri] @ *OTH* II, 1, 112

hovel **HUHV**-uhl [ˈhʌv-əl] or **HAHV**-___ [ˈhɑv-___]

howbeit always scans to how-**BEET** [hɑʊ-ˈbit]

howe'er how-**AIR** [hɑʊ-ˈɛɚ]

howlet **HOW**-lit [ˈhɑʊ-lɪt]

howsoe'er **HOW**-soh-air [ˈhɑʊ-sou-ɛɚ]

howsoever **HOW**-soh-ehv-er [ˈhɑʊ-sou-ɛv-ɚ]

howsome'er **HOW**-suhm-air [ˈhɑʊ-səm-ɛɚ]

hoxes **HAHKS**-iz [ˈhɑks-ɪz]

Hoy-day **HOY**-day [ˈhɔɪ-deɪ]

hugger-mugger **HUHG**-er-**MUHG**-er [ˈhʌg-ɚ-mʌg-ɚ]

Hugh Rebeck HYOO REE-behk [hju] [ˈri-bɛk]

humane **HYOO**-mayn [ˈhju-meɪn] scans to hyoo-**MAYN** [hju-ˈmeɪn] e.g. @ *MAC* III, 4, 76

humblebee **HUHM**-buhl-bee [ˈhʌm-bəl-bi]

Hume, John *(2HVI)* HYOOM [hjum]

Humphrey HUHM-free ['hʌm-fri] scans to **HUHM**-fuh-ree
['hʌm-fə-ri]
    Humphrey of Gloucester, afterward Duke *(2HIV, HV,*
1HVI, 2HVI) scans e.g. @ *2HVI* I, 1, 160 **GLAHS**-ter
['glɑs-tɚ] scans to **GLAHS**-i-ter ['glɑs-ɪ-tɚ] or
GLAH-sis-ter ['glɑ-sɪs-tɚ] e.g. @ *1HVI* I, 3, 6
    Humphrey, Lord Stafford *(2HVI)* **STAAF**-erd ['stæf-ɚd]

Hungerford HUHNG-ger-ferd ['hʌŋ-gɚ-fɚd]

Huntingdon HUHNT-ing-duhn ['hʌnt-ɪŋ-dən]

hurricano huh-ri-KAY-noh [hə-rɪ-'keɪ-nou]

huswife / huswive HUHZ-if ['hʌz-ɪf] or **HUHS**-weyef
['hʌs-waɪf]

Hybla HEYE-bluh ['haɪ-blə]

Hydra HEYE-druh ['haɪ-drə]

hyen HEYE-uhn ['haɪ-ən] or heye-EEN [haɪ-'in]

Hymen HEYE-muhn ['haɪ-mən] or ___-mehn [___-mɛn]
    Hymen *(AYL, 2NOB)*

Hymenaeus HEYE-muh-NEE-uhs [haɪ-mə-'ni-əs]

hyperbole heye-PER-buh-lee [haɪ-'pɚ-bə-li]

hyperbolical HEYE-per-BAH-li-k(uh)l [haɪ-pɚ-'bɑ-lɪ-kl̩]

Hyperion heye-PI-ree-uhn [haɪ-'pɪ-ri-ən] scans to __-PI-
ryuhn [__-'pɪ-rjən] e.g. @ *HAM* III, 4, 57

Hyrcan elides with "th" to form <u>TH</u>ER-kuhn ['ðɚ-kən]

Hyrcania scans to her-KAY-nyuh [hɚ-'keɪ-njə]

Hyrcanian always elides with "the" to form <u>th</u>er-KAY-nyuhn
[ðɚ-'keɪ-njən]

hyssop HIS-uhp [ˈhɪs-əp]

I'ld EYELD [aɪld]

i'th ITH [ɪð]

Iachimo *(CYM)* YAHK-i-moh [ˈjɑk-ɪ-moʊ] scans to YAHK-moh [ˈjɑk-moʊ] @ II, 5, 14

Iago *(OTH)* ee-AH-goh [i-ˈɑ-goʊ] scans to YAH-goh [ˈjɑ-goʊ] e.g. @ V, 2, 155

Icarus IK-uh-ruhs [ˈɪk-ə-rəs]

Iden, Alexander *(2HVI)* EYE-d(uh)n AAL-ig-ZAAN-der [ˈaɪ-dn̩] [æl-ɪg-ˈzæn-dɚ]

ides EYEDZ [aɪdz]

idolatrous scans to eye-DAHL-truhs [aɪ-ˈdɑl-trəs]

ignis fatuus IG-nuhs FAACH-wuhs [ˈɪg-nəs] [ˈfætʃ-wəs]

ignominy IG-nuh-min-ee [ˈɪg-nə-mɪn-i]

ignomy IG-nuh-mee [ˈɪg-nə-mi]

Ilion IL-ee-uhn [ˈɪl-i-ən] scans to IL-yuhn [ˈɪl-jən] or possibly EYEL-__-__ [ˈaɪl-__-__] scans to EYEL-__ [ˈaɪl-__] e.g. @ *T&C* II, 2, 109

Ilium IL-ee-uhm [ˈɪl-i-əm] scans to IL-yuhm [ˈɪl-jəm] or possibly EYEL-__-__ [ˈaɪl-__-__] scans to EYEL-__ [ˈaɪl-__] e.g. @ *T&C* I, 1, 97

illustrate (adj) i-LUHS-trit [ɪ-ˈlʌs-trɪt]

illustrated (part) scans to i-LUHS-tray-tid [ɪ-ˈlʌs-treɪ-tɪd]

Illyria i-LI-ree-uh [ɪ-ˈlɪ-ri-ə] scans to __-LI-ryuh [__-ˈlɪ-rjə] @ *12th* I, 2, 2

Illyrian i-LEA-ryuhn [ɪ-'lɪ-rjən]

imbar im-BAHR [ɪm-'bɑɚ]

imbrue im-BR$\overline{OO}$ [ɪm-'bru]

immanity i-MAAN-i-tee [ɪ-'mæn-ɪ-ti]

immask i-MAASK [ɪ-'mæsk]

immoment im-MOH-muhnt [ɪm-'moʊ-mənt]

immure i-MY$\widetilde{OO}$R [ɪ-'mjʊɚ]

Imogen *(CYM)* IM-uh-jin ['ɪm-ə-ʤɪn] scans to IM-jin ['ɪm-ʤɪn] e.g. @ V, 1, 10

impare (adj) scans to IM-pair ['ɪm-pɛɚ]

impartment im-PAHRT-muhnt [ɪm-'pɑɚt-mənt]

impasted im-PAYST-id [ɪm-'peɪst-ɪd]

imperator IM-puh-RAH-tawr [ɪm-pə-'rɑ-tɔɚ] or __-__-__-ter [__-__-__-tɚ]

imperceiverant IM-per-SEEV-uh-ruhnt [ɪm-pɚ-'siv-ə-rənt] or __-__-SEHV-__-__ [__-__-'sɛv-__-__]

imperious im-PI-ree-uhs [ɪm-'pɪ-ri-əs] scans to __-PI-ryuhs [__-'pɪ-rjəs] e.g. @ *A&C* IV, 15, 23

impeticos im-PEHT-i-kohz [ɪm-'pɛt-ɪ-koʊz]

impious im-PEE-uhs [ɪm-'pi-əs] or __-PEYE-__ [__-'paɪ-__] scans to IM-pyuhs ['ɪm-pjəs] e.g. @ *1HVI* V, 1, 2

implacable im-PLAAK-uh-b(uh)l [ɪm-'plæk-ə-bl̩] or __-PLAYK-__-__ [__-'pleɪk-__-__]

implorators scans to im-PLAWR-terz [ɪm-'plɔɚ-tɚz]

import (n) always scans to im-PAWRT [ɪm-'pɔɚt]

import (v) im-PAWRT [ɪm-'pɔɚt]

importunacy IM-pawr-TY͞OON-uh-see [ɪm-pɔɚ-'tɪun-ə-si]
scans to ___-___-TY͞OON-see [___-___-'tɪun-si]
@ *TIMON* II, 2, 41

importunate im-PAWR-chuh-nit [ɪm-'pɔɚ-tʃə-nɪt]

importune im-PAWR-ty͞on [ɪm-'pɔɚ-tɪun] or ___-___-
chuhn [___-___-tʃən]

importunity im-pawr-TY͞OON-i-tee [ɪm-pɔɚ-'tɪun-ɪ-ti]

imposthume im-PAHS-ty͞om [ɪm-'pɑs-tjum]

imprese IM-preez ['ɪm-priz] or ___-prehs [___-prɛs]

impress (n) im-PREHS [ɪm-'prɛs]

impress (v) im-PREHS [ɪm-'prɛs] scans to IM-prehs
['ɪm-prɛs] @ *LEAR* V, 3, 50

impressure im-PREHSH-er [ɪm-'prɛʃ-ɚ]

imprimis im-PREYE-mis [ɪm-'praɪ-mɪs]

impudency IM-pyuh-duhn-see ['ɪm-pjə-dən-si]

impugn im-PY͞OON [ɪm-'pjun]

in't INT [ɪnt]

incarnadine in-KAHR-nuh-deyen [ɪn-'kɑɚ-nə-daɪn] or
__-__-__-deen [__-__-__-din]

incidency IN-si-dehn-see ['ɪn-sɪ-dɛn-si]

inclips in-KLIPS [ɪn-'klɪps]

incony in-KUHN-ee [ɪn-'kʌn-i] possibly scans to INK-nee
['ɪnk-ni] or INGK-___ ['ɪŋk-___] @ *LLL* III, 1, 127

Inde IND [ɪnd] in *TEMP*, probably EYEND [aɪnd] in *LLL*,
and either in *AYL*

---

indenture in-DEHN-cher [ɪn-'dɛn-tʃɚ]

India IN-dee-uh ['ɪn-di-ə] scans to IN-dyuh ['ɪn-djə]
  e.g. @ *T&C* I, 1, 96

indict in-DEYET [ɪn-'daɪt]

indictment in-DEYET-muhnt [ɪn-'daɪt-mənt]

indigest IN-di-jehst ['ɪn-dɪ-ʤɛst]

indign in-DEYEN [ɪn-'daɪn]

indissoluble scans to in-DI-sahl-Y͞OO-b(uh)l [ɪn-'dɪ-sɑl-ju-bl̩]

indite in-DEYET [ɪn-'daɪt]

indrenched in-DREHNCHT [ɪn-'drɛntʃt]

indubitate in-DY͞OO-bi-tit [ɪn-'dɪu-bɪ-tɪt]

indue in-DY͞OO [ɪn-'dɪu]

inexecrable in-EHK-si-kruh-b(uh)l [ɪn-'ɛk-sɪ-krə-bl̩]

inexorable in-EHK-si-ruh-b(uh)l [ɪn-'ɛk-sɪ-rə-bl̩]

infamonize in-FAA-muh-neyez [ɪn-'fæ-mə-naɪz]

infer in-FER [ɪn-'fɝ]

ingener IN-jin-er ['ɪn-ʤɪn-ɚ]

ingenious in-JEEN-yuhs [ɪn-'ʤin-jəs]

ingot ING-guht ['ɪŋ-gət]

inheritrix in-HEH-ri-triks [ɪn-'hɛ-rɪ-trɪks]

injurious in-J͞OO-ree-uhs [ɪn-'ju-ri-əs] scans to __-J͞OO-ryuhs
  [__-'ʤu-rjəs] e.g. @ *MID* III, 2, 195

inkle ING-k(uh)l ['ɪŋ-kl̩]

inly IN-lee ['ɪn-li]

inoculate i-NAHK-yuh-layt [ɪ-'nɑk-jə-leɪt]

insanie in-SAYN-ee [ɪn-'seɪn-i]

insatiate always scans to in-SAY-shuht [ɪn-'seɪ-ʃət]

insisture in-SIS-cher [ɪn-'sɪs-tʃɚ] or __-__-choor [__-__-tʃʊɚ]

intendment in-TEHND-muhnt [ɪn-'tɛnd-mənt]

intenible scans to in-TEHN-b(uh)l [ɪn-'tɛn-bl̩]

inter in-TER [ɪn-'tɝ]

inter'gatory in-TER-guh-TAW-ree [ɪn-'tɝ-gə-tɔ-ri]

intercessors IN-ter-SEHS-erz [ɪn-tɚ-'sɛs-ɚ-z]

interim IN-tuh-ruhm ['ɪn-tə-rəm]scans to IN-truhm ['ɪn-trəm] e.g. @ *OTH* I, 3, 258

intermit IN-ter-mit ['ɪn-tɚ-mɪt]

interposer IN-ter-POHZ-er [ɪn-tɚ-'pouz-ɚ]

interpreter in-TER-pri-ter [ɪn-'tɝ-prɪ-tɚ]

interrogatories in-tuh-RAHG-uh-TAW-reez [ɪn-tə-'rɑg-ə-tɔ-riz] scans to ___-TER-guh-TAW-___ [___-'tɝ-gə-tɔ-___] @ *CYM* V, 5, 392

intertissued IN-ter-TI-shōōd [ɪn-tɚ-'tɪ-ʃud]

intervallums IN-ter-VAAL-uhmz [ɪn-tɚ-'væl-əmz]

intestate in-TEHS-tit [ɪn-'tɛs-tɪt]

intestine in-TEHS-tin [ɪn-'tɛs-tɪn]

intil in-TIL [ɪn-'tɪl]

intituled in-TICH-ōōld [ɪn-'tɪtʃ-uld] or __-TIT-yōōld [__-'tɪt-juld]

intrenchant in-TREHN-chuhnt [ɪn-'trɛn-tʃənt]

EE i be/ I ɪ bit/ EH ɛ bet/ AA æ bat/ ŌŌ u boot / Ō͞O ʊ book/ AW ɔ bought/ AH ɑ father/ ER ɝ bird/ UH ʌ cup/ AY eɪ bay/ EYE aɪ bite/ OY ɔɪ boy/ OH ou boat/ OW aʊ how/ YŌŌ ɪu duke/ EAR ɪɚ beer/ AIR ɛɚ bear/ ŌŌR ʊɚ tour/ AWR ɔɚ bore/ AHR ɑɚ bar/ NG ŋ king/ SH ʃ ship/ ZH ʒ vision/ TH θ thirty/ TH ð then/ CH tʃ child/ J ʤ just/ For complete list, see Key to Pronunciation p. 2.

intrinse in-TRINZ [ɪn-'trɪnz] or __-TRINS [__-'trɪns]

intrinsicate in-TRIN-si-kit [ɪn-'trɪn-sɪ-kɪt]

inundation in-uhn-DAY-shuhn [ɪn-ən-'deɪ-ʃən]

inure i-NYŌOR [ɪ-'njʊɚ]

invectively in-VEHK-tiv-lee [ɪn-'vɛk-tɪv-li]

inveigled in-VAY-guhld [ɪn-'veɪ-gəld]

Inverness in-ver-NEHS [ɪn-vɚ-'nɛs]

inviolable always scans to in-VEYE-luh-b(uh)l [ɪn-'vaɪ-lə-bḷ]

inward (the interior or a confidant) IN-werd ['ɪn-wɚd]

inwards (the bowels or innards) IN-erdz ['ɪn-ɚdz]

Io EYE-oh ['aɪ-oʊ]

Ionia eye-OH-nee-uh [aɪ-'oʊ-ni-ə]

Ionian scans to and elides with "the" to form theye-OH-nyuhn [ðaɪ-'oʊ-njən]

Ipswich IP-switch ['ɪp-swɪtʃ] or ___-sij [___-sɪdʒ]

Iras *(A&C)* EYE-ruhs ['aɪ-rəs]

ire EYER [aɪɚ]

ireful EYER-fuhl ['aɪɚ-fəl]

Ireland EYER-luhnd ['aɪɚ-lənd] scans to EYE-ruh-luhnd ['aɪ-rə-lənd] e.g. @ *1HVI* I, 1, 192

Iris EYE-ris ['aɪ-rɪs]
  Iris *(TEMP)*

iron EYERN [aɪɚn] scans to EYE-ruhn ['aɪ-rən] e.g. @ *MID* II, 1, 196

irregulous scans to i-REHG-luhs [ɪ-'rɛg-ləs]

irreparable i-REHP-uh-ruh-b(uh)l [ɪ-'rɛp-ə-rə-bḷ]

irrevocable i-REHV-uh-kuh-b(uh)l [ɪ-'rɛv-ə-kə-bl̩]

Isabel *(HV)* IZ-uh-behl ['ɪz-ə-bɛl]

Isabella *(MM)* IZ-uh-BEHL-uh [ɪz-ə-'bɛl-ə] also called "Isabel" IZ-uh-behl ['ɪz-ə-bɛl] scans to IZ-behl ['ɪz-bɛl] @ II, 2, 67

Isbel IZ-behl ['ɪz-bɛl]

Iscariot is-KAA-ree-uht [ɪs-'kæ-ri-ət]

Isidore IZ-uh-dawr ['ɪz-ə-dɔɚ]

Isis EYE-sis ['aɪ-sɪs]

Isle of Man EYEL uhv MAAN ['aɪl] [əv] [mæn]

issue ISH-o͞o ['ɪʃ-u]

iterance scans to I-truhns ['ɪ-trəns]

iteration it-uh-RAY-shuhn [ɪt-ə-'reɪ-ʃən]

Ithaca ITH-i-kuh ['ɪθ-ɪ-kə]

i-wis / iwis i-WIS [ɪ-'wɪs]

jackanapes JAAK-uh-nayps ['ʤæk-ə-neɪps]

Jacob JAY-kuhb ['ʤeɪ-kəb]

Jamy *(HV)* JAY-mee ['ʤeɪ-mi]

Janus JAY-nuhs ['ʤeɪ-nəs]

Japhet JAY-feht ['ʤeɪ-fɛt]

Jaquenetta *(LLL)* JAAK-wuh-NEH-tuh [ʤæk-wə-'nɛ-tə]

Jaques JAY-kweez ['ʤeɪ-kwiz] or JAY-kwis ['ʤeɪ-kwɪs] possibly scan to JAYKS [ʤeɪks] or JAAKS [ʤæks] when it's the last word in verse line

---

EE i be/ I ɪ bit/ EH ɛ bet/ AA æ bat/ O͞O u boot/ O͝O ʊ book/ AW ɔ bought/ AH ɑ father/ ER ɝ bird/ UH ʌ cup/ AY eɪ bay/ EYE aɪ bite/ OY ɔɪ boy/ OH oʊ boat/ OW aʊ how/ YO͞O ɪu duke/ EAR ɪɚ beer/ AIR ɛɚ bear/ O͞OR ʊɚ tour/ AWR ɔɚ bore/ AHR ɑɚ bar/ NG ŋ king/ SH ʃ ship/ ZH ʒ vision/ TH θ thirty/ T̲H̲ ð then/ CH ʧ child/ J ʤ just/ For complete list, see Key to Pronunciation p. 2.

Jaques *(AYL)*
Jaques de Boys *(AYL)* JAYKS [ʤeɪks] or JAAKS [ʤæks]
    duh-**BOYZ** [də-'bɔɪz] or ___-**BOYS** [___-bɔɪs]
Jaques le Grand luh GRAAND [lə] [grænd]

Jasons JAY-s(uh)nz ['ʤeɪ-sn̩z]

jaunce JAWNS [ʤɔns]

jauncing JAWN-sing ['ʤɔn-sɪŋ]

Jephtha JEHF-tuh ['ʤɛf-tə]

Jephthah JEHF-thuh ['ʤɛf-θə]

jerkin JER-kin ['ʤɝ-kɪn]

Jeronimy juh-RAH-nuh-mee [ʤə-'rɑ-nə-mi]

Jerusalem juh-ROO-suh-luhm [ʤə-'ru-sə-ləm]

jesses JEHS-iz ['ʤɛs-ɪz]

Jessica *(MVEN)* JEHS-i-kuh ['ʤɛs-ɪ-kə] scans to JEHS-kuh
    ['ʤɛs-kə] @ V, 1, 21

Jesu JAY-zyoo ['ʤeɪ-zju] or ___-syoo [___-sju] or ___-zoo
    [___-zu] or ___-soo [___-su] or YAY-___ ['jeɪ-___]

jewel JOO-uhl ['ʤu-əl] scans to JOOL [ʤul]
    e.g. @ *KJ* V, 1, 40

Jewess JOO-is ['ʤu-ɪs]

Jewry JOO-ree ['ʤu-ri]

Jezebel JEHZ-uh-behl ['ʤɛz-ə-bɛl]

Job JOHB [ʤoʊb]

jocund JAH-kuhnd ['ʤa-kənd]

John JAHN [ʤan]
    John of Gaunt, Duke of Lancaster *(RII)* GAWNT [gɔnt]
    LAANG-kuhs-ter ['læŋ-kəs-tɚ] or __-kaas-__
    [__-kæs-__]

John, Don *(MADO)*
John, Duke of Bedford *(HV)*
John, Friar *(R&J)*
John, King *(KJ)*

joinder JOYN-der ['dʒɔɪn-dɚ]

jointress JOYN-truhs ['dʒɔɪn-trəs]

jointure JOYN-cher ['dʒɔɪn-tʃɚ]

jollity JAHL-i-tee ['dʒal-ɪ-ti]

Joshua JAHSH-yo͞o-uh ['dʒaʃ-ju-ə]

Jourdain, Margery *(2HVI)* jer-DAYN MAHR-juh-ree
[dʒɚ-'deɪn] ['maɚ-dʒə-ri]

Jove JOHV [dʒouv]

Jud-as JO͞OD-aas ['dʒud-æs]

Judas JO͞O-duhs ['dʒu-dəs]

Jude JO͞OD [dʒud]

Judean scans to JO͞O-dyuhn ['dʒu-djən]

judicious jo͞o-DISH-uhs [dʒu-'dɪʃ-əs]

Julia *(2GEN)* JO͞OL-yuh ['dʒul-jə] scans to JO͞OL-ee-uh
['dʒul-i-ə] e.g. @ V, 4, 99

Juliet JO͞OL-yeht ['dʒul-jɛt] scans to JO͞OL-ee-eht ['dʒul-i-ɛt]
Juliet *(MM)* also called "Julietta" jo͞ol-YEHT-uh
[dʒul-'jɛt-ə]
Juliet *(R&J)* scans e.g. @ V, 3, 73, also called "Jule"
JO͞OL [dʒul] @ I, 3, 43

Julio Romano JO͞O-lee-oh ro-MAHN-oh ['dʒu-li-ou]
[rou-'man-ou]

Julius Caesar JOOL-yuhs SEE-zer ['ʤul-jəs] ['si-zɚ]
    Julius Caesar *(JC)*

July joo-LEYE [ʤu-'laɪ] scans to JOO-leye ['ʤu-laɪ]
    e.g. @ *HVIII* I, 1, 154

Junius JOON-yuhs ['ʤun-jəs]
    Junius Brutus *(COR)* BROO-tuhs ['bru-təs]

Juno JOO-noh ['ʤu-noʊ]
    Juno *(TEMP)*

Jupiter JOO-pi-ter ['ʤu-pɪ-tɚ] possibly scans to JOOP-ter
    ['ʤup-tɚ] @ *CYM* II, 3, 125

jure JOOR [ʤuɚ]

Justeius juhs-TEE-uhs [ʤəs-'ti-əs]

justicer JUHS-ti-ser ['ʤʌs-tɪ-sɚ]

justle JUHS-uhl ['ʤʌs-əl]

justs JUHSTS [ʤʌsts] (archaic form of "jousts")

juvenal JOO-vuh-nuhl ['ʤu-və-nəl]

kam KAAM [kæm]

Kated KAYT-id ['keɪt-ɪd]

Katharine KAATH-uh-rin ['kæθ-ə-rɪn] scans to KAATH-rin
    ['kæθ-rɪn]
    Katharine *(LLL)* scans @ V, 2, 47

Katherine KAATH-uh-rin ['kæθ-ə-rɪn] scans to KAATH-rin
    ['kæθ-rɪn]
    Katherine *(HV)*
    Katherine *(HVIII)*
    Katherine *(SHR)* scans @ II, 1, 184, also called
        "Katherina" KAATH-uh-REE-nuh [kæθ-ə-'ri-nə] or
        KAAT-__-__-__ [kæt-__-__-__] and "Kate" KAYT
        [keɪt]

kecksies KEHKS-eez ['kɛks-iz]

Keech KEECH [kitʃ]

keel KEEL [kil]

Keisar KEYE-zer ['kaɪ-zɚ]

ken / kenn KEHN [kɛn]

Kent KEHNT [kɛnt]
 Kent, Earl of *(LEAR)* disguised as "Caius" KEYE-uhs
  ['kaɪ-əs] or KAY-___ ['keɪ-___]

Kentishman KEHNT-ish-muhn ['kɛnt-ɪʃ-mən]

kern KERN [kɝn]

kersey KER-zee ['kɝ-zi]

Ketly KEHT-lee ['kɛt-li]

kibe KEYEB [kaɪb]

kickshaws KIK-shawz ['kɪk-ʃɔz]

Kildare kil-DAIR [kɪl-'dɛɚ]

killen KIL-uhn ['kɪl-ən]

Killingworth KIL-ing-werth ['kɪl-ɪŋ-wɚθ]

kiln-hole KILN-hohl ['kɪln-hoʊl]

Kimbolton KIM-uhl-tuhn ['kɪm-əl-tən] or KIM-bohl-___
 ['kɪm-boʊl-___]

kine KEYEN [kaɪn]

kinred KIN-rid ['kɪn-rɪd]

kirtle KER-t(uh)l ['kɝ-tl̩]

kissing-comfits KIS-ing-KUHM-fits ['kɪs-ɪŋ-kʌm-fɪts]

EE i be/ I ɪ bit/ EH ɛ bet/ AA æ bat/ OO u boot / OO ʊ book/ AW ɔ bought/ AH ɑ father/ ER ɝ bird/
UH ʌ cup/ AY eɪ bay/ EYE aɪ bite/ OY ɔɪ boy/ OH oʊ boat/ OW aʊ how/ YOO ɪu duke/ EAR ɪɚ
beer/ AIR ɛɚ bear/ OOR ʊɚ tour/ AWR ɔɚ bore/ AHR ɑɚ bar/ NG ŋ king/ SH ʃ ship/ ZH ʒ vision/
TH θ thirty/ TH ð then/ CH tʃ child/ J ʤ just/ For complete list, see Key to Pronunciation p. 2.

145

knapped NAAPT [næpt]

knave NAYV [neɪv]

knoll NOHL [noʊl]

koth-a KOHTH-uh ['koʊθ-ə] variant of "quoth-a"
KWOHTH-uh ['kwoʊθ-ə] which is a variant of "quoth he"
KWOHTH-hee ['kwoʊθ-hi]

La Far luh FAHR [lə] [fɑɚ]

Laban LAY-buhn ['leɪ-bən]

Labeo scans to LAY-byoh ['leɪ-bjoʊ]

Labienus LAA-bi-EE-nuhs [læ-bɪ-'i-nəs]

labyrinth LAAB-uh-rinth ['læb-ə-rɪnθ]

Lacedaemon LAAS-i-DEE-muhn [læs-ɪ-'di-mən]

Lacies LAY-seez ['leɪ-siz]

lade LAYD [leɪd]

lading LAYD-ing ['leɪd-ɪŋ]

Lady Brach BRAACH [brætʃ]

Laertes lay-AIR-teez [leɪ-'ɛɚ-tiz] or __-ER-__ [__-'ɝ-__]
Laertes *(HAM)*

Lafew *(AW)* luh-FYOO [lə-'fju]

lakin LAY-kin ['leɪ-kɪn]

Lambert's LAAM-berts ['læm-bɚts]

lambkins LAAM-kinz ['læm-kɪnz]

lamentable luh-MEHN-tuh-b(uh)l [lə-'mɛn-tə-bl̩] scans to
LAAM-uhn-__-__ ['læm-ən-__-__] e.g. @ *RII* V, 1, 44

lamentings luh-MEHNT-ingz [lə-'mɛnt-ɪŋz]

Lammas Eve LAA-muhs EEV ['læ-məs] [iv]

146

Lammastide LAA-muhs-teyed ['læ-məs-taɪd]

Lamord luh-MAWRD [lə-'mɔɚd]

lampass LAAM-puhs ['læm-pəs]

Lancaster LAANG-kuhs-ter ['læŋ-kəs-tɚ] or __-kaas-__
   [__-kæs-__]
   Lancaster, John, Prince of *(1HIV, 2HIV)*

lanched LAANCHT [læntʃt]

Langley LAANG-lee ['læŋ-li]

Langton LAANG-tuhn ['læŋ-tən]

languor LAANG-ger ['læŋ-gɚ]

lanthorn LAANT-hawrn ['lænt-hɔɚn] or LAAN-tern
   ['læn-tɚn]

Lapland LAAP-laand ['læp-lænd]

largess always scans to LAHR-jehs ['laɚ-dʒɛs]

'larum LAH-ruhm ['la-rəm] or LAA-___ ['læ-___]

lascivious luh-SIV-ee-uhs [lə-'sɪv-i-əs] scans to ___-SIV-yuhs
   [___-'sɪv-jəs] e.g. @ *RIII* I, 1, 13

lath LAATH [læθ]

latten bilbo LAA-t(uh)n BIL-boh ['læ-tn̩] ['bɪl-boʊ]

latter LAAT-er ['læt̮-ɚ]

lattice LAAT-is ['læt̮-ɪs]

laud LAWD [lɔd]

Launce *(2GEN)* LAWNS [lɔns] or LAANS [læns] or
   LAHNS [lɑns]

EE i be/ I ɪ bit/ EH ɛ bet/ AA æ bat/ OO u boot / OO ʊ book/ AW ɔ bought/ AH ɑ father/ ER ɝ bird/
UH ʌ cup/ AY eɪ bay/ EYE aɪ bite/ OY ɔɪ boy/ OH oʊ boat/ OW ɑʊ how/ YOO ɪu duke/ EAR ɪɚ
beer/ AIR ɛɚ bear/ OOR ʊɚ tour/ AWR ɔɚ bore/ AHR ɑɚ bar/ NG ŋ king/ SH ʃ ship/ ZH ʒ vision/
TH θ thirty/ TH ð then/ CH tʃ child/ J dʒ just/ For complete list, see Key to Pronunciation p. 2.

laund LAWND [lɔnd]

Laurence, Friar LAW-ruhns ['lɔ-rəns]
   Laurence, Friar *(R&J)*

Lavatch *(AW)* luh-VAACH [lə-'vætʃ] or ___-VAHCH
   [___-'vɑtʃ]

lave LAYV [leɪv]

Lavinia *(TITUS)* luh-VIN-ee-uh [lə-'vɪn-i-ə] scans to
   ___-VIN-yuh [__-'vɪn-jə] e.g. @ I, 1, 55

lavolt luh-VOHLT [lə-'voʊlt]

lavoltas luh-VOHL-tuhz [lə-'voʊl-təz]

lazar LAA-zer ['læ-zɚ] or LAY-__ ['leɪ-__]

Lazarus LAAZ-uh-ruhs ['læz-ə-rəs]

Le Beau *(AYL)* luh BOH [lə] [boʊ], Folio spelling "Le Beu"
   suggests luh BYO͞O [lə] [bju]

Le Bon luh BOHN [lə] [boʊn]

Le Fer luh FAIR [lə] [fɛɚ]

Le Port Blanc luh pawrt BLAANGK [lə] [pɔɚt] [blæŋk]

Le Roy luh ROY [lə] [rɔɪ]

Leah LEE-uh ['li-ə]

Leander lee-AAN-der [li-'æn-dɚ]

Lear, King of Britain *(LEAR)* LEAR [lɪɚ]

leas LEEZ [liz]

leasing (lying) LEEZ-ing ['liz-ɪŋ]

leathern LEH<u>TH</u>-ern ['lɛð-ɚn]

leavy LEE-vee ['li-vi]

Leda LEE-duh ['li-də]

leet LEET [lit]

legate / Legate LEHG-it [ˈlɛg-ɪt]

legative LEHG-uh-tiv [ˈlɛg-ə-tɪv]

legerity luh-JEH-ri-tee [lə-ˈʤɛ-rɪ-ti]

legitimation luh-JIT-uh-**MAY**-shuhn [lə-ʤɪt-ə-ˈmeɪ-ʃən]

Leicester LEHS-ter [ˈlɛs-tɚ]

Leicestershire LEHS-ter-sher [ˈlɛs-tɚ-ʃɚ] or ___-___-shear [__-__-ʃɪɚ]

leiger LEH-jer [ˈlɛ-ʤɚ] or LEE-___ [ˈli-__]

leisure LEE-zher [ˈli-ʒɚ] or LEH-___ [ˈlɛ-__]

leman LEHM-uhn [ˈlɛm-ən] or LEEM-___ [ˈlim-__]

Lena, Popilius *(JC)* LEE-nuh, always scans to poh-**PI**-lyuhs [ˈli-nə] [poʊ-ˈpɪ-ljəs]

lenity LEHN-i-tee [ˈlɛn-ɪ-ti]

Lennox *(MAC)* LEHN-uhks [ˈlɛn-əks]

lenten LEHN-tuhn [ˈlɛn-tən]

Leonardo *(MVEN)* scans to lee-**NAHR**-doh [li-ˈnɑɚ-doʊ]

Leonati lee-uh-**NAY**-teye [li-ə-ˈneɪ-taɪ]

Leonato *(MADO)* LEE-uh-**NAH**-toh [li-ə-ˈnɑ-toʊ]

Leonine *(PER)* LEE-uh-neyen [ˈli-ə-naɪn]

Leontes *(WT)* lee-**AHN**-teez [li-ˈɑn-tiz] also called "Sicilia" si-**SIL**-ee-uh [sɪ-ˈsɪl-i-ə] scans to __-**SIL**-yuh [__-ˈsɪl-yuh] @ I, 2, 217

Lepidus, M. Aemilius *(A&C, JC)* see "M. Aemilius Lepidus"

EE i be/ I ɪ bit/ EH ɛ bet/ AA æ bat/ OO u boot / ŌO ʊ book/ AW ɔ bought/ AH ɑ father/ ER ɚ bird/ UH ʌ cup/ AY eɪ bay/ EYE aɪ bite/ OY ɔɪ boy/ OH oʊ boat/ OW aʊ how/ YOO ɪu duke/ EAR ɪɚ beer/ AIR ɛɚ bear/ ŌOR ʊɚ tour/ AWR ɔɚ bore/ AHR ɑɚ bar/ NG ŋ king/ SH ʃ ship/ ZH ʒ vision/ TH θ thirty/ TH ð then/ CH ʧ child/ J ʤ just/ For complete list, see Key to Pronunciation p. 2.

lest LEHST [lɛst]

Lestrale LEH-strahl [ˈlɛ-strɑl] scans to leh-STRAHL [lɛ-ˈstrɑl]
@ *HV* IV, 8, 95

lethe / Lethe LEE-thee [ˈli-θi]

leviathan / Leviathan luh-VEYE-uh-thuhn [lə-ˈvaɪ-ə-θən]

levy LEHV-ee [ˈlɛv-i]

Lewis L$\overline{\text{OO}}$S [lus] scans to L$\overline{\text{OO}}$-is [ˈlu-ɪs]
Lewis XI *(3HVI)* scans @ III, 3, 169 and possibly III, 3, 23
Lewis, the Dauphin *(HV)* DAW-fin [ˈdɔ-fɪn]
Lewis, the Dauphin *(KJ)* some editions "Dolphin"
DAHL-fin [ˈdɑl-fɪn]

libbard's LIB-erdz [ˈlɪb-ɚ-dz]

libertine LIB-er-teen [ˈlɪb-ɚ-tin] or ___-___-teyen
[___-___-taɪn]

Libya LIB-ee-uh [ˈlɪb-i-ə] scans to LIB-yuh [ˈlɪb-jə]
e.g. @ *WT* V, 1, 165

licentious leye-SEHN-shuhs [laɪ-ˈsɛn-ʃəs] scans to ___-___-
shee-uhs [__-__-ʃi-əs] @ *CE* II, 2, 130

Lichas LEYE-kuhs [ˈlaɪ-kəs]

lictors LIK-terz [ˈlɪk-tɚz]

lief LEEF [lif]

liege LEEJ [lidʒ]

lieger LEE-jer [ˈli-dʒɚ]

lien (part) (to be at rest in a horizontal position) LEYEN
[laɪn]

liest LEYEST [laɪst]

lieu L$\overline{\text{OO}}$ [lu]

lieutenantry lōō-TEHN-uhn-tree [lu-'tɛn-ən-tri] scans to ___-TEHN-tree [___-'tɛn-tri] @ *A&C* III, 11, 39

lieve LEEV [liv]

Ligarius *(JC)* li-GEH-ree-uhs [lɪ-'gɛ-ri-əs] scans to ___-GEH-ryuhs [___-'gɛ-rjəs] e.g. @ II, 1, 215

liggens LIG-uhnz ['lɪg-ənz]

limbeck LIM-behk ['lɪm-bɛk]

Limbo LIM-boh ['lɪm-boʊ]

Limbo Patrum LIM-boh PAA-truhm ['lɪm-boʊ] ['pæ-trəm]

lime LEYEM [laɪm]

Limehouse (a section of London) LIM-uhs ['lɪm-əs]

limekiln LEYEM-kiln ['laɪm-kɪln]

limned LIMD [lɪmd]

Lincoln, Bishop of *(HVIII)* LING-kuhn ['lɪŋ-kən]

Lincolnshire LING-kuhn-sher ['lɪŋ-kən-ʃɚ] or ___-___-shear [___-___-ʃɪɚ]

lineal LIN-ee-uhl ['lɪn-i-əl] scans to LIN-yuhl ['lɪn-jəl] e.g. @ *2HIV* IV, 5, 45

lineally scans to LIN-yuh-lee ['lɪn-jə-li]

lineament LIN-ee-uh-muhnt ['lɪn-i-ə-mənt] scans to LIN-yuh-___ ['lɪn-jə-___] e.g. @ *R&J* I, 3, 83

Lingard LING-gahrd ['lɪŋ-gɑɚ-d]

lings LINGZ [lɪŋz]

linsey-woolsey LIN-zee-WŎŎL-zee ['lɪn-zi-wʊl-zi]

EE i be/ I ɪ bit/ EH ɛ bet/ AA æ bat/ ŌŌ u boot / ŎŎ ʊ book/ AW ɔ bought/ AH ɑ father/ ER ɝ bird/ UH ʌ cup/ AY eɪ bay/ EYE aɪ bite/ OY ɔɪ boy/ OH oʊ boat/ OW aʊ how/ YŌŌ ɪu duke/ EAR ɪɚ beer/ AIR ɛɚ bear/ ŌOR ʊɚ tour/ AWR ɔɚ bore/ AHR ɑɚ bar/ NG ŋ king/ SH ʃ ship/ ZH ʒ vision/ TH θ thirty/ TH ð then/ CH tʃ child/ J ʤ just/ For complete list, see Key to Pronunciation p. 2.

151

Lionel LEYE-uh-n(uh)l [ˈlaɪ-ə-n]]

lither LITH-er [ˈlɪð-ɚ]

litigious li-TIJ-uhs [lɪ-ˈtɪʤ-əs]

Litio see "Hortensio"

live (adv) (gladly, willingly) LEEV [liv] or possibly LEEF [lif]

livelong LIV-lawng [ˈlɪv-lɔŋ]

Livia LIV-ee-uh [ˈlɪv-i-ə]

loach LOHCH [loʊʧ]

loath LOHTH [loʊθ]

loathe LOHTH [loʊð]

loathly LOHTH-lee [ˈloʊð-li] or LOHTH-___ [ˈloʊθ-___]

loathness LOHTH-nis [ˈloʊð-nɪs] or LOHTH-__ [ˈloʊθ-__]

lockram LAHK-ruhm [ˈlɑk-rəm]

lodestar LOHD-stahr [ˈloʊd-stɑɚ]

Lodovico *(OTH)* LOH-doh-VEE-koh [loʊ-doʊ-ˈvi-koʊ] or ___- duh-___-___ [___-də-___-___]

Lodowick LOH-duh-wik [ˈloʊ-də-wɪk] or LAH-___-___ [ˈlɑ-___-___]

loggets LAHG-its [ˈlɑg-ɪts]

Lombardy LAHM-bahr-dee [ˈlɑm-bɑɚ-di]

Longaville *(LLL)* LAWNG-uh-vil [ˈlɔŋ-ə-vɪl] or ___-___-veyel [___-___-vaɪl] @ IV, 3, 128 and V, 2, 53 for rhyme

loofed LUHFT [lʌft]

lop LAHP [lɑp]

Lord Mayor of London LUHN-duhn [ˈlʌn-dən]

Lord Mayor of London *(HVIII)*
Lord Mayor of London *(RIII)*

Lorenzo *(MVEN)* luh-**REHN**-zoh [lə-'rɛn-zou] or
   loh-___-___ [lou-___-___]

Lorraine scans to **LOH**-rayn ['lou-reɪn]

louse (v) (to have lice) **LOWZ** [lɑuz]

lout LOWT [lɑut]

Louvre LŌŌV-er ['luv-ɚ] or ___-ruh [___-rə] possibly
   LUHV-er ['lʌv-ɚ] @ *HV* II, 4, 132

Lovel / Lovell LUHV-uhl ['lʌv-əl]
   Lovel, Lord *(RIII)*
   Lovell, Sir Thomas *(HVIII)*

love-monger LUHV-muhng-ger ['lʌv-məŋ-gɚ] or
   ___-mahng-___ [___-mɑŋ-___]

lower / low'r / lour (to frown) LOWR [lɑuɚ]

lown (a man of low station) LŌŌN [lun] and possibly
   LOWN [lɑun] @ *OTH* II, 3, 87 for rhyme

lozel LOH-z(uh)l ['lou-zl̩]

lubber LUHB-er ['lʌb-ɚ]

Luccicos loo-CHEE-kuhs [lu-'tʃi-kəs]

Luce LŌŌS [lus]
   Luce *(CE)*

Lucentio loo-**SEHN**-shee-oh [lu-'sɛn-ʃi-ou] scans to
   ___- **SEHN**-shyoh [___-'sɛn-ʃjou]
   Lucentio *(SHR)* scans @ II, 1, 101 later posing as
   "Cambio" **KAAM**-bee-oh ['kæm-bi-ou] scans to
   KAAM-byoh ['kæm-bjou] @ IV, 4, 105

EE i be/ I ɪ bit/ EH ɛ bet/ AA æ bat/ ŌŌ u boot / ŌŌ ʊ book/ AW ɔ bought/ AH ɑ father/ ER ɝ bird/
UH ʌ cup/ AY eɪ bay/ EYE aɪ bite/ OY ɔɪ boy/ OH ou boat/ OW ɑu how/ YŌŌ ɪu duke/ EAR ɪə
beer/ AIR ɛə bear/ ŌŌR ʊə tour/ AWR ɔə bore/ AHR ɑə bar/ NG ŋ king/ SH ʃ ship/ ZH ʒ vision/
TH θ thirty/ TH ð then/ CH tʃ child/ J dʒ just/ For complete list, see Key to Pronunciation p. 2.

153

luces $\overline{\text{LOO}}$S-iz ['lus-ɪz]

Lucetta *(2GEN)* loo-SEHT-uh [lu-'sɛt-ə]

Luciana *(CE)* $\overline{\text{LOO}}$-see-**AH**-nuh [lu-si-'ɑ-nə]

Lucianus $\overline{\text{LOO}}$-shee-**AY**-nuhs [lu-ʃi-'eɪ-nəs] or __-see-__-__
[__-si-__-__] or __-__-**AH**-__ [__-__-'ɑ-__]

Lucifer $\overline{\text{LOO}}$-si-fer ['lu-sɪ-fɚ]

Lucilius loo-**SIL**-ee-uhs [lu-'sɪl-i-əs] scans to ___-**SIL**-yuhs
[__-'sɪl-jəs]
Lucilius *(JC)* scans @ V, 3, 106
Lucilius *(TIMON)*

Lucina loo-**SEYE**-nuh [lu-'saɪ-nə]

Lucio $\overline{\text{LOO}}$-see-oh ['lu-si-oʊ] or loo-**SEE**-___ [lu-'si-__] in
prose, scans to $\overline{\text{LOO}}$-syoh ['lu-sjoʊ] or $\overline{\text{LOO}}$-shyoh
['lu-ʃjoʊ]
Lucio *(MM)* scans @ I, 2, 171

Lucius $\overline{\text{LOO}}$-shuhs ['lu-ʃəs] scans to $\overline{\text{LOO}}$-shee-uhs ['lu-ʃi-əs]
Lucius *(JC)*
Lucius *(TIMON)* scans @ III, 4, 2
Lucius *(TITUS)* scans @ IV, 4, 78
Lucius Pella **PEH**-luh ['pɛ-lə]

lucre $\overline{\text{LOO}}$-ker ['lu-kɚ]

Lucrece loo-**KREES** [lu-'kris] scans to $\overline{\text{LOO}}$-krees ['lu-kris]
e.g. @ *TITUS* IV, 1, 64

Lucretia's loo-**KREE**-shuhz [lu-'kri-ʃəz]

Lucullus *(TIMON)* loo-**KUHL**-uhs [lu-'kʌl-əs]

Lucy, Sir William *(1HVI)* $\overline{\text{LOO}}$-see ['lu-si]

Lud LUHD [lʌd]

Ludlow LUHD-loh ['lʌd-loʊ]

Luna $\overline{\text{LOO}}$-nuh ['lu-nə]

154

lunes LO͞ONZ [lunz]

Lupercal LO͞O-per-kaal ['lu-pɚ-kæl]

lustre LUHS-ter ['lʌs-tɚ]

Lycaonia LEYE-kay-**OH**-nee-uh [laɪ-keɪ-'oʊ-ni-ə]

Lychorida *(PER)* leye-**KAW**-ri-duh [laɪ-'kɔ-rɪ-də]

Lycurguses leye-**KER**-guhs-iz [laɪ-'kɝ-gəs-ɪz]

Lydia **LI**-dee-uh ['lɪ-di-ə]

lym LIM [lɪm]

Lymoges, Duke of Austria *(KJ)* li-**MOH**-zhiz [lɪ-'moʊ-ʒɪz]
possibly scans to **LI**-moh-__ ['lɪ-moʊ-__] @ III, 1, 114 or
li-**MOHZH** [lɪ-'moʊʒ] if headless line

Lynn LIN [lɪn]

Lysander *(MID)* leye-**SAAN**-der [laɪ-'sæn-dɚ]

Lysimachus *(PER)* leye-**SIM**-uh-kuhs [laɪ-'sɪm-ə-kəs]

M. Aemilius Lepidus **MAHR**-kuhs ee-**MIL**-i-uhs ['mɑɚ-kəs]
[i-'mɪl-ɪ-əs] or i-__-__-__ [ɪ-__-__-__] **LEH**-pi-duhs
['lɛ-pɪ-dəs] scans to leh-**PI**-__ [lɛ-'pɪ-__]
M. Aemilius Lepidus *(A&C)*
M. Aemilius Lepidus *(JC)* scans @ III, 2, 264

Mab MAAB [mæb]

Macbeth maak-**BEHTH** [mæk-'bɛθ]
Macbeth *(MAC)* may have rhymed @ I, 1, 7 to "heath"
Macbeth, Lady *(MAC)*

Maccabaeus MAAK-uh-**BEE**-uhs [mæk-ə-'bi-əs]

Macdonwald maak-**DAHN**-uhld [mæk-'dɑn-əld]

EE i be/ I ɪ bit/ EH ɛ bet/ AA æ bat/ O͞O u boot / O͝O ʊ book/ AW ɔ bought/ AH ɑ father/ ER ɝ bird/ UH ʌ cup/ AY eɪ bay/ EYE aɪ bite/ OY ɔɪ boy/ OH oʊ boat/ OW ɑʊ how/ YO͞O ɪu duke/ EAR ɪɚ beer/ AIR ɛɚ bear/ O͞OR ʊɚ tour/ AWR ɔɚ bore/ AHR ɑɚ bar/ NG ŋ king/ SH ʃ ship/ ZH ʒ vision/ TH θ thirty/ TH ð then/ CH ʧ child/ J ʤ just/ For complete list, see Key to Pronunciation p. 2.

Macduff maak-DUHF [mæk-'dʌf]
Macduff *(MAC)*
Macduff, Lady *(MAC)*

Macedon MAAS-i-dahn ['mæs-ɪ-dɑn]

Machiavel MAAK-ee-uh-vehl ['mæk-i-ə-vɛl] scans to
___-yuh-vehl [___-jə-vɛl] e.g. @ *1HVI* V, 4, 74

machinations MAAK-uh-NAY-shuhnz [mæk-ə-'neɪ-ʃənz]

Macmorris *(HV)* muhk-MAW-ris [mək-'mɔ-rɪs] or
maak-___-___ [mæk-___-___]

maculate MAAK-yuh-lit ['mæk-jə-lɪt]

maculation MAAK-yuh-LAY-shuhn [mæk-jə-'leɪ-ʃən]

madding MAAD-ing ['mæd-ɪŋ]

Madeira muh-DI-ruh [mə-'dɪ-rə]

madrigals MAAD-ri-g(uh)lz ['mæd-rɪ-g̩z]

Maecenas *(A&C)* mee-SEE-nuhs [mi-'si-nəs] or mi-___-___
[mɪ__-__]

magistrates MAAJ-i-strayts ['mædʒ-ɪ-streɪts]

magnanimity MAAG-ni-NIM-i-tee [mæg-nɪ-'nɪm-ɪ-ti]

magnanimous maag-NAAN-uh-muhs [mæg-'næn-ə-məs]

magnifico maag-NIF-i-koh [mæg-'nɪf-ɪ-koʊ]

Magnus MAAG-nuhs ['mæg-nəs]

Mahomet MAY-uh-meht ['meɪ-ə-mɛt]

Mahu MAH-hoo ['mɑ-hu]

Maidenhead / maidenhead MAY-d(uh)n-hehd ['meɪ-dn̩-hɛd]

maidenliest MAY-d(uh)n-lee-ist ['meɪ-dn̩-li-ɪst]

Maine MAYN [meɪn]

maintain mayn-TAYN [meɪn-'teɪn] scans to MAYN-tayn ['meɪn-teɪn] e.g. @ *1HVI* I, 1, 71

malapert MAAL-uh-pert ['mæl-ə-pɚt]

Malcolm *(MAC)* MAAL-kuhm ['mæl-kəm]

maledictions MAAL-i-DIK-shuhnz [mæl-ɪ-'dɪk-ʃənz]

malefactor MAAL-uh-faak-ter ['mæl-ə-fæk-tɚ]

malkin MAWL-kin ['mɔl-kɪn]

Mall MAWL [mɔl] or MAHL [mɑl]

mallicholy MAAL-i-kah-lee ['mæl-ɪ-kɑ-li]

mallows MAAL-ohz ['mæl-ouz]

malmsey MAHM-zee ['mɑm-zi]

Malvolio *(12th)* maal-VOH-lee-oh [mæl-'vou-li-ou] scans to __-VOH-lyoh [__-'vou-ljou] e.g. @ V, 1, 268

Mamillius *(WT)* muh-MIL-ee-uhs [mə-'mɪl-i-əs] scans to __-MIL-yuhs [__-'mɪl-jəs] @ I, 2, 210

mammet MAAM-it ['mæm-ɪt]

mammocked MAAM-uhkt ['mæm-əkt]

mamm'ring MAAM-ring ['mæm-rɪŋ]

manage MAAN-ij ['mæn-ɪʤ]

mandragora maan-DRAAG-uh-ruh [mæn-'dræg-ə-rə]

manikin MAAN-i-kin ['mæn-ɪ-kɪn]

Manningtree MAAN-ing-tree ['mæn-ɪŋ-tri]

mansionry MAAN-chuhn-ree ['mæn-ʧən-ri]

EE i be/ I ɪ bit/ EH ɛ bet/ AA æ bat/ O͞O u boot / O͞O ʊ book/ AW ɔ bought/ AH ɑ father/ ER ɝ bird/ UH ʌ cup/ AY eɪ bay/ EYE aɪ bite/ OY ɔɪ boy/ OH ou boat/ OW aʊ how/ Y͞OO ɪu duke/ EAR ɪɚ beer/ AIR ɛɚ bear/ O͞OR ʊɚ tour/ AWR ɔɚ bore/ AHR ɑɚ bar/ NG ŋ king/ SH ʃ ship/ ZH ʒ vision/ TH θ thirty/ T̲H̲ ð then/ CH ʧ child/ J ʤ just/ For complete list, see Key to Pronunciation p. 2.

157

Mantua MAAN-choo-wuh ['mæn-tʃu-wə] scans to **MAAN**-chwuh ['mæn-tʃwə] or **MAAN**-tyoo-uh ['mæn-tju-ə] scans to **MAAN**-tyuh ['mæn-tjə] e.g. @ *R&J* III, 3, 169

Mantuan MAAN-choo-wuhn ['mæn-tʃu-wən]

mapp'ry MAAP-ree ['mæp-ri]

mar MAHR [mɑɚ]

Marcade *(LLL)* MAHR-kuh-dee ['mɑɚ-kə-di]

Marcellus mahr-SEHL-uhs [mɑɚ-'sɛl-əs]
Marcellus *(HAM)*

Marchioness MAHR-shuh-nis ['mɑɚ-ʃə-nɪs]

marchpane MAHRCH-payn ['mɑɚtʃ-peɪn]

Marcians MAHR-shuhnz ['mɑɚ-ʃənz]

Marcus MAHR-kuhs ['mɑɚ-kəs]
Marcus Crassus **KRAAS**-uhs ['kræs-əs]
Marcus Octavius scans to ahk-**TAYV**-yuhs [ak-'teɪv-jəs]

Mardian *(A&C)* MAHR-dee-uhn ['mɑɚ-di-ən] scans to **MAHR**-dyuhn ['mɑɚ-djən] @ I, 5, 8

Margarelon *(T&C)* MAHR-guh-reh-luhn ['mɑɚ-gə-rɛ-lən]

Margaret MAHR-guh-rit ['mɑɚ-gə-rɪt] scans to **MAHR**-grit ['mɑɚ-grɪt]
Margaret *(1HVI)* scans e.g. @ V, 3, 51
Margaret *(2HVI)*
Margaret *(3HVI)* scans e.g. @ I, 1, 228
Margaret *(MADO)*
Margaret *(RIII)* scans e.g. @ I, 2, 93

margent MAHR-juhnt ['mɑɚ-ʤənt]

Margery MAHR-juh-ree ['mɑɚ-ʤə-ri]

Maria muh-REYE-uh [mə-'raɪ-ə]
Maria *(LLL)* possibly __-REE-__ [__-'rɪ-__]
Maria *(12th)*

Marian MAA-ree-uhn ['mæ-ri-ən] scans to MAA-ryuhn ['mæ-rjən] or **MEH-__-__** ['mɛ-__-__] scans to **MEH-__** ['mɛ-__] e.g. @ *CE* III, 1, 31

Mariana MEH-ri-**AA**-nuh [mɛ-rɪ-'æ-nə] or MAA-__-__-__ [mæ-__-__-__]
Mariana *(AW)*
Mariana *(MM)*

Marina *(PER)* muh-**REE**-nuh [mə-'ri-nə]

marjoram **MAHR**-juh-ruhm ['mɑɚ-ʤə-rəm]

Mark Antony *(A&C)* MAHRK **AAN**-tuh-nee [mɑɚk] ['æn-tə-ni] scans to **AANT**-nee ['ænt-ni] e.g. @ II, 1, 39; also called "Antonio" scans to aan-**TOHN**-yoh [æn-'toʊn-joʊ] @ II, 2, 7, and "Antonius" scans to aan-**TOHN**-yuhs [æn-'toʊn-jəs] e.g. @ I, 1, 56 (for the name in JC, see "Antonius, Marcus")

Marle MAHRL [mɑɚl]

marmoset **MAHR**-muh-seht ['mɑɚ-mə-sɛt]

Marquess **MAHR**-kwis ['mɑɚ-kwɪs]

Marquis **MAHR**-kwis ['mɑɚ-kwɪs]

marriage **MAA**-rij ['mæ-rɪʤ] scans to **MAA**-ree-ij ['mæ-ri-ɪʤ] e.g. @ *R&J* IV, 1, 11

Mars MAHRZ [mɑɚz]

Marseilles mahr-**SAYLZ** [mɑɚ-'seɪlz] scans to mahr-**SEHL**-uhs [mɑɚ-'sɛl-əs] e.g. @ *AW* IV, 4, 9 (if French pronunciation is preferred in prose mahr-**SAY** [mɑɚ-'seɪ])

Marshal **MAHR**-sh(uh)l ['mɑɚ-ʃl̩] scans to **MAHR**-uh-sh(uh)l ['mɑɚ-ə-ʃl̩] e.g. @ *1HIV* IV, 4, 2
Marshal *(PER)*

EE i be/ I ɪ bit/ EH ɛ bet/ AA æ bat/ O͞O u boot / O͞O ʊ book/ AW ɔ bought/ AH ɑ father/ ER ɝ bird/ UH ʌ cup/ AY eɪ bay/ EYE aɪ bite/ OY ɔɪ boy/ OH oʊ boat/ OW aʊ how/ Y͞O͞O ɪu duke/ EAR ɪɚ beer/ AIR ɛɚ bear/ O͞OR ʊɚ tour/ AWR ɔɚ bore/ AHR ɑɚ bar/ NG ŋ king/ SH ʃ ship/ ZH ʒ vision/ TH θ thirty/ T̲H̲ ð then/ CH ʧ child/ J ʤ just/ For complete list, see Key to Pronunciation p. 2.

Marshal, Lord *(RII)*

Marshalsea MAHR-sh(uh)l-see ['mɑɚ-ʃl̩-si]

Mar-text, Sir Oliver *(AYL)* MAHR-tehkst AH-li-ver ['mɑɚ-tɛkst] ['ɑ-lɪ-vɚ]

martial / Martial MAHR-sh(uh)l ['mɑɚ-ʃl̩]

Martino mahr-TEE-noh [mɑɚ-'ti-nou]

Martius *(TITUS)* MAHR-shuhs ['mɑɚ-ʃəs]

martlemas MAHR-t(uh)l-muhs ['mɑɚ-tl̩-məs]

martlet MAHRT-lit ['mɑɚt-lɪt]

Marullus *(JC)* muh-RUHL-uhs [mə-'rʌl-əs]

Masham MAASH-uhm ['mæʃ-əm] or MAAS-___ ['mæs-___]

masque MAASK [mæsk]

masquers MAASK-erz ['mæsk-ɚz]

massy MAAS-ee ['mæs-i]

masterdom MAAS-ter-duhm ['mæs-tɚ-dəm]

mastic MAAS-tik ['mæs-tɪk]

mastiff MAAS-tif ['mæs-tɪf]

matin MAA-tin ['mæ-tɪn]

mattock MAAT-uhk ['mæt-ək]

Mauchus MAW-kuhs ['mɔ-kəs]

Maud MAWD [mɔd]

Maudlin MAWD-lin ['mɔd-lɪn]

maugre MAW-ger ['mɔ-gɚ]

Mauritania MAW-ri-TAY-nee-uh [mɔ-rɪ-'teɪ-ni-ə]

maw MAW [mɔ]

mawkin MAW-kin ['mɔ-kɪn]

Mayor
    of Coventry *(3 HVI)* KUHV-uhn-tree ['kʌv-ən-tri]
    of London *(1HVI)*
    of Saint Albans *(2HVI)* AWL-buhnz ['ɔl-bənz]
    of York *(3HVI)*

mazzard MAAZ-erd ['mæz-ɚd]

meacock MEE-kahk ['mi-kɑk]

mead MEED [mid]

meanwhile always scans to meen-HWEYEL [min-'hwaɪl]

Mede MEED [mid]

Medea mi-DEE-uh [mɪ-'di-ə]

Media MEE-dee-uh ['mi-di-ə] scans to MEE-dyuh ['mi-djə]
    @ *A&C* III, 6, 14

medicinable / med'cinable MEHD-sin-uh-b(uh)l
    ['mɛd-sɪn-ə-bl̩] possibly scans to ___-sin-b(uh)l
    [__-sɪn-bl̩] e.g. @ *T&C* III, 3, 44

medicinal scans to MEHD-si-n(uh)l ['mɛd-sɪ-nl̩]

meditance MEHD-i-tuhns ['mɛd-ɪ-təns]

Mediterranean MEHD-i-tuh-RAY-nee-uhn [mɛd-ɪ-tə-'reɪ-ni-ən]
    possibly scans to MEHD-tuh-ray-nyuhn ['mɛd-tə-reɪ-njən]
    @ *TEMP* I, 2, 234

medlar MEHD-ler ['mɛd-lɚ]

meed MEED [mid]

meiny MAY-nee ['meɪ-ni]

Meisen MEYE-s(uh)n ['maɪ-sn̩]

Meleager MEH-lee-AY-jer [mɛ-li-'eɪ-ʤɚ]

Melford MEHL-ferd ['mɛl-fɚd]

mell MEHL [mɛl]

mellifluous muh-LIF-loo-uhs [mə-'lɪf-lu-əs]

Melun *(KJ)* muh-LOON [mə-'lun]

Menaphon MEHN-uh-fuhn ['mɛn-ə-fən]

Menas MEEN-uhs ['min-əs]
Menas *(A&C)*

Menecrates muh-NEHK-ruh-teez [mə-'nɛk-rə-tiz]
Menecrates *(A&C)*

Menelaus MEHN-uh-LAY-uhs [mɛn-ə-'leɪ-əs]
Menelaus *(T&C)*

Menenius Agrippa *(COR)* muh-NEE-nee-uhs uh-GRIP-uh
[mə-'ni-ni-əs] [ə-'grɪp-ə] scans to ___-NEE-nyuhs
[___-'ni-njəs] @ III, 3, 7

Menon MEE-nahn ['mi-nɑn]

Menteith mehn-TEETH [mɛn-'tiθ]
Menteith *(MAC)*

Mephistophilus MEHF-uh-STAHF-i-luhs [mɛf-ə-'stɑf-ɪ-ləs]

mercatante mer-kuh-TAHN-tay [mɚ-kə-'tɑn-teɪ]

Mercatio mer-KAY-shee-oh [mɚ-'keɪ-ʃi-oʊ]

mercer / Mercer *(TIMON)* MER-ser ['mɝ-sɚ]

Mercurial mer-KYOO-ree-uhl [mɚ-'kjʊ-ri-əl]

Mercury MER-kyuh-ree ['mɝ-kjə-ri]

Mercutio *(R&J)* mer-KYOO-shee-oh [mə-'kju-ʃi-oʊ] scans
to ___-KYOO-shyoh [___-'kju-ʃjoʊ] e.g. @ I, 2, 68

mere (only or absolute) MEAR [mɪɚ]

162

mered (to mark a boundary) scans to **MI**-rid ['mɪ-rɪd]

meritorious MEH-ri-**TAW**-ree-uhs [mɛ-rɪ-'tɔ-ri-əs]

Merlin MER-lin ['mɝ-lɪn]

Merops MEH-rahps ['mɛ-rɑps] or ___-rohps [___-roʊps]

Merriman MEH-ri-muhn ['mɛ-rɪ-mən]

mervailous scans to mer-**VAYL**-uhs [mɚ-'veɪl-əs]

Mesena mi-**SEE**-nuh [mɪ-'si-nə] Folio spelling, most editions "Misena"

Mesopotamia scans to MEHS-uh-puh-**TAYM**-yuh [mɛs-ə-pə-'teɪm-jə]

Messala *(JC)* meh-**SAH**-luh [mɛ-'sɑ-lə] or __-**SAY**-__ [__-'seɪ-__]

Messaline MEHS-uh-leen ['mɛs-ə-lin]

Messina muh-**SEEN**-uh [mə-'sin-ə] possibly scans to **MEH**-sin-___ ['mɛ-sɪn-___] @ *MADO* V, 4, 123

metamorphose MEHT-uh-**MAWR**-fohz [mɛt-ə-'mɔɚ-foʊz]

Metamorphosis MEHT-uh-**MAWR**-fuh-sis [mɛt-ə-'mɔɚ-fə-sɪs]

mete MEET [mit]

metheglin muh-**THEHG**-lin [mə-'θɛg-lɪn]

methought mi-**THAWT** [mɪ-'θɔt]

mettle MEH-t(uh)l ['mɛ-tl̩]

Metullus Cimber *(JC)* mi-**TEHL**-uhs SIM-ber [mɪ-'tɛl-əs] ['sɪm-bɚ]

mew MYOO [mju]

EE i be/ I ɪ bit/ EH ɛ bet/ AA æ bat/ OO u boot / OO ʊ book/ AW ɔ bought/ AH ɑ father/ ER ɝ bird/ UH ʌ cup/ AY eɪ bay/ EYE aɪ bite/ OY ɔɪ boy/ OH oʊ boat/ OW aʊ how/ YOO ɪu duke/ EAR ɪɚ beer/ AIR ɛɚ bear/ OOR ʊɚ tour/ AWR ɔɚ bore/ AHR ɑɚ bar/ NG ŋ king/ SH ʃ ship/ ZH ʒ vision/ TH θ thirty/ TH ð then/ CH tʃ child/ J dʒ just/ For complete list, see Key to Pronunciation p. 2.

mewling MYOO-ling ['mju-liŋ]

Michael, Sir *(1HIV)* MEYE-kuhl ['maɪ-kəl]

Michaelmas MIK-uhl-muhs ['mɪk-əl-məs]

micher MICH-er ['mɪtʃ-ɚ]

miching mallecho MICH-ing MAAL-uh-koh ['mɪtʃ-ɪŋ]
    ['mæl-ə-koʊ]

mickle MIK-uhl ['mɪk-əl]

Milan MI-luhn ['mɪ-lən] possibly scans to mi-LAAN [mɪ-'læn]
    or __-LAHN [__-'lɑn] @ *TEMP* II, 1, 128

Milan, Duke of *(2GEN)* MI-luhn ['mɪ-lən]

milch MILCH [mɪltʃ]

Milford MIL-ferd ['mɪl-fɚd]

Milo MEYE-loh ['maɪ-loʊ]

Minerva mi-NER-vuh [mɪ-'nɝ-və]

minikin MIN-i-kin ['mɪn-ɪ-kɪn]

minim MIN-uhm ['mɪn-əm]

minim-rest MIN-uhm-rehst ['mɪn-əm-rɛst]

minimus MIN-uh-muhs ['mɪn-ə-məs]

minion MIN-yuhn ['mɪn-jən] scans to MIN-ee-uhn
    ['mɪn-i-ən] e.g. @ *KJ* II, 1, 392

ministration MIN-i-STRAY-shuhn [mɪn-ɪ-'streɪ-ʃən]

Minola, Baptista *(SHR)* MIN-uh-luh baap-TIS-tuh
    ['mɪn-ə-lə] [bæp-'tɪs-tə]

Minos MEYE-nahs ['maɪ-nɑs] or ___-nohs [___-noʊs]

Minotaurs MIN-uh-tawrz ['mɪn-ə-tɔɚz]

minstrelsy MIN-struhl-see ['mɪn-strəl-si]

minutely (continual) **MIN**-it-lee ['mɪn-ɪt-li]

mirable **MI**-ruh-b(uh)l ['mɪ-rə-bl̩]

Miranda *(TEMP)* mi-**RAAN**-duh [mɪ-'ræn-də]

miry **MEYE**-ree ['maɪ-ri]

Misanthropos mi-**SAAN**-throh-pahs [mɪ-'sæn-θroʊ-pɑs] or
___-**ZAAN**-__-__ [__-'zæn-__-__]

mischievous **MIS**-chi-vuhs ['mɪs-tʃɪ-vəs]

misconster mis-**KAHN**-ster [mɪs-'kɑn-stɚ]

misconst'red mis-**KAHN**-sterd [mɪs-'kɑn-stɚd]

misconstrue always scans to mis-**KAHN**-strōō
[mɪs-'kɑn-stru]

miscreant **MIS**-kree-uhnt ['mɪs-kri-ənt]

miscreate **MIS**-kree-ayt ['mɪs-kri-eɪt]

misprise see "misprize"

misprised (mistaken) scans to **MIS**-preyezd ['mɪs-praɪzd]
@ *MID* III, 2, 74

misprision mis-**PRIZH**-uhn [mɪs-'prɪʒ-ən]

misprize / misprise (to undervalue) mis-**PREYEZ** [mɪs-'praɪz]

Mithridates **MITH**-ri-**DAY**-teez [mɪθ-rɪ-'deɪ-tiz]

Mitigation **MI**-ti-**GAY**-shuhn [mɪ-tɪ-'geɪ-ʃən]

mobled **MOH**-blid ['moʊ-blɪd] or **MOH**-b(uh)ld ['moʊ-bl̩d]
or **MAH**-___ ['mɑ-___]

Mockwater **MAHK**-waw-ter ['mɑk-wɔ-tɚ] or **MUHK**-__-__
['mʌk-__-__] or **MAYK**-__-__ ['meɪk-__-__]

Modena moh-DEE-nuh [mou-'di-nə]

modicum MAHD-i-kuhm ['mɑd-ɪ-kəm]

Modo MOH-doh ['mou-dou]

moe MOH [mou]

moi'ty MOY-tee ['mɔɪ-ti]

moiety MOY-i-tee ['mɔɪ-ɪ-ti] scans to **MOY**-tee ['mɔɪ-ti]
e.g. @ *WT* III, 2, 38

mollification MAHL-uh-fi-KAY-shuhn [mɑl-ə-fɪ-'keɪ-ʃən]

mome MOHM [moum]

momentany MOH-muhn-tuhn-ee ['mou-mən-tən-i]

Monarcho muh-NAHR-koh [muh-'naɚ-kou] or mah-__-__
[mɑ-__-__]

'mong MUHNG [mʌŋ]

'mongst MUHNGST [mʌŋst]

Monmouth MAHN-muhth ['mɑn-məθ]

Monsieur mahn-SOO-er [mɑn-'su-ɚ] (if French pronunciation is preferred mi-SYER [mɪ-'sjɝ])

monstrous MAHN-struhs ['mɑn-strəs] scans to **MAHNS**-
tuh-ruhs ['mɑns-tə-rəs] e.g. @ *OTH* II, 3, 207

monstruosity MAHN-stroo-AH-si-tee [mɑn-stru-'ɑ-sɪ-ti]

Montacute, Thomas, Earl of Salisbury *(HVIII)* MAHN-tuh-
kyoot ['mɑn-tə-kjut]

Montague MAHN-tuh-gyoo ['mɑn-tə-gju]
Montague *(R&J)*
Lady Montague *(R&J)*

Montano *(OTH)* mahn-TAAN-oh [mɑn-'tæn-ou] or
___-TAHN-___ [___-'tɑn-___]

montant MAHN-tuhnt [ˈmɑn-tənt]

Montferrat mahnt-fuh-**RAAT** [mɑnt-fə-ˈræt]

Montgomery, Sir John *(3HVI)* muhnt-**GUHM**-ree [mənt-ˈgʌm-ri] scans to __-__-uh-ree [__-__-ə-ri] @ IV, 7, 40

Montjoy *(HV)* **MAHNT**-joy [ˈmɑnt-ʤɔɪ] scans to mahnt-**JOY** [mɑnt-ˈʤɔɪ] @ III, 5, 61

moor / Moor MŌOR [mʊɚ]

Moorfields MŌOR-feeldz [ˈmʊɚ-fildz]

mop (n) (a grimace) MAHP [mɑp]

mop (v) (to make a face) MAHP [mɑp]

mope (v) (to be gloomy) MOHP [moʊp]

Mopsa *(WT)* MAHP-suh [ˈmɑp-sə]

Mordake MAWR-dayk [ˈmɔɚ-deɪk] possibly **MER**-dahk [ˈmɝ-dɑk] in keeping with "Murdocke," original name in Holinshed

More MAWR [mɔɚ]

Morisco muh-**RIS**-koh [mə-ˈrɪs-koʊ]

Morocco, Prince of *(MVEN)* muh-**RAH**-koh [mə-ˈrɑ-koʊ]

mort MAWRT [mɔɚt]

Mortimer MAWR-ti-mer [ˈmɔɚ-tɪ-mɚ]
    Mortimer, Edmund, Earl of March *(1HIV, 1HVI)*
        MAHRCH [mɑɚtʃ]
    Mortimer, Lady *(1HIV)*
    Mortimer, Sir Hugh *(3HVI)*
    Mortimer, Sir John *(3HVI)*

mortise MAWR-tis [ˈmɔɚ-tɪs]

EE i be/ I ɪ bit/ EH ɛ bet/ AA æ bat/ ŌŌ u boot / ŌŌ ʊ book/ AW ɔ bought/ AH ɑ father/ ER ɝ bird/ UH ʌ cup/ AY eɪ bay/ EYE aɪ bite/ OY ɔɪ boy/ OH oʊ boat/ OW aʊ how/ YŌŌ ɪu duke/ EAR ɪə beer/ AIR ɛə bear/ ŌŌR ʊə tour/ AWR ɔə bore/ AHR ɑə bar/ NG ŋ king/ SH ʃ ship/ ZH ʒ vision/ TH θ thirty/ TH ð then/ CH tʃ child/ J ʤ just/ For complete list, see Key to Pronunciation p. 2.

167

Morton MAWR-t(uh)n ['mɔɚ-tn̩]
Morton *(2HIV)*
Morton, John, Bishop of Ely *(RIII)* EE-lee ['i-li]

mose MOHZ [mouz]

mote MOHT [mout]

Moth MAWTH [mɔθ] or MAHTH [maθ]
Moth *(LLL)* probably MOHT [mout] as in "mote" (a speck)
Moth *(MID)*

motley MAHT-lee ['mɑt-li]

mought MOWT [mɑut] or MAWT [mɔt]

Mouldy, Ralph *(2HIV)* MOHLD-ee ['mould-i]

mounched MUHNCHT [mʌntʃt]

Mounsieur Basimecu MOWN-sear BAAZ-i-muh-kōō
['mɑun-sɪɚ] ['bæz-ɪ-mə-ku]

mountant MOWN-tuhnt ['mɑun-tənt]

Mountanto mown-TAHN-toh [mɑun-'tan-tou]

mountebank MOWN-tuh-baangk ['mɑun-tə-bæŋk]

mouth (n) MOWTH [mɑuθ]

mouth (v) MOW<u>TH</u> [mɑuð]

mow (n) (grimace) MOW [mɑu]

mow (v) (to cut down) MOH [mou]

Mowbray MOH-bray ['mou-breɪ] or ___-bree [___-bri]
Mowbray, John, Duke of Norfolk *(3HVI)* NAWR-fuhk
['nɔɚ-fək]
Mowbray, Lord *(2HIV)*
Mowbray, Thomas, Duke of Norfolk *(RII)*

moy MOY [mɔɪ]

Moyses MOY-zehz ['mɔɪ-zɛz]

Mugs MUHGZ [mʌgz]

muleter MYOOL-ter ['mjul-tɚ]

Muliteus scans to MYOO-li-tyuhs ['mju-lɪ-tjəs]

mulled MUHLD [mʌld]

Mulmutius muhl-MYOO-shuhs [məl-'mju-ʃəs]

multipotent muhl-TIP-uh-tuhnt [məl-'tɪp-ə-tənt]

multitudinous always scans to muhl-ti-TYOOD-nuhs [məl-tɪ-'tɪud-nəs]

muniments MYOO-ni-muhnts ['mju-nɪ-mənts]

mure MYOOR [mjʊɚ]

murk MERK [mɝk]

murrain MUH-rin ['mʌ-rɪn] or ME(r)-___ ['mɝ-___]

murrion MUH-rin ['mʌ-rɪn] or ME(r)-___ ['mɝ-___]

murther MER-ther ['mɝ-ðɚ]

muscadel MUHS-kuh-dehl ['mʌs-kə-dɛl]

Muscovites MUHS-kuh-veyets ['mʌs-kə-vaɪts]

Muscovits MUHS-kuh-vits ['mʌs-kə-vɪts]

Muscovy MUHS-kuh-vee ['mʌs-kə-vi]

mushrumps MUHSH-ruhmps ['mʌʃ-rəmps]

musit MYOO-zit ['mju-zɪt]

Muskos MUHS-kohs ['mʌs-koʊs]

muss MUHS [mʌs]

EE i be/ I ɪ bit/ EH ɛ bet/ AA æ bat/ OO u boot / OO ʊ book/ AW ɔ bought/ AH ɑ father/ ER ɝ bird/
UH ʌ cup/ AY eɪ bay/ EYE aɪ bite/ OY ɔɪ boy/ OH oʊ boat/ OW aʊ how/ YOO ɪu duke/ EAR ɪɚ
beer/ AIR ɛɚ bear/ OOR ʊɚ tour/ AWR ɔɚ bore/ AHR ɑɚ bar/ NG ŋ king/ SH ʃ ship/ ZH ʒ vision/
TH θ thirty/ TH ð then/ CH ʧ child/ J ʤ just/ For complete list, see Key to Pronunciation p. 2.

mustachio muh-STAA-shee-oh [mə-'stæ-ʃi-oʊ] or __-STAH-__-__ [__-'stɑ-__-__] or __-STAA-shyoh [__-'stæ-ʃjoʊ] or __-STAH-shyoh [__-'stɑ-ʃjoʊ]

Mustardseed *(MID)* MUHS-terd-seed ['mʌs-tɚd-sid]

muster MUHS-ter ['mʌs-tɚ]

mutine MYOO-tin ['mju-tɪn]

mutineer MYOO-t(uh)n-ear ['mju-tn̩-ɪɚ]

Mutius *(TITUS)* MYOO-shuhs ['mju-ʃəs] scans to MYOO-shee-uhs ['mju-ʃi-əs] @ I, 1, 392

Myrmidons MER-mi-dahnz ['mɝ-mɪ-dɑnz] or __-__- duhnz [__-__-dənz]

Mytilen MIT-i-lehn ['mɪt-ɪ-lɛn]

Mytilene MIT-i-LEE-nee [mɪt-ɪ-'li-ni]

Mytilin MIT-i-lin ['mɪt-ɪ-lɪn]

Naiades NEYE-aadz ['naɪ-ædz]

Naples NAY-p(uh)lz ['neɪ-pl̩z]

narcissus / Narcissus nahr-SIS-uhs [nɑɚ-'sɪs-əs]

Nathaniel *(LLL)* nuh-THAAN-yuhl [nə-'θæn-jəl]

naught NAWT [nɔt]

Navarre see "Ferdinand"

nave NAYV [neɪv]

nay NAY [neɪ]

nayward NAY-werd ['neɪ-wɚd]

Nazarite NAAZ-uh-reyet ['næz-ə-raɪt]

ne NEE [ni]

ne'er NAIR [nɛɚ]

ne'ertheless NAIR-<u>th</u>uh-lehs ['nɛɚ-ðə-lɛs]

neaf NEEF [nif]

Neapolitan NEE-uh-**PAHL**-i-tuhn [ni-ə-'pɑl-ɪ-tən]

neatherd NEET-herd ['nit-hɚd]

neb NEHB [nɛb]

Nebuchadnezzar NEHB-uh-kuhd-**NEHZ**-er
 [nɛb-ə-kəd-'nɛz-ɚ]

necessitied nuh-**SEHS**-i-teed [nə-'sɛs-ɪ-tid]

Nedar NEED-er ['nid-ɚ] or **NEHD-__** ['nɛd-__]

needle NEE-d(uh)l ['ni-dl̩] scans to one syllable NEELD
 [nild] or NEEL [nil] e.g. @ *MID* III, 2, 204

neele NEEL [nil]

neeze NEEZ [niz]

neglection ni-**GLEHK**-shuhn [nɪ-'glɛk-ʃən]

neif NEEF [nif]

neigh NAY [neɪ]

Nell *(CE)* NEHL [nɛl]

Nemean always scans to **NEE**-myuhn ['ni-mjən]

Nemesis NEHM-i-sis ['nɛm-ɪ-sɪs]

Neoptolemus NEE-uhp-**TAHL**-i-muhs [ni-əp-'tɑl-ɪ-məs]

Neptune NEHP-tyoon ['nɛp-tɪun]

Nereides NI-ree-idz ['nɪ-ri-ɪdz] or NI-ree-i-deez ['nɪ-ri-ɪ-diz]

Nerissa *(MVEN)* nuh-**RIS**-uh [nə-'rɪs-ə]

Nero NI-roh ['nɪ-roʊ]

EE i be/ I ɪ bit/ EH ɛ bet/ AA æ bat/ OO u boot / OO ʊ book/ AW ɔ bought/ AH ɑ father/ ER ɝ bird/
UH ʌ cup/ AY eɪ bay/ EYE aɪ bite/ OY ɔɪ boy/ OH oʊ boat/ OW aʊ how/ YOO ɪu duke/ EAR ɪɚ
beer/ AIR ɛɚ bear/ OOR ʊɚ tour/ AWR ɔɚ bore/ AHR ɑɚ bar/ NG ŋ king/ SH ʃ ship/ ZH ʒ vision/
TH θ thirty/ TH ð then/ CH tʃ child/ J ʤ just/ For complete list, see Key to Pronunciation p. 2.

171

Nervii NER-vee-eye ['nɝ-vi-aɪ]

Nessus NEHS-uhs ['nɛs-əs]

Nestor NEHS-ter ['nɛs-tə-] or ___-tawr [___-tɔə-]
Nestor *(T&C)*

nether NETH-er ['nɛð-ə-]

Nevil NEH-vuhl ['nɛ-vəl] or ___-vil [___-vɪl]
Nevil, John, Marquess of Montague *(3HVI)* MAHN-tuh-
gyoo ['mɑn-tə-gju]
Nevil, Ralph, Earl of Westmoreland *(3HVI)* WEHST-mer-
luhnd ['wɛst-mə-lənd]
Nevil, Richard, Earl of Salisbury *(2HVI)* SAWLZ-buh-ree
['sɔlz-bə-ri] scans to SAWLZ-bree ['sɔlz-bri] e.g. @ I, 3, 72
Nevil, Richard, Earl of Warwick *(2HVI, 3HVI)* WAW-rik
['wɔ-rɪk] or WAH-__ ['wɑ-__]

Newgate NYOO-gayt ['nɪu-geɪt] or ___-guht [___-gət]

newsmonger NYOOZ-muhng-ger ['nɪuz-məŋ-gə-] or ___-
mahng-__ [___-mɑŋ-__]

newt NYOOT [nɪut]

new-trothed scans to nyoo-TROHTH-id [nɪu-'troʊð-ɪd]

Nicander neye-KAAN-der [naɪ-'kæn-də-]

Nicanor *(COR)* neye-KAY-ner [naɪ-'keɪ-nə-]

Nicholas Henton scans to NIK-luhs HEHN-t(uh)n ['nɪk-ləs]
['hɛn-tn̩] @ *HVIII* I, 2, 147

niggard NIG-erd ['nɪg-ə-d]

Nilus NEYE-luhs ['naɪ-ləs]

ninny / Ninny NI-nee ['nɪ-ni]

Ninus NEYEN-uhs ['naɪn-əs] or NIN-__ ['nɪn-__]

Niobe NEYE-oh-bee ['naɪ-oʊ-bi] or ___- uh-__ [___-ə-__]
in the plural scans to NEYE-bees ['naɪ-biz] @ *T&C* V, 10, 19

Nob NAHB [nɑb]

noblesse NOH-blehs ['noʊ-blɛs]

noddle NAH-d(uh)l ['nɑ-dl̩]

noddy NAH-dee ['nɑ-di]

noes NOHZ [noʊz]

noisome NOY-suhm ['nɔɪ-səm]

nole NOHL [noʊl]

nonage NAH-nij ['nɑ-nɪdʒ]

nonce NAHNS [nɑns]

nonino nah-nee-NOH [nɑ-ni-'noʊ]

nonpareil nahn-puh-REHL [nɑn-pə-'rɛl] or ___-___-RAYL [___-___-'reɪl]

nook-shotten no͞ok-SHAH-t(uh)n [nʊk-'ʃɑ-tn̩]

Norbery, Sir John scans to nawr-BREE [nɔɚ-'bri]

Norfolk, Duke of NAWR-fuhk ['nɔɚ-fək]
    Norfolk, Duke of *(HVIII)*
    Norfolk, Duke of *(RIII)*

Normandy NAWR-muhn-dee ['nɔɚ-mən-di]

Northampton nawr-THAAMP-t(uh)n [nɔɚ-'θæmp-tn̩] or nawrth-HAAMP-___ [nɔɚθ-'hæmp-___]

Northamptonshire nawr-THAAMP-t(uh)n-sher [nɔɚ-'θæmp-tn̩-ʃɚ] or nawrth-HAAMP-___-___ [nɔɚθ-'hæmp-___-___] or ___-___-___-shear [___-___-___-ʃɪɚ]

Northumberland nawr-THUHM-ber-luhnd [nɔɚ-'θʌm-bɚ-lənd]

EE i be/ I ɪ bit/ EH ɛ bet/ AA æ bat/ O͞O u boot/ OO ʊ book/ AW ɔ bought/ AH ɑ father/ ER ɝ bird/ UH ʌ cup/ AY eɪ bay/ EYE aɪ bite/ OY ɔɪ boy/ OH oʊ boat/ OW aʊ how/ YO͞O ɪu duke/ EAR ɪɚ beer/ AIR ɛɚ bear/ O͞OR ʊɚ tour/ AWR ɔɚ bore/ AHR ɑɚ bar/ NG ŋ king/ SH ʃ ship/ ZH ʒ vision/ TH θ thirty/ <u>TH</u> ð then/ CH tʃ child/ J dʒ just/ For complete list, see Key to Pronunciation p. 2.

Northumberland, Earl of *(RII, 1HIV, 2HIV)* possibly scans to nawr-THUM-bluhnd [nɔɚ-'θʌm-blənd] @ *1HIV* V, 5, 37
Northumberland, Lady *(2HIV)*

Norweyan nawr-WAY-uhn [nɔɚ-'weɪ-ən]

notary NOHT-uh-ree ['noʊt-ə-ri] scans to NOHT-ree ['noʊt-ri] @ *MVEN* I, 3, 140

not'st (to observe) NOHTST [noʊtst]

nought NAWT [nɔt]

novice NAH-vis ['nɑ-vɪs]

novum NOH-vuhm ['noʊ-vəm]

noyance NOY-uhns ['nɔɪ-əns]

nullity NUHL-i-tee ['nʌl-ɪ-ti]

Numa NYOO͞-muh ['nɪu-mə]

nuncio scans to NUHN-syoh ['nʌn-sjoʊ]

nuncle NUHNG-k(uh)l ['nʌŋ-kl̩]

nuptial NUHP-shuhl ['nʌp-ʃəl] scans to NUHP–shee-uhl ['nʌp-ʃi-əl] e.g. @ *TEMP* V, 1, 308

Nurse NERS [nɝs]
Nurse *(R&J)*
Nurse *(TITUS)*

Nym NIM [nɪm]
Nym *(HV, MW)*

nymph NIMF [nɪmf]
Nymphs *(TEMP)*

O (an interjection) OH [oʊ]

o' (abbreviation for "of" or "on") uh [ə]

o'er AWR [ɔɚ]

o'th UH<u>TH</u> [ʌð]

Oatcake, Hugh OHT-kayk HY$\overline{OO}$ ['oʊt-keɪk] [hju]

oathable OH<u>TH</u>-uh-b(uh)l ['oʊð-ə-bļ]

oath OH<u>TH</u> [oʊθ]

oaths OH<u>TH</u>Z [oʊðz]

ob. (abbreviation for "obolus") AHB-uh-luhs ['ɑb-ə-ləs]

obduracy AHB-dy$\overline{oo}$-ruh-see ['ɑb-djʊ-rə-si]

obdurate ahb-DY$\overline{OO}$-rit [ab-'djʊ-rɪt] scans to AHB-dy$\overline{oo}$-___ ['ɑb-djʊ-___] @ *2GEN* IV, 2, 119

obeisance scans to oh-BAY-uh-suhns [oʊ-'beɪ-ə-səns] if the line @ *SHR* Ind, 1, 107 is an Epic Caesura, or possibly OH-bay-suhns ['oʊ-beɪ-səns]

Oberon *(MID)* OH-buh-rahn ['oʊ-bə-rɑn]

Obidicut oh-BID-i-kuht [oʊ-'bɪd-ɪ-kət]

oblations oh-BLAY-shuhnz [oʊ-'bleɪ-ʃənz]

obliquy / obloquy AHB-luh-kwee ['ɑb-lə-kwi]

obscure (adj) ahb-SKY$\overline{OO}$R [ab-'skjʊɚ] scans to AHB-sky$\overline{oo}$r ['ɑb-skjʊɚ] e.g. @ *HAM* IV, 5, 211

obsequies AHB-si-kweez ['ɑb-sɪ-kwiz]

obsequious ahb-SEE-kwee-uhs [ab-'si-kwi-əs] or uhb-___-___-___ [əb-___-___-___]

obsequiously scans to ahb-SEE-kwuhs-lee [ab-'si-kwəs-li]

observants (n) AHB-zer-vuhnts ['ɑb-zɚ-vənts]

obstinacy always scans to AHB-stin-AY-see [ɑb-stɪn-'eɪ-si]

EE i be/ I ɪ bit/ EH ɛ bet/ AA æ bat/ $\overline{OO}$ u boot / $\overline{OO}$ ʊ book/ AW ɔ bought/ AH ɑ father/ ER ɝ bird/ UH ʌ cup/ AY eɪ bay/ EYE aɪ bite/ OY ɔɪ boy/ OH oʊ boat/ OW aʊ how/ Y$\overline{OO}$ ɪu duke/ EAR ɪə beer/ AIR ɛə bear/ $\overline{OO}$R ʊə tour/ AWR ɔɚ bore/ AHR ɑɚ bar/ NG ŋ king/ SH ʃ ship/ ZH ʒ vision/ TH θ thirty/ <u>TH</u> ð then/ CH tʃ child/ J dʒ just/ For complete list, see Key to Pronunciation p. 2.

occident AHK-suh-duhnt ['ɑk-sə-dənt] or __-__-dehnt [__-__-dɛnt]

ocean OH-shuhn ['oʊ-ʃən] scans to OH-shee-uhn ['oʊ-ʃi-ən] e.g. @ *HV* III, 1, 14

Octavia *(A&C)* ahk-TAYV-ee-uh [ɑk-'teɪv-i-ə] scans to ___-TAY-vyuh [___-'teɪ-vjə] e.g. @ II, 2, 119

Octavius ahk-TAYV-ee-uhs [ɑk-'teɪv-i-əs] scans to __-TAY-vyuhs [__-'teɪ-vjəs]
Octavius Caesar *(A&C)*
Octavius Caesar *(JC)* scans @ III, 1, 276

ocular scans to AHK-ler ['ɑk-lɚ]

odoriferous OH-duh-RIF-uh-ruhs [oʊ-də-'rɪf-ə-rəs] scans to __-__-RIF-ruhs [__-__-'rɪf-rəs] @ *KJ* III, 4, 26

'od's / 'ods / od's (corruption of "God's") AHDZ [ɑdz]

'ods nouns (corruption of "God's wounds") AHDZ NO͞ ONZ [ɑdz] [nunz]

oeillades uh-YAHDZ [ə-'jɑdz] or IL-ee-yuhdz ['ɪl-i-jədz] @ *MW* I, 3, 54

oes OHZ [oʊz]

offal AWF-uhl ['ɔf-əl]

offendress uh-FEHN-dris [ə-'fɛn-drɪs]

Old Shepherd SHEHP-erd ['ʃɛp-ɚd]
Old Shepherd *(1HVI)*
Old Shepherd *(WT)*

Oliver *(AYL)* AH-li-ver ['ɑ-lɪ-vɚ]

Olivia *(12th)* oh-LIV-ee-uh [oʊ-'lɪv-i-ə] scans to __-LIV-yuh [__-'lɪv-jə] e.g. @ I, 1, 20

Olympus oh-LIM-puhs [oʊ-'lɪm-pəs] or uh-___-___ [ə-___-___]

omittance oh-MI-tuhns [oʊ-'mɪ-təns]

oneyers WUHN-yerz ['wʌn-jɚz]

ope OHP [oʊp]

operance AHP-uh-ruhns ['ɑp-ə-rəns]

operant always scans to AHP-ruhnt ['ɑp-rənt]

Ophelia *(HAM)* oh-FEEL-yuh [oʊ-'fil-jə] scans to __-__-ee-uh [__-__-i-ə] e.g. @ IV, 5, 158

opinion uh-PIN-yuhn [ə-'pɪn-jən] scans to __-__-ee-yuhn [__-__-i-jən] e.g. @ *1HIV* V, 4, 47

opportune always scans to ah-PAWR-tyōōn [ɑ-'pɔɚ-tɪun]

opprobriously scans to uh-PROH-bruhs-lee [ə-'proʊ-brəs-li]

oppugnancy uh-PUHG-nuhn-see [ə-'pʌg-nən-si]

oracle AW-ruh-k(uh)l ['ɔ-rə-kl̩] scans to AWR-k(uh)l ['ɔɚ-kl̩] @ *WT* III, 2, 126

orator AW-ruh-ter ['ɔ-rə-tɚ] or AH-__-__ ['ɑ-__-__]

ordain awr-DAYN [ɔɚ-'deɪn] scans to AWR-dayn ['ɔɚ-deɪn] @ *TITUS* V, 3, 22

ordinance AWR-d(uh)n-uhns ['ɔɚ-dn̩-əns]

ordinant AWR-d(uh)n-uhnt ['ɔɚ-dn̩-ənt]

ordnance AWRD-nuhns ['ɔɚd-nəns]

ordure AWR-jer ['ɔɚ-ʤɚ]

orgulous AWR-gyuh-luhs ['ɔɚ-gjə-ləs]

orisons AW-ri-zuhnz ['ɔ-rɪ-zənz]

Orlando *(AYL)* awr-LAAN-doh [ɔɚ-'læn-doʊ]

Orleans AWR-lee-uhnz ['ɔɚ-li-ənz] scans to **AWR**-lyuhnz ['ɔɚ-ljənz] or ___-leenz [___-linz]
   Orleans, Duke of *(HV)* scans @ *HV* II, 4, 5

Orodes ah-ROH-deez [ɑ-'roʊ-diz]

Orpheus always scans to **AWR**-fyuhs ['ɔɚ-fjəs] or ___-fyo͞os [___-fjus]

Orsino *(12th)* awr-SEE-noh [ɔɚ-'si-noʊ]

ort AWRT [ɔɚt]

orthography awr-THAHG-ruh-fee [ɔɚ-'θɑg-rə-fi]

osier OH-zher ['oʊ-ʒɚ]

osprey AHS-pree ['ɑs-pri] or ___-pray [___-preɪ]

Osric *(HAM)* AHZ-rik ['ɑz-rɪk] or AHS-___ ['ɑs-___]

Ossa AH-suh ['ɑ-sə]

ostent always scans to ah-STEHNT [ɑ-'stɛnt]

ostler / Ostler *(1HIV)* AHS-ler ['ɑs-lɚ]

Oswald *(LEAR)* AHZ-wawld ['ɑz-wɔld]

Othello *(OTH)* oh-THEHL-oh [oʊ-'θɛl-oʊ]

Ottoman AH-tuh-muhn ['ɑ-tə-mən]

Ottomites AH-tuh-meyets ['ɑ-tə-maɪts]

ouches OWCH-iz ['aʊtʃ-ɪz]

ought AWT [ɔt]

ounce OWNTS [aʊnts]

ouphs OWFS [aʊfs] or O͞OFS [ufs]

ousel O͞O-zuhl ['u-zəl]

outdure OWT-dyo͞or ['aʊt-djuɚ]

Overdone, Mistress *(MM)* OH-ver-duhn ['oʊ-vɚ-dən]

overscutched OH-ver-skuhcht ['oʊ-vɚ-skətʃt]

Ovid AH-vid ['ɑ-vɪd]

Ovidius Naso oh-VID-ee-uhs NAY-zoh [oʊ-'vɪd-i-əs] ['neɪ-zoʊ]

Owen OH-in ['oʊ-in]

Oxford AHKS-ferd ['ɑks-fɚd]

Oxfordshire AHKS-ferd-sher ['ɑks-fɚd-ʃɚ] or __-__-shear [__-__-ʃɪɚ]

oxlips AHKS-lips ['ɑks-lɪps]

oyes oh-YEHZ [oʊ-'jɛz] or __-YEHS [__-'jɛs] scans to OH-yehz ['oʊ-jɛz] or OH-yehs ['oʊ-jɛs] @ *MW* V, 5, 39

Pacorus PAAK-uh-ruhs ['pæk-ə-rəs]

paction PAAK-shuhn ['pæk-ʃən]

paddock / Paddock PAAD-uhk ['pæd-ək]

Padua PAA-dyoo-uh ['pæ-dju-ə] scans to PAA-dywuh ['pæ-djwə] or __-joo-uh [__-dʒu-ə] scans to __-jwuh [__-dʒwə] e.g. @ *MVEN* III, 4, 49

Page PAYJ [peɪdʒ]
  Page *(MW)*
  Page, Anne *(MW)*
  Page, Mistress *(MW)*
  Page, William *(MW)*

Palamades PAAL-uh-MEE-deez [pæl-ə-'mi-diz]

Palamon *(2NOB)* PAAL-uh-muhn ['pæl-ə-mən] scans to PAAL-muhn ['pæl-mən] or __-__-mahn [__-__-mɑn] scans to __-mahn [__-mɑn] e.g. @ V, 3, 51

EE i be/ I ɪ bit/ EH ɛ bet/ AA æ bat/ OO u boot / OO ʊ book/ AW ɔ bought/ AH ɑ father/ ER ɝ bird/ UH ʌ cup/ AY eɪ bay/ EYE aɪ bite/ OY ɔɪ boy/ OH oʊ boat/ OW aʊ how/ YOO ɪu duke/ EAR ɪɚ beer/ AIR ɛɚ bear/ OOR ʊɚ tour/ AWR ɔɚ bore/ AHR ɑɚ bar/ NG ŋ king/ SH ʃ ship/ ZH ʒ vision/ TH θ thirty/ TH ð then/ CH tʃ child/ J dʒ just/ For complete list, see Key to Pronunciation p. 2.

Palatine PAAL-uh-teyen ['pæl-ə-taɪn]

Palestine PAAL-i-steyen ['pæl-ɪ-staɪn]

palfrey PAWL-free ['pɔl-fri]

palisadoes PAAL-i-SAY-dohz [pæl-ɪ-'seɪ-douz]

Pallas PAAL-uhs ['pæl-əs] or ___-aas [___-æs]

palliament scans to PAAL-yuh-muhnt ['pæl-jə-mənt]

palmer PAHM-er ['pɑm-ɚ]

palsy PAWL-zee ['pɔl-zi]

palter PAWL-ter ['pɔl-tɚ]

paltry PAWL-tree ['pɔl-tri]

paly PAY-lee ['peɪ-li]

Pandar PAAN-der ['pæn-dɚ]

Pandarus PAAN-duh-ruhs ['pæn-də-rəs]
  Pandarus *(T&C)* also called "Pandar" PAAN-der ['pæn-dɚ]

pander / Pander *(PER)* PAAN-der ['pæn-dɚ]

Pandulph, Cardinal *(KJ)* PAAN-duhlf ['pæn-dəlf]

pannier PAAN-yer ['pæn-jɚ] or ___-ee-er [___-i-ɚ]

Pannonians paa-NOH-nyuhnz [pæ-'nou-njənz] or
  puh-__-__ [pə-__-__]

Pansa PAAN-zuh ['pæn-zə] or ___-suh [___-sə]

pantaloon paan-tuh-LO͞ON [pæn-tə-'lun]

Pantheon scans to PAAN-thyuhn ['pæn-θjən] @ *TITUS* I, 1,
  245 and paan-THEE-uhn [pæn-'θi-ən] or ___-THEE-ahn
  [___-'θi-ɑn] @ *TITUS* I, 1, 336

Panthino *(2GEN)* paan-THEE-noh [pæn-'θi-nou]

pantler PAANT-ler ['pænt-lɚ]

Papal Legate *(1HVI)* PAY-puhl LEHG-it ['peɪ-pəl] ['lɛg-ɪt]

Paphlagonia PAAF-luh-GOH-nee-uh [pæf-lə-'goʊ-ni-ə]

Paphos PAY-fohs ['peɪ-foʊs]

papist PAY-pist ['peɪ-pɪst]

Paracelsus PAA-ruh-SEHL-suhs [pæ-rə-'sɛl-səs]

paragon PAA-ruh-gahn ['pæ-rə-gɑn] or PEH-__-__ ['pɛ-__-__]

paramour PAA-ruh-mo͞or ['pæ-rə-mʊɚ] or PEH-___-___ ['pɛ-___-___]

parapets PAA-ruh-pehts ['pæ-rə-pɛts]

paraquito PAA-ruh-KEE-toh [pæ-rə-'ki-toʊ]

Parca PAHR-kuh ['pɑɚ-kə]

pard PAHRD [pɑɚd]

Paris PAA-ris ['pæ-rɪs]
    Paris *(R&J)*
    Paris *(T&C)*

Paris-ward PAA-ris-werd ['pæ-rɪs-wɚd]

paritors PAA-ri-tawrz ['pæ-rɪ-tɔɚz] or __-__-terz [__-__-tɚz]

Park-ward PAHRK-werd ['pɑɚk-wɚd]

parle PAHRL [pɑɚl]

parley PAHR-lee ['pɑɚ-li]

parlous PAHR-luhs ['pɑɚ-ləs]

parmacity PAHR-muh-SI-tee [pɑɚ-mə-'sɪ-ti]

Parolles *(AW)* puh-ROHL-iz [pə-'roʊl-ɪz] or __-__-eez [__-__-iz] or __-RAHL-is [__-'rɑl-ɪs]

EE i be/ I ɪ bit/ EH ɛ bet/ AA æ bat/ O͞O u boot / OO ʊ book/ AW ɔ bought/ AH ɑ father/ ER ɝ bird/ UH ʌ cup/ AY eɪ bay/ EYE aɪ bite/ OY ɔɪ boy/ OH oʊ boat/ OW aʊ how/ YO͞O ɪu duke/ EAR ɪɚ beer/ AIR ɛɚ bear/ O͞OR ʊɚ tour/ AWR ɔɚ bore/ AHR ɑɚ bar/ NG ŋ king/ SH ʃ ship/ ZH ʒ vision/ TH θ thirty/ TH ð then/ CH ʧ child/ J ʤ just/ For complete list, see Key to Pronunciation p. 2.

Parthia PAHR-thee-uh ['pɑɚ-θi-ə] scans to **PAHR**-thyuh ['pɑɚ-θjə] e.g. @ *A&C* II, 3, 32

Parthian always scans to **PAHR**-thyuhn ['pɑɚ-θjən]

partisan PAHR-ti-zuhn ['pɑɚ-tɪ-zən] or __-__-zaan [__-__-zæn]

Partlet PAHRT-lit ['pɑɚt-lɪt]

pash PAASH [pæʃ]

passado puh-SAH-doh [pə-'sɑ-doʊ]

passant PAAS-uhnt ['pæs-ənt]

passy measures pavin PAAS-ee MEHZH-erz PAA-vin ['pæs-i] ['mɛʒ-ɚz] ['pæ-vɪn]

pastern PAAS-tern ['pæs-tɚn]

pasty (a pie) PAAS-tee ['pæs-ti]

Patchbreech PAACH-brich ['pætʃ-brɪtʃ] or ___-breech [___-brɪtʃ]

pate PAYT [peɪt]

patens PAA-t(uh)nz ['pæ-tn̩z]

patent PAAT-uhnt ['pæt-ənt] or PAYT-___ ['peɪt-___]

patience / Patience PAY-shuhns ['peɪ-ʃəns] scans to PAY-shee-uhns ['peɪ-ʃi-əns]
Patience *(HVIII)* scans @ IV, 2, 165

patrician puh-TRI-shuhn [pə-'tri-ʃən] scans to __-__-shee-uhn [__-__-ʃi-ən] @ *COR* V, 6, 82

patrimony PAA-tri-moh-nee ['pæ-trɪ-moʊ-ni]

Patroclus *(T&C)* puh-TROHK-luhs [pə-'troʊk-ləs] or ___-TRAHK-___ [___-'trɑk-___]

Paulina *(WT)* paw-LEYE-nuh [pɔ-'laɪ-nə] (paw-LEE-nuh [pɔ-'li-nə] is sometimes heard)

paunch / Paunch PAWNCH [pɔntʃ]

pax PAAKS [pæks]

peascod PEEZ-kahd ['piz-kɑd]

pease PEEZ [piz]

Peaseblossom *(MID)* PEEZ-blah-suhm ['piz-blɑ-səm]

pedant / Pedant PEH-d(uh)nt ['pɛ-dn̩t]
  Pedant *(SHR)*, later posing as Vincentio vin-**SEHN**-shee-oh
  [vɪn-'sɛn-ʃi-ou] scans to ___-**SEHN**-shyoh
  [___-'sɛn-ʃjou] @ I, 1, 192

pedantical puh-**DAAN**-ti-k(uh)l [pə-'dæn-tɪ-kl̩]

pedlar PEHD-ler ['pɛd-lɚ]

Pedro, Don, Prince of Arragon *(MADO)* PAY-droh AA-ruh-
  gahn ['peɪ-drou] ['æ-rə-gɑn]

Peesel PI-s(uh)l [pɪ-sl̩] or ___-z(uh)l [___-zl̩] or PEE-s(uh)l
  ['pi-sl̩] or ___-z(uh)l [___-zl̩]

Pegasus PEHG-uh-suhs ['pɛg-ə-səs]

peise PEEZ [piz] or PAYZ [peɪz]

peize PEEZ [piz]

pelf PEHLF [pɛlf]

Pelion PEE-lee-uhn ['pi-li-ən] scans to PEE-lyuhn ['pi-ljən]
  @ *HAM* V, 1, 240

Peloponnesus pehl-OH-puh-NEE-suhs [pɛl-ou-pə-'ni-səs]

Pelops PEE-lahps ['pi-lɑps]

Pembroke PEHM-brŏŏk ['pɛm-brʊk] or ___-brohk
  [___-broʊk]

EE i be/ I ɪ bit/ EH ɛ bet/ AA æ bat/ O͞O u boot / O͝O ʊ book/ AW ɔ bought/ AH ɑ father/ ER ɝ bird/
UH ʌ cup/ AY eɪ bay/ EYE aɪ bite/ OY ɔɪ boy/ OH ou boat/ OW aʊ how/ YO͞O ɪu duke/ EAR ɪə
beer/ AIR ɛə bear/ O͞OR ʊə tour/ AWR ɔə bore/ AHR ɑə bar/ NG ŋ king/ SH ʃ ship/ ZH ʒ vision/
TH θ thirty/ T̲H̲ ð then/ CH tʃ child/ J dʒ just/ For complete list, see Key to Pronunciation p. 2.

Pembroke, Earl of *(KJ)*

pence PEHNS [pɛns]

Pendragon pehn-DRAAG-uhn [pɛn-'dræg-ən]

penetrative PEHN-i-tray-tiv ['pɛn-ɪ-treɪ-tɪv]

penitential PEHN-i-TEHN-shuhl [pɛn-ɪ-'tɛn-ʃəl]

penner PEHN-er ['pɛn-ɚ]

pennons PEHN-uhnz ['pɛn-ənz]

pennyworth PEHN-ee-werth ['pɛn-i-wɚ-θ] or PEHN-erth
['pɛn-ɚ-θ]

Pentapolis pehn-TAA-puh-luhs [pɛn-'tæ-pə-ləs]

Pentecost PEHN-ti-kahst ['pɛn-tɪ-kɑst]

Penthesilea PEHN-theh-si-LEE-uh [pɛn-θɛ-sɪ-'li-ə]

penurious scans to peh-NYOOR-yuhs [pɛ-'njʊɚ-jəs]

penury PEHN-yoo-ree ['pɛn-ju-ri] scans to PEHN-ree
['pɛn-ri] e.g. @ *R&J* V, 1, 49

Pepin PEHP-in ['pɛp-ɪn]

per se per-SAY [pɚ-'seɪ] or __-SEE [__-'si]

peradventure per-aad-VEHN-cher [pɚ-æd-'vɛn-tʃɚ]

Percy PER-see ['pɝ-si]
    Percy, Henry *(RII, 1HIV)* also called "Hotspur" HAHT-sper
        ['hɑt-spɚ]
    Percy, Henry, Earl of Northumberland *(RII, 1HIV, 2HIV)*
        nawr-THUHM-ber-luhnd [nɔɚ-'θʌm-bɚ-lənd]
    Percy, Lady *(1HIV, 2HIV)*
    Percy, Thomas, Earl of Worcester *(1HIV)* WOOS-ter
        ['wʊs-tɚ] scans to WOO-sis-ter ['wu-sɪs-tɚ] @ I, 3, 15
    Percy, Henry, Earl of Northumberland *(3HVI)*

perdie per-DEE [pɚ-'di]

Perdita *(WT)* PER-di-tuh [ˈpɝ-dɪ-tə]

perdition per-DISH-uhn [pɚ-ˈdɪʃ-ən]

perdu per-DYOO [pɚ-ˈdɪu] possibly scans to PER-dyoo [ˈpɝ-dɪu] @ *LEAR* IV, 7, 35

perdurable per-DYOO-ruh-b(uh)l [pɚ-ˈdɪu-rə-bl̩] scans to PER-dyoo-__-__ [ˈpɝ-dɪu-__-__] @ *HV* IV, 5, 8

perdurably scans to PER-dyoo-ruh-blee [ˈpɝ-dɪu-rə-bli]

perdy per-DEE [pɚ-ˈdi]

peregrinate PEH-ri-gri-nayt [ˈpɛ-rɪ-grɪ-neɪt]

peremptory puh-REHMP-tuh-ree [pə-ˈrɛmp-tə-ri] scans to PEH-ruhmp-taw-ree [ˈpɛ-rəmp-tɔ-ree] e.g. @ *LLL* IV, 3, 221 and PREHMP-tuh-ree [ˈprɛmp-tə-ri] @ *1HIV* I, 3, 17, and possibly PREHMP-tree [ˈprɛmp-tri] @ *2HVI* III, 1, 8

perfect (v) always scans to PER-fehkt [ˈpɝ-fɛkt]

perfecter PER-fehk-ter [ˈpɝ-fɛk-tɚ]

perfidious per-FID-ee-uhs [pɚ-ˈfɪd-i-əs] scans to __-FID-yuhs [__-ˈfɪd-jəs] @ *TEMP* I, 2, 68

perfit PER-fit [ˈpɝ-fɪt]

perfume (n) PER-fyoom [ˈpɝ-fjum] e.g. @ *HAM* I, 3, 9 and per-FYOOM [pɚ-ˈfjum] e.g. @ *SHR* I, 1, 172

perfume (v) per-FYOOM [pɚ-ˈfjum] scans to PER-fyoom [ˈpɝ-fjum] @ *2HIV* III, 1, 12

periapts PEH-ree-ahpts [ˈpɛ-ri-ɑpts]

Pericles *(PER)* PEH-ri-kleez [ˈpɛ-rɪ-kliz] possibly scans to peh-RI-__ [pɛ-ˈrɪ-__] @ II, 3, 81

Perigenia PEH-ri-JEEN-yuh [pɛ-rɪ-ˈdʒin-jə]

EE i be/ I ɪ bit/ EH ɛ bet/ AA æ bat/ OO u boot / OO ʊ book/ AW ɔ bought/ AH ɑ father/ ER ɝ bird/ UH ʌ cup/ AY eɪ bay/ EYE aɪ bite/ OY ɔɪ boy/ OH oʊ boat/ OW aʊ how/ YOO ɪu duke/ EAR ɪɚ beer/ AIR ɛɚ bear/ OOR ʊɚ tour/ AWR ɔɚ bore/ AHR ɑɚ bar/ NG ŋ king/ SH ʃ ship/ ZH ʒ vision/ TH θ thirty/ TH ð then/ CH tʃ child/ J dʒ just/ For complete list, see Key to Pronunciation p. 2.

Perigort scans to PAIR-gawrt ['pɛɚ-gɔɚt]

perilous scans to PAIR-luhs ['pɛɚ-ləs] e.g. @ *HV* Pro, 22

perishen PEH-ri-shun ['pɛ-rɪ-ʃən]

periwig PEH-ri-wig ['pɛ-rɪ-wɪg]

perjure (n) or (v) PER-jer ['pɝ-ʤɚ]

Perk, Gilbert PAHRK [pɑɚk]

Perkes PAHRKS [pɑɚks]

peroration PEH-ruh-RAY-shuhn [pɛ-rə-'reɪ-ʃən]

perpend per-PEHND [pɚ-'pɛnd]

perpetuity per-pi-TYŌŌ-i-tee [pɚ-pɪ-'tɪu-ɪ-ti] scans to
___-___-TYŌŌ-tee [___-___-'tɪu-ti] @ *CYM* V, 4, 6

Perseus PER-see-uhs ['pɝ-si-əs] scans to PER-syuhs
['pɝ-sjəs] e.g. @ *T&C* I, 3, 42

persever per-SEHV-er [pɚ-'sɛv-ɚ]

perseverance per-SEHV-uh-ruhns [pɚ-'sɛv-ə-rəns] scans to
___-SEHV-ruhns [___-'sɛv-rəns] e.g. @ *MAC* IV, 3, 93

Persia PER-zhuh ['pɝ-ʒə]

persistive per-SIS-tiv [pɚ-'sɪs-tɪv]

personated PER-suhn-ay-tid ['pɝ-sən-eɪ-tɪd]

perspective always scans to PER-spehk-tiv ['pɝ-spɛk-tɪv]

perspicuous per-SPIK-yōō-uhs [pɚ-'spɪk-ju-əs]

pertaunt-like PAIR-tawnt-leyek ['pɛɚ-tɔnt-laɪk] or
PER-___-___ ['pɝ-___-___]

perturbation per-ter-BAY-shuhn [pɚ-tɚ-'beɪ-ʃən]

perusal puh-RŌŌ-z(uh)l [pə-'ru-zl̩]

pestiferous pehs-TIF-uh-ruhs [pɛs-'tɪf-ə-rəs] scans to ___-TIF-ruhs [___-'tɪf-rəs] @ *1HVI* III, 1, 15

petar pi-TAHR [pɪ-'tɑɚ]

Peter of Pomfret *(KJ)* PAHM-frit ['pɑm-frɪt] or PUHM-___ ['pʌm-___]

Peto PEE-toh ['pi-toʊ]
 Peto *(1HIV, 2HIV)*

Petrarch PEE-trahrk ['pi-trɑɚk] or PEH-___ ['pɛ-___]

Petruchio pi-TROO-kee-oh [pɪ-'tru-ki-oʊ] scans to ___-TROO-kyoh [___-'tru-kjoʊ] or ___-___-chee -___ [___-___-tʃi-___] scans to ___-TROO-chyoh [___-'tru-tʃjoʊ]
 Petruchio *(SHR)* scans e.g. @ I, 2, 128

pettitoes PEH-tee-tohz ['pɛ-ti-toʊz]

Phaeton FAY-i-tuhn ['feɪ-ɪ-tən]

phantasime faan-TAAZ-uhm [fæn-'tæz-əm]

phantasma faan-TAAZ-muh [fæn-'tæz-mə]

Pharamond FAA-ruh-mahnd ['fæ-rə-mɑnd] or ___-___-muhnd [___-___-mənd]

Pharaoh FEH-roh ['fɛ-roʊ] or FAY-___ ['feɪ-___] or FAA-___ ['fæ-___]

Pharsalia fahr-SAYL-yuh [fɑɚ-'seɪl-jə]

Pheazar FEE-zer ['fi-zɚ]

Phebe *(AYL)* FEE-bee ['fi-bi]

Phebes (v) FEE-beez ['fi-biz]

pheese FEEZ [fiz]

EE i be/ I ɪ bit/ EH ɛ bet/ AA æ bat/ OO u boot / OO ʊ book/ AW ɔ bought/ AH ɑ father/ ER ɝ bird/ UH ʌ cup/ AY eɪ bay/ EYE aɪ bite/ OY ɔɪ boy/ OH oʊ boat/ OW aʊ how/ YOO ɪu duke/ EAR ɪɚ beer/ AIR ɛɚ bear/ OOR ʊɚ tour/ AWR ɔɚ bore/ AHR ɑɚ bar/ NG ŋ king/ SH ʃ ship/ ZH ʒ vision/ TH θ thirty/ TH ð then/ CH tʃ child/ J ʤ just/ For complete list, see Key to Pronunciation p. 2.

Phibbus FIB-uhs ['fɪb-əs]

Philadelphos FIL-uh-DEHL-fuhs [fɪl-ə-'dɛl-fəs] or
___-___-___-fahs [__-__-__-fɑs]

Philario *(CYM)* scans to fi-LAHR-yoh [fɪ-'lɑɚ-joʊ]

Philarmonus FIL-ahr-MOHN-uhs [fil-ɑɚ-'moʊn-əs]

Philemon fi-LEE-muhn [fɪ-'li-mən] or feye-___-___
[faɪ-___-___]
Philemon *(PER)*

Philip FI-lip ['fɪ-lɪp]
Philip the Bastard *(KJ)*
Philip, King *(KJ)*

Philippan fi-LIP-uhn [fɪ-'lɪp-ən]

Philippe (female name in 2HVI) FI-lip ['fɪ-lip]

Philippi fi-LIP-eye [fɪ-'lɪp-aɪ]

Phillida FIL-i-duh ['fɪl-ɪ-də]

Philo *(A&C)* FEYE-loh ['faɪ-loʊ]

Philomel / Philomele FIL-uh-mehl ['fɪl-ə-mɛl]

Philomela FIL-uh-MEE-luh [fɪl-ə-'mi-lə]

Philostrate *(MID)* FI-luh-strayt ['fɪ-lə-streɪt]

Philoten FI-luh-tin ['fɪ-lə-tɪn] or FEYE-__-__ ['faɪ-__-__]

Philotus *(TIMON)* fi-LOH-tuhs [fɪ-'loʊ-təs] or feye-___-___
[faɪ-___-___]

phlegmatic flehg-MAAT-ik [flɛg-'mæt-ɪk]

Phoebe FEE-bee ['fi-bi]

Phoebus FEE-buhs ['fi-bəs]

Phoenicia fi-NEE-shuh [fɪ-'ni-ʃə] or fuh-__-__ [fə-__-__]

Phoenicians fi-NEE-shuhnz [fɪ-'ni-ʃənz] or fuh-__-__
  [fə-__-__]

Phoenix FEE-niks ['fi-nɪks]

Photinus FOH-ti-nuhs ['foʊ-tɪ-nəs] or FAH-__-__ ['fɑ-__-__]

Phrygia FRIJ-ee-uh ['frɪʤ-i-ə] scans to FRIJ-yuh ['frɪʤ-jə]
  e.g. @ *T&C* Pro, 7

Phrygian always scans to FRIJ-yuhn ['frɪʤ-jən]

Phrynia *(TIMON)* FRI-nee-uh ['frɪ-ni-ə]

Picardy PIK-er-dee ['pɪk-ɚ-di]

Pickt-hatch PIKT-haach ['pɪkt-hæʧ]

pied PEYED [paɪd]

piedness PEYED-nuhs ['paɪd-nəs]

pight PEYET [paɪt]

Pigrogromitus PI-groh-GRAHM-i-tuhs [pɪ-groʊ-'grɑm-ɪ-təs]

Pilate PEYE-luht ['paɪ-lət]

Pilch PILCH [pɪlʧ]

pilcher PILCH-er ['pɪlʧ-ɚ]

Pillicock PIL-i-kahk ['pɪl-ɪ-kɑk]

pillory PIL-uh-ree ['pɪl-ə-ri]

Pimpernell PIM-per-nehl ['pɪm-pɚ-nɛl]

Pinch, Doctor *(CE)* PINCH [pɪnʧ]

Pindarus *(JC)* PIN-duh-ruhs ['pɪn-də-rəs]

pinion PIN-yuhn ['pɪn-jən]

EE i be/ I ɪ bit/ EH ɛ bet/ AA æ bat/ O͞O u boot / O͝O ʊ book/ AW ɔ bought/ AH ɑ father/ ER ɝ bird/
UH ʌ cup/ AY eɪ bay/ EYE aɪ bite/ OY ɔɪ boy/ OH oʊ boat/ OW aʊ how/ YO͞O ɪu duke/ EAR ɪɚ
beer/ AIR ɛɚ bear/ O͞OR ʊɚ tour/ AWR ɔɚ bore/ AHR ɑɚ bar/ NG ŋ king/ SH ʃ ship/ ZH ʒ vision/
TH θ thirty/ TH̲ ð then/ CH ʧ child/ J ʤ just/ For complete list, see Key to Pronunciation p. 2.

pinnace PIN-uhs ['pɪn-əs]

pioned PEYE-uhn-id ['paɪ-ən-ɪd]

pioner PEYE-uh-ner ['paɪ-ə-nɚ] scans to PEYE-ner ['paɪ-nɚ] @ *OTH* III, 3, 346

pippin PIP-in ['pɪp-ɪn]

Pirithous *(2NOB)* peye-RI-thoh-uhs [paɪ-'rɪ-θou-əs] scans to PEYE-ri-thuhs ['paɪ-rɪ-θəs] or __-__-thōos [__-__-θus] e.g. @ I, 1, 207

Pisa PEE-zuh ['pi-zə]

Pisanio *(CYM)* pi-ZAHN-ee-oh [pɪ-'zɑn-i-ou] scans to ___-ZAHN-yoh [___-'zɑn-jou] e.g. @ III, 5, 56

pish PISH [pɪʃ]

pismires PIS-meyerz ['pɪs-maɪɚ-z] or PIZ-___ ['pɪz-___]

Pistol PIS-t(uh)l ['pɪs-tl̩]
   Pistol *(2HIV, HV, MW)*

pitchy PICH-ee [pɪtʃ-i]

pith PITH [pɪθ]

Pittie-ward PIT-ee-werd ['pɪt-i-wɚd] or possibly PEHT-__-__ ['pɛt-__-__] many emendations including "Petty-ward"

Pius PEYE-uhs ['paɪ-əs]

pizzle PIZ-uhl ['pɪz-əl]

Placentio scans to pluh-SEHN-shyoh [plə-'sɛn-ʃjou]

plaguy PLAY-gee ['pleɪ-gi]

plaints PLAYNTS [pleɪnts]

planched PLAANCH-id ['plæntʃ-ɪd]

plantage PLAAN-tij ['plæn-tɪdʒ]

Plantagenet plaan-**TAAJ**-uh-nit [plæn-'tædʒ-ə-nɪt] scans to
___-**TAAJ**-nit [___-'tædʒ-nɪt]
    Plantagenet, Edward, Earl of Warwick *(RIII)* **WAW**-rik
        ['wɔ-rɪk] or **WAH**-___ ['wɑ-___]
    Plantagenet, Richard, afterwards Duke of Gloucester, and
        Richard III *(2HVI, 3HVI, RIII)* **GLAHS**-ter ['glɑs-tɚ]
        scans to **GLAHS**-i-ter ['glɑs-ɪ-tɚ] or **GLAH**-sis-ter
        ['glɑ-sɪs-tɚ] @ *RIII* III, 4, 46
    Plantagenet, Richard, afterwards Duke of York *(1HVI,*
        2HVI, 3HVI) scans @ *3HVI* III, 1, 140, possibly
        scans to PLAAN-tuh-**JEHN**-it [plæn-tə-'dʒen-ɪt]
        @ *1HVI* III, 1, 149

plantain PLAAN-tuhn ['plæn-tən] possibly plaan-**TAYN**
[plæn-'teɪn] @ *LLL* III, 1, 66, 67

plash PLAASH [plæʃ]

Plashy PLAASH-ee ['plæʃ-i]

plated PLAY-tid ['pleɪ-tɪd]

plats PLAATS [plæts]

plausive PLAW-ziv ['plɔ-zɪv] or ___-siv [___-sɪv]

Plautus PLAW-tuhs ['plɔ-təs]

play-feres PLAY-fearz ['pleɪ-fɪɚ-z]

pleached PLEECHT [plitʃt]

plebeians pli-**BEE**-uhnz [plɪ-'bi-ənz] scans to **PLEHB**-yuhnz
['plɛb-jənz] e.g. @ *COR* I, 9, 7 and possibly scans to
PLEH-bee-uhnz ['plɛ-bi-ənz] @ *A&C* IV, 12, 34 (if "to
the" elides to one syllable)

plebeii PLEE-bee-eye ['pli-bi-aɪ] or **PLEH**-___-___ ['plɛ-___-___]

plebs PLEHBZ [plɛbz]

EE i be/ I ɪ bit/ EH ɛ bet/ AA æ bat/ O͞O u boot / O͞O ʊ book/ AW ɔ bought/ AH ɑ father/ ER ɝ bird/
UH ʌ cup/ AY eɪ bay/ EYE aɪ bite/ OY ɔɪ boy/ OH oʊ boat/ OW aʊ how/ YO͞O ɪu duke/ EAR ɪɚ
beer/ AIR ɛɚ bear/ O͞OR ʊɚ tour/ AWR ɔɚ bore/ AHR ɑɚ bar/ NG ŋ king/ SH ʃ ship/ ZH ʒ vision/
TH θ thirty/ TH ð then/ CH tʃ child/ J dʒ just/ For complete list, see Key to Pronunciation p. 2.

191

pleurisy PLOO͞-ri-see [ˈpluˑrɪ-si]

plied PLEYED [plaɪd]

plies PLEYEZ [plaɪz]

plight PLEYET [plaɪt]

plummet PLUHM-it [ˈplʌm-ɪt]

plurisy PLOO͞-ri-see [ˈpluˑrɪ-si]

Plutus PLOO͞-tuhs [ˈplu-təs]

Po POH [poʊ]

pocky PAHK-ee [ˈpɑk-i]

poesy POH-i-zee [ˈpoʊ-ɪ-zi] or ___-___-see [___-___-si] scans
    to POH-zee [ˈpoʊ-zi] or ___-see [___-si] @ *SHR* I, 1, 36

Poictiers poy-TEARZ [pɔɪ-ˈtɪɚ-z]

Poins POYNZ [pɔɪnz]
    Poins *(1HIV, 2HIV)*

point-devise POYNT-di-veyes [ˈpɔɪnt-dɪ-vaɪs]

Poitiers poy-TEARZ [pɔɪ-ˈtɪɚ-z] scans to POY-tearz [ˈpɔɪ-tɪɚ-z]
    @ *KJ* I, 1, 11

Polacks POH-laaks [ˈpoʊ-læks]

poleaxe POHL-aaks [ˈpoʊl-æks]

pole-clipt POHL-klipt [ˈpoʊl-klɪpt]

Polemon pah-LEH-muhn [pɑ-ˈlɛ-mən] or ___-LEE-___
    [___-li-___]

politic PAH-li-tik [ˈpɑ-lɪ-tɪk]

politicly PAHL-uh-tik-lee [ˈpɑl-ə-tɪk-li] scans to PAHL-tik-lee
    [ˈpɑl-tɪk-li] @ *SHR* IV, 1, 175

Polixenes puh-LIKS-uh-neez [pə-ˈlɪks-ə-niz] scans to
    ___-LIKS-neez [___-ˈlɪks-niz]

Polixenes *(WT)* scans e.g. @ I, 2, 351 also called "Bohemia"
boh-HEE-mee-uh [boʊ-'hi-mi-ə] scans to
___-HEE-myuh [___-'hi-mjə] e.g. @ IV, 4, 581

pollaxe POHL-aaks ['poʊl-æks]

polled POHLD [poʊld]

Polonius *(HAM)* puh-LOH-nyuhs [pə-'loʊ-njəs] possibly
___-___-nee-uhs [___-___-ni-əs] in prose

poltroons scans to POHL-trōōnz ['poʊl-trunz]

Polydamas pah-LID-uh-muhs [pɑ-'lɪd-ə-məs]

Polyxena puh-LIKS-uh-nuh [pə-'lɪks-ə-nə] or pah-___-___-___
[pɑ-___-___-___] or poh-___-___-___ [poʊ-___-___-___]

pomander POH-maan-der ['poʊ-mæn-dɚ]

pomegranate PAHM-graan-it ['pɑm-græn-ɪt] scans to
___-GRAAN-___ [___-'græn-___] @ *R&J* III, 5, 4

pomewater POHM-waw-ter ['poʊm-wɔ-tɚ]

Pomfret PAHM-frit ['pɑm-frɪt] or PUHM-___ ['pʌm-___]

Pomgarnet PAHM-gahr-nit ['pɑm-gɑɚ-nɪt]

pommel PAHM-uhl ['pɑm-əl]

Pompey PAHM-pee ['pɑm-pi]
Pompey *(MM)*

Pompion PUHMP-ee-uhn ['pʌmp-i-ən] or PUHMP-yuhn
['pʌmp-jən]

poniard PAHN-yerd ['pɑn-jɚd]

Pont PAHNT [pɑnt]

Pontic PAHN-tik ['pɑn-tɪk]

EE i be/ I ɪ bit/ EH ɛ bet/ AA æ bat/ ŌŌ u boot / OO ʊ book/ AW ɔ bought/ AH ɑ father/ ER ɝ bird/
UH ʌ cup/ AY eɪ bay/ EYE aɪ bite/ OY ɔɪ boy/ OH oʊ boat/ OW aʊ how/ YŌŌ ɪu duke/ EAR ɪɚ
beer/ AIR ɛɚ bear/ ŌŌR ʊɚ tour/ AWR ɔɚ bore/ AHR ɑɚ bar/ NG ŋ king/ SH ʃ ship/ ZH ʒ vision/
TH θ thirty/ <u>TH</u> ð then/ CH tʃ child/ J dʒ just/ For complete list, see Key to Pronunciation p. 2.

Ponton de Santrailles PAHN-tuhn duh-SAAN-trayl-eez ['pɑn-tən] [də-'sæn-treɪl-iz]

popingay PAHP-in-gay ['pɑp-ɪn-geɪ] some editions "popinjay" PAHP-in-jay ['pɑp-ɪn-ʤeɪ]

popish POHP-ish ['poʊp-ɪʃ]

pop'rin PAHP-rin ['pɑp-rɪn]

porpentine / Porpentine PAWR-puhn-teyen ['pɔ˞-pən-taɪn]

porringer PAW-rin-jer ['pɔ-rɪn-ʤ˞] or PAH-___-___ ['pɑ-___-___]

portage PAWR-tij ['pɔ˞-tɪʤ]

portance PAWR-t(uh)ns ['pɔ˞-tn̩s]

portcullised pawrt-KUHL-ist [pɔ˞t-'kʌl-ɪst]

portent always scans to pawr-TEHNT [pɔ˞-'tɛnt]

portentous pawr-TEHN-tuhs [pɔ˞-'tɛn-təs]

Porter *(MAC)* PAWR-ter ['pɔ˞-t˞]

Portia PAWR-shuh ['pɔ˞-ʃə] scans to PAWR-shee-uh ['pɔ˞-ʃi-ə]
Portia *(JC)*
Portia *(MVEN)* scans e.g. @ I, 1, 66

portraiture PAWR-tri-cho͞or ['pɔ˞-trɪ-tʃʊ˞] or ___-___-cher [___-___-tʃ˞]

posset PAHS-it ['pɑs-ɪt]

postern POH-stern ['poʊ-st˞n] or PAH-___ ['pɑ-___]

posthaste pohst-HAYST [poʊst-'heɪst]

Posthumus Leonatus *(CYM)* pahs-TYO͞O-muhs LEE-oh-NAH-tuhs [pɑs-'tɪu-məs] [li-oʊ-'nɑ-təs] scans to PAHS-tyo͞o-___ ['pɑs-tɪu-___] @ IV, 2, 320 and possibly PAHS-tymuhs ['pɑs-tjməs] @ I, 1, 41

posy POH-zee ['poʊ-zi]

194

potations poh-TAY-shuhnz [poʊ-'teɪ-ʃənz]

potch PAHCH [pɑtʃ]

potentate POH-t(uh)n-tayt ['poʊ-tṇ-teɪt]

pothecary PAHTH-uh-keh-ree ['pɑθ-ə-kɛ-ri] scans to
_____-uh-kree [___-ə-kri] @ *R&J* V, 3, 289

pother PAH<u>TH</u>-er ['pɑð-ɚ]

Potpan PAHT-paan ['pɑt-pæn]

pottle PAH-t(uh)l ['pɑ-tḷ]

poulter POHL-ter ['poʊl-tɚ]

poultice POHL-tis ['poʊl-tɪs]

Poultney POHLT-nee ['poʊlt-ni]

pouncet POWN-sit ['paʊn-sɪt]

pox PAHKS [pɑks]

Poysam POY-suhm ['pɔɪ-səm]

practic PRAAK-tik ['præk-tɪk]

practisants PRAAK-ti-suhnts ['præk-tɪ-sənts]

praemunire PREE-myōō-NEYE-ree [pri-mju-'naɪ-ri]

praetor PREE-ter ['pri-tɚ]

Prague PRAHG [prɑg]

prank PRAANGK [præŋk]

Prat PRAAT [præt]

prate PRAYT [preɪt]

prater PRAY-ter ['preɪ-tɚ]

EE i be/ I ɪ bit/ EH ɛ bet/ AA æ bat/ ŌŌ u boot / ŌŌ ʊ book/ AW ɔ bought/ AH ɑ father/ ER ɝ bird/
UH ʌ cup/ AY eɪ bay/ EYE aɪ bite/ OY ɔɪ boy/ OH oʊ boat/ OW aʊ how/ YŌŌ ɪu duke/ EAR ɪɚ
beer/ AIR ɛɚ bear/ ŌŌR ʊɚ tour/ AWR ɔɚ bore/ AHR ɑɚ bar/ NG ŋ king/ SH ʃ ship/ ZH ʒ vision/
TH θ thirty/ <u>TH</u> ð then/ CH tʃ child/ J dʒ just/ For complete list, see Key to Pronunciation p. 2.

prattle PRAA-t(uh)l ['præ-tl̩]

prayer (one who offers a petition to heaven) PRAIR [prɛɚ]
scans to **PRAY**-er ['preɪ-ɚ] e.g. @ *R&J* I, 5, 105

prayer (a petition to heaven) PRAIR [prɛɚ] scans to **PRAY**-er
['preɪ-ɚ] e.g. @ *TITUS* III, 1, 75

preambulate pree-AAM-byo͞o-layt [pri-'æm-bju-leɪt]

precedence scans to pri-SEE-duhns [prɪ-'si-dəns]

precedent (adj) pri-SEE-duhnt [prɪ-'si-dənt]

precedent (n) PREHS-i-duhnt ['prɛs-ɪ-dənt]

precept PREE-sehpt ['pri-sɛpt]

preceptial pree-SEHP-chuhl [pri-'sɛp-tʃəl]

precinct scans to pree-SINGKT [pri-'sɪŋkt]

precipitance pri-SIP-i-tuhns [prɪ-'sɪp-ɪ-təns]

precisian pri-SIZH-uhn [prɪ-'sɪʒ-ən]

preeminence pree-EHM-i-nuhns [pri-'ɛm-ɪ-nəns]

preferment pri-FER-muhnt [prɪ-'fɝ-mənt]

preformed scans to pree-FAWRM-id [pri-'fɔɚm-ɪd]

prejudicates pri-JO͞O-di-kayts [prɪ-'dʒu-dɪ-keɪts]

prelate PREHL-it ['prɛl-ɪt]

premised scans to pri-MEYEZ-id [prɪ-'maɪz-ɪd]

prenominate pree-NAHM-i-nit [pri-'nɑm-ɪ-nɪt] scans to __-
NAHM-nit [__-'nɑm-nɪt] @ *HAM* II, 1, 43

prentice PREHN-tis ['prɛn-tɪs]

prenzie PREHN-zee ['prɛn-zi]

prerogative pri-RAHG-uh-tiv [prɪ-'rɑg-ə-tɪv]

presage (n) PREH-sij ['prɛ-sɪʤ] scans to pri-SAYJ [prɪ-'seɪʤ] @ *RII* II, 2, 142

presage (v) pri-SAYJ [prɪ-'seɪʤ]

prescience PREH-shee-uhns ['prɛ-ʃi-əns] or PREE-___-___ ['pri-___-___] scans to pri-SHEE-___ ['prɪ-'ʃi-___] @ *T&C* I, 3, 199

prescript PREE-skript ['pri-skrɪpt]

presentment pri-ZEHNT-muhnt [prɪ-'zɛnt-mənt]

prest PREHST [prɛst]

presurmise pree-ser-MEYEZ [pri-sɚ-'maɪz]

pretense PREE-tehns ['pri-tɛns] scans to pri-TEHNS [prɪ-'tɛns] e.g. @ *MAC* II, 3, 127

Priam PREYE-uhm ['praɪ-əm]
　　Priam *(T&C)* possibly scans to PREYEM [praɪm] @ Pro, 15; also called "Priamus" PREYE-uhm-uhs ['praɪ-əm-əs]

Priapus preye-AY-puhs [praɪ-'eɪ-pəs]

pricket PRIK-it ['prɪk-ɪt]

primer PREYEM-er ['praɪm-ɚ]

primero pri-MEH-roh [prɪ-'mɛ-roʊ]

primest PREYEM-ist ['praɪm-ɪst]

primogenity PREYE-moh-JEHN-i-tee [praɪ-moʊ-'ʤɛn-ɪ-ti]

primy PREYE-mee ['praɪ-mi]

princox PRIN-kahks ['prɪn-kɑks] or PRING -___ ['prɪŋ-___]

prioress PREYE-uh-ris ['praɪ-ə-rɪs]

EE i be/ I ɪ bit/ EH ɛ bet/ AA æ bat/ OO u boot / OO ʊ book/ AW ɔ bought/ AH ɑ father/ ER ɝ bird/ UH ʌ cup/ AY eɪ bay/ EYE aɪ bite/ OY ɔɪ boy/ OH oʊ boat/ OW aʊ how/ YOO ɪu duke/ EAR ɪə beer/ AIR ɛə bear/ OOR ʊɚ tour/ AWR ɔɚ bore/ AHR ɑɚ bar/ NG ŋ king/ SH ʃ ship/ ZH ʒ vision/ TH θ thirty/ TH ð then/ CH ʧ child/ J ʤ just/ For complete list, see Key to Pronunciation p. 2.

priory PREYE-uh-ree ['praɪ-ə-ri] scans to PREYE-ree ['praɪ-ri] @ *CE* V, 1, 37

Priscian PRISH-ee-uhn ['prɪʃ-i-ən]

prithee PRI-<u>thee</u> ['prɪ-ði]

prived scans to PREYE-vid ['praɪ-vɪd]

privilege PRIV-lij ['prɪv-lɪdʒ] scans to PRIV-uh-lij ['prɪv-ə-lɪdʒ] e.g. @ *MID* I, 1, 41

privily PRIV-i-lee ['prɪv-ɪ-li]

privity PRIV-i-tee ['prɪv-ɪ-ti]

privy PRIV-ee ['prɪv-i]

probal PROH-b(uh)l ['proʊ-bl̩]

proceed pruh-SEED [prə-'sid] scans to PROH-seed ['proʊ-sid] e.g. @ *2HVI* I, 3, 147

proconsul proh-KAHN-s(uh)l [proʊ-'kɑn-sl̩]

procreant PROH-kree-uhnt ['proʊ-kri-ənt]

Procrus PROH-kris ['proʊ-krɪs]

Proculeius *(A&C)* PROH-kyo͞o-LEE-uhs [proʊ-kju-'li-əs]

procurator PRAHK-yuh-ray-ter ['prɑk-jə-reɪ-tɚ]

prodigal PRAHD-i-guhl ['prɑd-ɪ-gəl] scans to PRAHD-guhl ['prɑd-gəl] @ *MVEN* II, 5, 15

prodigious pruh-DIJ-uhs [prə-'dɪdʒ-əs] or proh-___-___ [proʊ-___-___]

proditor PRAH-di-ter ['prɑ-dɪ-tɚ]

proface proh-FAYS [proʊ-'feɪs]

profanation PRAH-fuh-NAY-shuhn [prɑ-fə-'neɪ-ʃən] scans to ___-___-___-shee-uhn [___-___-___-ʃi-ən] @ *MM* II, 2, 128

proffer PRAHF-er ['prɑf-ɚ]

profound pruh-FOWND [prə-'faʊnd] scans to
PROH-fownd ['proʊ-faʊnd] e.g. @ *HAM* IV, 1, 1

progenitors proh-JEHN-i-terz [proʊ-'ʤɛn-ɪ-tɚz]

progeny PRAHJ-i-nee ['praʤ-ɪ-ni]

Progne PRAHG-nee ['prag-ni]

prognostication prahg-NAH-sti-KAY-shuhn
[prag-nɑ-stɪ-'keɪ-ʃən]

prolixious proh-LIK-shuhs [proʊ-'lɪk-ʃəs]

prolixity proh-LIK-si-tee [proʊ-'lɪk-sɪ-ti]

prologue / Prologue PROH-lahg ['proʊ-lag]

Promethean always scans to proh-MEE-thyuhn
[proʊ-'mi-θjən] or pruh-___-___ [prə-___-___]

Prometheus scans to proh-MEE-thyuhs [proʊ-'mi-θjəs] or
pruh-___-___ [prə-___-___]

prompture PRAHMP-cher ['pramp-ʧɚ]

promulgate scans to pruh-MOOL-gayt [prə-'mʊl-geɪt]

propagate PRAH-puh-gayt ['pra-pə-geɪt]

propend proh-PEHND [proʊ-'pɛnd]

propension proh-PEHN-shuhn [proʊ-'pɛn-ʃən]

prophecy (n) PRAHF-i-see ['praf-ɪ-si]

prophesier PRAHF-i-seye-er ['praf-ɪ-saɪ-ɚ]

prophesy (v) PRAHF-i-seye ['praf-ɪ-saɪ]

prophetess PRAHF-i-tis ['praf-ɪ-tɪs]

propinquity proh-PING-kwi-tee [proʊ-'pɪŋ-kwɪ-ti]

EE i be/ I ɪ bit/ EH ɛ bet/ AA æ bat/ OO u boot / OO ʊ book/ AW ɔ bought/ AH ɑ father/ ER ɝ bird/
UH ʌ cup/ AY eɪ bay/ EYE aɪ bite/ OY ɔɪ boy/ OH oʊ boat/ OW aʊ how/ YOO ɪu duke/ EAR ɪɚ
beer/ AIR ɛɚ bear/ OOR ʊɚ tour/ AWR ɔɚ bore/ AHR ɑɚ bar/ NG ŋ king/ SH ʃ ship/ ZH ʒ vision/
TH θ thirty/ TH ð then/ CH ʧ child/ J ʤ just/ For complete list, see Key to Pronunciation p. 2.

Propontic pruh-**PAHN**-tik [prə-'pɑn-tɪk]

propugnation PROH-puhg-**NAY**-shuhn [proʊ-pəg-'neɪ-ʃən]

prorogue pruh-**ROHG** [prə-'roʊg] or proh-___ [proʊ-___]

proselytes PRAH-suh-leyets ['prɑ-sə-laɪts]

Proserpina proh-**SER**-pi-nuh [proʊ-'sɝ-pɪ-nə]

Proserpine PRAH-ser-peyen ['prɑ-sɚ-paɪn]

Prospero *(TEMP)* PRAHS-puh-roh ['prɑs-pə-roʊ] scans to
PRAHS-proh ['prɑs-proʊ] e.g. @ I, 2, 20 also called
"Prosper" PRAHS-per ['prɑs-pɚ] @ II, 2, 2

protest (n) always scans to proh-**TEHST** [proʊ-'tɛst]

Proteus PROH-tee-uhs ['proʊ-ti-əs] scans to **PROH**-tyuhs
['proʊ-tjəs]
Proteus *(2GEN)* scans e.g. @ I, 1, 56

protractive proh-**TRAAK**-tiv [proʊ-'træk-tɪv]

provand PRAHV-uhnd ['prɑv-ənd]

provender PRAHV-uhn-der ['prɑv-ən-dɚ]

proverbed PRAH-verbd ['prɑ-vɚbd]

providently PRAHV-i-duhnt-lee ['prɑv-ɪ-dənt-li]

Provincial proh-**VIN**-shuhl [proʊ-'vɪn-ʃəl]

proviso pruh-**VEYE**-zoh [prə-'vaɪ-zoʊ]

Provost *(MM)* PROH-vohst ['proʊ-voʊst]

prowess PROW-is ['praʊ-ɪs] scans to PROWS [praʊs]
@ *MAC* V, 8, 41

Prudence PR$\overline{OO}$-d(uh)ns ['pru-dn̩s]

prun'st PR$\overline{OO}$NST [prunst]

Psalmist SAHM-ist ['sɑm-ɪst]

psalteries SAWL-tuh-reez ['sɔl-tə-riz]

Ptolemy TAHL-uh-mee ['tɑl-ə-mi] possibly scans to
  TAHL-mee ['tɑl-mi] @ *A&C* I, 4, 6; in plural scans to
  TAHL-meez ['tɑl-miz] @ *A&C* III, 12, 18

Publicola puhb-LIK-uh-luh [pəb-'lɪk-ə-lə]

Publius PUHB-lee-uhs ['pʌb-li-əs] scans to PUHB-lyuhs
    ['pʌb-ljəs]
  Publius *(JC)*
  Publius *(TITUS)* scans @ IV, 3, 25

Puck (Robin Goodfellow) *(MID)* PUHK [pʌk] RAH-bin
  GŌŌD-feh-loh ['rɑ-bɪn] ['gʊd-fɛ-lou]

pudder PUHD-er ['pʌd-ɚ]

pudency PYŌŌ-d(uh)n-see ['pju-dn̩-si]

pugging PUHG-ing ['pʌg-ɪŋ]

puisny PYŌŌ-nee ['pju-ni]

puissance PYŌŌ-i-suhns ['pju-ɪ-səns] scans to PYŌŌ-suhns
    ['pju-səns] or PWEE-suhns ['pwi-səns] e.g. @ *2HIV* II, 3, 52

puissant always scans to PYŌŌ-suhnt ['pju-sənt] or
  PWEE-suhnt ['pwi-sənt]

puling PYŌŌL-ing ['pjul-ɪŋ]

pulsidge PUHL-sij ['pʌl-sɪʤ]

pumpion PUHMP-yuhn ['pʌmp-jən]

punto PUHN-toh ['pʌn-tou] or POON-___ ['pʊn-___]

punto reverso PUHN-toh or POON-___ ri-VER-soh
    ['pʌn-tou] or ['pʊn-___] [rɪ-'vɝ-sou]

pur PER [pɝ]

EE i be/ I ɪ bit/ EH ɛ bet/ AA æ bat/ ŌŌ u boot / ŌŌ ʊ book/ AW ɔ bought/ AH ɑ father/ ER ɝ bird/
UH ʌ cup/ AY eɪ bay/ EYE aɪ bite/ OY ɔɪ boy/ OH ou boat/ OW aʊ how/ YŌŌ ɪu duke/ EAR ɪɚ
beer/ AIR ɛɚ bear/ ŌŌR ʊɚ tour/ AWR ɔɚ bore/ AHR ɑɚ bar/ NG ŋ king/ SH ʃ ship/ ZH ʒ vision/
TH θ thirty/ TH ð then/ CH ʧ child/ J ʤ just/ For complete list, see Key to Pronunciation p. 2.

201

purblind PER-bleyend ['pɝ-blaɪnd]

purgation per-GAY-shuhn [pɚ-'geɪ-ʃən]

purgative scans to PERG-tiv ['pɝg-tɪv]

purlieus PERL-yōōz ['pɝl-juz]

purport per-PAWRT [pɚ-'pɔɚt]

purpose (v) PER-puhs ['pɝ-pəs]

pursents per-SEHNTS [pɚ-'sɛnts]

pursuivant PER-swi-vuhnt ['pɝ-swɪ-vənt]

pursy PER-see ['pɝ-si]

purveyor scans to PER-vay-er ['pɝ-veɪ-ɚ]

pusillanimity PYŌŌ-suh-luh-NIM-i-tee [pju-sə-lə-'nɪm-ɪ-ti]

pussel PUH-suhl ['pʌ-səl]

puttock PUHT-uhk ['pʌt-ək]

Pygmalion's pig-MAYL-yuhnz [pɪg-'meɪl-jənz]

pyramides pi-RAAM-i-deez [pɪ-'ræm-ɪ-diz]

pyramis PI-ruh-mis ['pɪ-rə-mɪs]

Pyramus PI-ruh-muhs ['pɪ-rə-məs]

Pyrenean PI-ruh-NEE-uhn [pɪ-rə-'ni-ən]

Pyrrhus PI-ruhs ['pɪ-rəs]

Pythagoras pi-THAAG-uh-ruhs [pɪ-'θæg-ə-rəs]

quaff KWAHF [kwɑf]

quagmire KWAAG-meyer ['kwæg-maɪɚ]

qualm KWAHM [kwɑm]

qualmish KWAHM-ish ['kwɑm-ɪʃ]

quarrelous scans to **KWAWR**-luhs ['kwɔɚ-ləs]

quat KWAHT [kwɑt]

quatch KWAHCH [kwɑtʃ]

quean KWEEN [kwin]

queasy KWEE-zee ['kwi-zi]

Queen KWEEN [kwin]
   Queen *(CYM)*
   Queen *(RII)*

quell KWEHL [kwɛl]

quern KWERN [kwɝn]

questant KWEHS-tuhnt ['kwɛs-tənt]

questrists KWEHS-trists ['kwɛs-trɪsts]

Queubus KY$\overline{\text{OO}}$-buhs ['kju-bəs]

Quickly KWIK-lee ['kwɪk-li]
   Quickly, Mistress / Hostess *(1HIV, 2HIV, HV, MW)*

quiddities KWID-i-teez ['kwɪd-ɪ-tiz]

quietus kweye-EE-tuhs [kwaɪ-'i-təs]

quillets KWIL-its ['kwɪl-ɪts]

quillities KWIL-i-teez ['kwɪl-ɪ-tiz]

Quinapalus kwin-AAP-uh-luhs [kwɪn-'æp-ə-ləs]

Quince, Peter / Prologue *(MID)* KWINS [kwɪns]

quintain KWIN-tuhn ['kwɪn-tən]

quintessence kwin-TEHS-uhns [kwɪn-'tɛs-əns] scans to
   KWIN-tuh-suhns ['kwɪn-tə-səns] @ *AYL* III, 2, 133

EE i be/ I ɪ bit/ EH ɛ bet/ AA æ bat/ $\overline{\text{OO}}$ u boot / $\breve{\text{OO}}$ ʊ book/ AW ɔ bought/ AH ɑ father/ ER ɝ bird/
UH ʌ cup/ AY eɪ bay/ EYE aɪ bite/ OY ɔɪ boy/ OH oʊ boat/ OW aʊ how/ Y$\overline{\text{OO}}$ ɪu duke/ EAR ɪɚ
beer/ AIR ɛɚ bear/ $\overline{\text{OO}}$R ʊɚ tour/ AWR ɔɚ bore/ AHR ɑɚ bar/ NG ŋ king/ SH ʃ ship/ ZH ʒ vision/
TH θ thirty/ <u>TH</u> ð then/ CH tʃ child/ J ʤ just/ For complete list, see Key to Pronunciation p. 2.

Quintus KWIN-tuhs ['kwɪn-təs]
  Quintus *(TITUS)*

quire KWEYER [kwaɪɚ]

quittance KWIT-uhns ['kwɪt-əns]

quoif KWOYF [kwɔɪf]

quoit KWOYT [kwɔɪt]

quondam KWAHN-duhm ['kwɑn-dəm] or ___-daam
  [___-dæm]

quotidian kwoh-TID-ee-uhn [kwoʊ-'tɪd-i-ən]

rabblement RAA-b(uh)l-muhnt ['ræ-bl̩-mənt]

Rafe RAYF [reɪf]

Ragozine RAAG-uh-zeen ['ræg-ə-zin]

raiment RAY-muhnt ['reɪ-mənt]

Rainold Lord Cobham REH-nuhld KAHB-uhm ['rɛ-nəld]
  ['kɑb-əm]

Rambures raam-BOORZ [ræm-'bʊɚz] scans to
  RAAM-boorz ['ræm-bʊɚz] @ *HV* III, 5, 43 with
  "Jacques" two syllables

rampallian raam-PAAL-yuhn [ræm-'pæl-jən]

rampired RAAM-peyerd ['ræm-paɪɚd]

Ramston, Sir John scans to raams-TUHN [ræms-'tʌn]

rancor RAANG-ker ['ræŋ-kɚ]

randon RAAN-duhn ['ræn-dən]

rapier RAYP-yer ['reɪp-jɚ]

Rapine RAYP-eyen ['reɪp-aɪn] or ___-in [___-ɪn] or
  RAAP-eyen ['ræp-aɪn] or ___-in [___-ɪn]

rase RAYZ [reɪz]

204

Ratcliffe, Sir Richard *(RIII)* RAAT-klif ['ræt-klɪf]

ratsbane RAATS-bayn ['ræts-beɪn]

raught RAWT [rɔt]

ravel RAAV-uhl ['ræv-əl]

raven (n) (a black bird) RAYV-uhn ['reɪv-ən]

raven (v) (to devour greedily) RAAV-uhn ['ræv-ən]

Ravenspurgh RAA-vuhn-sperg ['ræ-vən-spɚg] scans to RAAVN-sperg ['rævn-spɚg] or RAY-vuhn-sperg ['reɪ-vən-spɚg] scans to RAYVN-___ ['reɪvn-___] e.g. @ *3HVI* IV, 7, 8

ravin (adj) (ravenous) RAAV-uhn ['ræv-ən]

raze (v) RAYZ [reɪz]

razes (n) RAYZ-iz ['reɪz-ɪz]

razure RAY-zher ['reɪ-ʒɚ]

Readins REHD-inz ['rɛd-ɪnz]

rearward REAR-werd ['rɪɚ-wɚd]

reave REEV [riv]

rebato ri-BAH-toh [rɪ-'bɑ-toʊ]

recant ri-KAANT [rɪ-'kænt]

recantation REE-kaan-TAY-shuhn [ri-kæn-'teɪ-ʃən]

recanter ri-KAANT-er [rɪ-'kænt-ɚ]

receptacle always scans to REE-sehp-tuh-k(uh)l ['ri-sɛp-tə-kl̩]

rechate ri-CHAYT [rɪ-'tʃeɪt]

EE i be/ I ɪ bit/ EH ɛ bet/ AA æ bat/ OO u boot / OO ʊ book/ AW ɔ bought/ AH ɑ father/ ER ɝ bird/ UH ʌ cup/ AY eɪ bay/ EYE aɪ bite/ OY ɔɪ boy/ OH oʊ boat/ OW aʊ how/ YOO ɪu duke/ EAR ɪɚ beer/ AIR ɛɚ bear/ OOR ʊɚ tour/ AWR ɔɚ bore/ AHR ɑɚ bar/ NG ŋ king/ SH ʃ ship/ ZH ʒ vision/ TH θ thirty/ TH ð then/ CH tʃ child/ J dʒ just/ For complete list, see Key to Pronunciation p. 2.

205

recking REHK-ing ['rɛk-ɪŋ]

recognizance ri-KAHG-ni-zuhns [rɪ-'kɑg-nɪ-zəns]

recomforture ri-KUHM-fuh-cher [rɪ-'kʌm-fə-tʃɚ]

recompense REHK-uhm-pehns ['rɛk-əm-pɛns]

recompt ri-KOWNT [rɪ-'kɑunt] (archaic form of "recount" stems from Latin "computare," to count)

record (n) REH-kerd ['rɛ-kɚd] scans to ruh-KAWRD [rə-'kɔɚd] e.g. @ *RIII* IV, 4, 28

recordation REH-kawr-DAY-shuhn [rɛ-kɔɚ-'deɪ-ʃən]

recourse REE-kawrs ['ri-kɔɚs] scans to ri-KAWRS [rɪ-'kɔɚs] e.g. @ *T&C* V, 3, 55

recreant REHK-ree-uhnt ['rɛk-ri-ənt] scans to REHK-ruhnt ['rɛk-rənt] e.g. @ *KJ* III, 1, 129

recreate (to refresh oneself by diversion) REH-kree-ayt ['rɛ-kri-eɪt]

recure ree-KYOOR [ri-'kjuɚ] or ri-___ [rɪ-'___]

rede REED [rid]

redound ri-DOWND [rɪ-'dɑund]

redress (n) REE-drehs ['ri-drɛs] scans to ri-DREHS [rɪ-'drɛs] e.g. @ *RII* II, 3, 171

redress (v) ri-DREHS [rɪ-'drɛs]

reechy REE-chee ['ri-tʃi]

reeking REEK-ing ['rik-ɪŋ]

reeky REEK-ee ['rik-i]

refelled ri-FEHLD [rɪ-'fɛld]

reflex (n) or (v) ri-FLEHKS [rɪ-'flɛks]

reformation REH-fer-**MAY**-shuhn [rɛ-fɚ-'meɪ-ʃən] scans to
___-__-___-shee-uhn [__-__-__-ʃi-ən] @ *LLL* V, 2, 859

refractory ri-**FRAAK**-tuh-ree [rɪ-'fræk-tə-ri]

reft REHFT [rɛft]

refuge (v) REH-fyōoj ['rɛ-fjuʤ] or possibly scans to
reh-**FYŌOJ** [rɛ-'fjuʤ] @ *RII* V, 5, 26

Regan *(LEAR)* REE-guhn ['ri-gən]

regent / Regent REE-juhnt ['ri-ʤənt]

region REE-juhn ['ri-ʤən] scans to REE-jee-uhn ['ri-ʤi-ən]
e.g. @ *JC* V, 1, 3

regreet (n) ri-**GREET** [rɪ-'grit]

reguerdon ree-**GER**-d(uh)n [ri-'gɝ-dṇ]

Reignier RAYN-yer ['reɪn-jɚ]
Reignier, Duke of Anjou *(1HVI)* AAN-jōo ['æn-ʤu] scans
to aan-**JŌO** [æn-'ʤu] e.g. @ V, 3, 95

rejoindure ri-**JOYN**-dyōor [rɪ-'ʤɔɪn-djuɚ]

rejourn ree-**JERN** [ri-'ʤɝn]

relume ri-**LŌOM** [rɪ-'lum]

remediate ri-**MEE**-dee-it [rɪ-'mi-di-ɪt] or scans to
___-**MEE**-dyuht [__-'mi-djət]

remembrancer ri-**MEHM**-bruhns-er [rɪ-'mɛm-brəns-ɚ]

remissness ri-**MIS**-nis [rɪ-'mɪs-nɪs]

remuneration ri-**MYŌO**-nuh-**RAY**-shuhn [rɪ-mju-nə-'reɪ-ʃən]

rend REHND [rɛnd]

EE i be/ I ɪ bit/ EH ɛ bet/ AA æ bat/ ŌO u boot / ŌO ʊ book/ AW ɔ bought/ AH ɑ father/ ER ɝ bird/
UH ʌ cup/ AY eɪ bay/ EYE aɪ bite/ OY ɔɪ boy/ OH oʊ boat/ OW aʊ how/ YŌO ɪu duke/ EAR ɪɚ
beer/ AIR ɛɚ bear/ ŌOR ʊɚ tour/ AWR ɔɚ bore/ AHR ɑɚ bar/ NG ŋ king/ SH ʃ ship/ ZH ʒ vision/
TH θ thirty/ TH ð then/ CH tʃ child/ J ʤ just/ For complete list, see Key to Pronunciation p. 2.

renegado REH-ni-GAY-doh [rɛ-nɪ-'geɪ-doʊ] or
___-___-GAH-___ [___-___-'gɑ-___]

renege ri-NEHG [rɪ-'nɛg] or __-NIG [__-'nɪg]

repast ri-PAAST [rɪ-'pæst]

repasture ri-PAAS-cher [rɪ-'pæs-tʃɚ]

repine ri-PEYEN [rɪ-'paɪn]

reprehend reh-pri-HEHND [rɛ-prɪ-'hɛnd]

reprobate REH-pruh-bayt ['rɛ-prə-beɪt]

repugn ri-PYO͞ON [rɪ-'pjun]

repugnancy ri-PUHG-nuhn-see [rɪ-'pʌg-nən-si]

repulse ri-PUHLS [rɪ-'pʌls]

repured ri-PYOͦO-rid [rɪ-'pjʊ-rɪd]

repute ri-PYO͞OT [rɪ-'pjut]

requit ri-KWIT [rɪ-'kwɪt]

requital ri-KWEYE-t(uh)l [rɪ-'kwaɪ-tl̩]

requite ri-KWEYET [rɪ-'kwaɪt] scans to REE-kweyet
['ri-kwaɪt] @ *TIMON* IV, 3, 518

reremice REAR-meyes ['rɪɚ-maɪs]

resorters ri-ZAWR-terz [rɪ-'zɔɚ-tɚz]

respite (n) or (v) REHS-pit ['rɛs-pɪt]

restem ree-STEHM [ri-'stɛm]

restorative ri-STAW-ruh-tiv [rɪ-'stɔ-rə-tɪv]

retires ri-TEYERZ [rɪ-'taɪɚz]

revel REHV-uhl ['rɛv-əl]

reveller REHV-uh-ler ['rɛv-ə-lɚ]

208

revenue REHV-uh-nyōō ['rɛv-ə-nɪu] scans to ri-VEHN-yōō [rɪ-'vɛn-ju] e.g. @ *A&C* III, 6, 30

reverb ri-VERB [rɪ-'vɝb]

reverberate (adj) scans to ri-VER-brit [rɪ-'vɝ-brɪt]

reversion ri-VER-zhuhn [rɪ-'vɝ-ʒən]

Reynaldo *(HAM)* ri-NAHL-doh [rɪ-'nɑl-doʊ] or __-NAAL-__ [__-'næl-__]

Rheims REEMZ [rimz]

Rhenish REHN-ish ['rɛn-ɪʃ]

Rhesus REE-suhs ['ri-səs]

rheum RŌŌM [rum]

rheumatic rōō-MAAT-ik [ru-'mæt-ɪk] scans to RŌŌ-muh-tik ['ru-mə-tɪk] @ *MID* II, 1, 105

rheumy RŌŌM-ee ['rum-i]

Rhodes ROHDZ [roʊdz]

Rhodope ROHD-uh-pee ['roʊd-ə-pi]

rhubarb RŌŌ-bahrb ['ru-bɑɚb]

Rialto ree-AAL-toh [ri-'æl-toʊ]

ribald RI-buhld ['rɪ-bəld]

riband / ribband RIB-uhnd ['rɪb-ənd]

ribaudred possibly ri-BAW-drid [rɪ-'bɔ-drɪd] if "death is" contracts to one syllable. Many editors emend with "ribald."

Rice ap Thomas REYES aap TAH-muhs [raɪs] [æp] ['tɑ-məs]

Richard RICH-erd ['rɪtʃ-ɚd]
   Richard II *(RII)*
   Richard, afterward Duke of Gloucester *(2HVI, 3HVI)*
   Richard, Duke of Gloucester, afterwards King Richard III
      (RIII)
   Richard, Duke of York *(RIII)*

riggish RIG-ish ['rɪg-ɪʃ]

rigol RI-guhl ['rɪ-gəl]

Rinaldo *(AW)* ri-NAHL-doh [rɪ-'nɑl-doʊ] or ___-NAAL-___
   [___-'næl-___]

rivage RIV-ij ['rɪv-ɪdʒ]

rivality reye-VAAL-i-tee [raɪ-'væl-ɪ-ti]

rivalled REYE-vuhld ['raɪ-vəld]

rive REYEV [raɪv]

rivelled RI-vuhld ['rɪ-vəld]

rivo (an exclamation) possibly REE-voh ['ri-voʊ]

roan ROHN [roʊn]

Robin *(MW)* RAH-bin ['rɑ-bɪn]

robustious roh-BUHS-chuhs [roʊ-'bʌs-tʃəs]

Roderigo RAH-duh-REE-goh [rɑ-də-'ri-goʊ] scans to
      rah-DREE-___ [rɑ-'dri-___]
   Roderigo *(OTH)* scans @ I, 1, 182

roe ROH [roʊ]

Rogero roh-JEH-roh [roʊ-'dʒɛ-roʊ]

rogue ROHG [roʊg]

roisting ROYST-ing ['rɔɪst-ɪŋ]

romage RUHM-ij ['rʌm-ɪdʒ]

Rome ROHM [roʊm] except RŌOM [rum] @ *KJ* III, 1, 180 and *JC* I, 2, 156, and possibly *JC* III, 1, 288, in keeping with Elizabethan pun of contempt

Romeo *(R&J)* ROH-mee-oh ['roʊ-mi-oʊ] scans to ROHM-yoh ['roʊm-joʊ] e.g. @ I, 1, 114

Romish ROH-mish ['roʊ-mɪʃ]

ronyon RUHN-yuhn ['rʌn-jən]

rood RŌOD [rud]

rooky RŎOK-ee ['rʊk-i]

ropery ROHP-uh-ree ['roʊp-ə-ri]

Rosalind / Rosalinde *(AYL)* RAHZ-uh-lind ['rɑz-ə-lɪnd] except RAHZ-uh-leyend ['rɑz-ə-laɪnd] to accommodate rhymes @ III, 2, 83 and ff

Rosalinda RAHZ-uh-LIN-duh [rɑz-ə-'lɪn-də]

Rosaline RAH-zuh-leyen ['rɑ-zə-laɪn]
Rosaline *(LLL)*

Roscius RAHSH-ee-uhs ['rɑʃ-i-əs] scans to RAHSH-yuhs ['rɑʃ-jəs] @ *3HVI* V, 6, 10

rosemary ROHZ-muh-ree ['roʊz-mə-ri] or ___-meh-___ [___-mɛ-___]

Rosencrantz *(HAM)* ROH-zuhn-KRAANTS ['roʊ-zən-krænts] or ___-z(uh)n-___ [___-zn̩-___]

Ross RAWS [rɔs] or RAHS [rɑs]
Ross *(MAC)*
Ross, Lord *(RII)*

Rossillion roh-SIL-yuhn [roʊ-'sɪl-jən] possibly scans to ROH-sil-___ ['roʊ-sɪl-___] @ *AW* V, 1, 29

EE i be/ I ɪ bit/ EH ɛ bet/ AA æ bat/ ŌO u boot / ŎO ʊ book/ AW ɔ bought/ AH ɑ father/ ER ɝ bird/ UH ʌ cup/ AY eɪ bay/ EYE aɪ bite/ OY ɔɪ boy/ OH oʊ boat/ OW aʊ how/ YŌO ɪu duke/ EAR ɪɚ beer/ AIR ɛɚ bear/ ŌOR ʊɚ tour/ AWR ɔɚ bore/ AHR ɑɚ bar/ NG ŋ king/ SH ʃ ship/ ZH ʒ vision/ TH θ thirty/ T̲H̲ ð then/ CH tʃ child/ J ʤ just/ For complete list, see Key to Pronunciation p. 2.

Rossillion, Bertram, Count of *(AW)* **BER**-truhm
['bɝ-trəm]
Rossillion, Countess of *(AW)*

Rotherham, Thomas, Archbishop of York *(RIII)*
RAHTH-uh-ruhm ['rað-ə-rəm]

Rouen **ROH**-uhn ['roʊ-ən] scans to **ROHN** [roʊn]
e.g. @ *1HVI* III, 2, 17

Rouge-mount **ROOZH**-mownt ['ruʒ-moʊnt]

roundel **ROWN**-d(uh)l ['raʊn-dl̩]

roundure **ROWN**-jer ['raʊn-ʤɚ]

rouse ROWZ [raʊz]

Roussi roo-**SEE** [ru-'si]

rout ROWT [raʊt]

rove ROHV [roʊv]

rowel ROWL [raʊl] or scans to **ROW**-uhl ['raʊ-əl]

rowel-head **ROW**-uhl-hehd ['raʊ-əl-hɛd]

Rowland **ROH**-luhnd ['roʊ-lənd]
Rowland de Boys duh-**BOYZ** [də-'bɔɪz] or __-**BOYS**
[__-'bɔɪs]

roynish **ROYN**-ish ['rɔɪn-ɪʃ]

ruddock **RUHD**-uhk ['rʌd-ək]

rudesby **ROODZ**-bee ['rudz-bi]

rue ROO [ru]

Rugby *(MW)* **RUHG**-bee ['rʌg-bi]

ruin **ROO**-in ['ru-ɪn]

ruinate **ROO**-i-nayt ['ru-ɪ-neɪt]

ruminate **ROO**-muh-nayt ['ru-mə-neɪt]

Rumor *(2HIV)* ROO-mer ['ru-mɚ]

runagate RUHN-uh-gayt ['rʌn-ə-geɪt] scans to RUHN-gayt ['rʌn-geɪt] @ *CYM* I, 6, 137

runnion RUHN-yuhn ['rʌn-jən]

Russia RUHSH-uh ['rʌʃ-ə] scans to RUHSH-ee-uh ['rʌʃ-i-ə] @ *MM* II, 1, 127

rustically RUHS-ti-kuh-lee ['rʌs-tɪ-kə-li]

ruth ROOTH [ruθ]

ruthful ROOTH-fuhl ['ruθ-fəl]

Rutland RUHT-luhnd ['rʌt-lənd]

ruttish RUHT-ish ['rʌt-ɪʃ]

Rycas REYE-kuhs ['raɪ-kəs]

s. (abbreviation for "shilling") SHIL-ing ['ʃɪl-ɪŋ]

Saba SAH-buh ['sɑ-bə] or SAY-___ ['seɪ-__]

Sackerson SAAK-er-suhn ['sæk-ɚ-sən]

sacring SAYK-ring ['seɪk-rɪŋ]

saffron SAAF-ruhn ['sæf-rən]

Sagittary SAAJ-i-teh-ree ['sædʒ-ɪ-tɛ-ri] scans to SAAJ-i-tree ['sædʒ-ɪ-tri] @ *OTH* I, 1, 157

sain SAYN [seɪn]

Saint Albans SAYNT AWL-buhnz [seɪnt] ['ɔl-bənz]

Saint Denis SAYNT DEHN-is [seɪnt] ['dɛn-ɪs]

Saint Jaques SAYNT JAY-kweez [seɪnt] ['dʒeɪ-kwiz]

Sala SAY-luh ['seɪ-lə] or SAA-___ ['sæ-__]

EE i be/ I ɪ bit/ EH ɛ bet/ AA æ bat/ OO u boot/ OO ʊ book/ AW ɔ bought/ AH ɑ father/ ER ɝ bird/ UH ʌ cup/ AY eɪ bay/ EYE aɪ bite/ OY ɔɪ boy/ OH oʊ boat/ OW aʊ how/ YOO ɪu duke/ EAR ɪɚ beer/ AIR ɛɚ bear/ OOR ʊɚ tour/ AWR ɔɚ bore/ AHR ɑɚ bar/ NG ŋ king/ SH ʃ ship/ ZH ʒ vision/ TH θ thirty/ TH ð then/ CH tʃ child/ J dʒ just/ For complete list, see Key to Pronunciation p. 2.

Salerio *(MVEN)* always scans to suh-**LEH**-ryoh [sə-'lɛ-rjoʊ] or ___-**LI**-___ [___-'lɪ-___]

Salic **SAY**-lik ['seɪ-lɪk] or **SAA**-___ ['sæ-___]

Salisbury **SAWLZ**-buh-ree ['sɔlz-bə-ri] scans to **SAWLZ**-bree ['sɔlz-bri]
    Salisbury *(HV)*
    Salisbury *(RII)*
    Salisbury, Earl of *(KJ)* scans e.g. @ IV, 2, 162

sallet **SAAL**-it ['sæl-ɪt]

sally (n) or (v) **SAAL**-ee ['sæl-i]

Saltiers (possible corruption of "Satyrs") **SAYL**-terz ['seɪl-tɚz] or **SAAL**-___ ['sæl-___]

saltpetre **SAWLT**-pee-ter ['sɔlt-pi-tɚ]

salve **SAAV** [sæv] possibly **SAHL**-vay ['sɑl-veɪ]
    @ *LLL* III, 1, 65, 67

Samingo suh-**MING**-goh [sə-'mɪŋ-goʊ]

sampire **SAAM**-peyer ['sæm-paɪɚ]

Sampson *(R&J)* **SAMP**-suhn ['sæmp-sən]

sanctuarize scans to **SAANGK**-choo-reyez ['sæŋk-tʃu-raɪz]

Sandal **SAAN**-d(uh)l ['sæn-dl̩]

Sandys, Lord *(HVIII)* **SAANDZ** [sændz] also called "Sir Walter Sandys"

sanguine **SAANG**-gwin ['sæŋ-gwɪn]

sans **SAANZ** [sænz]

sapient scans to **SAY**-pyuhnt ['seɪ-pjənt]

Saracens **SAA**-ruh-suhnz ['sæ-rə-sənz]

sarcenet **SAHRS**-nit ['sɑɚs-nɪt]

Sardians SAHR-dee-uhnz ['sɑɚ-di-ənz] or ___-di-___
[___-dɪ-___]

Sardinia scans to sahr-DI-nyuh [sɑɚ-'dɪ-njə]

Sardis SAHR-dis ['sɑɚ-dɪs]

Sarum SEH-ruhm ['sɛ-rəm]

sate SAYT [seɪt]

satiate scans to SAY-shuht ['seɪ-ʃət]

satiety suh-TEYE-i-tee [sə-'taɪ-ɪ-ti] scans to ___-TEYE-tee
[___-'taɪ-ti] @ *SHR* I, 1, 24

satisfice SAAT-is-feyes ['sæt-ɪs-faɪs]

Saturninus *(TITUS)* SAA-ter-NEYE-nuhs [sæ-tɚ-'naɪ-nəs]
also called "Saturnine" SAA-ter-neyen ['sæ-tɚ-naɪn]

satyr SAY-ter ['seɪ-tɚ] or SAA-___ ['sæ-___]

saucily SAW-si-lee ['sɔ-sɪ-li]

savor SAY-ver ['seɪ-vɚ]

Savoy suh-VOY [sə-'vɔɪ]

Saxons SAAK-suhnz ['sæk-sənz]

Saxony SAAK-suh-nee ['sæk-sə-ni]

'sblood (corruption of "God's blood") ZBLUHD [zblʌd] or
SBLUHD [sblʌd]

scabbard SKAAB-erd ['skæb-ɚd]

scaffoldage SKAAF-uhl-dij ['skæf-əl-dɪdʒ]

Scales, Lord Thomas *(2HVI)* SKAYLZ [skeɪlz]

scall SKAWL [skɔl]

EE i be/ I ɪ bit/ EH ɛ bet/ AA æ bat/ OO u boot / OO ʊ book/ AW ɔ bought/ AH ɑ father/ ER ɝ bird/
UH ʌ cup/ AY eɪ bay/ EYE aɪ bite/ OY ɔɪ boy/ OH oʊ boat/ OW aʊ how/ YOO ɪu duke/ EAR ɪɚ
beer/ AIR ɛɚ bear/ OOR ʊɚ tour/ AWR ɔɚ bore/ AHR ɑɚ bar/ NG ŋ king/ SH ʃ ship/ ZH ʒ vision/
TH θ thirty/ TH ð then/ CH ʧ child/ J ʤ just/ For complete list, see Key to Pronunciation p. 2.

215

scambling SKAAM-bling ['skæm-blɪŋ]

scamels SKAAM-uhlz ['skæm-əlz] or SKAYM-___
['skeɪm-___]

scantling SKAANT-ling ['skænt-lɪŋ]

scaped SKAYPT [skeɪpt]

Scarus *(A&C)* SKEH-ruhs ['skɛ-rəs]

scath SKAATH [skæθ]

scathe SKAY<u>TH</u> [skeɪð]

scathful SKAATH-fuhl ['skæθ-fəl]

sceptre SEHP-ter ['sɛp-tɚ]

'schew SCHOO [stʃu]

sciatica seye-**AAT**-i-kuh [saɪ-'æt-ɪ-kə]

scimitar SIM-i-ter ['sɪm-ɪ-tɚ] or ___-___-tahr [___-___-tɑɚ]

scion SEYE-uhn ['saɪ-ən]

sconce SKAHNS [skɑns]

Scone SKOON [skun]

scorpion always scans to **SKAWR**-pyuhn ['skɔɚ-pjən]

scotch SKAHCH [skɑtʃ]

scour SKOWR [skɑʊɚ]

scourge SKERJ [skɝdʒ]

scrimers SKRIM-erz ['skrɪm-ɚz] or SKREEM-__
['skrim-__]

scrip SKRIP [skrɪp]

scrippage SKRIP-ij ['skrɪp-ɪdʒ]

scrivener scans to **SKRIV**-ner ['skrɪv-nɚ]

Scroop SKR$\overline{OO}$P [skrup]
Scroop, Lord *(HV)*
Scroop, Richard, Archbishop of York *(1HIV, 2HIV)*
Scroop, Sir Stephen *(RII)*

scrowl SKROHL [skroʊl]

scroyles SKROYLZ [skrɔɪlz]

sculls SKUHLZ [skʌlz]

scullion SKUHL-yuhn ['skʌl-jən]

scurril SKE(r)-ruhl ['skɜ-rəl] or SKUH-ruhl ['skʌ-rəl]

scurrility skuh-RIL-i-tee [skə-'rɪl-ɪ-ti]

scut SKUHT [skʌt]

scutcheon SKUHCH-uhn ['skʌtʃ-ən]

Scylla SIL-uh ['sɪl-ə]

scythe SEYE<u>TH</u> [saɪð]

Scythia always scans to SI-thyuh ['sɪ-θjə]

Scythian always scans to SI-thyuhn ['sɪ-θjən]

'sdeath (corruption of "God's death") ZDEHTH [zdɛθ] or SDEHTH [sdɛθ]

se'nnight SEHN-eyet ['sɛn-aɪt] or ___-it [___-ɪt]

Sea Captain *(12th)* SEE KAAP-t(uh)n [si] ['kæp-tn̩]

Seacole, George SEE-kohl ['si-koʊl]

sea-marge SEE-mahrj ['si-mɑɚʤ]

Sebastian si-BAAS-chuhn [sɪ-'bæs-tʃən] or ___-___-tyuhn [___-___-tjən]
Sebastian *(TEMP)*
Sebastian *(12th)*

---

sectary SEHK-tuh-ree ['sɛk-tə-ri]

secure (adj) si-**KYOOR** [sɪ-'kjʊɚ] scans to SI-kyoor ['sɪ-kjʊɚ] e.g. @ *HAM* I, 5, 61

sedge SEHJ [sɛʤ]

sedgy SEHJ-ee ['sɛʤ-i]

seel SEEL [sil]

seely SEE-lee ['si-li]

Seely, Sir Bennet SEE-lee ['si-li]

seld SEHLD [sɛld]

Seleucus *(A&C)* suh-**LOO**-kuhs [sə-'lu-kəs]

semblable SEHM-bluh-b(uh)l ['sɛm-blə-bl̩]

semblably SEHM-bluh-blee ['sɛm-blə-bli]

semblance SEHM-bluhns ['sɛm-bləns] scans to SEHM-buh-luhns ['sɛm-bə-ləns] e.g. @ *CE* V, 1, 359

semblative SEHM-bluh-tiv ['sɛm-blə-tɪv]

Semiramis suh-**MI**-ruh-mis [sə-'mɪ-rə-mɪs]

Sempronius sehm-**PROH**-nee-uhs [sɛm-'proʊ-ni-əs] scans to ___-**PROH**-nyuhs [___-'proʊ-njəs]
　Sempronius *(TIMON)* scans @ III, 4, 110
　Sempronius *(TITUS)* scans @ IV, 3, 10

sempster SEHMP-ster ['sɛmp-stɚ]

Seneca SEHN-i-kuh ['sɛn-ɪ-kə]

seniory SEEN-yuh-ree ['sin-jə-ri]

senna SEHN-uh ['sɛn-ə]

Sennois SEH-noyz ['sɛ-nɔɪz]

Senoys SEH-noyz ['sɛ-nɔɪz]

sententious sehn-TEHN-chuhs [sɛn-'tɛn-tʃəs]

sentinel SEHN-tuh-nuhl ['sɛn-tə-nəl]

Septentrion sehp-TEHN-tri-uhn [sɛp-'tɛn-trɪ-ən] or
__-__-__-ahn [__-__-__-ɑn]

sepulchre (n) SEHP-uhl-ker ['sɛp-əl-kɚ] scans to
seh-PUHL-__ [sɛ-'pʌl-__] @ *RII* I, 3, 196

sepulchre (v) seh-PUHL-ker [sɛ-'pʌl-kɚ]

sequent SEE-kwuhnt ['si-kwənt]

sequester (n) SEE-kwehs-ter ['sɪ-kwɛs-tɚ]

sequester (v) see-KWEHS-ter [si-'kwɛs-tɚ] scans to
SEE-kwehs-___ ['si-kwɛs-___] @ *TITUS* II, 3, 75

sequestration SEE-kwi-STRAY-shuhn [si-kwɪ-'streɪ-ʃən]

sere SEAR [sɪɚ]

serpigo ser-PEYE-goh [sɚ-'paɪ-gou] or __-PEE-__ [__-'pi-__]

servile SER-veyel ['sɝ-vaɪl] or ___-vuhl [___-vəl]

Servilius *(TIMON)* ser-VIL-ee-uhs [sɚ-'vɪl-i-əs] scans to
___-VIL-yuhs [___-'vɪl-jəs] @ III, 4, 77

servitor SER-vuh-ter ['sɝ-və-tɚ]

sessa SEHS-uh ['sɛs-ə]

Sestos SEHS-tuhs ['sɛs-təs] or ___-tohs [___-tous]

Setebos SEHT-i-bahs ['sɛt-ɪ-bɑs]

sev'night / sev'n-night SEHV-neyet ['sɛv-naɪt] or
SEHN-neyet ['sɛn-naɪt]

severally SEHV-uh-ruh-lee ['sɛv-ə-rə-li] scans to
SEHV-ruh-___ ['sɛv-rə-___] @ *CYM* V, 5, 397

EE i be/ I ɪ bit/ EH ɛ bet/ AA æ bat/ OO u boot/ OO ʊ book/ AW ɔ bought/ AH ɑ father/ ER ɝ bird/
UH ʌ cup/ AY eɪ bay/ EYE aɪ bite/ OY ɔɪ boy/ OH ou boat/ OW aʊ how/ YOO ɪu duke/ EAR ɪɚ
beer/ AIR ɛɚ bear/ OOR ʊɚ tour/ AWR ɔɚ bore/ AHR ɑɚ bar/ NG ŋ king/ SH ʃ ship/ ZH ʒ vision/
TH θ thirty/ TH ð then/ CH tʃ child/ J ʤ just/ For complete list, see Key to Pronunciation p. 2.

Severn SEHV-ern ['sɛv-ən]

sexton / Sexton SEHKS-tuhn ['sɛks-tən]
  Sexton *(MADO)*

Sextus Pompeius *(A&C)* SEHKS-tuhs pahm-PEE-uhs
  ['sɛks-təs] [pɑm-'pi-əs]

Seyton *(MAC)* SEE-t(uh)n ['si-tn̩] or possibly SAY-___
  ['seɪ-___]

'sfoot (corruption of "Christ's foot") SFŌŌT [sfʊt]

Shadow, Simon *(2HIV)* SHAA-doh SEYE-muhn ['ʃæ-doʊ]
  ['saɪ-mən]

Shafalus SHAA-fuh-luhs ['ʃæ-fə-ləs]

Shallow SHAA-loh ['ʃæ-loʊ]
  Shallow *(2HIV, MW)*

shealed SHEELD [ʃild]

shearman SHEAR-muhn ['ʃɪə-mən]

sheath SHEETH [ʃiθ]

sheathe SHEE<u>TH</u> [ʃið]

sheepcote SHEEP-koht ['ʃip-koʊt] or ___-kaht [___-kɑt]

Sheffield SHEHF-eeld ['ʃɛf-ild]

shelvy SHEHLV-ee ['ʃɛlv-i]

shent SHEHNT [ʃɛnt]

Sheriff of Wiltshire *(RIII)* WILT-sher ['wɪlt-ʃə] or
  ___-shear [___-ʃɪə]

sherris SHEH-ris ['ʃɛ-rɪs]

shipwrack SHIP-raak ['ʃɪp-ræk]

shire SHEYER [ʃaɪə]

shive SHEYEV [ʃaɪv]

shoal SHOHL [ʃoul]

shog SHAHG [ʃɑg]

shoon SHO͞ON [ʃun]

shotten SHAH-t(uh)n ['ʃɑ-tn̩]

shoughs SHUHFS [ʃʌfs] or SHAHKS [ʃɑks] (form of "shock-dog")

shove-groat SHUHV-groht ['ʃʌv-groʊt]

Shrewsbury SHRO͞OZ-buh-ree ['ʃruz-bə-ri] or SHROHZ-___-___ ['ʃroʊz-___-___] possibly SHRO͞OZ-bree ['ʃruz-bri] or SHROHZ-___ ['ʃroʊz-___] in prose

shrieve SHREEV [ʃriv]

shrift SHRIFT [ʃrɪft]

shrive SHREYEV [ʃraɪv]

shriver SHREYEV-er ['ʃraɪv-ɚ]

shroud SHROWD [ʃraʊd]

Shrove SHROHV [ʃroʊv]

shrow SHROH [ʃroʊ]

shrowd SHROHD [ʃroʊd]

Shylock *(MVEN)* SHEYE-lahk ['ʃaɪ-lɑk]

sib SIB [sɪb]

sibyl / Sibyl SIB-uhl ['sɪb-əl]

Sibylla si-BIL-uh [sɪ-'bɪl-ə]

Sicil SIS-uhl ['sɪs-əl]

EE i be/ I ɪ bit/ EH ɛ bet/ AA æ bat/ O͞O u boot / O͝O ʊ book/ AW ɔ bought/ AH ɑ father/ ER ɝ bird/ UH ʌ cup/ AY eɪ bay/ EYE aɪ bite/ OY ɔɪ boy/ OH oʊ boat/ OW aʊ how/ YO͞O ɪu duke/ EAR ɪə beer/ AIR ɛɚ bear/ O͞OR ʊə tour/ AWR ɔɚ bore/ AHR ɑɚ bar/ NG ŋ king/ SH ʃ ship/ ZH ʒ vision/ TH θ thirty/ <u>TH</u> ð then/ CH ʧ child/ J ʤ just/ For complete list, see Key to Pronunciation p. 2.

221

Sicilia si-SIL-ee-uh [sɪ-'sɪl-i-ə] scans to ___-SIL-yuh
  [___-'sɪl-jə] e.g. @ *WT* I, 2, 146 and scans to SI-sil-___
  ['sɪ-sɪl-___] @ *WT* IV, 4, 582

Sicilius always scans to si-SIL-yuhs [sɪ-'sɪl-jəs]

Sicils SIS-uhlz ['sɪs-əlz]

Sicily SIS-uh-lee ['sɪs-ə-li] scans to SIS-lee ['sɪs-li]
  @ *A&C* II, 6, 7

Sicinius Velutus *(COR)* si-SIN-ee-uhs vuh-LŌO-tuhs
  [sɪ-'sɪn-i-əs] [və-'lu-təs]

sicklied SIK-leed ['sɪk-lid]

sicles SI-k(uh)lz ['sɪ-kl̩z]

Sicyon always scans to SIS-yuhn ['sɪs-jən] or SISH-___ ['sɪʃ-___]

siege SEEJ [siʤ]

Siena see-EHN-uh [si-'ɛn-ə]

sieve SIV [sɪv]

signor SEEN-yawr ['sin-jɔɚ] scans to seen-YAWR [sin-'jɔɚ]
  e.g. @ *MVEN* I, 1, 73 (sometimes spelled "signior")

signory SEEN-yuh-ree ['sin-jə-ri] (sometimes spelled
  "signiory")

Silence *(2HIV)* SEYE-luhns ['saɪ-ləns]

Silius SIL-yuhs ['sɪl-jəs]

sillily SI-li-lee ['sɪ-lɪ-li]

Silvia *(2GEN)* SIL-vee-uh ['sɪl-vi-ə] scans to SIL-vyuh
  ['sɪl-vjə] e.g. @ II, 4, 46

Silvius SIL-vee-yuhs ['sɪl-vi-jəs] scans to SIL-vyuhs ['sɪl-vjəs]
  Silvius *(AYL)* scans e.g. @ III, 5, 123

Simon Catling KAAT-ling ['kæt-lɪŋ]

Simonides *(PER)* seye-**MAHN**-uh-deez [saɪ-'mɑn-ə-diz]

simony SEYE-muh-nee ['saɪ-mə-ni] or SIM-uh-___ ['sɪm-ə-___]

Simpcox, Saunder *(2HVI)* SIMP-kahks SAWN-der ['sɪmp-kɑks] ['sɔn-dɚ]

Simple *(MW)* SIM-p(uh)l ['sɪm-pl̩]

simular SIM-yuh-ler ['sɪm-jə-lɚ] or ___-___-lahr [___-___-lɑɚ] scans to SIM-ler ['sɪm-lɚ] or ___-lahr [___-lɑɚ] @ *CYM* V, 5, 200

Sinel SI-nuhl ['sɪ-nəl] or SEYE-___ ['saɪ-___]

sinew SIN-yoo ['sɪn-ju]

sinister SIN-i-ster ['sɪn-ɪ-stɚ] scans to si-NIS-ter [sɪ-'nɪs-tɚ] e.g. @ *HV* II, 4, 85

sink-a-pace SINGK-uh-pays ['sɪŋk-ə-peɪs]

Sinon SEYE-nuhn ['saɪ-nən]

sire SEYER [saɪɚ]

sirrah SI-ruh ['sɪ-rə]

sith SITH [sɪθ]

sithence SITH-uhns ['sɪθ-əns]

situate SICH-oo-wayt ['sɪtʃ-u-weɪt] or ___-___-wit [___-___-wɪt] scans to SICH-wit ['sɪtʃ-wɪt] @ *CE* II, 1, 16

Siward, Earl of Northumberland *(MAC)* SYOO-erd nawr-**THUHM**-ber-luhnd ['sɪu-ɚd] [nɔɚ-'θʌm-bɚ-lənd]

sixpence SIKS-puhnts ['sɪks-pənts]

skains-mates SKAYNZ-mayts ['skeɪnz-meɪts]

EE i be/ I ɪ bit/ EH ɛ bet/ AA æ bat/ OO u boot / OO ʊ book/ AW ɔ bought/ AH ɑ father/ ER ɝ bird/ UH ʌ cup/ AY eɪ bay/ EYE aɪ bite/ OY ɔɪ boy/ OH oʊ boat/ OW aʊ how/ YOO ɪu duke/ EAR ɪɚ beer/ AIR ɛɚ bear/ OOR ʊɚ tour/ AWR ɔɚ bore/ AHR ɑɚ bar/ NG ŋ king/ SH ʃ ship/ ZH ʒ vision/ TH θ thirty/ TH ð then/ CH tʃ child/ J ʤ just/ For complete list, see Key to Pronunciation p. 2.

skein SKAYN [skeɪn]

skimble-skamble SKIM-b(uh)l-SKAAM-b(uh)l
['skɪm-bl̩-skæm-bl̩]

skirr SKER [skɝ]

skittish SKI-tish ['skɪ-tɪʃ]

Skogan SKAH-guhn ['skɑ-gən]

skyey SKEYE-ee ['skaɪ-i]

slake SLAYK [sleɪk]

slaver (v) (to smear with saliva) SLAAV-er ['slæv-ɚ]

slavish SLAY-vish ['sleɪ-vɪʃ]

slay SLAY [sleɪ]

sleave SLEEV [sliv]

sleided SLEED-id ['slid-ɪd]

sleight SLEYET [slaɪt]

Slender *(MW)* SLEHN-der ['slɛn-dɚ]

slew SLO͞O [slu]

'slid (corruption of "God's eyelid") ZLID [zlɪd] or SLID
[slɪd]

'slight (corruption of "God's light") ZLEYET [zlaɪt] or
SLEYET [slaɪt]

slily SLEYE-lee ['slaɪ-li]

slish SLISH [slɪʃ]

sloth SLAWTH [slɔθ] or SLAHTH [slɑθ] or SLOHTH
[sloʊθ]

slough (skin of a snake) SLUHF [slʌf]

slough (a place of deep mud) SLO͞O [slu] @ *MW* IV, 5, 58

224

slovenly SLUHV-uhn-lee [ˈslʌv-ən-li]

slovenry SLUHV-uhn-ree [ˈslʌv-ən-ri]

slubber SLUHB-er [ˈslʌb-ɚ]

sluggard SLUHG-erd [ˈslʌg-ɚd]

sluice SLŌOS [slus]

Sly, Christopher *(SHR)* SLEYE [slaɪ]

Smalus SMAY-luhs [ˈsmeɪ-ləs]

smatch SMAACH [smætʃ]

smatter SMAAT-er [ˈsmæt-ɚ]

smit SMIT [smɪt]

smote SMOHT [smoʊt]

Smulkin SMUHL-kin [ˈsmʌl-kɪn]

smutched SMUHCHT [smʌtʃt]

snaffle SNAA-f(uh)l [ˈsnæ-fl̩]

Snare *(2HIV)* SNAIR [snɛɚ]

sneap SNEEP [snip]

sneck SNEHK [snɛk]

Snout, Tom / Wall *(MID)* SNOWT [snaʊt]

Snug / Lion *(MID)* SNUHG [snʌg]

Socrates SAHK-ruh-teez [ˈsɑk-rə-tiz]

soe'er soh-AIR [soʊ-ˈɛɚ]

soho (a cry of sportsmen) soh-HOH [soʊ-ˈhoʊ]

soilure SOYL-yer [ˈsɔɪl-jɚ]

EE i be/ I ɪ bit/ EH ɛ bet/ AA æ bat/ ŌO u boot / ŌO ʊ book/ AW ɔ bought/ AH ɑ father/ ER ɝ bird/
UH ʌ cup/ AY eɪ bay/ EYE aɪ bite/ OY ɔɪ boy/ OH oʊ boat/ OW aʊ how/ YŌO ɪu duke/ EAR ɪɚ
beer/ AIR ɛɚ bear/ ŌOR ʊɚ tour/ AWR ɔɚ bore/ AHR ɑɚ bar/ NG ŋ king/ SH ʃ ship/ ZH ʒ vision/
TH θ thirty/ TH ð then/ CH tʃ child/ J dʒ just/ For complete list, see Key to Pronunciation p. 2.

sojourn (n) SOH-jern ['soʊ-ʤə-n]

sojourn (v) SOH-jern ['soʊ-ʤə-n] scans to soh-**JERN**
  [soʊ-'ʤɜ-n] @ *MID* III, 2, 171

sojourner SOH-jer-ner ['soʊ-ʤə-nə] or soh-**JER**-ner
  [soʊ-'ʤɜ-nə]

Sol SAHL [sɑl]

solace SAHL-is ['sɑl-ɪs]

Solanio *(MVEN)* suh-**LAHN**-ee-oh [sə-'lɑn-i-oʊ]

sold'rest SAHD-rist ['sɑd-rɪst]

solder SAHD-er ['sɑd-ə]

soldier SOHL-jer ['soʊl-ʤə] scans to SOHL-jee-er ['soʊl-ʤi-ə]
  e.g. @ *COR* I, 1, 111

solemnized SAH-lehm-neyezd ['sɑ-lɛm-naɪzd] scans to suh-
  LEHM-neye-zid [sə-'lɛm-naɪ-zɪd] e.g. @ *LLL* II, 1, 42

solidares SAH-luh-dairz ['sɑ-lə-dɛə-z]

Solinus *(CE)* suh-**LEYE**-nuhs [sə-'laɪ-nəs]

Solomon SAHL-uh-muhn ['sɑl-ə-mən]

Solon SOH-lahn ['soʊ-lɑn] or ___-luhn [___-lən]

solus SOH-luhs ['soʊ-ləs]

Solyman SAHL-i-muhn ['sɑl-ɪ-mən]

Somervile *(3HVI)* SUHM-er-vil ['sʌm-ə-vɪl]

Somme SAHM [sɑm]

sonance SOH-nuhns ['soʊ-nəns]

sonties SAHN-teez ['sɑn-tiz]

sooth SOOTH [suθ]

soothe SOOTH [suð]

Soothsayer SOOTH-say-er ['suθ-seɪ-ɚ] scans to SOOTH-sair ['suθ-sɛɚ]
    Soothsayer *(A&C)*
    Soothsayer *(CYM)* scans @ V, 5, 426
    Soothsayer *(JC)*

sop SAHP [sɑp]

sophister SAHF-is-ter ['sɑf-ɪs-tɚ]

Sophy SOH-fee ['sou-fi]

sorel SAW-ruhl ['sɔ-rəl]

sortance SAWR-t(uh)ns ['sɔɚ-tn̩s]

Sossius SOH-shuhs ['sou-ʃəs]

Soto SOH-toh ['sou-tou]

sottish SAHT-ish ['sɑt-ɪʃ]

sound (to swoon) SOOND [sund] variant of "swoon" SWOON [swun]

souse SOWS [saʊs]

Southam SUH_TH_-uhm ['sʌð-əm] or SOW_TH_-uhm ['saʊð-əm]

Southampton sowth-HAAMP-tuhn [saʊθ-'hæmp-tən]

Southwark SUH_TH_-erk ['sʌð-ɚk]

Southwell, John *(2HVI)* SUH_TH_-uhl ['sʌð-əl] or SOW_TH_-wuhl ['saʊθ-wəl]

sovereign SAHV-uh-rin ['sɑv-ə-rɪn] scans to SAHV-rin ['sɑv-rɪn] e.g. @ *KJ* V, 1, 4

sowl SOWL [saʊl]

EE i be/ I ɪ bit/ EH ɛ bet/ AA æ bat/ OO u boot / OO ʊ book/ AW ɔ bought/ AH ɑ father/ ER ɝ bird/ UH ʌ cup/ AY eɪ bay/ EYE aɪ bite/ OY ɔɪ boy/ OH ou boat/ OW aʊ how/ YOO ɪu duke/ EAR ɪɚ beer/ AIR ɛɚ bear/ OOR ʊɚ tour/ AWR ɔɚ bore/ AHR ɑɚ bar/ NG ŋ king/ SH ʃ ship/ ZH ʒ vision/ TH θ thirty/ TH ð then/ CH tʃ child/ J dʒ just/ For complete list, see Key to Pronunciation p. 2.

227

sow-skin SOW-skin ['sɑʊ-skɪn]

Sowter SOO-ter ['su-tɚ] or SOW-__ ['sɑʊ-__]

Sparta SPAHR-tuh ['spɑɚ-tə]

spavin SPAAV-in ['spæv-ɪn]

Speed *(2GEN)* SPEED [spid]

speken SPEEK-uhn ['spik-ən]

sperr SPER [spɝ] some editions "spar" SPAHR [spɑɚ]

spherical SFI-ri-k(uh)l ['sfɪ-rɪ-kl̩]

sphery SFI-ree ['sfɪ-ri]

Sphinx SFINGKS [sfɪŋks]

spigot SPIG-uht ['spɪg-ət]

spilth SPILTH [spɪlθ]

Spinii SPI-nee-eye ['spɪ-ni-aɪ] or SPEYE-__-__ ['spaɪ-__-__]

spiritualty scans to SPEAR-chool-tee ['spɪɚ-tʃul-ti]

spital SPI-t(uh)l ['spɪ-tl̩]

splay SPLAY [spleɪ]

spleeny SPLEEN-ee [splin-i]

splenitive SPLEHN-i-tiv ['splɛn-ɪ-tiv]

spousal SPOW-zuhl ['spɑʊ-zəl]

sprat SPRAAT [spræt]

springe SPRINJ [sprɪndʒ]

spriting SPREYET-ing ['spraɪt-ɪŋ]

spur SPER [spɝ]

Spurio SPYOO-ree-oh ['spjʊ-ri-oʊ]

Squele SKWEEL [skwil]

squier SKWEYER [skwaɪɚ]

squiny SKWIN-ee ['skwɪn-i]

squire SKWEYER [skwaɪɚ]

Stafford STAAF-erd ['stæf-ɚd]
    Stafford, Humphrey, Duke of Buckingham *(2HVI)*
        BUHK-ing-uhm ['bʌk-ɪŋ-əm]
    Stafford, Lord Humphrey *(3HVI)*
    Stafford, Sir Humphrey *(2HVI)*
    Stafford, William *(2HVI)*

Staffordshire STAAF-erd-sher ['stæf-ɚd-ʃɚ] or __-__-shear
    [__-__-ʃɪɚ]

staider STAYD-er ['steɪd-ɚ]

Staines STAYNZ [steɪnz]

stanchless STAWNCH-lis ['stɔntʃ-lɪs] or STAANCH-___
    ['stæntʃ-___]

staniel STAAN-yuhl ['stæn-jəl]

Stanley STAAN-lee ['stæn-li]
    Stanley, John *(2HVI)*
    Stanley, Lord, Earl of Derby *(RIII)* DAHR-bee ['dɑɚ-bi]
        or DER-___ ['dɝ-___]
    Stanley, Sir William *(3HVI)*

stanzo STAAN-zoh ['stæn-zoʊ]

stark-nak'd stahrk-NAYKT [stɑɚk-'neɪkt]

Starveling, Robin / Moonshine *(MID)* STAHRV-ling
    ['stɑɚv-lɪŋ]

Statilius stuh-TIL-yuhs [stə-'tɪl-jəs]

statist STAY-tist ['steɪ-tɪst]

EE i be/ I ɪ bit/ EH ɛ bet/ AA æ bat/ O͞O u boot / O͝O ʊ book/ AW ɔ bought/ AH ɑ father/ ER ɝ bird/
UH ʌ cup/ AY eɪ bay/ EYE aɪ bite/ OY ɔɪ boy/ OH oʊ boat/ OW aʊ how/ YO͞O ɪu duke/ EAR ɪɚ
beer/ AIR ɛɚ bear/ O͞OR ʊɚ tour/ AWR ɔɚ bore/ AHR ɑɚ bar/ NG ŋ king/ SH ʃ ship/ ZH ʒ vision/
TH θ thirty/ T̲H̲ ð then/ CH tʃ child/ J ʤ just/ For complete list, see Key to Pronunciation p. 2.

statue STAACH-o͞o ['stætʃ-u] scans to STAA-cho͞o-uh ['stæ-tʃu-ə] e.g. @ *JC* II, 2, 76

staunch STAWNCH [stɔntʃ] or STAHNCH [stantʃ]

stave STAYV [steɪv]

stead STEHD [stɛd]

stealth STEHLTH [stɛlθ]

stelled STEHL-id ['stɛl-ɪd]

stepdame STEHP-daym ['stɛp-deɪm]

Stephano *(MVEN)* steh-FAH-noh [stɛ-'fɑ-noʊ]

Stephano *(TEMP)* STEH-fuh-noh ['stɛ-fə-noʊ]

stigmatic always scans to STIG-muh-tik ['stɪg-mə-tɪk]

stigmatical stig-MAAT-i-k(uh)l [stɪg-'mæt-ɪ-kl̩]

stile STEYEL [staɪl]

stilly STIL-ee ['stɪl-i]

stithy STITH-ee ['stɪð-i]

stoccadoes stuh-KAH-dohz [stə-'kɑ-doʊz]

Stokesly STOHKS-lee ['stoʊks-li]

stomacher STUHM-uh-ker ['stʌm-ə-kɚ] scans to STUHM-ker ['stʌm-kɚ] @ *CYM* III, 4, 84

stonish STAHN-ish ['stɑn-ɪʃ]

stoup STO͞OP [stup]

stover STOH-ver ['stoʊ-vɚ]

Strachy STRAYCH-ee ['streɪtʃ-i]

strappado struh-PAH-doh [strə-'pɑ-doʊ] or ___-PAY-___ [___-'peɪ-___]

strategem STRAAT-uh-juhm ['stræt-ə-ʤəm]

Strato *(JC)* STRAY-toh ['streɪ-toʊ]

strawy STRAW-ee ['strɔ-i]

strew STRO͞O [stru]

strewments STRO͞O-muhnts ['stru-mənts]

stricture STRIK-cher ['strɪk-tʃɚ]

stroken STROHK-uhn ['stroʊk-ən]

strond / Strond STRAHND [strɑnd] often emended to "strand" STRAAND [strænd]

strooken STRO͞OK-uhn ['strʊk-ən]

strossers STRAWS-erz ['strɔs-ɚz] or STRAHS-__ ['strɑs-__]

strove STROHV [stroʊv]

strow STROH [stroʊ]

strown STROHN [stroʊn]

strucken STRUHK-uhn ['strʌk-ən]

Stygian scans to STIJ-yuhn ['stɪdʒ-jən]

Styx STIKS [stɪks]

subcontracted scans to SUHB-kuhn-traakt-id ['sʌb-kən-trækt-ɪd]

suborn suh-BAWRN [sə-'bɔɚn]

subornation suhb-awr-NAY-shuhn [səb-ɔɚ-'neɪ-ʃən]

subsequent scans to suhb-SEE-kwehnt [səb-'si-kwɛnt]

substractors suhb-STRAAK-terz [sʌb-'stræk-tɚz]

subtile SUH-t(uh)l ['sʌ-tl̩] or SUHB-___ ['sʌb-__]

EE i be/ I ɪ bit/ EH ɛ bet/ AA æ bat/ O͞O u boot / OO ʊ book/ AW ɔ bought/ AH ɑ father/ ER ɝ bird/ UH ʌ cup/ AY eɪ bay/ EYE aɪ bite/ OY ɔɪ boy/ OH oʊ boat/ OW aʊ how/ YO͞O ɪu duke/ EAR ɪɚ beer/ AIR ɛɚ bear/ O͞OR ʊɚ tour/ AWR ɔɚ bore/ AHR ɑɚ bar/ NG ŋ king/ SH ʃ ship/ ZH ʒ vision/ TH θ thirty/ TH ð then/ CH tʃ child/ J dʒ just/ For complete list, see Key to Pronunciation p. 2.

subtile-witted SUH-t(uh)l-WIT-id ['sʌ-tl̩-wɪt-ɪd] or
  SUHB-__-__-__ ['sʌb-__-__-__]

subtilly always scans to SUHT-lee ['sʌt-li]

successantly suhk-SEHS-uhnt-lee [sək-'sɛs-ənt-li]

succor SUHK-er ['sʌk-ɚ]

sue SOO [su] or SYOO [sɪu]

Suffolk SUHF-uhk ['sʌf-ək]
  Suffolk, Duke of *(HVIII)*

Sulla SUH-luh ['sʌ-lə]

sully SUHL-ee ['sʌl-i]

sumpter SUHMP-ter ['sʌmp-tɚ]

sunder SUHN-der ['sʌn-dɚ]

sup SUHP [sʌp]

superfluity SOO-per-FLOO-i-tee [su-pɚ-'flu-ɪ-ti] or
  syoo-__-__-__-__ [sɪu-__-__-__-__]

supernal soo-PER-nuhl [su-'pɝ-nəl] or syoo-__-__
  [sɪu-__-__]

suppliance suh-PLEYE-uhns [sə-'plaɪ-əns]

suppliant SUHP-lee-uhnt ['sʌp-li-ənt] scans to SUHP-lyuhnt
  ['sʌp-ljənt] e.g. @ *AW* V, 3, 134

supplyant suh-PLEYE-uhnt [sə-'plaɪ-ənt]

supplyment suh-PLEYE-muhnt [sə-'plaɪ-mənt]

supportance suh-PAWR-tuhns [sə-'pɔɚ-təns]

supposal suh-POH-z(uh)l [sə-'poʊ-zl̩]

supreme soo-PREEM [su-'prim] or syoo-___ [sɪu-___]
  scans to SOO-preem ['su-prim] or SYOO-___ ['sɪu-___]
  e.g. @ *RIII* III, 7, 118

sur-additon SER-uh-di-shuhn ['sɝ-ə-dɪ-ʃən]

surcease always scans to ser-SEES [sɚ-'sis]

surety (n) SHŎŎ-ri-tee ['ʃʊ-rɪ-ti] scans to SHŎŎR-tee
['ʃʊɚ-ti] e.g. @ *HV* V, 2, 356

surety (v) always scans to SHŎŎR-tee ['ʃʊɚ-ti]

surfeit SER-fit ['sɝ-fɪt]

surplice SER-plis ['sɝ-plɪs]

sur-reined SER-raynd ['sɝ-reɪnd]

Surrey SUH-ree ['sʌ-ri] or SE(r)-___ ['sɝ-___]
Surrey, Duke of *(RII)*
Surrey, Earl of *(2HIV)*
Surrey, Earl of *(HVIII)*
Surrey, Earl of *(RIII)*

survey (n) SER-vay ['sɝ-veɪ] scans to ser-VAY [sɚ-'veɪ]
e.g. @ *AW* V, 3, 16

survey (v) ser-VAY [sɚ-'veɪ]

surveyor ser-VAY-er [sɚ-'veɪ-ɚ] scans to SER-vay-er
['sɝ-veɪ-ɚ] @ *HVIII* I, 1, 222

suspect (n) always scans to suh-SPEHKT [sə-'spɛkt]

suspiration suhs-pi-RAY-shuhn [səs-pɪ-'reɪ-ʃən]

suspire suh-SPEYER [sə-'spaɪɚ]

sutler SUHT-ler ['sʌt-lɚ]

Sutton Co'fil' SUH-t(uh)n KOH-fil ['sʌ-tn̩] ['koʊ-fɪl]

swain SWAYN [sweɪn]

sware SWAIR [swɛɚ]

---

swart SWAWRT [swɔɚt]

swarth SWAWRTH [swɔɚθ]

swarthy SWAWR-<u>thee</u> ['swɔɚ-ði] or ___-thee [___-θi]

swashers SWAH-sherz ['swɑ-ʃɚz]

swath (n) (swaddling clothes) SWAWTH [swɔθ] or
  SWAHTH [swɑθ]

swath (n) (the stroke of a scythe) SWAWTH [swɔθ] or
  SWAHTH [swɑθ]

Sweno SWEE-noh ['swi-nou]

swinge SWINJ [swɪnʤ]

swinish SWEYE-nish ['swaɪ-nɪʃ]

Swinstead SWIN-stehd ['swɪn-stɛd]

Swithold SWI<u>TH</u>-uhld ['swɪð-əld] or **SWITH-**___ [swɪθ-___]
  or **SWIT-**___ ['swɪt-___]

Switzers SWIT-serz ['swɪt-sɚz]

swoln / swol'n SWOHLN [swouln]

swoon SWO͞ON [swun]

sword SAWRD [sɔɚd]

sworder SAWRD-er ['sɔɚd-ɚ]

swound SWOWND [swɑund] most editions alter to
  "swoond" SWO͞OND [swund]

'swounds (corruption of "God's wounds") ZO͞ONDZ [zundz]

Sycorax SIK-uh-raaks ['sɪk-ə-ræks] scans to SIK-raaks
  ['sɪk-ræks] @ *TEMP* I, 2, 258

syllogism SIL-uh-ji-zuhm ['sɪl-ə-ʤɪ-zəm]

synod SIN-uhd ['sɪn-əd] or ___-ahd [___-ɑd]

Syracusa SI-ruh-**KYOO**-zuh [sɪ-rə-'kju-zə]

Syracuse SI-ruh-kyōoz ['sɪ-rə-kjuz]

Syracusian SI-ruh-**KYOO**-zhuhn [sɪ-rə-'kju-ʒən]

Syria SI-ree-uh ['sɪ-ri-ə] scans to SI-ryuh ['sɪ-rjə]
  e.g. @ *A&C* III, 1, 18

T (the letter) TEE [ti]

tabor TAY-ber ['teɪ-bɚ]

tabourines TAA-buh-reenz ['tæ-bə-rinz]

taciturn TAAS-i-tern ['tæs-ɪ-tɚn]

taffeta TAAF-i-tuh ['tæf-ɪ-tə]

taffety TAAF-i-tee ['tæf-ɪ-ti]

taincture TAYNGK-cher ['teɪŋk-tʃɚ]

taint TAYNT [teɪnt]

Talbonites TAWL-buh-neyets ['tɔl-bə-naɪts] or TAAL-__-__
  ['tæl-__-__]

Talbot TAWL-buht ['tɔl-bət] or TAAL-___ ['tæl-___]
  Talbot, John *(1HVI)*
  Talbot, Lord, Earl of Shrewsbury *(1HVI)*

Tamora *(TITUS)* TAAM-uh-ruh ['tæm-ə-rə] scans to
  TAAM-ruh ['tæm-rə] e.g. @ I, 1, 318

Tamworth TAAM-werth ['tæm-wɚθ]

tanlings TAAN-lingz ['tæn-lɪŋz]

taper TAY-per ['teɪ-pɚ]

tapster / Tapster TAAP-ster ['tæp-stɚ]

EE i be/ I ɪ bit/ EH ɛ bet/ AA æ bat/ OO u boot / OO ʊ book/ AW ɔ bought/ AH ɑ father/ ER ɝ bird/
UH ʌ cup/ AY eɪ bay/ EYE aɪ bite/ OY ɔɪ boy/ OH oʊ boat/ OW aʊ how/ YOO ɪu duke/ EAR ɪɚ
beer/ AIR ɛɚ bear/ OOR ʊɚ tour/ AWR ɔɚ bore/ AHR ɑɚ bar/ NG ŋ king/ SH ʃ ship/ ZH ʒ vision/
TH θ thirty/ TH ð then/ CH tʃ child/ J dʒ just/ For complete list, see Key to Pronunciation p. 2.

Tarentum tuh-REHN-tuhm [tə-'rɛn-təm]

targe TAHRJ [taɚʤ] in plural scans to one syllable
   TAHRJZ [taɚʤz] @ *A&C* II, 6, 39

Tarpeian tahr-PEE-uhn [taɚ-'pi-ən]

Tarquin TAHR-kwin ['taɚ-kwɪn]

tarre TAHR [taɚ]

tarriance TAA-ree-uhns ['tæ-ri-əns]

Tartar TAHR-ter ['taɚ-tɚ]

tattling TAA-t(uh)l-ing ['tæ-tl̩-ɪŋ]

Taurus TAW-ruhs ['tɔ-rəs]
   Taurus *(A&C)*

tawny TAW-nee ['tɔ-ni]

Tearsheet TAIR-sheet ['tɛɚ-ʃit]
   Tearsheet, Doll *(2HIV)*

teat TEET [tit]

Telamon scans to TEHL-muhn ['tɛl-mən]

Telamonius TEHL-uh-MOH-nee-uhs [tɛl-ə-'mou-ni-əs]

Tellus TEHL-uhs ['tɛl-əs]

temperality TEHM-puh-RAAL-i-tee [tɛm-pə-'ræl-ɪ-ti]

temporal TEHM-puh-ruhl ['tɛm-pə-rəl]

Tenantius tuh-NAAN-shuhs [tə-'næn-ʃəs]

tench TEHNCH [tɛnʧ]

tendance TEHN-duhns ['tɛn-dəns]

Tenedos TEHN-uh-dohs ['tɛn-ə-dous] or ___-___-dahs
   [___-___-dɑs] or ___-___-duhs [___-___-dəs]

tenure TEHN-yer ['tɛn-jɚ] or ___-yo͞or [___-jʊɚ]

tercel TER-suhl ['tɝ-səl]

Tereus TEAR-yo͞os ['tɪɚ-jus] or ___-yuhs [__-jəs]

termagant / Termagant TER-muh-guhnt ['tɝ-mə-gənt]

terrene TEH-reen ['tɛ-rin]

terrestrial tuh-REHS-tree-uhl [tə-'rɛs-tri-əl] scans to ___-REHS-truhl [__-'rɛs-trəl] @ *RII* III, 2, 41

tertian TER-shuhn ['tɝ-ʃən]

tester TEHS-ter ['tɛs-tɚ]

testerned TEHS-ternd ['tɛs-tɚnd]

testril TEHS-truhl ['tɛs-trəl]

tetchy TEHCH-ee ['tɛtʃ-i]

tetter TEHT-er ['tɛt-ɚ]

Tewksbury / Tewkesbury TYO͞OKS-buh-ree ['tɪuks-bə-ri]

Thaisa *(PER)* thay-I-suh [θeɪ-'ɪ-sə] scans to THAY-i-___ ['θeɪ-ɪ-___] e.g. @ V, 1, 212

Thaliard *(PER)* THAAL-yerd ['θæl-jɚd]

Thames TEHMZ [tɛmz]

Thane THAYN [θeɪn]

Tharsus TAHR-suhs ['tɑɚ-səs]

Thasos THAY-sahs ['θeɪ-sɑs] or ___-sohs [__-soʊs]

theatre THEE-uh-ter ['θi-ə-tɚ] scans to THEE-ter ['θi-tɚ] @ *KJ* II, 1, 375

Theban THEE-buhn ['θi-bən]

EE i be/ I ɪ bit/ EH ɛ bet/ AA æ bat/ O͞O u boot / O͝O ʊ book/ AW ɔ bought/ AH ɑ father/ ER ɝ bird/ UH ʌ cup/ AY eɪ bay/ EYE aɪ bite/ OY ɔɪ boy/ OH oʊ boat/ OW aʊ how/ YO͞O ɪu duke/ EAR ɪɚ beer/ AIR ɛɚ bear/ O͞OR ʊɚ tour/ AWR ɔɚ bore/ AHR ɑɚ bar/ NG ŋ king/ SH ʃ ship/ ZH ʒ vision/ TH θ thirty/ TH ð then/ CH tʃ child/ J dʒ just/ For complete list, see Key to Pronunciation p. 2.

237

Thebes THEEBZ [θibz] scans to **THEE**-buhs ['θi-bəs]
@ *2NOB* I, 2, 15

thee T̲H̲EE [ði]

thence T̲H̲EHNS [ðɛns]

theoric THEE-uh-rik ['θi-ə-rɪk] possibly scans to **THEE**-rik
['θi-rɪk] @ *OTH* I, 1, 24

thereat t̲h̲eh-RAAT [ðɛ-'ræt]

Thersites ther-SEYE-teez [θɚ-'saɪ-tiz]
Thersites *(T&C)*

Theseus THEE-see-uhs ['θi-si-əs] scans to **THEE**-syuhs
['θi-sjəs]
Theseus *(MID)* scans @ I, 1, 20
Theseus *(2NOB)*

Thessalian scans to theh-SAYL-yuhn [θɛ-'seɪl-jən]

Thessaly THEHS-uh-lee ['θɛs-ə-li] possibly scans to
THEHS-lee ['θɛs-li] @ *A&C* IV, 13, 2

Thetis THEE-tis ['θi-tɪs]

thews THYO̅O̅Z [θɪuz]

Thidias *(A&C)* THID-ee-uhs ['θɪd-i-əs] scans to **THID**-yuhs
['θɪd-jəs] @ III, 13, 73

thine T̲H̲EYEN [ðaɪn]

Thisbe THIZ-bee ['θɪz-bi]

thither THI-t̲h̲er ['θɪ-ðɚ]

thitherward THI-t̲h̲er-werd ['θɪ-ðɚ-wɚd]

Thoas THOH-uhs ['θou-əs]

Thomas TAH-muhs ['tɑ-məs]
Thomas *(MM)*
Thomas of Clarence *(2HIV)*

thorough (prep) or (adv) (through) THUH-roh ['θʌ-roʊ] or THE(r)-roh ['θɜ-roʊ]

Thracian THRAY-shuhn ['θreɪ-ʃən]

thrall THRAWL [θrɔl]

thrasonical thruh-SAHN-i-kuhl [θrə-'sɑn-ɪ-kəl] or thray-__-__-__ [θreɪ-__-__-__]

threepence THRUH-puhnts ['θrʌ-pənts] or THRI-___ ['θrɪ-___] or THREE-___ ['θri-___]

threepenny THREHP-uh-nee ['θrɛp-ə-ni]

thrice THREYES [θraɪs]

throe THROH [θroʊ]

throstle THRAH-s(uh)l ['θrɑ-sl̩]

throughfare THROO-fair ['θru-fɛɚ]

throughly THROO-lee ['θru-li]

thrum THRUHM [θrʌm]

Thump, Peter *(2HVI)* THUHMP [θʌmp]

Thurio *(2GEN)* THYOO-ree-oh ['θju-ri-oʊ] scans to THYOOR-yoh ['θjuɚ-joʊ] e.g. @ II, 6, 39

thwack THWAAK [θwæk]

thwart THWAWRT [θwɔɚt]

thyme TEYEM [taɪm]

Tib TIB [tɪb]

Tiber TEYE-ber ['taɪ-bɚ]

Tiberio teye-BI-ree-oh [taɪ-'bɪ-ri-oʊ]

EE i be/ I ɪ bit/ EH ɛ bet/ AA æ bat/ OO u boot / OO ʊ book/ AW ɔ bought/ AH ɑ father/ ER ɝ bird/ UH ʌ cup/ AY eɪ bay/ EYE aɪ bite/ OY ɔɪ boy/ OH oʊ boat/ OW aʊ how/ YOO ɪu duke/ EAR ɪɚ beer/ AIR ɛɚ bear/ OOR ʊɚ tour/ AWR ɔɚ bore/ AHR ɑɚ bar/ NG ŋ king/ SH ʃ ship/ ZH ʒ vision/ TH θ thirty/ TH ð then/ CH tʃ child/ J dʒ just/ For complete list, see Key to Pronunciation p. 2.

ticed TEYEST [taɪst]

Tiger TEYE-ger ['taɪ-gɚ]

tilly-fally TIL-ee-FAAL-ee ['tɪl-i-fæl-i]

tilth TILTH [tɪlθ]

tiltyard TILT-yahrd ['tɪlt-jaɚd]

Timandra *(TIMON)* ti-MAAN-druh [tɪ-'mæn-drə]

Timbria scans to TIM-bruh ['tɪm-brə]

Timon TEYE-muhn ['taɪ-mən]
    Timon *(TIMON)*

tinct TINGKT [tɪŋkt]

tincture TINGK-cher ['tɪŋk-tʃɚ]

tirra-lyra TI-ruh-LI-ruh ['tɪ-rə-lɪ-rə]

tirrits TI-rits ['tɪ-rɪts]

tis TIZ [tɪz]

tisick / Tisick TIZ-ik ['tɪz-ɪk]

Titan TEYE-t(uh)n ['taɪ-tn̩]

Titania *(MID)* ti-TAHN-yuh [tɪ-'tɑn-jə] scans to
    __-__-ee-uh [__-__-i-ə] e.g. @ II, 1, 60 (ti-TAYN-yuh
    [tɪ-'teɪn-jə] and teye-__-__ [taɪ-__-__] are sometimes heard)

tithe TEYE<u>TH</u> [taɪð]

Titinius *(JC)* ti-TI-nee-uhs [tɪ-'tɪ-ni-əs] scans to __-TI-nyuhs
    [__-'tɪ-njəs] e.g. @ IV, 2, 52

tittles TI-t(uh)lz ['tɪ-tl̩z]

Titus TEYE-tuhs ['taɪ-təs]
    Titus *(TIMON)*
    Titus Andronicus *(TITUS)* aan-DRAHN-i-kuhs
        [æn-'drɑn-ɪ-kəs]
    Titus Lartius *(COR)* LAHR-shuhs ['lɑɚ-ʃəs]

to't TŌŌT [tut]

toaze TOHZ [touz] or TOWZ [tɑuz]

tod (n) or (v) TAHD [tad]

tofore tōō-FAWR [tu-'fɔɚ] or tuh-___ [tə-___]

toge TOHG [toug]

toged scans to TOH-gid ['tou-gɪd]

Toledo tuh-LEE-doh [tə-'li-dou]

Tomyris TAHM-uh-ris ['tɑm-ə-rɪs]

Topas TOH-paaz ['tou-pæz] or ___-paas [___-pæs]

topmast TAHP-muhst ['tɑp-məst] or ___-maast [___-mæst]

topsail TAHP-s(uh)l ['tɑp-sļ] or ___-sayl [___-seɪl]

tortive TAWR-tiv ['tɔɚ-tɪv]

Toryne TAH-rin ['tɑ-rɪn] or TOH-___ ['tou-___]

tost TAWST [tɔst]

Touchstone *(AYL)* TUHCH-stohn ['tʌtʃ-stoun]

Touraine always scans to TŌŌ-rayn ['tu-reɪn]

tourney TER-nee ['tɝ-ni]

Tours TŌŌR [tuɚ]

touse TOWZ [tɑuz]

toward (adj) TAWRD [tɔɚd] scans to TOH-erd ['tou-ɚd]
@ *3HVI* II, 2, 66

toward (adv) TAWRD [tɔɚd] scans to TOH-erd ['tou-ɚd]
e.g. @ *HAM* I, 1, 77

---

toward (prep) TAWRD [tɔɚd] scans to **TOH**-erd [ˈtoʊ-ɚd]
e.g. @ *2HVI* II, 1, 195

towardly TAWRD-lee [ˈtɔɚd-li] or possibly **TOH**-erd-lee
[ˈtoʊ-ɚd-li] @ *TIMON* III, 1, 32

towards (adv) TAWRDZ [tɔɚdz] @ *R&J* I, 5, 122

towards (prep) TAWRDZ [tɔɚdz] scans to **TOH**-erdz
[ˈtoʊ-ɚdz] e.g. @ *RIII* IV, 5, 17

traduced truh-DYO͞OST [trə-ˈdɪust]

traducement truh-DYO͞OS-muhnt [trə-ˈdɪus-mənt]

tragedian truh-JEE-dee-uhn [trə-ˈʤi-di-ən]

traitress TRAY-truhs [ˈtreɪ-trəs]

traject TRAA-jehkt [ˈtræ-ʤɛkt]

Tranio *(SHR)* TRAH-nee-oh [ˈtrɑ-ni-oʊ] scans to
TRAH-nyoh [ˈtrɑ-njoʊ] e.g. @ I, 1, 17 later posing as
"Lucentio" lo͞o-SEHN-shee-oh [lu-ˈsɛn-ʃi-oʊ] scans to
___-SEHN-shyoh [___-ˈsɛn-ʃjoʊ]

translate always scans to traanz-LAYT [trænz-ˈleɪt]

transportance traans-PAWR-tuhns [træns-ˈpɔɚ-təns]

Transylvanian TRAAN-sil-VAY-nyuhn [træn-sɪl-ˈveɪ-njən]

travail (n) truh-VAYL [trə-ˈveɪl] scans to **TRAAV**-uhl
[ˈtræv-əl] or ___-ayl [___-eɪl] e.g. @ *HVIII* V, 1, 71

travail (v) truh-VAYL [trə-ˈveɪl] scans to **TRAAV**-uhl
[ˈtræv-əl] or ___-ayl [___-eɪl] e.g. @ *AW* II, 3, 157

Travers *(2HIV)* TRAAV-erz [ˈtræv-ɚz]

traverse (adv) or (v) truh-VERS [trə-ˈvɝs]

traversed TRAAV-erst [ˈtræv-ɚst]

treachers TREHCH-erz [ˈtrɛʧ-ɚz]

treatise TREE-tis ['tri-tɪs]

Trebonius *(JC)* tri-**BOH**-nee-uhs [trɪ-'boʊ-ni-əs] scans to
__-**BOH**-nyuhs [__-'boʊ-njəs] e.g. @ I, 3, 148

tremor cordis TREH-mer KAWR-dis ['trɛ-mɚ] ['kɔɚ-dɪs]

trencher TREHN-cher ['trɛn-tʃɚ]

Tressel *(RIII)* TREHS-uhl ['trɛs-əl]

treys TRAYZ [treɪz]

tribunal treye-**BYOON**-uhl [traɪ-'bjun-əl]

tribune TRIB-yoon ['trɪb-jun]

trice TREYES [traɪs]

tricksy TRIK-see ['trɪk-si]

trier TREYER [traɪɚ]

Trigon TREYE-guhn ['traɪ-gən]

Trinculo *(TEMP)* TRING-kyuh-loh ['trɪŋ-kjə-loʊ]

tripartite scans to TREYE-pahr-teyet ['traɪ-pɑɚ-taɪt]

Tripoli scans to TRIP-lee ['trɪp-li]

Tripolis TRIP-uh-lis ['trɪp-ə-lɪs]

Triton TREYE-t(uh)n ['traɪ-tn̩]

triumphers treye-**UHMF**-erz [traɪ-'ʌmf-ɚ-z]

triumvirate treye-**UHM**-vuh-rit [traɪ-'ʌm-və-rɪt]

triumviry treye-**UHM**-vuh-ree [traɪ-'ʌm-və-ri]

trod TRAHD [trɑd]

Troien TROY-uhn ['trɔɪ-ən]

EE i be/ I ɪ bit/ EH ɛ bet/ AA æ bat/ OO u boot / ŌŌ ʊ book/ AW ɔ bought/ AH ɑ father/ ER ɝ bird/
UH ʌ cup/ AY eɪ bay/ EYE aɪ bite/ OY ɔɪ boy/ OH oʊ boat/ OW aʊ how/ YOO ɪu duke/ EAR ɪɚ
beer/ AIR ɛɚ bear/ ŌŌR ʊɚ tour/ AWR ɔɚ bore/ AHR ɑɚ bar/ NG ŋ king/ SH ʃ ship/ ZH ʒ vision/
TH θ thirty/ TH ð then/ CH tʃ child/ J ʤ just/ For complete list, see Key to Pronunciation p. 2.

Troilus TROY-luhs [ˈtrɔɪ-ləs] scans to TROY-uh-luhs [ˈtrɔɪ-ə-ləs] or possibly TROH-luhs [ˈtroʊ-ləs] scans to TROH-uh-luhs [ˈtroʊ-ə-ləs]
　　Troilus *(T&C)* scans e.g. @ IV, 4, 31

troll TROHL [troʊl]

tropically TROH-pik-lee [ˈtroʊ-pɪk-li] as in "trope" or TRAA-__-__ [ˈtræ-__-__] if punning on "Mousetrap" @ *HAM* III, 2, 229

troth TROHTH [troʊθ] or TRAHTH [trɑθ]

troublous TRUHB-luhs [ˈtrʌb-ləs]

trough TRAWF [trɔf] or TRAHF [trɑf]

trow TROH [troʊ]

Troy TROY [trɔɪ]

Troyan see "Troien"

truckle-bed TRUHK-uhl-behd [ˈtrʌk-əl-bɛd]

trudge TRUHJ [trʌʤ]

trull TRUHL [trʌl]

trumpery TRUHM-puh-ree [ˈtrʌm-pə-ri] scans to TRUHM-pree [ˈtrʌm-pri] e.g. @ *TEMP* IV, 1, 186

truncheon TRUHN-chuhn [ˈtrʌn-ʧən]

Tubal *(MVEN)* TYOO-b(uh)l [ˈtɪu-bl̩]

tucket TUHK-it [ˈtʌk-ɪt]

Tullus Aufidius *(COR)* TUH-luhs aw-FID-ee-uhs [ˈtʌ-ləs] [ɔ-ˈfɪd-i-əs] scans to __-FID-yuhs [__-ˈfɪd-jəs] e.g. @ I, 1, 224

Tully TUHL-ee [ˈtʌl-i]

tumult TYOO-muhlt [ˈtɪu-məlt]

tun-dish TUHN-dish [ˈtʌn-dɪʃ]

Tunis TYŌŌ-nis ['tɪu-nɪs]

tupping TUHP-ing ['tʌp-ɪŋ]

turfy TER-fee ['tɝ-fi]

Turlygod TER-li-gahd ['tɝ-lɪ-gɑd]

Turph TERF [tɝf]

turpitude TER-pi-tyōōd ['tɝ-pɪ-tɪud]

turqoise TER-koyz ['tɝ-kɔɪz]

turquoise TER-koyz ['tɝ-kɔɪz] or ___-kwoyz [___-kwɔɪz]

Tuscan TUHS-kuhn ['tʌs-kən]

tush TUHSH [tʌʃ]

tut TUHT [tʌt]

twain TWAYN [tweɪn]

twere TWER [twɝ]

twiggen TWIG-uhn ['twɪg-ən]

twit TWIT [twɪt]

'twixt TWIKST [twɪkst]

twopences TUHP-uhnts-iz ['tʌp-ənts-ɪz]

Tybalt *(R&J)* TIB-uhlt ['tɪb-əlt]

Tyburn TEYE-bern ['taɪ-bɚn]

Tyke TEYEK [taɪk]

Typhon TEYE-fahn ['taɪ-fɑn]

Tyre TEYER [taɪɚ] possibly scans to TEYE-er ['taɪ-ɚ]
  @ *PER* II, 3, 81

EE i be/ I ɪ bit/ EH ɛ bet/ AA æ bat/ ŌŌ u boot / ŌŌ ʊ book/ AW ɔ bought/ AH ɑ father/ ER ɝ bird/ UH ʌ cup/ AY eɪ bay/ EYE aɪ bite/ OY ɔɪ boy/ OH oʊ boat/ OW aʊ how/ YŌŌ ɪu duke/ EAR ɪɚ beer/ AIR ɛɚ bear/ ŌŌR ʊɚ tour/ AWR ɔɚ bore/ AHR ɑɚ bar/ NG ŋ king/ SH ʃ ship/ ZH ʒ vision/ TH θ thirty/ TH ð then/ CH tʃ child/ J ʤ just/ For complete list, see Key to Pronunciation p. 2.

Tyrian always scans to TI-ryuhn ['tɪ-rjən]

Tyrrel, Sir James *(RIII)* TI-ruhl ['tɪ-rəl]

Tyrus TEYE-ruhs ['taɪ-rəs]

'ud's UHDZ [ʌdz]

Ulysses yo͞o-LIS-eez [ju-'lɪs-iz]
Ulysses *(T&C)*

umber UHM-ber ['ʌm-bɚ]

umbrage UHM-brij ['ʌm-brɪdʒ]

Umfrevile uhm-FREHV-uhl [əm-'frɛv-əl] possibly scans to
UHM-fruh-vuhl ['ʌm-frə-vəl]

unaneled uhn-uh-NEELD [ən-ə-'nild]

unchary uhn-CHEH-ree [ən-'tʃɛ-ri] or __-CHAA-__
[__-'tʃæ-__]

uncleanly uhn-KLEHN-lee [ən-'klɛn-li]

unclew uhn-KLO͞O [ən-'klu]

uncouth (unfamiliar) UHN-ko͞oth ['ʌn-kuθ]

unction UHNGK-shuhn ['ʌŋk-ʃən]

unctuous scans to UHNGK-chuhs ['ʌŋk-tʃəs]

under-skinker UHN-der-SKING-ker ['ʌn-dɚ-skɪŋ-kɚ]

undescried uhn-di-SKREYED [ən-dɪ-'skraɪd]

uneath uhn-EETH [ən-'iθ]

unfeignedly uhn-FAYN-id-lee [ən-'feɪn-ɪd-li]

unfrequented always scans to UHN-free-kwehnt-id
['ʌn-fri-kwɛnt-ɪd]

ungenitured uhn-JEHN-i-cherd [ən-'dʒɛn-ɪ-tʃɚd]

unhouseled uhn-HOW-zuhld [ən-'haʊ-zəld]

unlineal scans to uhn-LIN-yuhl [ən-'lɪn-jəl]

unmitigable uhn-MIT-i-guh-b(uh)l [ən-'mɪt-ɪ-gə-bl̩]

unplausive uhn-PLAW-ziv [ən-'plɔ-zɪv]

unrecuring uhn-ri-KYOO-ring [ən-rɪ-'kjʊ-rɪŋ]

unseminared uhn-SEHM-i-nahrd [ən-'sɛm-ɪ-nɑɚd]

unstaid uhn-STAYD [ən-'steɪd]

unstanch uhn-STAWNCH [ən-'stɔntʃ] or ___-STAANCH [___-'stæntʃ]

untoward scans to UHN-tawrd ['ʌn-tɔɚd] @ *SHR* IV, 5, 78 and uhn-TOH-erd [ən-'toʊ-ɚd] @ *KJ* I, 1, 243

unwappered uhn-WAHP-erd [ən-'wɑp-ɚd]

unwonted uhn-WAWNT-id [ən-'wɔnt-ɪd] or ___-WOHNT-___ [___-'woʊnt-___]

upon uh-PAHN [ə-'pɑn] scans to UH-pahn ['ʌ-pɑn] e.g. @ *12th* V, 1, 93

Urchinfield ER-chin-feeld ['ɝ-tʃɪn-fild]

Ursa Major ER-suh MAY-jer ['ɝ-sə] ['meɪ-dʒɚ]

Ursula ER-suh-luh ['ɝ-sə-lə] scans to ERS-luh ['ɝs-lə] Ursula *(MADO)* scans @ III, 1, 34, also called "Ursley" ERS-lee ['ɝs-li] @ III, 1, 4

Urswick, Christopher *(RIII)* ERZ-ik ['ɝz-ɪk] or ERS-___ ['ɝs-___]

usance YOO-zuhns ['ju-zəns]

usurer YOO-zhuh-rer ['ju-ʒə-rɚ]

usurp yoo-ZERP [ju-'zɝp] or ___-SERP [___-'sɝp]

---

usurpation YŌŌ-zer-**PAY**-shuhn [ju-zɚ-'peɪ-ʃən] scans to
__-__-__-shee-uhn [__-__-__-ʃi-ən] e.g. @ *KJ* II, 1, 9

usury YŌŌ-zhuh-ree ['ju-ʒə-ri]

ut UHT [ʌt] or ŌŌT [ʊt]

Utis YŌŌ-tis ['ju-tɪs]

vagary VAY-guh-ree ['veɪ-gə-ri]

vails VAYLZ [veɪlz]

vainglory vayn-**GLAW**-ree [veɪn-'glɔ-ri] or **VAYN**-glaw-__
['veɪn-glɔ-__] scans to second syllable stress @ *HVIII* III,
1, 127

valance VAAL-uhns ['væl-əns]

valanced VAAL-uhnst ['væl-ənst]

Valdes VAAL-deez ['væl-diz]

vale VAYL [veɪl]

Valence VAAL-uhns ['væl-əns]

Valencius vuh-**LEHN**-shee-uhs [və-'lɛn-ʃi-əs]

Valentine VAAL-uhn-teyen ['væl-ən-taɪn]
Valentine *(TITUS)*
Valentine *(12th)*
Valentine *(2GEN)* possibly scans to **VAALN**-teyen
['væln-taɪn] @ I, 2, 38, also called "Valentinus"
VAAL-uhn-**TEYE**-nuhs [væl-ən-'taɪ-nəs]

Valentio scans to vuh-**LEHN**-shyoh [və-'lɛn-ʃjoʊ]

Valeria *(COR)* vuh-**LI**-ree-uh [və-'lɪ-ri-ə] scans to
___-**LI**-ryuh [___-'lɪ-rjə] e.g. @ I, 3, 41

Valerius vuh-**LI**-ree-uhs [və-'lɪ-ri-əs] scans to ___-**LI**-ryuhs
[___-'lɪ-rjəs]
Valerius *(2NOB)*
Valerius scans @ *2GEN* V, 3, 8

valor / valour VAAL-er ['væl-ɚ]

vant VAANT [vænt]

vantbrace VAANT-brays ['vænt-breɪs]

Vapians VAY-pee-uhnz ['veɪ-pi-ənz]

varlet VAHR-lit ['vaɚ-lɪt]

varletry VAHR-li-tree ['vaɚ-lɪ-tri]

varletto vahr-LEHT-oh [vaɚ-'lɛt-oʊ]

Varrius VAA-ree-uhs ['væ-ri-əs] scans to VAA-ryuhs ['væ-rjəs]
Varrius *(A&C)*
Varrius *(MM)* scans @ IV, 5, 1

Varro VAA-roh ['væ-roʊ]
Varro *(JC)*

vassal VAAS-uhl ['væs-əl]

vassalage VAA-suh-lij ['væ-sə-lɪdʒ]

vastidity vaas-TID-uh-tee [væs-'tɪd-ə-ti]

Vaudemont VOH-duh-mahnt ['voʊ-də-mɑnt]

Vaughan, Sir Thomas *(RIII)* VAWN [vɔn] scans to VAW-uhn
['vɔ-ən] e.g. @ V, 3, 143

vaultages VAWL-tij-iz ['vɔl-tɪdʒ-ɪz]

Vaumond VAW-muhnd ['vɔ-mənd]

vaunt VAWNT [vɔnt]

Vaux VAWKS [vɔks] or VAHKS [vɑks]
Vaux *(2HVI)*
Vaux, Sir Nicholas *(HVIII)*

vaward VOW-erd ['vaʊ-ɚd] or ___-awrd [___-ɔɚd]

---

vegetives VEHJ-i-tivz ['vɛʤ-ɪ-tɪvz]

velure veh-LOOR [vɛ-'lʊɚ]

vendible VEHN-duh-b(uh)l ['vɛn-də-bl̩]

venerable VEHN-uh-ruh-b(uh)l ['vɛn-ə-rə-bl̩]

venew VEHN-yoo ['vɛn-ju]

veneys VEHN-eez ['vɛn-iz]

venial scans to VEEN-yuhl ['vin-jəl]

Venice, Duke of VEHN-is ['vɛn-ɪs]
    Venice, Duke of *(MVEN)*
    Venice, Duke of *(OTH)*

ventages VEHN-tij-iz ['vɛn-tɪʤ-ɪz]

Ventidius vehn-TID-ee-uhs [vɛn-'tɪd-i-əs] scans to
    ___-TID-yuhs [___-'tid-jəs]
    Ventidius *(A&C)* scans @ II, 3, 31
    Ventidius *(TIMON)* scans @ I, 2, 9

venturous VEHN-chuh-ruhs ['vɛn-ʧə-rəs] scans to
    VEHNCH-ruhs ['vɛnʧ-rəs] e.g. @ *MID* IV, 1, 34

Venus VEE-nuhs ['vi-nəs]

Ver VER [vɝ]

verbatim ver-BAY-tim [vɝ-'beɪ-tɪm]

Verdun ver-DUHN [vɚ-'dʌn]

verdure VER-jer ['vɝ-ʤɚ]

Verger VER-jer ['vɝ-ʤɚ]

Verges *(MADO)* VER-jis ['vɝ-ʤɪs]

verier VEH-ree-er ['vɛ-ri-ɚ] scans to VAIR-yer ['vɛɚ-jɚ]
    @ *WT* I, 2, 66

veriest VEH-ree-ist ['vɛ-ri-ɪst] scans to VAIR-yist ['vɛɚ-jɪst]
    e.g. @ *CYM* V, 3, 77

Vernon VER-nuhn ['vɜ-nən]
Vernon *(1HVI)*
Vernon, Sir Richard *(1HIV)*

Verolles vuh-RAH-luhs [və-'rɑ-ləs] or __-ROH-leez [__-'roʊ-liz]

Verona vuh-ROH-nuh [və-'roʊ-nə]

Veronesa VEH-ruh-NEHS-uh [vɛ-rə-'nɛs-ə]

versal VER-suhl ['vɜ-səl]

vestal / Vestal VEHS-t(uh)l ['vɛs-tl̩]

vesture VEHS-cher ['vɛs-tʃə]

via VEE-uh ['vi-ə] or VEYE-__ ['vaɪ-__]

vial VEYEL [vaɪl] scans to VEYE-uhl ['vaɪ-əl] e.g. @ *A&C* I, 3, 63

viand VEYE-uhnd ['vaɪ-ənd]

Vicar VIK-er ['vɪk-ə]

vicegerent veyes-JI-ruhnt [vaɪs-'dʒɪ-rənt]

Viceroy VEYES-roy ['vaɪs-rɔɪ]

victual VI-t(uh)l ['vɪ-tl̩]

victuallers VIT-lerz ['vɪt-lə-z]

videlicet vi-DEHL-i-seht [vɪ-'dɛl-ɪ-sɛt]

vie VEYE [vaɪ]

vild VEYELD [vaɪld]

villagery VIL-ij-ree ['vɪl-ɪdʒ-ri]

Villiago vil-ee-YAH-goh [vɪl-i-'jɑ-goʊ]

EE i be/ I ɪ bit/ EH ɛ bet/ AA æ bat/ OO̅ u boot / OO̅ ʊ book/ AW ɔ bought/ AH ɑ father/ ER ɝ bird/
UH ʌ cup/ AY eɪ bay/ EYE aɪ bite/ OY ɔɪ boy/ OH oʊ boat/ OW aʊ how/ YOO̅ ɪu duke/ EAR ɪə
beer/ AIR ɛə bear/ OO̅R ʊə tour/ AWR ɔə bore/ AHR ɑə bar/ NG ŋ king/ SH ʃ ship/ ZH ʒ vision/
TH θ thirty/ TH̲ ð then/ CH tʃ child/ J dʒ just/ For complete list, see Key to Pronunciation p. 2.

251

Vincentio vin-SEHN-shee-oh [vɪn-ˈsɛn-ʃi-ou] scans to
　　___-SEHN-shyoh [___-ˈsɛn-ʃjou]
　　Vincentio *(MM)*
　　Vincentio *(SHR)* scans @ I, 1, 192

vindicative vin-DIK-uh-tiv [vɪn-ˈdɪk-ə-tɪv]

vinewd'st VIN-yo͞odst [ˈvɪn-judst]

Vintner *(1HIV)* VINT-ner [ˈvɪnt-nɚ]

viol VEYE-uhl [ˈvaɪ-əl]

Viola *(12th)* VEYE-uh-luh [ˈvaɪ-ə-lə] scans to VEYE-luh
　　[ˈvaɪ-lə] @ V, 1, 236

viol-de-gamboys VEYE-uhl-duh-GAAM-boyz
　　[ˈvaɪ-əl-də-gæm-bɔɪz]

Violenta *(AW)* VEYE-uh-LEHN-tuh [vaɪ-ə-ˈlɛn-tə]

violently VEYE-luhnt-lee [ˈvaɪ-lənt-li] scans to
　　VEYE-uh-lehnt-__ [ˈvaɪ-ə-lɛnt-__] @ *CE* I, 1, 102

Virgilia *(COR)* ver-JIL-ee-uh [vɚ-ˈdʒɪl-i-ə]

virginalling VER-jin-uhl-ing [ˈvɝ-dʒɪn-əl-ɪŋ] or possibly
　　scans to VER-jin-ling [ˈvɝ-dʒɪn-lɪŋ]

Virginius ver-JI-nee-uhs [vɚ-ˈdʒɪ-ni-əs] scans to __-JI-nyuhs
　　[__-ˈdʒɪ-njəs] @ *TITUS* V, 3, 50

Virgo VER-goh [ˈvɝ-gou]

visage VIZ-ij [ˈvɪz-ɪdʒ]

Viscount Rochford VEYE-kownt RAHCH-ferd [ˈvaɪ-kaunt]
　　[ˈratʃ-fɚd]

visor VEYE-zer [ˈvaɪ-zɚ]

Vitruvio vi-TRO͞O-vee-oh [vɪ-ˈtru-vi-ou]

viz. (that is) VIZ [vɪz]

vizaments VEYE-zuh-muhnts [ˈvaɪ-zə-mənts]

vizard VIZ-erd ['vɪz-ə-d] or ___-ahrd [___-aə-d]

vizor VEYE-zer ['vaɪ-zə-]

Volquessen vahl-KEHS-uhn [vɑl-'kɛs-ən]

Volsce VAHLS [vɑls] in plural **VAHLS**-iz ['vɑls-ɪz]

Volscian VAHL-shuhn ['vɑl-ʃən]

Voltemand *(HAM)* VAHL-ti-maand ['vɑl-tɪ-mænd]

volubility VAHL-yōō-BIL-i-tee [vɑl-ju-'bɪl-ɪ-ti]

voluble VAHL-yuh-b(uh)l ['vɑl-jə-b̩l] possibly scans to
 vahl-YŌŌ-___ [vɑl-'ju-___] @ *2NOB* I, 2, 67

Volumnia *(COR)* vuh-LUHM-nee-uh [və-'lʌm-ni-ə]

Volumnius *(JC)* vuh-LUHM-nee-uhs [və-'lʌm-ni-əs] scans to
 __-LUHM-nyuhs [__-'lʌm-njəs] @ V, 5, 15

vot'ress VOH-tris ['voʊ-trɪs]

votaress VOH-tuh-ris ['voʊ-tə-rɪs]

votarist VOH-tuh-rist ['voʊ-tə-rɪst] scans to VOH-trist
 ['voʊ-trɪst] @ *MM* I, 4, 5

votary VOH-tuh-ree ['voʊ-tə-ri]

vouchsafe vowch-SAYF [vaʊtʃ-'seɪf] scans to VOWCH-sayf
 ['vaʊtʃ-seɪf] @ *LLL* V, 2, 210

vox VAHKS [vɑks]

Vulcan VUHL-kuhn ['vʌl-kən]

waft WAHFT [wɑft] or WAAFT [wæft]

waftage WAHF-tij ['wɑf-tɪdʒ] or WAAFT-___ ['wæf-___]

wafter WAHFT-er ['wɑft-ə-] or WAAFT-___ ['wæft-___]

EE i be/ I ɪ bit/ EH ɛ bet/ AA æ bat/ ŌŌ u boot / OO ʊ book/ AW ɔ bought/ AH ɑ father/ ER ɝ bird/
UH ʌ cup/ AY eɪ bay/ EYE aɪ bite/ OY ɔɪ boy/ OH oʊ boat/ OW aʊ how/ YŌŌ ɪu duke/ EAR ɪə
beer/ AIR ɛə bear/ ŌŌR ʊə tour/ AWR ɔə bore/ AHR ɑə bar/ NG ŋ king/ SH ʃ ship/ ZH ʒ vision/
TH θ thirty/ TH ð then/ CH tʃ child/ J dʒ just/ For complete list, see Key to Pronunciation p. 2.

wain WAYN [weɪn]

wainropes WAYN-rohps ['weɪn-roʊps]

wainscot WAYN-skuht ['weɪn-skət] or ___-skaht [___-skɑt]

Wallon / Walloon wah-LŌŌN [wɑ-'lun]

wan (adj) (pale) WAHN [wɑn]

wan / wanned (v) (to become pale) WAHN [wɑn] / WAHND [wɑnd]

wane (n) (a decrease) WAYN [weɪn]

wane / waned (v) (to decrease, to lessen) WAYN [weɪn] / WAYND [weɪnd]

wanion WAHN-yuhn ['wɑn-jən]

wanny WAHN-ee ['wɑn-i]

wanton WAHN-tuhn ['wɑn-tən]

wappened WAHP-uhnd ['wɑp-ənd]

warder / Warder WAWR-der ['wɔɚ-dɚ]

ware / Ware WAIR [wɛɚ]

warily WEH-ri-lee ['wɛ-rɪ-li]

warr'st WAWRST [wɔɚst]

warrener WAW-rehn-er ['wɔ-rɛn-ɚ]

warrior WAW-ree-er ['wɔ-ri-ɚ] scans to **WAWR-yer** ['wɔɚ-jɚ] e.g. @ *1HVI* II, 3, 82

Wart, Thomas *(2HIV)* WAWRT [wɔɚt]

Warwick WAW-rik ['wɔ-rɪk] or **WAH-___** ['wɑ-___] Warwick, Earl of *(2HIV, HV)*

Warwickshire WAW-rik-sher ['wɔ-rɪk-ʃɚ] or __-__-shear [__-__-ʃɪɚ] or **WAH-__-__** ['wɑ-__-__]

Washford WAWSH-ferd ['wɔʃ-fɚd]

wassail WAH-suhl ['wɑ-səl]

wast WUHST [wʌst] or WAHST [wɑst]

Waterford WAW-ter-ferd ['wɔ-tɚ-fɚd]

Waterton, Sir Robert WAW-ter-t(uh)n ['wɔ-tɚ-tn̩]

wawl WAWL [wɔl]

we'ld WEELD [wild]

weal WEEL [wil]

wealsmen WEELZ-muhn ['wilz-mən]

wean WEEN [win]

ween WEEN [win]

weet WEET [wit]

Weird Sisters *(MAC)* WEARD SIS-terz [wɪɚd] ['sɪs-tɚz]
scans to WEE-erd ['wi-ɚd] or WI-___ ['wɪ-___]
e.g. @ II, 1, 20

welkin WEHL-kin ['wɛl-kɪn]

wench WEHNCH [wɛntʃ]

wend WEHND [wɛnd]

weraday WEH-ruh-day ['wɛ-rə-deɪ]

wesand WEE-z(uh)nd ['wi-zn̩d]

Westminster WEHST-min-ster ['wɛst-mɪn-stɚ]
Westminster, Abbot of *(RII)*

Westmoreland WEHST-mer-luhnd ['wɛst-mɚ-lənd]
Earl of Westmoreland *(1HIV, 2HIV, HV)*

EE i be/ I ɪ bit/ EH ɛ bet/ AA æ bat/ OO u boot / OO ʊ book/ AW ɔ bought/ AH ɑ father/ ER ɝ bird/
UH ʌ cup/ AY eɪ bay/ EYE aɪ bite/ OY ɔɪ boy/ OH oʊ boat/ OW aʊ how/ YOO ɪu duke/ EAR ɪɚ
beer/ AIR ɛɚ bear/ OOR ʊɚ tour/ AWR ɔɚ bore/ AHR ɑɚ bar/ NG ŋ king/ SH ʃ ship/ ZH ʒ vision/
TH θ thirty/ TH ð then/ CH tʃ child/ J dʒ just/ For complete list, see Key to Pronunciation p. 2.

wether WEH<u>TH</u>-er ['wɛð-ɚ]

whales-bone HWAYL-is-bohn ['hweɪl-ɪs-boʊn]

whate'er hwuht-AIR [hwət-'ɛɚ]

whatsoe'er HWUHT-soh-air ['hwʌt-soʊ-ɛɚ]

whatsome'er HWUHT-suhm-air ['hwʌt-səm-ɛɚ]

whatsomever HWUHT-suhm-ehv-er ['hwʌt-səm-ɛv-ɚ]

whe'r HWAIR [hwɛɚ]

Wheeson HWEE-suhn ['hwi-sən]

whelk (n) HWEHLK [hwɛlk]

whelked (v) HWEHLKT [hwɛlkt]

whelm HWEHLM [hwɛlm]

whelp HWEHLP [hwɛlp]

whet HWEHT [hwɛt]

whether HWEH<u>TH</u>-er ['hwɛð-ɚ] scans to HWAIR [hwɛɚ]
  e.g. @ *HAM* II, 2, 17

whetstone HWEHT-stohn ['hwɛht-stoʊn]

whey HWAY [hweɪ]

whiffler HWI-fler ['hwɪ-flɚ]

whilere hweyel-AIR [hwaɪl-'ɛɚ]

whiles HWEYELZ [hwaɪlz]

whilst HWEYELST [hwaɪlst]

whirligig HWER-li-gig ['hwɝ-lɪ-gɪg]

whirring HWE(r)-ring ['hwɝ-rɪŋ]

whist HWIST [hwɪst]

whit HWIT [hwɪt]

Whitefriars scans to hweyet-FREYE-erz [hwaɪt-'fraɪ-ɚ-z]

whither HWITH-er ['hwɪð-ɚ] scans to HWAIR [hwɛɚ-]
  @ *COR* IV, 1, 34

whiting HWEYET-ing ['hwaɪt-ɪŋ]

whiting-time HWEYET-ing-teyem ['hwaɪt-ɪŋ-taɪm]

Whitmore, Walter *(2HVI)* HWIT-mawr WAW-ter
  ['hwɪt-mɔɚ] ['wɔ-tɚ] (The meaning of the passage in
  IV, 1 depends on the "Walter"/"water" homonym.)

whitsters HWEYET-sterz ['hwaɪt-stɚ-z]

Whitsun HWIT-suhn ['hwɪt-sən]

whoremonger HAWR-muhng-ger ['hɔɚ-mən-gɚ] or
  ___-mahng-___ [___-mɑŋ-___]

whoreson HAWR-s(uh)n ['hɔɚ-sn̩]

whorish HAW-rish ['hɔ-rɪʃ]

whosoe'er HOO-soh-air ['hu-soʊ-ɛɚ-]

Widow WID-oh ['wɪd-oʊ]
  Widow *(AW)*
  Widow *(SHR)*

wield WEELD [wild]

wight WEYET [waɪt]

William *(AYL)* WIL-yuhm ['wɪl-jəm]

Williams, Michael *(HV)* WIL-yuhmz ['wɪl-jəmz]

Willoughby, Lord *(RII)* WIL-uh-bee ['wɪl-ə-bi]

wilt WILT [wɪlt]

Wiltshire WILT-sher ['wɪlt-ʃɚ-] or ___-shear [___-ʃɪɚ-]

EE i be/ I ɪ bit/ EH ɛ bet/ AA æ bat/ OO u boot / OO ʊ book/ AW ɔ bought/ AH ɑ father/ ER ɝ bird/
UH ʌ cup/ AY eɪ bay/ EYE aɪ bite/ OY ɔɪ boy/ OH oʊ boat/ OW aʊ how/ YOO ɪu duke/ EAR ɪɚ
beer/ AIR ɛɚ bear/ OOR ʊɚ tour/ AWR ɔɚ bore/ AHR ɑɚ bar/ NG ŋ king/ SH ʃ ship/ ZH ʒ vision/
TH θ thirty/ TH ð then/ CH ʧ child/ J ʤ just/ For complete list, see Key to Pronunciation p. 2.

Winchester WIN-chehs-ter ['wɪn-ʧɛs-tɚ] or ___-chis-___
[___-ʧɪs-___]

Wincot WING-kuht ['wɪŋ-kət]

wind (n) (a current of air) WIND [wɪnd]

wind (v) (to blow) WIND [wɪnd]

wind (v) (to turn or twist) WEYEND [waɪnd]

windlasses WIND-luhs-iz ['wɪnd-ləs-ɪz]

windring WEYEND-ring ['waɪnd-rɪŋ]

Windsor WIN-zer ['wɪn-zɚ]

Wingham WING-uhm ['wɪŋ-əm]

winnow WIN-oh ['wɪn-ou]

wist WIST [wɪst]

withal wi<u>th</u>-AWL [wɪð-'ɔl]

withers WI<u>TH</u>-erz ['wɪð-ɚz]

Wittenberg WI-t(uh)n-berg ['wɪ-tn̩-bɚg]

wittol WI-t(uh)l ['wɪ-tl̩]

wittolly WI-t(uh)l-ee ['wɪ-tl̩-i]

wo't see "woo't"

Wolsey, Cardinal *(HVIII)* WO͝OL-zee ['wʊl-zi]

wolt WOHLT [woult] or WO͝OLT [wʊlt]

womby WO͞O-mee ['wu-mi]

Woncot WO͝ONG-kuht ['wʊŋ-kət] or **WAHNG-**___
['wɑŋ-___]

wont WAWNT [wɔnt] or WOHNT [wount]

woo't / wo't WO͞OT [wʊt]

woodbine WŎOD-beyen ['wʊd-baɪn]

Woodeville / Woodville WŎOD-vil ['wʊd-vɪl] scans to
   WŎOD-uh-vil ['wʊd-ə-vɪl]
   Woodville, Anthony, Earl Rivers *(RIII)* scans @ I, 1, 67
   Woodville, Richard *(1HVI)*

wooer WŌO-er ['wu-ɚ]

woosel WŌO-z(uh)l ['wu-z̩l]

Worcester WŎOS-ter ['wʊs-tɚ]

workyday WERK-ee-day ['wɝk-i-deɪ]

worship WER-ship ['wɝ-ʃɪp]

wor'st WAWRST [wɔɚst]

worsted-stocking WŌOST-id-STAHK-ing ['wʊst-ɪd-stak-ɪŋ]
   or WERST-__-__-__ ['wɝst-__-__-__]

wort (beer) WERT [wɝt]

worts (cabbages) WERTS [wɝts]

wot WAHT [wɑt] or WAWT [wɔt]

wound (n) (a break in the flesh) WŌOND [wund] possibly
   WOWND [waʊnd] @ *RII* III, 2, 139 and *PER* IV, Cho, 23

wound (v) (turned or twisted) WOWND [waʊnd]

wrack RAAK [ræk]

wrath RAATH [ræθ]

wreak REEK [rik]

wreath (n) REETH [riθ]

wreathe (v) REE̲T̲H̲ [rið]

EE i be/ I ɪ bit/ EH ɛ bet/ AA æ bat/ ŌO u boot / ŎO ʊ book/ AW ɔ bought/ AH ɑ father/ ER ɝ bird/
UH ʌ cup/ AY eɪ bay/ EYE aɪ bite/ OY ɔɪ boy/ OH oʊ boat/ OW aʊ how/ YŌO ɪu duke/ EAR ɪɚ
beer/ AIR ɛɚ bear/ ŌOR ʊɚ tour/ AWR ɔɚ bore/ AHR ɑɚ bar/ NG ŋ king/ SH ʃ ship/ ZH ʒ vision/
TH θ thirty/ T̲H̲ ð then/ CH tʃ child/ J ʤ just/ For complete list, see Key to Pronunciation p. 2.

259

wrest REHST [rɛst]

writhled RI-thuhld ['rɪ-θəld]

wroath ROHTH [rouθ]

wrought RAWT [rɔt]

Wye WEYE [waɪ]

Xanthippe zaan-TIP-ee [zæn-'tɪp-i]

yare YAIR [jɛɚ] or YAHR [jɑɚ]

yaw YAW [jɔ]

yclad ee-KLAAD [i-'klæd]

ycleped ee-KLEEPT [i-'klipt] scans to ee-KLIP-id [i-'klɪp-ɪd]
    @ *LLL* V, 2, 591 to make sense of "clipt" in next line

ye YEE [ji]

ye're YER [jɝ]

yea YAY [jeɪ]

Yed YEHD [jɛd]

Yedward YEHD-werd ['jɛd-wɚd]

ye'll YEEL [jil]

yeoman YOH-muhn ['jou-mən]

yerk YERK [jɝk]

yest YEHST [jɛst]

yesty YEHS-tee ['jɛs-ti]

ye've YEEV [jiv]

yew YOO [ju]

yon YAHN [jɑn]

yond YAHND [jɑnd]

yonder YAHND-er ['jɑnd-ɚ]

Yorick YAW-rik ['jɔ-rɪk]

York YAWRK [jɔɚk]
York, Duchess of *(RII, RIII)*
York, Duke of *(HV)*

Yorkshire YAWRK-sher ['jɔɚk-ʃɚ] or ___-shear [___-ʃɪɚ]

you'ld YOOLD [juld]

Young Cato *(JC)* KAY-toh ['keɪ-toʊ]

Young Lucius *(TITUS)* LOO-shuhs ['lu-ʃəs]

Young Marcius *(COR)* MAHR-shuhs ['mɑɚ-ʃəs]

Young Siward *(MAC)* SYOO-erd ['sɪu-ɚd]

younker YUHNG-ker ['jʌŋ-kɚ]

y-ravished ee-RAA-vish-id [i-'ræ-vɪʃ-ɪd]

yslacked ee-SLAAK-id [i-'slæk-ɪd]

zealous ZEHL-uhs ['zɛl-əs]

zed ZEHD [zɛd]

Zenelophon zeh-NEHL-uh-fahn [zɛ-'nɛl-ə-fɑn]

zephyrs ZEHF-erz ['zɛf-ɚz]

zounds (corruption of "God's wounds") ZOONDZ [zundz]
or possibly ZOWNDZ [zaʊndz]

---

latin

C

O that's the Latin word
Love's Labor's Lost III, 1, 129

In an attempt at consistency, the following pronunciations are rendered into what is commonly referred to as "restored" or classical Latin. Many Latin words and phrases have entered the English language. Clearly, it is best to pronounce these in the manner with which the audience is most familiar. Thus, while the letter *c* is always hard in classical Latin pronunciation, names such as Caesar and Cicero should be pronounced as they are commonly sounded in English with the soft *c*. These pronunciations reflect what is called "Anglicized" Latin, which was the form of Latin pronunciation prevalent in Britain until the end of the 19th century, when a movement arose to "restore" or codify Latin pronunciation. To complicate matters further, there is another form of pronunciation, church Latin, which is Italianate in style, and which some may find to be appropriate for ecclesiastical references or greetings. The greatest problem with the classical pronunciation is the use of the *w* for the *v*, producing **WAY**-nee, **WEE**-dee, **WEE**-kee for Caesar's famous quote "Veni, vidi, vici." In this case, we have provided a pronunciation more common for American ears, **VAY**-nee, **VEE**-dee, **VEE**-chee, which is church Latin. Readers should feel free, if they prefer, to use the *v* sound whenever the *w* sound appears. If a pronunciation is other than classical, we have indicated such in parentheses. We have included blunders and those instances where a character's incorrect use of Latin suggests a pronunciation. Finally, it might be good to remember that, in the words of *A Dictionary of Latin Words and Phrases*, "anything goes" in the pronunciation of Latin.

We have alphabetized this section by individual word, phrase, or sentence, used the respelling system exclusively to avoid the confusion that might be engendered by long phonetic transcriptions, and entered all monosyllabic words in lower case letters to present this information as clearly as possible.

Accommodo
  ah-**KAHM**-ah-doh

accusativo
  ah-ko͞o-zuh-**TEE**-woh

Ad Jovem, ad Apollinem, ad martem
  ahd **YOH**-wehm, ahd ah-**PAHL**-i-nehm, ahd **MAHR**-tehm

Ad manes fratrum
  ahd **MAHN**-ays **FRAH**-tro͞om

Adsum
  AHD-so͞om

Aio te, Aeacida, romanos vincere posse
  AH-ee-oh tay, eye-**AH**-kee-duh, roh-**MAHN**-ohs
  WINGK-er-ay **PAHS**-ay

Armigero
  ahr-mi-**JI**-roh

Ave
  AH-vay

Ave-Maries
  AH-vay **MEH**-reez (church Latin)

EE be/ I bit/ EH bet/ AA bat/ O͞O boot / O͝O book/ AW bought/ AH father/ ER bird/ UH cup/ AY bay/ EYE bite/ OY boy/ OH boat/ OW how/ YO͞O duke/ EAR beer/ AIR bear/ O͞OR tour/ AWR bore/ AHR bar/ NG king/ SH ship/ ZH vision/ TH thirty/ T̲H̲ then/ CH child/ J just/ For complete list, see Key to Pronunciation p. 2.

Benedicite
　　bay-nay-**DEE**-chee-tay　(church Latin)

Bis coctus
　　bis **KAHK**-to͞os

bona terra, mala gens
　　BAHN-ah　**TEH**-rah,　**MAH**-lah　gayns

bone for bene
　　BAHN-ay　fawr　**BEHN**-ay

Bonos dies　(blunder for "bonus dies")
　　possibly **BOH**-nohs　**DEE**-ehs

candidatus
　　kahn-di-**DAH**-to͞os

canus　(blunder for "canis")
　　possibly　**KAHN**-uhs

caret
　　KAHR-eht

caveto　(blunder for "cavete")
　　possibly　kuh-**VEH**-toh

coelo　(blunder for "caelo")
　　possibly　**KEE**-loh

Coram　(blunder for "quorum")
　　possibly　**KAW**-ruhm

cucullus non facit monachum
　　ko͞o-**KO͞OL**-o͞os　nahn　**FAH**-kit　**MAHN**-ah-ko͞om

Cum multis aliis
　　ko͞om　**MO͞OL**-tees　**AHL**-i-ees

cum privilegio ad imprimendum solum
　　ko͞om　pree-wi-**LAY**-gee-yoh　ahd　im-pri-**MEHN**-do͞om
　　SOH-lo͞om

Custalorum (blunder for "custus rotulorum")
   possibly kuhs-tuh-LAW-ruhm

Di faciant laudis summa sit ista tuae
   DEE FAHK-ee-ahnt **LOW**-dis **SŌŌM**-ah sit **IS**-tah **TŌŌ**-eye

Dii boni
   DEE-ee **BAHN**-ee

Dii deaeque omnes
   DEE-ee day-**EYE**-kway **AHM**-nays

diluculo surgere
   dee-**LŌŌ**-kōō-loh sōōr-**GEH**-ray

Dives
   DEE-wis or **DEYE**-veez (Anglicized Latin)

Ecce signum
   EHK-ay **SIG**-nōōm

Ego et Rex meus
   EHG-oh eht rayks **MEH**-ōōs

ergo
   ER-goh

Et bonum quo antiquius eo melius
   eht **BAHN**-ōōm kwoh ahn-**TEE**-kwi-ōōs **EH**-oh **MEHL**-i-ōōs

Et cetera
   eht **KEHT**-eh-ruh

Et opus exegi, quod nec Jovis ira, nec ignis
   eht **AHP**-ōōs ehks-**AY**-gee, kwahd nehk **YAH**-wis **EE**-rah,
   nehk **IG**-nis

et tu Brute
   eht tōō **BRŌŌ**-tay or possibly scans to brōō-**TAY**

EE be/ I bit/ EH bet/ AA bat/ ŌŌ boot / ŌŌ book/ AW bought/ AH father/ ER bird/ UH cup/
AY bay/ EYE bite/ OY boy/ OH boat/ OW how/ YŌŌ duke/ EAR beer/ AIR bear/ ŌŌR tour/
AWR bore/ AHR bar/ NG king/ SH ship/ ZH vision/ TH thirty/ T̲H̲ then/ CH child/ J just/ For
complete list, see Key to Pronunciation p. 2.

facere
    FAHK-eh-ray

Facile precor gelida quando pecas omnia sub umbra ruminat
    FAH-ki-lay PREHK-awr GEHL-i-dah KWAHN-doh
    PEHK-ahs AHM-nay sōob ŌOM-brah RŌO-mi-naht

Gallia
    GAAL-ee-yuh or scans to GAAL-yuh e.g. @ *1HVI* IV, 7, 48

genitivo hujus
    gehn-i-TEE-woh HŌO-yōos

Haud credo
    hohd KRAY-doh   (spoken so that Dull can misunderstand
    as "old gray doe" @ *LLL* IV, 2, 12)

Hic et ubique
    heek eht ōō-BEE-kway

Hic ibat Simois, hic est Sigeia tellus; Hic steterat Priami regia
celsa senis
    heek I-baat SIM-oh-is,
    heek ehst si-GAY-i-uh TEHL-ōōs;
    heek STEHT-eh-raht PREE-ah-mee RAY-gee-ah KEHL-
    sah SEHN-is

Hic jacet
    heek YAH-keht

hic, haec, hoc
    heek, hayk, hahk

Homo
    HOH-moh

honorificabilitudinitatibus
    AHN-eh-ri-fi-KAA-bi-li-TŌO-di-ni-TAA-ti-buhs (Anglicized
    Latin)

horum, harum, horum
    HAW-rōom, HAH-rōom, HAW-rōom

Hysterica passio
    hi-**STEH**-ri-kah **PAH**-see-yoh

imitari
    im-i-**TAH**-ree

imprimis
    im-**PREE**-mis

in capite
    in **KAHP**-i-tay

In hac spe vivo
    in hahk spay **WEE**-woh

In limbo Patrum
    in **LIM**-boh **PAH**-tr$\overline{oo}$m

In terram Salicam mulieres ne succedant
    in **TEH**-rahm **SAHL**-i-kahm m$\overline{oo}$-**LEE**-eh-rays nay
    s$\overline{oo}$k-**KAY**-dahnt

In via
    in **WEE**-uh or **VEE**-uh or **VEYE**-uh

Integer vitae, scelerisque purus, Non eget Mauri jaculis nec arcu
    in-**TEHG**-er **WEE**-teye skehl-i-**RIS**-kway **P$\overline{OO}$**-r$\overline{oo}$s,
    nahn **EHG**-eht **MOW**-ree **YAHK**-$\overline{oo}$-lees nehk **AHRK**-$\overline{oo}$

Invitis nubibus
    in-**WEE**-t$\overline{oo}$s **N$\overline{OO}$**-bi-b$\overline{oo}$s

Ipse
    IP-say

ipso facto
    IP-soh **FAHK**-toh or **FAAK**-toh

Ira furor brevis est
    EE-rah **F$\overline{OO}$**-rawr **BREH**-wis ehst

EE be/ I bit/ EH bet/ AA bat/ $\overline{OO}$ boot / $\breve{OO}$ book/ AW bought/ AH father/ ER bird/ UH cup/
AY bay/ EYE bite/ OY boy/ OH boat/ OW how/ Y$\overline{OO}$ duke/ EAR beer/ AIR bear/ $\overline{OO}$R tour/
AWR bore/ AHR bar/ NG king/ SH ship/ ZH vision/ TH thirty/ <u>TH</u> then/ CH child/ J just/ For
complete list, see Key to Pronunciation p. 2.

Item (used to enumerate)
  I-tehm

Lapis
  LAH-pis

Laus deo, bone, intelligo
  lows **DAY**-yoh, **BAHN**-ay, in-**TEHL**-i-goh

Lege, domine
  LEHG-ay, **DAHM**-i-nay

Leo-natus
  LAY-oh-**NAH**-tōōs

Lux tua vita mihi
  lōōks **TŌŌ**-ah **WEE**-tah **MI**-hee

Magni dominator poli, tam lentus audis scelera? tam lentus vides
  MAHG-nee dohm-i-**NAH**-tawr **PAHL**-ee,
  tahm **LEHN**-tōōs **OW**-dees **SKEHL**-eh-rah?
  tahm **LEHN**-tōōs **WID**-ays

manu cita
  MAHN-ōō **KIT**-ah

manus
  MAHN-ōōs

Me pompae provexit apex
  may **PAHM**-peye proh-**WEHK**-sit **AH**-pehks

Medice, te ipsum
  MEHD-i-kay, tay **IP**-sōōm

Mehercle
  may-**HERK**-lay

Memento mori
  meh-**MEHN**-toh **MAW**-ree

Mollis aer
  MAHL-is **AH**-air

Mulier
  MŌOL-ee-er

ne intelligis, domine
  nay in-**TEHL**-i-gis, **DAHM**-i-nay

nominativo
  noh-min-ah-**TEE**-woh

Non nobis
  nahn **NOH**-bees

Novi hominen tanquam te
  NOH-wee **HAHM**-i-nehm **TAHNG**-kwahm tay

obsque hoc nihil est
  AHBS-kway hahk **NEE**-hil ehst

omne bene
  AHM-nay **BEHN**-ay

ostentare
  ahs-tehn-**TAH**-ray

Ovidius Naso
  oh-**WID**-ee-ōōs **NAH**-soh or oh-**VID**-ee-uhs **NAY**-zoh
  (Anglicized Latin)

paene gelidus timor occupat artus
  PEYE-nay **GEHL**-i-dōōs **TIM**-awr **AHK**-ōō-paht **AHR**-tōōs

passio
  PAHS-ee-oh

pauca
  POW-kah

pauca verba
  POW-kah **WAIR**-bah

EE be/ I bit/ EH bet/ AA bat/ ŌŌ boot / ŌŌ book/ AW bought/ AH father/ ER bird/ UH cup/
AY bay/ EYE bite/ OY boy/ OH boat/ OW how/ YŌŌ duke/ EAR beer/ AIR bear/ ŌŌR tour/
AWR bore/ AHR bar/ NG king/ SH ship/ ZH vision/ TH thirty/ T̲H̲ then/ CH child/ J just/ For
complete list, see Key to Pronunciation p. 2.

per se
  per say

Per Stygia, per manes vehor
  per **STIG**-ee-ah, per **MAHN**-ays **WEH**-hawr

perge
  PAIR-gay

pia mater
  PEE-uh **MAHT**-er

Praeclarissimus filius noster Henricus Rex Angliae et Heres
Franciae
  preye-klah-**RIS**-i-mo͞os **FEE**-lee-o͞os **NOH**-ster hehn-**REE**-ko͞os
  rayks **AHNG**-gli-eye eht **HAY**-rays **FRAHN**-ki-eye

praemunire
  preye-**MYO͞ON**-i-ray

primo, secundo, tertio
  PREE-moh, seh-**KO͞ON**-doh, **TAIR**-shee-oh

Priscian
  PRISH-ee-uhn

pro Deum, medius fidius
  proh **DAY**-o͞om, **MEHD**-ee-o͞os **FID**-ee-o͞os

pueritia
  po͞o-eh-**RIT**-ee-ah

pulcher
  PO͞OL-ker

quare
  KWAH-ray

quasi
  KWAH-zee

Qui me alit, me extinguit
  kwee may **AH**-lit, may ehk-**STING**-gwit

Qui passa
    kee **PAAS**-uh

qui, quae, quod
    kee, kay, kahd (to make the pun with keys, case, and cod)

quid for quo
    kwid fawr kwoh

quis
    kwis

Quo usque tandem
    kwoh O͞OS-kway **TAHN**-dehm

quoniam
    KWAHN-ee-ahm

Ratolorum (blunder for "Rotulorum")
    possibly raa-tuh-**LAW**-ruhm

Redime te captum quam queas minimo
    REHD-i-may tay **KAHP**-to͞om kwahm **KWAY**-ahs
    MIN-i-moh

respice finem
    REHS-pi-kay **FEE**-nehm

sancta majestas
    SAHNGK-tah mah-**YEHS**-tahs

sanguis
    SAHNG-gwis

satis quid sufficit
    SAHT-is kwid SO͞O-fi-kit

Se offendendo (blunder for "de defendendo")
    possibly say **OH**-fehn-dehn-doh

EE be/ I bit/ EH bet/ AA bat/ O͞O boot / O͝O book/ AW bought/ AH father/ ER bird/ UH cup/
AY bay/ EYE bite/ OY boy/ OH boat/ OW how/ YO͞O duke/ EAR beer/ AIR bear/ O͞OR tour/
AWR bore/ AHR bar/ NG king/ SH ship/ ZH vision/ TH thirty/ T̲H̲ then/ CH child/ J just/ For
complete list, see Key to Pronunciation p. 2.

271

semper idem
   SEHM-pair **EE**-dehm

Sic spectanda fides
   sik spehk-**TAHN**-dah **FID**-ehs

sine
   SEE-nay

singulariter
   sing-g$\overline{oo}$-**LAH**-ri-ter

sit fas aut nefas
   sit fahs awt **NEHF**-ahs

solus
   SOH-luhs

Stuprum
   ST$\overline{OO}$P-r$\overline{oo}$hm

suum cuique
   S$\overline{OO}$-$\overline{oo}$m **KWI**-kway

tanta est erga te mentis integritas, regina serenissima
   TAHN-tah ehst **ER**-gah tay **MEHN**-tis in-**TEHG**-ri-tahs,
   ray-**GEE**-nah seh-rehn-**IS**-i-mah

Tantaene animis coelestibus irae
   tahn-**TEYE**-nay **AHN**-i-mees keye-**LEHS**-ti-b$\overline{oo}$s **EE**-reye

Te Deum
   tay **DAY**-$\overline{oo}$m

terra
   TEH-rah

Terras Astrae reliquit
   TEH-rahs **AHS**-treye-uh rehl-**EE**-kwit

tertio
   TER-shee-oh

tremor cordis
   TREH-mer **KAWR**-dis

unguem
   O͞ONG-gwehm

veni, vidi, vici
   VAY-nee, **VEE**-dee, **VEE**-chee (church Latin)

Ver
   wair

Verba
   WAIR-bah

via
   WEE-uh or **VEE**-uh or **VEYE**-uh

videlicet
   vi-**DEHL**-i-sit (Anglicized Latin)

Video et gaudeo
   WID-ay-oh eht **GOW**-day-oh

videsne quis venit
   wid-**AYS**-nay kwis **WEHN**-it

Vir sapit qui pauca loquitur
   wear **SAHP**-it kwee **POW**-kah **LAH**-kwi-to͝or

viva voce
   WEE-wah **WOH**-kay or **VEE**-vah **VOH**-chay or
   VOH-chee (church Latin)

vocativo
   wohk-ah-**TEE**-woh

vocatur
   WOHK-ah-to͝or

vox
   wohks

EE be/ I bit/ EH bet/ AA bat/ O͞O boot / O͝O book/ AW bought/ AH father/ ER bird/ UH cup/
AY bay/ EYE bite/ OY boy/ OH boat/ OW how/ YO͞O duke/ EAR beer/ AIR bear/ O͞OR tour/
AWR bore/ AHR bar/ NG king/ SH ship/ ZH vision/ TH thirty/ T̲H̲ then/ CH child/ J just/ For
complete list, see Key to Pronunciation p. 2.

accents, dialects, and foreign languages

a great feast of language
Love's Labor's Lost V, 1, 35

In some plays, accents are required of characters whose native language is not English. This occurs in both *The Merry Wives of Windsor* and *Henry V*. In the former, Dr. Caius, the physician, speaks English with a French accent and Hugh Evans, the schoolmaster, speaks English with a Welsh accent. The text indicates the French accent with the substitution of *v* for *w*, and *t* or *d* for *th*. Sometimes an extra unstressed vowel sound is added to verbs. The Welsh accent is indicated by the substitution of *p* for *b*, *t* for *d*, and *g* for *k*. The sounds for *v* and *f* are transposed. Also, *s* and *sh* replace *z* and *zh*. In addition, the text indicates that the *w* sound at the beginning of words like *woman* disappears.

The different accents of the four captains in *Henry V* illuminate a central theme in the play. Fluellen, the second largest part, speaks with a Welsh accent. The printed text indicates the use of an Irish accent for MacMorris with the substitution of *ish* for *is* and *Chrish* for *Christ*, and a Scottish accent for Jamy with the repetition of *gud* for *good*. The text also indicates the use of *sall* for *shall* and the substitution of *ay* for *I*. If actors adopt the suggested nationalist accents for these characters, the question then is raised as to what to do with the speech of Gower, the Englishman. We would suggest that, in this one instance, an exception be made to our preference for American speech. The use of an English accent for Gower can accentuate the linguistic differences amongst the characters and point up the competing regional or national interests in both Shakespeare's and Henry's Britain, as well as reflect those of our own world.

In *Henry V*, both Katherine and Alice speak English with a French accent that is indicated with the substitution of *d* for *th* and *wat* for *what*. In turn, Henry's attempt to address Katherine in her native tongue provokes laughter on her part. There is no indication in the text about the accuracy of the Boy's French accent as he interprets between Pistol and the French soldier. However, he does seem to have achieved a basic familiarity with the language while on campaign.

In *Henry IV Part One*, there is no orthographic suggestion as to the adoption of an accent for the part of Glendower. An accent might be employed to excellent effect considering that he is a native speaker of Welsh. In addition, Hotspur seems to insult Glendower with the gibe that "no man speaks better Welsh." Productions have sometimes used a trace of a Spanish accent for Katherine in *Henry VIII*, and a French accent for the Queen in *Richard II* and for Margaret in the *Henry VI* trilogy.

Native speakers should be consulted for the French in *Henry V* and the Welsh exchanges between Glendower and Lady Mortimer in *Henry IV Part One*, as well as for the occasional Spanish and Italian in other plays.

The text of *King Lear* calls for a Somersetshire dialect when Edgar confronts Oswald. The text indicates this with the substitution of *z*'s for *s*'s and *v*'s for *f*'s among others. It is best learned from a native speaker or from a dialect tape.

Questions often arise as to the efficacy of a dialect in the portrayal of the rustic or lower class characters. Our preference is for the use of American speech rather than stage Cockney or generic lower-class English speech. A wide variety of American regional dialects is available. Their usefulness will depend on the setting and location of the stage action.

afterthoughts

what's past is prologue
The Tempest II, 1, 247

This section offers brief observations on the poetic diction of each play. Each entry notes the percentage of prose and/or verse in a given play, as well as the amount of rhyming verse, if significant. It also includes a sampling of contractions and of words that expand to fulfill the demands of the meter. Examples of words that require an unusual stress on either their first or second syllables follow. For example, *revenue* is pronounced today with a stress on its first syllable but often requires a stress on its second syllable in Shakespeare. We direct readers to the appropriate sections for accents, dialects, foreign languages, Latin, and words that might present unforseen difficulty.

All's Well That Ends Well

The amount of prose and verse in this play is almost equal. In the gulling of Parolles, the soldiers speak *linsey-woolsy* or *choughs' language* which are nonsense sounds meant to intimidate and frighten. Parolles understands the sounds as belonging to the *Muskos* regiment. This may indicate a Russian flavored pronunciation. *Lustick* is possibly Dutch, while *Mort du vinaigre*! is French. *Capriccio*, which scans to three syllables, is Italianate. The *s* in *rope's* @ IV, 2, 38 stands for "us." Some of the contractions include *I've* for *I have, you've* for *you have, I'd* for *I would,* and *he'd* for *he had.* *Soldier* expands to three syllables @ III, 2, 68. Words with a primary stress on the first syllable include *enjoined* @ III, 5, 90, *perfect* @ IV, 4, 4, and *perspective* @ V, 3, 48. Words with a primary stress on the second syllable include *exploit* @ I, 2, 17, *contract* @ II, 3, 177, and *assay* @ III, 7, 44. See dictionary entry for *baring* @ IV, 1, 47.

Antony and Cleopatra

90 percent of this late play is in verse. There are many epic caesuras and the highest number of shared lines of all of the plays. The text has numerous contractions including *he'd* for *he had, th'art* for *thou art, th'ast* for *thou hast,* and *I'll* for *I will.* Words that expand include *million, Asia, affections,* and *instruction.* Words with a primary stress on the first syllable include *condemned* @ I, 3, 49, *cement* @ II, 1, 48 and III, 2, 29, and *combating* @ III, 13, 79. Words with a primary stress on the second syllable include *revenue* @ III, 6, 30, *seaside* @ III, 11, 20, *triumphing* @ IV, 8, 16, and *record* @ IV, 9, 8. See dictionary entries for *buffet, prophesy,* and *eat* @ II, 2, 227. Note that *power* often scans to one syllable.

As You Like It

While more than half of the play is in prose, 10 percent of the play is in rhyme, some of which affords comic possibilities, including Celia's reading of Orlando's verse, which forces rhymes like *age/pilgrimage* and *slave/have.* The pronunciation of *Goths* is akin to GOHTS in order to make the pun with *goats. Sound* @ V, 2, 26 is often emended to indicate a pronunciation of SWŌŌNED. Words with a primary stress on the first syllable include *antique* @ II, 3, 57 and *upon* @ IV, 3, 150. Words with a primary stress on the second syllable include *exile* @ II, 1, 1, *translate* @ II, 1, 19, and *confines* @ II, 1, 24. *Dials* cans to one or two syllables. Words that expand include *promotion, intermission, observation,* and *reputation. Theatre* expands to three syllables @ II, 7, 137, as does *wrestler* @ II, 3, 70. See dictionary entries for *eat* @ I, 3, 70 and II, 7, 88 (second citation) and *victualled.*

The Comedy of Errors

65 percent of this play is in blank verse with few variants. Slightly more than 20 percent of the verse rhymes. Words that expand include *patience, violently, contagion, Asia,* and *children.* Words with a primary stress on the first syllable include *buffet* @ II, 2, 157 and *travail* @ V, 1, 402. Words with a primary stress on the second syllable include *bedtime* @ I, 2, 28, *sometimes* @ II, 2, 26, and *compact* @ II, 2, 160 and III, 2, 22. *Hour* scans to one or two syllables depending on the meter. Note that *situate* scans to two syllables @ II, 1, 16.

Coriolanus

Approximately 75 percent of this play is in verse. As with other late plays, the verse has many variations including epic caesuras, short lines, and hexameters. Contractions include *I've* for *I have, you've* for *you have,* and *I'd* for *I would.* Words that expand include *malicious, preparation, assembly,* and *violent.* Words with a primary stress on the first syllable include *antique* @ II, 3, 114, *extreme* @ IV, 5, 70, and *cement* @ IV, 6, 86. Words with a primary stress on the second syllable include *record* @ IV, 6, 50 and *increase* @ III, 3, 114. Note that the word *power,* used throughout the play, can have either one or two syllables.

Cymbeline

80 percent of the play is in blank verse. There are numerous contractions, such as *I'm* for *I am, I'll* for *I will,* and *we've* for *we have.* Some of the words that expand are *complexion, soldiers,* and *malefactions.* Words with a primary stress on the first syllable include *exquisite* @ III, 5, 71, *diseased* @ I, 6, 123, and *impious* @ III, 3, 6. Words with a primary stress on the second syllable include *contents* @ II, 2, 27, *maintop* @ IV, 2, 320, and *exiled* @ IV, 4, 26 and V, 4, 59. *Needle* scans to one syllable @ I, 1, 168. *Diamond,* used throughout the play, can be two or three syllables. See "Latin" section for the puns in Act V.

Hamlet

Two-thirds of the play is in blank verse and just under 30 percent is in prose. Contractions include *I'm* for *I am*, *I'll* for *I will*, and *we've* for *we have*. Some of the words that expand are *complexion*, *soldiers*, and *malefactions*. Words with a primary stress on the first syllable include *complete* @ I, 4, 52, *secure* @ I, 5, 61, and *absurd* @ III, 2, 57. Words with a primary stress on the second syllable include *character* @ I, 3, 59, *exploit* @ IV, 7, 63, and *absent* @ V, 2, 336. *Courage* @ I, 3, 65 is kuh-**RAHJ**. *Tropically* @ III, 2, 229 is either **TROH**-pik-lee in reference to the word *trope* or **TRAA**-pik-lee if punning on *The Mousetrap*, the play within the play. *As's* @ V, 2, 43 may be **AAZ**-iz to pun with "asses." *Chanson* @ II, 2, 409 could perhaps be the French shahn-**SOHN**, though the English **CHAAN**-suhn works equally well in this prose passage. See dictionary entry for *eat* @ IV, 3, 27.

Henry IV Part One

More than 40 percent of the play is in prose; the remainder is in blank verse with a small amount of rhyming verse. *Prisoners*, used throughout the play, scans to either two or three syllables. *Power* usually scans to one syllable. *Glendower* frequently scans to two syllables. Words that expand include *transformation, expedition, determination,* and *suggestion*, as well as *impatience, soldier,* and *physicians*. Words with a primary stress on the first syllable include *frontier* @ I, 3, 19 and *exact* @ IV, 1, 46. Words with a primary stress on the second syllable include *allies* @ I, 1, 16 and *portent(s)* @ II, 3, 59 and V, 1, 20. See dictionary entries for the abbreviations *s., d.,* and *ob.* in II, 4. For a discussion of Glendower, Lady Mortimer, and the use of the Welsh language, see "Accents, Dialects, and Foreign Languages."

Henry IV Part Two

This play features the highest percentage of prose of any of the histories. Words that expand include *rebellion, religion, destruction, foundation, commotion,* and *ocean*. Words with a primary stress on the second syllable include *access* @ IV, 1, 78, *instinct* @ I, 1, 86, and *retail* @ I, 1, 32. Pistol's fantastical language contains a blend of Italian and French. See dictionary entries for *victuallers,* *forgetive, gainsaid,* and *eat* @ IV, 5, 164.

Henry V

57 percent of this play is in verse. Contractions include *we're* for *we are, you'd* for *you would, we'll* for *we will,* and *what's* for *what is.* Some of the words that expand are *invention, million, convocation, ocean,* and *preparation.* Words with a primary stress on the first syllable include *perfected* @ I, 1, 69, *largess* @ IV, Cho, 43, and *Dauphin* @ I, 2, 222 and throughout the play. Words with a primary stress on the second syllable include *exploits* @ I, 2, 121, *assay* @ I, 2, 151, and *sinister* @ II, 4, 85. See dictionary entries for *accompt, puissance, puissant, Louvre, Lorraine,* and *executors.* Note that *Lewis* always scans to one syllable, and *Charles* often scans to one syllable. See "Accents, Dialects, and Foreign Languages" for a discussion of the accents used by the "Four Captains."

Henry VI Part One

The play is almost entirely in verse. It contains few variants and has the lowest number of short and shared lines of any of the plays. Contractions include *you've* for *you have, we're* for *we are,* and *I'm* for *I am.* Some of the words that expand are *faction, proclamation, religion, apprehension, coronation, leopard, creature,* and *marriage.* Words with a primary stress on the first syllable include *complete* @ I, 2, 83, *forlorn* @ I, 2, 19, and *travail* @ V, 4, 102. Words with a primary stress on the second syllable include *precinct* @ II, 1, 68 and *reflex* @ V, 4, 87. *Charles* always scans to one syllable except @ IV, 4, 26. *Henry* scans to either two or three syllables. *Prisoner,* used throughout the play, scans to two or three syllables. See dictionary entries for *victual* and *Dauphin.*

Henry VI Part Two

82 percent of this play is in blank verse. Contractions include *I'd* for *I would, he'd* for *he would, t'have* for *to have,* and *he's* for *he is.* Words that expand include *subornation, execution, ambition, patience, country,* and *statue.* Words with a primary stress on the

first syllable include *stigmatic* @ V, 1, 215, *forlorn* @ II, 4, 45 and @ III, 2, 77 (if *poisonous* is two syllables), and *corrosive* @ III, 2, 403. Words with a primary stress on the second syllable include *suspect* @ III, 2, 139 and *edict* @ III, 2, 258. *Henry* scans to either two or three syllables. Note that the Elizabethans probably pronounced *Walter* @ IV, 1, 14 as something like "water." It may be necessary to adopt this pronunciation to make complete sense of the passage. See dictionary entries for *Dauphin* and *eat* @ IV, 10, 37.

Henry VI Part Three
The play is almost entirely in verse. Contractions include *you're* for *you are* and *I'd* for *I had*. Words that expand include *rebellion, succession,* and *apprehension*. Words with a primary stress on the first syllable include *Archbishop* @ IV, 3, 53, *horizon* @ IV, 7, 81, and *farewell* @ V, 7, 45. Words with a primary stress on the second syllable include *forecast* @ V, 1, 42 and *crossbow* @ III, 1, 6. See dictionary entries for *recompt* and *desert* @ III, 3, 132.

Henry VIII
More than 95 percent of the play is in verse. There are numerous contractions contained in the text including *and't, in's, t'attach, y'are, be't,* and *t'oppose*. Additional contractions are *I'm* for *I am, they're* for *they are,* and *they'd* for *they would*. Some of the words that expand are *meditations, commission, business,* and *pernicious*. Words with a primary stress on the first syllable include *July* @ I, 1, 154 and *Archbishop* throughout. Words with a primary stress on the second syllable include *discourser* @ I, 1, 41, *advertise* @ II, 4, 176, and *travail* @ V, I, 71.

Julius Caesar
The majority of this play is in verse. Contractions include *I'll* for *I will* and *I'd* for *I had*. Words that expand include *destruction, insurrection,* and *emulation*. Words with a primary stress on the first syllable include *construe* @ I, 2, 45 and I, 3, 34, *upon* @ I, 2, 171, and *mischievous* @ II, 1, 33. Words with a primary stress on the second syllable include *sometimes* @ II, 1, 285, *exploit* @ II, 1, 317 and 318, and *portents* @ II, 2, 80. The word *not'st* @ V, 3,

22 means "to note." *Funeral*, *soldier*, and *prisoner* scan to two or three syllables. See dictionary entries for *prophesy*, *statue*, and *wind* @ IV, 1, 32.

King John

This is one of the few plays written entirely in verse. Contractions include *he's* for *he is* and *I'll* for *I shall*. Words that expand include *usurpation*, *occasion*, *generation*, *protection*, *desolation*, *minion*, *ocean*, and *destruction*. Words with a primary stress on the first syllable include *hospitable* @ II, 1, 244, *presage* @ III, 4, 158, *supreme* @ III, 1, 155, and *Milan* @ V, 2, 120. Words with a primary stress on the second syllable include *sunset* @ III, 1, 110 and *seaside* @ V, 7, 91. *Needle* @ V, 2, 157 elides to one syllable. The word *iron*, used throughout the play, is frequently disyllabic. See dictionary entries for *Cordelion*, *Absey*, *eat* @ I, 1, 234, and *lien* @ IV, 1, 50.

King Lear

70 percent of the play is in verse. The text has numerous shared lines and hexameters and the most short lines of all the plays. Contractions include *we've* for *we have*, *I'm* for *I am*, *be't* for *be it*, and *I'd* for *I would*. Words with a primary stress on the first syllable include *sincere* @ II, 2, 100, *lamentable* @ IV, 1, 5, and *proclaimed* @ IV, 6, 222. Words with a primary stress on the second syllable include *revenue* @ II, 1, 100, *contents* @ II, 4, 33, and *defects* @ IV, 1, 20. See dictionary entries for *champains*, *fut*, and *sepulchring*. See "Accents, Dialects, and Foreign Languages" for Edgar's dialect in IV, 6.

Love's Labor's Lost

Only 21 percent of this early play is in blank verse. 43 percent is in rhyme. Words that expand include *affections*, *lamentation*, and *reformation*. Words with a primary stress on the first syllable include *complete* @ I, 1, 133, *profound* @ IV, 3, 163, and *peremptory* @ IV, 3, 221. Words with a primary stress on the second syllable include *sometimes* @ IV, 1, 30, *retails* @ V, 2, 318, and *content* and *contents* @ V, 2, 515. Holofernes's vocabulary is Latinate and effulgent. His pedantry values silent consonants so that words like *debt* are pronounced DEHBT. The text abounds in puns and features *honorificabilitudinitatibus,* the longest word in Shakespeare. See dictionary entries for *ballet* @ I, 2, 103 and *eat* @ IV, 2, 24.

Macbeth

80 percent of the play is in verse. It has a high number of shared lines as well as numerous epic caesuras and short lines. Contractions include *we've* for *we have* and *they've* for *they have.* Some of the words that expand are *execution, reflection, entrance,* and *monstrous.* Words with a primary stress on the first syllable include *humane* @ III, 4, 76, *largess* @ II, 1, 14, and *obscure* @ II, 3, 55. Words with a primary stress on the second syllable include *th'access* @ I, 5, 42, *pretence* @ II, 3, 127, and *exploits* @ IV, 1, 144. *Weird,* spelled "weyward" in the Folio and used throughout the play, scans to one or two syllables, as does *Glamis. Scone,* which is the last word of the play, formerly rhymed with *one.* See dictionary entries for *gripe, buffets, minutely,* and *eat* @ II, 4, 18.

Measure for Measure

60 percent of the play is in blank verse. There are frequent epic caesuras and short lines. Contractions include *we've* for *we have, we're* for *we are, I've* for *I have, it's* for *it is,* and *th'art* for *thou art.* Words that expand include *commission, evasion, approbation, profanation,* and *Russia.* Words with a primary stress on the first syllable include *unsoiled* @ II, 4, 155, *compelled* @ II, 4, 57, and *chastisement* @ V, 1, 255. Words with a primary stress on the second syllable include *assay* @ I, 4, 76, *access* @ II, 2, 19, and *record* @ II, 2, 40. *Prayer* and *Friar* scan to one or two syllables. Note that *use* is a noun @ I, 3, 26. See dictionary entry for *accompt.*

The Merchant of Venice

Almost three-quarters of the play is in blank verse. 5 percent is in rhyme. Contractions include *you're* for *you are, I'm* for *I am, you'd* for *you had,* and *I've* for *I have.* Words that expand include *opinion, occasions, Christian,* and *companions.* Words that have a primary stress on the first syllable include *outside* @ I, 3, 98, *obscure* @ II, 7, 51, and *unthrift* @ V, 1, 16. Words that have a primary stress on the second syllable include *aspect* @ I, 1, 54, *obdurate* @ IV, 1, 8, and *highways* @ V, 1, 263. To get the maximum effect out of the rhyming joke @ V, 1, 305, consider pronouncing *clerk* with the English pronunciation KLAHRK starting at IV, 1, 392. *Le Bon* @ I, 2, 50 is probably "bone." Shylock might play with the word *pirates* as PEYE-raats @ I, 3, 22.

The Merry Wives of Windsor
86 percent of this play is in prose. Within the small amount of verse, some of the contractions are *I'd* for *I had*, *they're* for *they are*, and *we've* for *we have*. Words with a primary stress on the first syllable include *extreme* @ IV, 4, 11 and *unclean* @ IV, 4, 56. Words with a primary stress on the second syllable include *midnight* @ IV, 4, 28, *contents* @ IV, 6, 13, and *charactery* @ V, 5, 71 (if *flowers* is one syllable). See dictionary entry for *buffet*.

A Midsummer Night's Dream
Rhyming verse accounts for 45 percent of this play. Words that expand include *patience*, *dissension*, *derision*, *affection*, *confusion*, and *imagination*. Words with a primary stress on the first syllable include *rheumatic* @ II, 1, 105 and *misprised* @ III, 2, 74. Words with a primary stress on the second syllable include *edict* @ I, 1, 151, *midnight* @ I, 1, 223, and *compact* @ V, 1, 8. See the dictionary entries for *thorough* @ II, 1, 106, *eat* @ II, 2, 149, and *ballet* @ IV, 1, 212. Note that *childing* @ II, 1, 112 means pregnant or fruitful.

Much Ado About Nothing
Prose accounts for more than 70 percent of this play. Within the verse some of the contractions are *I'd* for *I would*, *we've* for *we have*, *you'll* for *you will*, and *I'm* for *I am*. Words that expand include *affection*, *complexion*, *gracious*, *apparitions*, *ostentation*, and *patience*. Words that have a primary stress on the first syllable include *betwixt* @ IV, 1, 82 and *unknown* @ IV, 1, 133. Words with a primary stress on the second syllable include *discourse* @ III, 1, 5 and *propose* @ III, 1, 12. See dictionary entries for *victual*, *pennyworth,* and *eat* @ IV, 1, 192.

Othello

Almost 80 percent of the play in verse. The prose is usually spoken by Iago and Roderigo. It has more epic caesuras than any other play, as well as numerous shared lines and short lines. Contractions include *I'm* for *I am*, *I'd* for *I had*, *we're* for *we are*, and *he's* for *he is*. Words that expand include *estimation, patience, satisfaction*, and *apprehension*. Words with a primary stress on the first syllable include *profane* @ I, 1, 114, *cashiered* @ II, 3, 357, *secure* @ IV, 1, 71, and *antique* @ V, 2, 217. Words with a primary stress on the second syllable include *demonstrate* @ I, 1, 61 and III, 3, 431, *affects* @ I, 3, 263, and *portents* @ V, 2, 45. See dictionary entries for *arithmetician, Moor,* and *close* (adj) @ V, 2, 335.

Pericles

Almost 60 percent of the play is in blank verse. 20 percent is in rhymed verse, an unusually high percentage for a late play. There are a large number of short and shared lines in those parts of the play attributed to Shakespeare. Words that expand are *perfections, companion, marriage, nation,* and *diamond*. Words with a primary stress on the first syllable include *respite* @ I, 1, 117, *entreat* @ II, 4, 45, and *travail* @ III, Cho, 52 and III, 1, 14. Words with a primary stress on the second syllable include *edict* @ I, 1, 112, *access* @ II, 5, 7, and *relapse* @ III, 2, 110.

Richard II

The play is entirely in verse. 20 percent of the verse rhymes and sometimes has the potential for comic effect. For example @ V, 3, 119, *pardonne moi* seems to rhyme with *destroy*, which might indicate the pronunciation. Words which expand include *physician, incision, admonition, succession, proportion, correction,* and *patience*. Words with a primary stress on the first syllable include *complot* @ I, 3, 189, *perspectives* @ II, 2, 18, and *delectable* @ II, 3, 7. Words with a primary stress on the second syllable include *record* @ IV, 1, 230, *contents* @ V, 2, 38 and *sepulchre* @ I, 3, 196. *High way* is two words with the second word in the stressed position @ I, 4, 4. Note that *bounty* expands to three syllables @ II,

3, 67 and *tears* is TAIRZ @ III, 3, 57. See dictionary entry for *eat* @ V, 5, 85.

Richard III
More than 98 percent of this early play is in verse. Contractions include *I'd* for *I had*, *I'm* for *I am*, and *you've* for *you have*. Some of the words that expand are *promotion, patient*, and *indignation*. Words with a primary stress on the first syllable include *curtailed* @ I, 1, 18, *excuse* @ I, 2, 84, *accessary* @ I, 2, 191, and *supreme* @ III, 7, 118. Words with a primary stress on the second syllable include *abjects* @ I, 1, 106, *suspects* @ I, 3, 88 and III, 5, 32, and *obdurate* @ I, 3, 346 and III, 1, 39. See dictionary entries for *prophesy* and *characters*.

Romeo and Juliet
71 percent of the play is in blank verse, with slightly over 16 percent in rhyme. The names of the title characters frequently scan to **ROHM**-yoh and **JOOL**-yeht. *Friar* scans to one or two syllables. Contractions include *I'd* for *I would*, *she'd* for *she would*, *I'm* for *I am*, *he's* for *he is*, and *it's* for *it is*. Words that expand include *marriage, invocation, substantial, lamentation,* and *patience*. Words with a primary stress on the first syllable include *confessor* @ II, 6, 21 and III, 3, 49, *unmade* @ III, 3, 70, *before* @ V, 3, 90, and *receptacle* @ IV, 3, 39. *Exile* always stresses on the first syllable except @ III, 3, 43. Words with a primary stress on the second syllable include *access* @ II, Cho, 9, *excess* @ II, 6, 33, and *baptized* @ II, 2, 50. Note the difference in pronunciation between *raven* (a bird) and *ravening* (devouring) @ III, 2, 76. See dictionary entries for *prayers, pennyworth*, and *close* (adj) @ III, 2, 5.

The Taming of the Shrew
72 percent of this early play is in blank verse. Contractions include *we'll* for *we will*, *it's* for *it is*, *you're* for *you are*, and *you've* for *you have*. Words that expand include *impatient, instructions, patience*, and *million*. Words with a primary stress on the first syllable include *commune* @ I, 1, 101, *largess* @ I, 2, 147, and *extreme*

@ II, 1, 135. Words with a primary stress on the second syllable include *absent* @ Ind, 2, 121, *defects* @ I, 2, 121, and *elsewhere* @ IV, 3, 6. See dictionary entries for *politicly, satiety, extempore,* and *eat* @ IV, 1, 184, first citation.

The Tempest

71 percent of this late play is in verse. There are numerous short and shared lines. The text has frequent contractions including *heard'st, saw'st, canst, hadst, seest, say'st,* and *call'dst.* Other possible contractions include *we're* for *we are, t'have* for *to have,* and *they're* for *they are.* Words that expand include *valiant, vineyard,* and *celebration.* Words with a primary stress on the first syllable include *perfected* @ I, 2, 79, *frustrate* @ III, 3, 10, and *humane* @ I, 2, 346. Words with a primary stress on the second syllable include *extirpate* @ I, 2, 125, *opportune* @ IV, 1, 26, and *solemnized* @ V, 1, 309. See dictionary entries for *aches* and *throughly.*

Timon of Athens

Two-thirds of the play is in blank verse. Almost 20 percent of the lines are short or shared. Contractions include *I'll* for *I will, I've* for *I have, I'd* for *I had, I'm* for *I am,* and *you're* for *you are.* Words that expand include *damnation, factions,* and *valiant.* Words with a primary stress on the first syllable include *austere* @ I, 1, 54, *condemn* @ III, 5, 53, and *detestable* @ IV, 1, 33. Words with a primary stress on the second syllable include *frequents* @ I, 1, 117, *precedent* @ I, 1, 133, and *aspect* @ II, 1, 28. See dictionary entries for *gramercy, triumphers,* and *aches.*

Titus Andronicus

More than 93 percent of the play is in blank verse. There are a few Latin words as well as one anachronistic greeting in French: *bon jour* @ I, 1, 497. Contractions include *they're* for *they are,* and *you're* for *you are. Emperor,* used throughout the play, scans to two or three syllables. Words that expand include *expiation, proclamations, million, impatient, spacious, execution, destruction, patience,* and *Empress.* Words with a primary stress on the first syllable include *abjectly* @ II, 3, 4, *sequestered* @ II, 3, 75, *obscure*

@ II, 3, 77, and *forlorn* @ II, 3, 153. Words with a primary stress on the second syllable include *triumpher* @ I, 1, 173, *conduct* @ IV, 4, 64, and *gramercy* @ I, 1, 498. Some editions substitute "raze" for *race* @ I, 1, 454. See dictionary entry for *prayer* @ III, 1, 75.

Troilus and Cressida

60 percent of the play is in verse. There are numerous epic caesuras and a large number of short and shared lines. The text has many multi-syllabic words that are unique to this play. Contractions include *I'm* for *I am*, *here's* for *here is*, *you're* for *you are*, and *I've* for *I have*. Words that expand include *approbation*, *oration*, *execution*, and *genius*. Words with a primary stress on the first syllable include *o'ertop* @ III, 3, 164, *complete* @ III, 3, 180 and IV, 1, 27, and *humane* @ IV, 1, 20 (in an epic caesura line). Words with a primary stress on the second syllable include *canonize* @ II, 2, 202, *characterless* @ III, 2, 180, and *sinister* @ IV, 5, 127. Note that *general* and *surety* can be two or three syllables. See dictionary entries for *dividable*, *prescience*, *subsequent*, and *multipotent*.

Twelfth Night

More than 60 percent of the play is in prose and just over 30 percent is in blank verse. Epic caesuras are frequent. Contractions include *I've* for *I have*, *I'd* for *I had*, and *she's* for *she is*. Words that expand include *country*, *remembrance*, *creatures*, *adorations*, and *distraction*. Words with a primary stress on the first syllable include *upon* @ III, 4, 198 and V, 1, 93 and *adverse* @ V, 1, 78. Words with a primary stress on the second syllable include *excess* @ I, 1, 2, *access* @ I, 4, 15, and *discourse* @ I, 4, 24. See dictionary entries for *comptible*, *champian*, and *convents*.

Two Gentlemen of Verona

More than two-thirds of this early play is in blank verse. Contractions include *I'm* for *I am*, *I'll* for *I will*, *you're* for *you are*, and *there's* for *there is*. Some of the words that expand include *protestation*, *expedition*, and *correction*. Words with a primary stress on the first syllable include *perfected* @ I, 3, 23, *extreme* @ II, 7, 22 (with *fire* scanning to two syllables), and *lamentable* @

IV, 4, 164. Words with a primary stress on the second syllable include *turmoil* @ II, 7, 37, *allied* @ IV, 1, 49, and *recourse* @ III, 1, 112. See dictionary entries for *throughly, unfrequented, sepulchre* (v), and *Milan*.

The Two Noble Kinsmen

The majority of the play is in blank verse. Contractions include *I'd* for *I would*, *she'd* for *she would*, *I've* for *I have*, *you've* for *you have,* and *I'd* for *I had*. *Iron* often scans to two syllables. Some of the words that expand include *imaginations, sufficient, position,* and *musicians*. Words with a primary stress on the first syllable include *farewell* @ II, 2, 179 and *confessed* @ III, 1, 35. Words with a primary stress on the second syllable include *success* @ V, 3, 69, *record* @ II, 2, 112, *edict* @ III, 6, 145 and 168, and *sinister* @ V, 3, 76. *Moor* @ III, 5, 117 tends towards MAWR and *is* towards IS to make the pun with *Morris*. *Hercules* @ I, 1, 66 is pronounced as ER-kleez. See dictionary entry for *victuals*.

The Winter's Tale

More than 70 percent of this play is in blank verse. Most of the prose occurs when the play shifts to Bohemia. As with other late plays, the verse has many variations including epic caesuras, short lines, and hexameters. Contractions include *I've* for *I have*, *I'd* for *I had,* and *I'll* for *I will*. Words that expand include *confirmation, proclamations, creature,* and *business*. Words with a primary stress on the first syllable include *July* @ I, 2, 168 and *unknown* @ IV, 4, 65 and 484. Words with a primary stress on the second syllable include *allied* @ I, 2, 338, *something* @ II, 2, 25, and *contract* @ IV, 4, 410. See dictionary entries for *gaoler* and *Saltiers*.

references

We turned o'er many books together
The Merchant of Venice IV, 1, 155

Abbott, E. A. *A Shakespearian Grammar*. New York: Dover Publications, 1966.

The American Heritage Dictionary of the English Language, 3rd Edition. Boston: Houghton Mifflin, 1992.

Allen, W. Sidney. *Vox Latina*. Cambridge: Cambridge University Press, 1965.

Attridge, Derek. *Poetic Rhythm: An Introduction*. Cambridge: Cambridge University Press, 1995.

Barton, John. *Playing Shakespeare*. London and New York: Methuen, 1984.

Berry, Cicely. *The Actor and the Text*. New York: Applause, 1992.

———. *Text in Action*. London: Virgin Publishing, 2001.

Cercignani, Fausto. *Shakespeare's Words and Elizabethan Pronunciation*. Oxford: Clarendon Press, 1981.

Colaianni, Louis. *Shakespeare's Names: A New Pronouncing Dictionary*. New York: Quite Specific Media Group, 1999.

Coye, Dale F. *Pronouncing Shakespeare's Words*. Westport, Conn.: Greenwood Press, 1998.

Dobson, E. J. *English Pronunciation, 1500–1700.* 2 vols. Oxford: Clarendon Press, 1968.

Ehrlich, Eugene. *Amo, Amas, Amat and More: How to Use Latin to Your Own Advantage and to the Astonishment of Others.* New York: Harper & Row, 1985.

Irvine, Theodora Ursula. *How to Pronounce the Names in Shakespeare.* Ann Arbor, Michigan: Gryphon Books, 1971.

Jones, Daniel. *English Pronouncing Dictionary*, 15th Edition. Edited by Peter Roach and James Hartmann. Cambridge: Cambridge University Press, 1997.

————. *Everyman's English Pronouncing Dictionary.* Extensively revised and edited by A.C. Gimson. London and Melbourne: J.M. Dent & Sons, 1986.

Kermode, Frank. *Shakespeare's Language.* New York: Farrar, Straus and Giroux, 2001.

Kökeritz, Helge. *Shakespeare's Names: A Pronouncing Dictionary.* New Haven: Yale University Press, 1959.

————. *Shakespeare's Pronunciation.* New Haven: Yale University Press, 1953.

McDonald, Russ. *The Bedford Companion to Shakespeare.* Boston and New York: Bedford Books of St. Martin's Press, 1996.

McLean, Margaret Prendergast. *Good American Speech.* New York: E.P. Dutton and Co., 1946.

Merriam-Webster's Collegiate Dictionary, 10th Edition. Springfield, Mass.: Merriam-Webster, 1993.

Morwood, James. *A Dictionary of Latin Words and Phrases.* Oxford and New York: Oxford University Press, 1998.

The Oxford English Dictionary, 2nd Edition. 20 vols. Oxford: Clarendon, 1989.

The Oxford Universal Dictionary, 3rd Edition. Oxford: Clarendon, 1944.

A Pronouncing Dictionary of American English. Editors John Samuel Kenyon and Thomas Albert Knott. Springfield, Mass.: G&C Merriam Co., 1953.

The Reader's Encyclopedia of Shakespeare. Editors Oscar James Campbell and Edward G. Quinn. New York: MJF Books, 1966.

Reading Shakespeare's Dramatic Language — A Guide. Editors Sylvia Adamson, Lynette Hunter, Lynne Magnusson, Ann Thompson, and Katie Wales. London: Thomson Learning, 2001.

Schmidt, Alexander. *Shakespeare Lexicon and Quotation Dictionary.* 2 Vols. New York: Dover Publications, 1971.

Shakespeare, William. *The First Folio of Shakespeare 1623.* Prepared and Introduced by Doug Moston. New York: Applause Books, 1995.

Shakespeare, William. *William Shakespeare: The Complete Works.* General Editor, Alfred Harbage. New York: The Viking Press, 1969.

Skinner, Edith. *Speak With Distinction.* Edited by Lilene Mansell. Revised by Timothy Monich and Lilene Mansell. New York: Applause, 1990.

Spain, Delbert. *Shakespeare Sounded Soundly.* Santa Barbara, California: Garland-Clarke Editions/Capra Press, 1988.

Tarlinskaja, Marina. *Shakespeare's Verse.* New York: Peter Lang, 1987.

Webster's Third New International Dictionary of the English Language. Springfield, Mass.: Merriam, 1961.

Wilkinson, L. P. *Golden Latin Artistry.* Cambridge: Cambridge University Press, 1963.

Wright, George T. *Shakespeare's Metrical Art.* Berkeley, California: University of California Press, 1988.

Other editions of Shakespeare consulted include *The Riverside Shakespeare* and *The Oxford Shakespeare,* as well as individual volumes in the following series: The Arden, Folger, Kittredge, New American Library, The New Cambridge, New Clarendon, New Penguin, and New Swan.

LOUIS SCHEEDER is a Master Teacher at New York University's Tisch School of the Arts and is the founder and director of The Classical Studio, an advanced training program in the Department of Drama. He has directed on, off, and off-off Broadway and at regional theaters in the United States and Canada. He has worked at the Royal Shakespeare Company, was associated with the Manitoba Theatre Centre, served as producer of the Folger Theatre Group, and teaches and coaches privately in New York City.

SHANE ANN YOUNTS teaches voice and text classes in the Graduate Acting Program of New York University, where she specializes in the texts of Shakespeare. She also teaches private classes and coaches actors for theater, film, and television at her Manhattan studio. She has served as voice consultant for Broadway, and off-Broadway productions, and at regional theaters including the Guthrie Theater, The Public Theater, and The Pearl Theatre. She has taught at The Public Theater's Summer Shakespeare Lab, the Guthrie Experience, The Juilliard School (Drama Division), the American Academy of Dramatic Arts, and NYU's Classical Studio.

all the words on stage
&

A COMPLETE PRONUNCIATION DICTIONARY FOR THE PLAYS OF WILLIAM SHAKESPEARE

Louis Scheeder
and Shane Ann Younts

CAREER DEVELOPMENT SERIES

A Smith and Kraus Book

Published by
Smith and Kraus, Inc.
177 Lyme Road, Hanover, New Hampshire 03755
www.SmithKraus.com

Cover and text design by Julia Hill Gignoux, Freedom Hill Design

First edition: March 2002
10 9 8 7 6 5 4 3 2 1

The Library of Congress Cataloging-In-Publication Data
Scheeder, Louis.
All the words on stage : the complete Shakespeare pronunciation dictionary / Louis
Scheeder and Shane Ann Younts. —1st ed.
p. cm. (Career development series)
Includes bibliographical references (p.).
ISBN 1-57525-263-5 (cloth)
ISBN 1-57525-214-7 (pbk.)
1. Shakespeare, William, 1564–1616—Language—Glossaries, etc.
2. English language—Early modern, 1500–1700—Pronunciation—Dictionaries.
I. Younts, Shane Ann. II. Title. III. Series.
PR3081 .S27 2001
822.3'3—dc21
Library of Congress Control Number: 2001020182